Indefinites and the Type of Sets

Explorations in Semantics

Series Editor: Susan Rothstein

Editorial Board

This exciting series features important new research by leading scholars in the field of semantics. Each volume focuses on a topic or topics central to the field, including dynamic semantics, aspect, focus, anaphora, and type-shifting, and offers a pedagogical component designed to introduce the topics addressed and situate the new research in the context of the field and previous research. The presentational style emphasizes student accessibility without compromising the sophistication of the research involved.

Explorations in Semantics is an excellent series for students and researchers in the field, as well as scholars in adjacent areas such as syntax, philosophy of language, and computational linguistics.

1 *Compositionality in Formal Semantics: Selected Papers of Barbara H. Partee*
  Barbara H. Partee

2 *Structuring Events: A Study in the Semantics of Lexical Aspect*
  Susan Rothstein

3 *Indefinites and the Type of Sets*
  Fred Landman

4 *Focus Sensitivity: Semantics and Pragmatics*
  David Beaver and Brady Clark

5 *The Proper Treatment of Events*
  Fritz Hamm and Michiel van Lambalgen

Indefinites and the Type of Sets

Fred Landman

Blackwell
Publishing

350 Main Street, Malden, MA 02148-5020, USA
108 Cowley Road, Oxford OX4 1JF, UK
550 Swanston Street, Carlton, Victoria 3053, Australia

First published 2004 by Blackwell Publishing Ltd

Library of Congress Cataloging-in-Publication Data

Landman, Fred.
    Indefinites and the type of sets / Fred Landman.
        p. cm. — (Explorations in semantics)
    Includes bibliographical references and index.
        ISBN 1-4051-1630-7 (alk. paper) — ISBN 1-4051-1631-5 (pbk. : alk. paper)
        1. Definiteness (Linguistics)   2. Grammar, Comparative and general—
Noun phrase.   3. Semantics.   I. Title.   II. Series.

P299.D43L36 2004
415—dc21

                                                                    2003010493

A catalogue record for this title is available from the British Library.

Set in 10/12.5pt Palatino
by Graphicraft Limited, Hong Kong
Printed and bound in the United Kingdom
by MPG Books Ltd, Bodmin, Cornwall

For further information on
Blackwell Publishing, visit our website:
http://www.blackwellpublishing.com

Contents

Acknowledgments

The oldest parts of this book go back to the spring of 1994. Coming to Israel, I landed during a big strike and the spring semester started months late. That spring I wrote a text to be used in my advanced semantics classes, which included a chapter on predicates and properties, basically a discussion of Partee's work on predication and Zimmermann's work on the objects of intensional verbs. I discussed the connection between *exactly/at least* readings and predicate/argument position, and gave a tentative analysis in an as yet embryonic adjectival theory of indefinites. Since this version was as logically incoherent as adjectival theories had been up to that time, the requirement of making this coherent set an agenda which ultimately resulted in chapter 2. The predication chapter of the 1994 text also had an extensive discussion of role predicates, their intensionality, and the need for a variable constraint on quantifying in, and in fact a lot of chapter 3 is already in that text in some form or other.

In 1995, Alex Grosu and I developed an analysis for what we later called maximalizing relative clauses. In the course of this work, we noted the similarity between the external definiteness effects in these relative clauses, and the facts for adverbial *time* noun phrases that Susan Rothstein discussed. In the context of this work we noted the interpretational definiteness effects for adverbial *time* noun phrases: definite ones are indirect counters, while indefinite ones are direct counters. This, of course, set the agenda for the last two chapters of this book, which provides an analysis of these constructions, but it is fair to say that it actually set the agenda for the whole book: to find a general analysis of definiteness effects in which these interpretational effects for adverbial *time* noun phrases can find a natural place.

That year, I presented the work on direct/indirect counting of adverbial *time* noun phrases in the spring in a meeting of the Semantics Circle, a group of semanticists who met at our house in Tel Aviv every other week. I also presented this work in the summer at the 10th IATL conference in Tel Aviv, and in the fall at the 10th Amsterdam Colloquium. A first layer of thanks go to Alex Grosu and Susan Rothstein for discussing these issues extensively with me, and to the audiences of the meetings mentioned for their comments.

Here things stayed for a while, since in 1996 I had other concerns: preparing and sending off my *Events and Plurality* book to be refereed, and changing diapers.

This is all prehistory. The current book was started early in 1997, during the semester break. The invaluable help of our babysitter, Sarah Aharon, and the good weather, gave me a daily slot between ten and three to sit on park benches and scribble yellow pads full. The heart of the book, the flip-flop analysis in chapter 5, the fitting of the analysis in the theory of event maximalization of my *Events and Plurality* book, and the core of chapters 7 and 8 was developed during that month. In the spring of that year, I presented the work at a colloquium at Tel Aviv University, and in the summer, in a class on events that I co-taught with Susan Rothstein at the Summer Institute of the LSA at Cornell University in Ithaca. A second layer of thanks go to, once again, Susan Rothstein for continuous daily discussion of these issues, culminating in our joint events seminar, and to the audiences, with special mention here to John Bowers (in Ithaca).

In the fall semester of 1997/1998 I had the good luck of co-directing with Edit Doron a Semantics Group at the Institute for Advanced Study at the Hebrew University of Jerusalem. A big thank-you is due to the Institute for its financial support, to the staff for creating a wonderfully supportive environment, and of course to my fellow semanticists who made the Group an unforgettable success.

During this semester I wrote two huge manuscripts, the first covering basically the material that had already been developed during that year. I presented this material at a conference we organized at the Institute during that fall. The second manuscript developed what is now chapter 6 (adjunction to saturated predicates), and chapter 9 (definiteness effects for relational nouns). I presented the material now in chapter 6 at a colloquium in Tel Aviv in the spring of 1998, and at SALT 8 at MIT. Again, many thanks to the audiences of these presentations, with special thanks to Maria Bittner, Veneeta Dayal, Edit Doron, Marc-Ariel Friedemann, Polly Jacobson, Angelika Kratzer, Manfred Krifka, Tali Siloni, and Anna Szabolsci. Even more direct thanks are due to Gennaro Chierchia and Hans Kamp: discussions with them (distributively) shaped the chapter on negation (chapter 8).

At this point (the beginning of the summer of 1998), the bulk of the material in this book existed in the form of these two circulating unwielding manuscripts, which I was ready to rewrite and turn into a book. But the other book intervened: that summer I finally received the referee reports of the *Events and Plurality* book, and I spent the summer, and the following semester writing the final version of that book. The spring semester of 1999 was, by necessity of a grant, dedicated to other research, so in the end I didn't get to start writing the book during 1998/1999.

What I did do, during that year, was teach a year-long seminar at Tel Aviv University. In that class, chapter 5 was reshaped into a form much closer to its present form. And, most importantly, I discovered the need to present a conceptual prehistory to the work, developing the Adjectival Theory in more detail, and comparing it with the Montague–Partee approach. Thus, the core of chapter 2 was developed during this seminar. Here many thanks go to the penetrating comments, skepticism, and encouragement of my students, Victoria Barabash, Shai Cohen, Gabi Danon, Yael Greenberg, Daphna Heller, Aldo Sevi, and Galit Sassoon.

By the summer of 1999 I was, thus, all ready to finally start writing but, again, things turned out differently. Due to another strike in the year before, that summer was very short, and because of a variety of interactions with the real world, it passed before any writing could be done. Correcting the proofs of the *Events and Plurality* book basically took care of the fall semester. By this time, I was feeling like a character in Luis Buñuel's film *Le Charme discret de la bourgeoisie* (in which a group of people is prevented from having dinner for the duration of the movie). But in 2000 things started moving again. That spring I wrote the paper on argument–predicate mismatches which is incorporated in chapter 2. I presented that paper that spring at the NP–DP conference in Antwerpen, and at a colloquium at Tel Aviv University; that summer I presented a version of it at IATL 14 at Tel Aviv University and again in February 2001 at a colloquium at ZAS in Berlin. Once more I profited greatly from the comments of the audiences of these talks; here, I mention in particular Manfred Krifka and Tanya Reinhart. An earlier version of chapter 2 was published as Landman (2003), and I am grateful to John Benjamins Publishing Company for permission to reuse this material here.

In the spring of 2000, I decided that the trick to get the material rewritten would be to think of it as a series of about ten little, semi-independent papers, the NP–DP paper being the first. While I was never serious about these really being independent papers, the trick worked very well: at the end of the summer, the material was rewritten as a series of ten papers, in which the structure of the present book becomes recognizable.

This is the right point to mention that from 1998 to 2000 and from 2000 to 2001, Alex Grosu and I received two grants from the Israel Science Foundation, the first on a Tripartite Typology of Relative Clause Constructions, and the second on Transparent Free Relatives. The first grant supported some of the work that I have mentioned (where it intersects with the problems of maximalizing relatives), the second grant supported some major work that I did on adverbial *time* noun phrases between the summer of 2000 and the spring of 2001. This financial support is gratefully acknowledged. Thanks to Alex Grosu for many discussions on topics intersecting with the topics in this book.

The work on adverbial *time* noun phrases just mentioned led to basically what is now chapters 10 and 11 (but at the time sat uncomfortably between the NP–DP paper and what is now chapter 5). I want to mention here three sources of inspiration for this work. In the first place, a talk on this class of expressions by Susan Rothstein at the Israel Science Foundation workshop on Relative Clauses that Alex Grosu and I organized in the summer of 2000. Secondly, the discussion of *time* phrases in Jenny Doetjes' dissertation, which she was kind enough to send to me. Thirdly, joint work and discussions with Alex Grosu on Transparent Free Relatives, which inspired my particular use of categorial grammar in chapter 11. I presented the new analysis of adverbial *time* phrases in the spring of 2001 in colloquiums at the Hebrew University of Jerusalem, Tel Aviv University, and the Technion in Haifa, and in a three-hour seminar at ZAS in Berlin. Again, thanks to the audiences, with once again special thanks to Manfred Krifka and Susan Rothstein.

The year 2001/2002 we spent on sabbatical in Holland. Many thanks to UIL-LOT in Utrecht for providing hospitality. Also thanks to my family in Holland and Belgium, and in particular to my daughter Dafna, for making this year for me, after 16 years of absence, an intensely Dutch experience.

When I started rewriting the material once more, the originally successful form of ten little papers became more and more of a burden. Due to the need for more structuring glue, commentary sections came into existence, and comments on comments, and the whole started to look like a postmodernist composition with optional parts, and various optional directions to read through the material. A colloquium at the University of Amsterdam, and a week-long series of lectures at the Winterschool in Leiden of the LOT Graduate School in Linguistics created a new structure. The talk in Amsterdam was basically written as a kind of résumé of what is now the first five chapters. It was by giving this talk that I realized that it would be best to move the *time* adverbial material to the end, and that in between what is now chapter 3 (on the Variable Constraint) and chapter 5 (the flip-flop analysis), there was a real need for a chapter making the comparison with analyses of the definiteness effect in terms of a weak–strong distinction. Initially sketched as part of the Amsterdam talk, much of the contents of chapter 4 developed in the course of the lectures in Leiden. I am very grateful to the audiences, in particular to Robert van Rooy. Also in Leiden, I realized the necessity of adding a prehistory to the prehistory, and start off the book with a discussion of the Adjectival Theory within the nominal domain, in the context of a presentation of the background theory of plurality.

With this structure in place, I reworked all the existing material extensively in the spring of 2002 (merging some chapters, splitting some others), ending up with the present book. Very helpful, in this process, was the possibility of making a different résumé, this time focusing on chapters 5 and 6, that I gave that spring as a colloquium at the University of Utrecht and at the University of Groningen, and a presentation at the conference on (Preferably) Non-lexical Semantics at the University of Paris VII, and again, in the fall of 2002 as a colloquium at Tel Aviv University. Again, many thanks to the audiences.

Yet another variant of the "Amsterdam" version was presented at the conference on "Existential sentences" at the University of Nancy in the fall of 2002. Here too, many thanks to the audience, with special thanks to Barbara Partee for several stimulating lunch discussions during this conference.

The fall of 2002 saw the resurrection of the bi-weekly Semantics Circle meetings at our house. This time I spaced a variant of the "Utrecht" version over three presentations. I am very grateful for the penetrating discussions with the audiences of these meetings: many thanks to Ron Artstein, Arik Cohen, Edit Doron, Yael Greenberg, Anita Mittwoch, and Susan Rothstein.

Finally, the comments of the referee at Blackwell Publishing have been extremely useful in writing the final version of this book.

This book is, more than any of my previous works, focused on (the semantic side of) the syntax–semantics relation. While my own views on this relation are (of course) peculiarly my own, I want to express my debt here to Barbara Partee and Gennaro Chierchia: my long exposure from close by to their virtuosity and depth in dealing with the syntax–semantics relation has influenced my own thinking in innumerable ways. Closer to home (well, in fact, at home) this work has benefitted in equally innumerable ways from daily critical interaction with Susan Rothstein. And from love, of course.

F. L.

Reading This Book
at Different Levels

This book is addressed to audiences at three levels of semantic skill:

- Group 1: people who have an elementary fluency in reading semantic types and expressions with λ-operators. I have in mind here people who have been able to digest a classic paper like Partee (1987).
- Group 2: people with a background in semantics who are familiar with semantic operations and semantic derivations involving λ-conversion.
- Group 3: specialists in semantics who will stoically brave any technical complexity.

I will first address a few general comments to the first group of readers. This book is at some places dense with semantic types and type logical expressions, which may be hard to read. However, I've made a habit of describing the content of these logical expressions informally as well, which means that if you read these logical expressions *and* their informal description, you will soon gain the required fluency in reading these expressions.

The book also contains many semantic derivations, derivations of the interpretations of complex expressions from the interpretations of the parts and the composing operations. These derivations are, of course, important in the arguments made in this book, and I am not advising readers to skip them, but they contain many reduction steps (usually with λ-conversion) in which a complex representation is shown to be equivalent to a somewhat more readable one. These reductions are there to help the readers, not to scare them away. If they don't help you, trust me that they do what I claim they do, and skip them. I have done my best to make sure that you can quite well follow the story without having gone through the reduction steps. This advice applies, of course, to the second group of readers as well, though they shouldn't have problems following the reductions.

I will indicate now which parts of the book are addressed to more specialized audiences, and can be skipped by those who want to get the general picture (though, of course, this will mean skipping some of the icing on the cake).

Chapter 1 contains the background theory of numerical expressions in the nominal domain. While the basic notions from the theory of Boolean algebras may be difficult for those not familiar with them, they should not be skipped. The chapter is meant to be self-contained, and these notions can readily be understood by looking at the pictures of Boolean algebras given. However, the discussion of *every three lions* ending the chapter is a piece of "icing" meant for the specialists, which can be skipped unproblematically.

In chapter 2, sections 2.6 (on conjunctive predicates) and 2.9 (on sentence adverbials inside noun phrases) are more difficult sections meant for the specialists, and can be skipped without losing track of the story. The reader may find section 2.5 difficult; 2.5 cannot be skipped though. While I have done my best to make the discussion as gentle as possible, 2.5 is difficult because it addresses a difficult problem, the solution to which is at the heart of the chapter, and at the heart of the book. Thus the readers should fasten their seatbelts and stay with me.

Chapter 3 consists of two parts. The first part, sections 3.1–3.3, contains the basic discussion of variable constraint effects, and should not be skipped. The second part, sections 3.4–3.5, is concerned with ways of avoiding variable constraint effects. The second part is a bit more specialized than the first part. I don't really think the second part should be skipped, but admittedly skipping it doesn't affect the main story line.

In chapter 4, the only thing that can be skipped is the compositional derivation of *more than half of the boys* and the final section, 4.8, on collectivity, which is, again, for the specialists.

Chapters 5 and 6 are the heart of the book. The technical heart is the operation of flip-flop in section 5.2. While this section may look difficult, I think it is less difficult than it looks. It can certainly not be skipped. The discussion of maximalization in section 5.3, which starts one page into the section, is very technical and difficult. In presentations based on the book I have alternated between the "Amsterdam" version, which presents basically chapters 1 to 5, ending with section 5.3, and the "Utrecht" version, which presents chapters 1 to 6, skipping section 5.3 (except for the first page). The maximalization part of section 5.3 is, in a way, the official implementation of the ideas expressed in section 2.5. On the assumption that the reader has read section 2.5, it is possible (though hazardous) for the reader to take the incorporation of these ideas into my event theory for granted, and skip to the next bit (section 5.4). Note that I am not advising readers to skip this part of section 5.3, but I will let them get away with it.

Several sections in chapter 6 are at the same technical level as section 5.2: that is, on going through them carefully, they turn out to be less difficult than they look at first sight. This is not the case for section 6.2, on predicate formation. The scope shift mechanism introduced there is just difficult. And the section cannot be skipped, because it is an essential part in the theory developed. This, then, is another seatbelt section. Sections 6.6 and 6.7 are, once again, "icing" sections, where 6.6 is more syntactically oriented, while 6.7 is more spiritual. Both can be skipped, though neither is technically difficult.

Chapter 7 addresses syntactic questions, and questions about the syntax–semantics interface. This chapter can be skipped by some more semantically oriented specialists (i.e. the ones who want to get to chapter 11 as soon as they can).

Chapter 8 consists of two parts. The first part, sections 8.1–8.4, presents the basic account of negative noun phrases. This part is not difficult and cannot be skipped. The second part, sections 8.5–8.6, deals with some complex cases. This part is **very** difficult, and meant for the fearless specialist.

While chapters 1 to 8 present the basic theory, chapters 9, 10, and 11 present further developments of the theory. However, even for those who only want to get to know the basic theory, I would advise reading sections 9.1 and 9.2 as well. These sections present the analysis of *have* and relational indefinites. The analysis in 9.2 is not easy, but should give way on careful study.

Section 9.3 concerns verbs of change of possession. Here 9.3.1 and 9.3.2 are not particularly difficult, while 9.3.3, containing the ultimate analysis, is, unfortunately, very difficult. Thus, 9.3 should be approached with caution. I am not saying by this that 9.3 is for the specialist only. The data discussed in 9.3 are fascinating, and should be of interest to anyone. But the semantic analysis they entail is complex. I can't help it.

Chapter 10, on definite *time* adverbials, is maybe a bit difficult, though not really more difficult than the papers by Rothstein (1995) and Grosu and Landman (1998) that it discusses.

Chapter 11, on indefinite *time* adverbials, is **hair-raisingly** difficult, and should only be approached with a long stick through heavy metal bars. It's very beautiful, though.

Introduction

In this introduction, I will call nominal expressions as they occur in argument position or predicate position **determiner phrases**, DPs. Thus, the italic phrases in (1) are determiner phrases: in argument position in (1a), in predicate position in (1b).

(1)a. *Most girls/the three girls/at most three girls* played in the street.
   b. At the party, the guests were *the girls from Dafna's class/at least three girls*.

The usage of the word **noun phrase**, NP, I will restrict here to nominal phrases inside determiner phrases. Thus, I will call the noun *girls* as it occurs in the expression *the three girls* a noun phrase, and I will call the phrase *three girls* in the same expression a noun phrase as well. The expression *the three girls* I will not here call a noun phrase. (This terminological purism will not extend into the book itself, though.)

This brings in a question about the expression *at least three girls* in (1b). It is a determiner phrase, since it occurs in predicate position, but *at least three girls* also occurs in it: the latter occurrence should be a noun phrase. I will avoid this conclusion by writing Ø *at least three girls* for the determiner phrase containing an empty determiner Ø and the noun phrase *at least three girls*.

I realize quite well that one can hardly adopt such terminology without committing oneself to a version of the theory of noun phrase structure underlying the terminology. I will gladly commit myself to some version of that theory in the chapters of this book (especially in chapters 1 and 2), and explain which aspects I feel strongly about (the NP–DP distinction), and which I am less strongly committed to (the extensive use of empty categories). But you can forget about this for the moment: at this stage, the only thing I need is terminological clarity.

Chapter 1 concerns the semantics of numerical noun phrases, like the noun phrase *three girls* inside the determiner phrase *the three girls*. The chapter gives an exposition of the theory of plurality, started in the work of Godehard Link (see Link 1983), in which the semantic domain of individuals forms a complete atomic Boolean algebra of singular individuals (atoms) and plural individuals (their sums), singular nouns denote sets of atoms, and pluralization is closure under sum. It is argued that this framework provides a natural and elegant setting for analyzing numerical phrases like *three, at most three,* and *at least three* semantically as intersective adjectives. This means that they are semantically analyzed as sets (of singularities and pluralities) that combine with the interpretation of the head noun phrase (which is also a set) through intersection. More precisely, the set interpretation of the numerical phrase shifts with the type shifting operation of **adjunction** to a modifier interpretation as a function from sets to sets (the function which maps the set denoted by the numerical phrase and any input set onto the intersection of the two). This means, then, that the noun phrase *three girls* in *the three girls* is itself interpreted at the type of sets. This we can call the **Adjectival Theory of Numerical Noun Phrases**. This analysis is hardly controversial: the adjectival behavior of numerical phrases inside determiner phrases has long been noted. To get the discussion off the ground, the first chapter discusses some solid evidence that favors the Adjectival Theory of Numerical Noun Phrases over some alternative analyses, like the ones presented by Barwise and Cooper (1981) and Keenan (1987).

This book is not concerned with the Adjectival Theory of Numerical Noun Phrases, but with the Adjectival Theory of Numerical, or more generally, Indefinite **Determiner Phrases**. Chapter 2 is concerned with the semantics of determiner phrases in argument position and in predicate position, the different interpretations that these expressions have in these positions, and the relations between these interpretations. The chapter argues (among other things) for a mismatch between the syntax and the semantics of the expressions in question:

1. There are systematic syntactic differences between numerical noun phrases and numerical determiner phrases, which are easy to account for if the first are indeed NPs and the second DPs. There are no detectable syntactic differences between numerical determiner phrases in argument or in predicate position. Thus, syntactically, predicates and arguments are DPs.
2. There are systematic semantic differences between numerical, or more generally, indefinite determiner phrases in argument position and in predicate position.
3. There are no semantic differences between numerical determiner phrases in predicate position and numerical noun phrases: numerical determiner phrases in predicate position and numerical noun phrases have the same semantics.

The Adjectival Theory of Indefinite Determiner Phrases takes the third fact as its starting point. Chapter 1 argues that numerical noun phrases have a set interpretation. Numerical determiner phrases in predicate position have the same semantics as numerical noun phrases. The null assumption would be that this is the case, because the process of forming a DP from the NP is semantically interpreted as identity. Since, with fact one, there is no syntactic difference between numerical determiner phrases in predicate or in argument position, it follows that numerical determiner phrases are generated as expressions with an interpretation at the type of sets. Once we have drawn this conclusion, we generalize this to indefinite determiner phrases in general, and we get the **Adjectival Theory of Indefinite Determiner Phrases**: indefinite determiner phrases are generated with their interpretation at the type of sets.

More generally, the Adjectival Theory assumes that different determiner phrases are generated with interpretations at different semantic types:

- **definite determiner phrases**, like *the three girls*, are generated with an interpretation at the type of individuals (type d);
- **indefinite determiner phrases**, like Ø *three girls*, are generated with an interpretation at the type of sets of individuals (type <d,t>);
- **quantificational determiner phrases**, like *every girl*, are generated with an interpretation at the type of generalized quantifiers over individuals (type <<d,t>,t>);

With Partee (1987), the assumption is that types d and <<d,t>,t> are appropriate types for argument interpretations, while <d,t> is the appropriate type for predicate interpretations. In the Adjectival Theory, quantificational determiner phrases and definites are generated with interpretations appropriate for argument interpretations, while indefinites are generated with interpretations appropriate for predicate interpretations.

But, of course, definites have predicate interpretations as well, and indefinites have argument interpretations as well. Following Partee (1987), we will assume that this is a matter of **type shifting**: the grammar contains a **type shifting theory**, a set of type shifting operations. These operations represent systematic interpretation shifts of expressions. Basically, the type shifting theory tells you which interpretation shifts are available to the grammar without cost. For determiner phrases, the relevant type shifting operations are discussed in Partee (1987): definites can shift from the argument type of individuals to the argument type of generalized quantifiers with the operation LIFT; definites can shift from the argument type of individuals to the predicate type with the operation IDENT; indefinites and definites can shift from the predicate type to the argument type of generalized quantifiers with the operation EC.

Unlike Partee's theory, the Adjectival Theory, in this version, has only lifting operations. This means that quantificational determiner phrases do not have default predicate interpretations. This aspect of the Adjectival Theory plays a crucial role throughout this book.

Traditionally (e.g. in the work of Montague 1973 and Partee 1987), predicate interpretations of determiner phrases are derived from argument interpretations, and it is assumed that the alternative strategy of deriving argument interpretations from predicate interpretations is logically untenable. This alternative strategy is, of course, precisely the Adjectival Theory of Indefinite Determiner Phrases, so traditionally it is assumed that the Adjectival Theory is logically untenable. The bulk of chapter 2 compares these two strategies.

It is argued that the logical problems facing the Adjectival Theory can be solved in a general way, by using the theory of event maximalization developed in Landman (2000). The resulting theory is logically coherent, but at the cost of some complexity, or more precisely, non-uniformity: not all noun phrases are analyzed semantically in exactly the same way. I argue that this is hardly a disadvantage, because I show that the Classical analysis – and, in fact, any analysis – must be complex and non-uniform in analogous ways. Ultimately, then, we are comparing two ways of setting up the grammar that are both logically coherent and complex. In a point by point comparison it is argued that the evidence actually favours the Adjectival Theory.

In chapter 3 I argue that the interpretation of determiner phrases in predicate position is sensitive to a constraint on variables. The issue is theory independent: e.g. the Classical Theory is as much in need of a constraint here as the Adjectival Theory. The constraint I propose is formulated in terms of type shifting: the **Variable Constraint** says that **variables** cannot be shifted from type a of a-individuals to the corresponding type $<a,t>$ of sets of a-individuals. The chapter discusses the effects of the constraint, and the available ways the grammar has to circumvent it (in particular, functional readings).

The importance of the Variable Constraint in this book is the following: the Variable Constraint, in combination with the Adjectival Theory, predicts a battery of semantic effects for determiner phrases with interpretations generated at the type of sets $<a,t>$. The most obvious context where this is relevant is predicate position, but, importantly, the theory predicts similar effects for any position where the interpretation is based on the type of sets.

The Adjectival Theory together with the Variable Constraint makes the following predictions for predicate position:

1. by default, quantificational determiner phrases are infelicitous in predicate position;
2. by default, determiner phrases filling predicate position cannot be given wide scope;
3. by default, relativization with the gap in predicate position is infelicitous;
4. by default, wh-questioning with the gap in predicate position is infelicitous.

In all these cases I say "by default" because the theory only predicts the relevant infelicity if and when the Variable Constraint is violated. The chapter discusses various situations where the grammar provides "rescue mechanisms," ways of avoiding conflict with the variable constraint, leading to certain types of examples which are felicitous.

At this point, *there*-insertion constructions enter the stage, and the well-known contrast in (2):

(2)a. #There was *every girl* in the garden.
  b. #There were *the three girls* in the garden.
  c.   There were *three girls* in the garden.

Let us, for the sake of this introduction, call *there* in the examples in (2) the **temporary subject** and the italic phrases the **delayed subjects**. The crucial observation is that, in these constructions, delayed subjects show exactly the same Variable Constraint effects as we find for determiner phrases in predicate position (i.e. 1–4 above), plus a definiteness effect:

5. By default, definite noun phrases are infelicitous as delayed subjects.

This means that given the Adjectival Theory with the Variable Constraint, there is every reason to assume that delayed subjects have an interpretation based on the type of sets.

Higginbotham (1987) and others have made a more precise assumption: they assume that *there*-insertion constructions are in fact predicate constructions, with the delayed subject being the predicate. I argue that this analysis is untenable when you look cross-linguistically: e.g. Dutch allows delayed subjects in any kind of verbal or predicative construction, and it just will not do to argue that these must be reanalyzed as structures in which the delayed subject is the predicate.

This brings us to chapter 4 where the main idea underlining the analysis of *there*-insertion constructions is proposed:

Proposal:
1. Delayed subjects are neither arguments nor predicates. They are **intersective adjuncts**: under certain circumstances determiner phrases with an interpretation at the type of sets can shift to delayed subjects with an interpretation as an intersective adjunct.

The interpretation of intersective adjuncts (like adjectives and adverbials) is accessed from the type of sets: the types of intersective adjuncts are derived from the type of sets through the general type shifting operation ADJOIN (from type $<a,t>$ to types $<<b^n,<a,t>>,<b^n,<a,t>>>$). It is shown that the Variable Constraint effects 1–4 for delayed subjects follow straightforwardly from this. The definiteness effect 5 does not as this requires a separate stipulation:

Proposal:
2. Only determiner phrases with an interpretation generated at the type of sets can shift to delayed subjects with an intersective adjunct interpretation.

This means that **indefinite** determiner phrases in delayed subject position can receive an interpretation as an intersective adjunct. While **definite** determiner phrases can receive a set interpretation in predicate position, they cannot receive an interpretation as an intersective adjunct in delayed subject position. **Quantificational** determiner phrases are already infelicitous in predicate position, so *a fortiori* they are infelicitous as delayed subjects.

The details of this proposal are worked out in later chapters. But first in chapter 4 alternative accounts of the Definiteness Effect are discussed, accounts based on a distinction between weak and strong determiner phrases. Such theories propose a semantic criterion (strength) that distinguishes definites and quantificational expressions from indefinites. Two kinds of theories are discussed: those that identify strength with **presuppositionality**, and those that identify weakness with **symmetry**.

Several arguments against such theories are discussed. For a start, we can already see from the above discussion that the weak–strong contrast puts the dividing line at the wrong place: it groups together definites and quantificational expressions, and separates out indefinites. But the parallel with predicate position shows that the major dividing line lies first between quantificational expressions and the rest, and only then between definites and indefinites.

The discussion of presuppositionality argues in two direction: it is shown that there are many types of quantificational expressions and definites which are arguably not presuppositional, but are nevertheless infelicitous as delayed subjects; vice versa, it is shown that there are indefinites which are arguably presuppositional, which are felicitous, or only slightly infelicitous as delayed subjects. Hence the effects of presuppositionality are not strong enough to explain the robust infelicity of the quantificational expressions and definites as delayed subjects.

The case against symmetry has some discussion of Dutch *sommige* (*some*), which is arguably symmetric, but infelicitous in predicative contexts and as delayed subjects. The more important case is the comparison between *most boys* and *more than half of the boys*. While *most boys* is infelicitous in predicative position and as delayed subject, *more than half of the boys* is fine in both contexts. But not only is *more than half of the boys* arguably non-symmetric, again arguably it has exactly the same argument interpretation as *most boys*. These facts are not just problematic for accounts identifying weakness with symmetry, but in fact for any account based on a semantically interpreted weak–strong distinction.

Chapter 5 provides the basics of my account of delayed subjects. Above, I already indicated how assuming that delayed subjects are adjuncts gives you the Variable Constraint effects and the definiteness effects. The question to be answered is: how can determiner phrases in the position of delayed subjects be adjuncts? Normally determiner phrases are not licensed in adjunct position. Why can they occur as adjuncts here?

The first step lies in a modification of what in syntax is called **Theta Theory**. Classical formulations of Theta Theory assume that determiner phrases must receive a thematic role, and can receive such a role in argument position, but not in adjunct position. I replace the latter assumption by a semantic constraint, which, I argue, has by and large the same effect: a role can only be assigned to a constituent if in the semantic interpretation of the complex the interpretation of that constituent restricts the value of that role in the appropriate way. I argue that in the normal case, this semantic constraint is satisfied if the constituent is in argument position, but not if it is in adjunct position. The second step will be to argue that the constraint is actually satisfied in the delayed subject position. In this chapter, I analyze the Dutch case in (3) (postponing the English cases to chapter 6).

(3) (dat) er   een meisje zingt.
     that there a   girl   sings

My proposal is that the determiner phrase *een meisje* in (3) is an adjunct on the verbal predicate *zingt*. But, and this is the crux of the matter, there is a type mismatch: the determiner phrase is of the type of sets of individuals, <d,t>, while the type of the verbal predicate is <d,<e,t>>, functions from individuals into sets of events. While the type shifting operation ADJUNCT can shift expressions denoting sets of individuals into modifiers of (functions from entities into) sets of individuals, it cannot shift them into modifiers of (functions from entities into) sets of events. Thus, type shifting is needed to resolve this mismatch. The mechanism I propose, which I call **flip–flop**, shifts the interpretation of the verbal predicate from type <d,<e,t>> to type <e,<d,t>> (and back), allowing the adjunction.

  I argue that this mechanism has several pleasing features: it uses an operation which is well attested in the semantics of passive; it can only operate high in the tree, at the level of one-place predicates (so you only get delayed subjects, not delayed objects); and importantly, it satisfies the constraint on thematic role assignment: i.e. exceptionally in adjunct position, the interpretation of these adjuncts will constrain the thematic role in the correct way, hence the role can be assigned to them.

  Having successfully adjoined the determiner phrase as a delayed subject, I discuss what happens higher in the tree. Since the subject thematic role has already been assigned to the delayed subject, no more role can be assigned to the external subject position. Since normal determiner phrases cannot occur in this position unless they are thematically licensed, the position must be filled by a non-thematic determiner phrase, also called a pleonastic.

  Two more things are done in chapter 5:

- The semantics of (3), with an adjoined subject and a pleonastic subject, is worked out by showing how it fits in the general theory of sentence interpretation with event maximalization of Landman (2000).
- Some thoughts are developed about the syntax of non-thematic determiner phrases, and their distribution in Dutch, German, English, and French. It is argued that the distribution of non-thematic determiner phrases in these languages is fruitfully characterized by assuming an ordered set of non-thematic determiner phrases {empty, last resort}, of which "empty" must be syntactically licensed (with parametric differences), and a non-thematic adverb (*there* in English) which can license "empty" (and of which the availability is parametrized). Thus, *there* is not a pleonastic determiner phrase: the pleonastic determiner phrase is [DP *there* [DP empty]]; *there* itself is an adverb.

  Chapter 6 deals with the nature of the predicates that allow adjoined subjects. It already basically follows from the nature of flip–flop that only semantically one-place predicates allow adjoined subjects. This means that the delayed subject cannot be adjoined below the VP level, say, directly to a transitive verb, because it's at the VP level that the interpretation reaches the stage of a one-place predicate.

It has long been known that in English (and French), adjoined subjects are allowed with (certain) unaccusative verbs and passives and with episodic predicates, but not with unergative verbs, transitive verbs, and not with non-episodic predicates. As is well known, in Dutch (and German), adjoined subjects are allowed basically with any verb (like the unergative verb *sing* in (3) above). I argue in chapter 6 that Dutch adjoined subjects are not sensitive to the episodic–non-episodic distinction either: you find felicitous adjoined subjects with non-episodic predicates as well (where the English counterpart is clearly infelicitous).

I take from Rothstein (2001) and Chierchia (1989) the distinction between **unsaturated** and **saturated** one-place predicates – which I formalize within the current event theory as a typal distinction between one-place predicates of type <d,<e,t>> (functions from individuals into sets of events) and of type <e,t> (sets of events) – and I take from them the assumption that the grammatical derivation at the level of the VP must go through a stage where the VP is interpreted as an unsaturated predicate (meaning that if it isn't, it must be shifted into one). Then I propose that while all verbs and predicates are derived with unsaturated interpretations (in which the argument structure is explicit in the type), unaccusatives, passives, and episodic predicates allow a second derivation with a saturated interpretation (in which the argument structure is typally implicit). The differences between Dutch and German on the one hand, and English and French on the other then lie in a semantic parameter: Dutch and German allow adjoined subjects for one-place predicates, both saturated and unsaturated, while English and French only allow adjoined subjects for saturated predicates.

There is a large literature on the syntax of Dutch *er*-insertion contexts. In chapter 7 I discuss, in relation to the present proposal, some of the pertinent issues that have been raised. On my proposal, the indefinite is adjoined to VP, while *er*, when present, is adjoined to an empty non-thematic DP in the external subject position.

I argue that there is strong evidence that the indefinite is inside the VP and that *er*, when present, is inside the external subject position. Concerning the indefinite, I argue that you can't really tell whether the indefinite is syntactically adjoined to VP, or in a syntactic VP-internal subject position, if you allow that the latter is semantically adjoined. Since I have shown how the adjoined indefinite is naturally thematically licensed in an adjoined position, I prefer to maintain here the connection between syntactic and semantic adjunction. Concerning *er*, I argue, against Bennis (1986), that *er* patterns with subjects and not with adverbials in normal adverbial position. But I agree with Bennis that we don't want to identify *er* with the subject: *er* is an adverbial, and adverbials do not make good subjects of the verbs they occur with (we need a DP). The proposal that *er* is adjoined to a non-thematic DP allows us to make the adverbial nature of *er* consistent with its distribution.

The other main issue discussed in this chapter is what has been called "semantic partitioning": the assumption that syntactic positions inside the VP are necessarily marked as "semantically weak," while positions outside the VP are marked as "semantically strong." I argue that some of the observed effects will follow from anybody's theory: anybody who assumes some correlation between the external subject position and a notion of topic will predict at least weak, pragmatic effects of "strength" for indefinites in the external subject position, and "weakness" for adjoined indefinites. Semantic partitioning assumes more: it assumes a grammatical correlation between these syntactic positions and semantic notions of weak and strong. I argue that this theory, insofar as it is testable, is false, and that attempts to remove the falsehood move it into the domain of the untestable.

Chapter 8 deals with problems of negative noun phrases, like *no girls*. The theory of event maximalization developed in Landman (2000), and modified in the present book in chapters 2 and 5, provides a semantics for a wide range of determiner phrases in argument position, predicate position, and adjoined position, including downward entailing ones like *at most three girls*. But it doesn't account for the semantics of negative determiner phrases, and in particular not for adjoined negative determiner phrases in *there*-insertion constructions. I argue in chapter 8 that an approach that will provide a correct semantics for negative noun phrases has long been proposed in the literature; I call it **semantic break-up**: the negative noun phrase is separated in a negation and an indefinite noun phrase (i.e. *no(t)* and *girls*), and the negation takes its scope independently from the remainder indefinite noun phrase. I argue that, while this approach may at first sight seem *ad hoc*, there are a lot of arguments in its favor, among which are several semantic arguments. I formulate the operation of semantic break-up as a type driven storage and retrieval operation (a negation of type <t,t> must be stored if the types do not match, and must be retrieved as soon as the types do match); I show how it accounts for negative determiner phrases in argument position, predicate position, and adjoined position; and I work out an account for various highly complex problems, like the problem of negative determiner phrases inside conjunctions, and negative noun phrases modified by *almost* and exception phrases.

With this, the discussion of *there*-insertion constructions ends. The remaining three chapters deal with definiteness effects in other constructions.

Chapter 9 deals with definiteness effects of relational determiner phrases. I argue that there are two connected sets of facts here. In the first place, with verbs like *have* relational determiner phrases show definiteness effects, as in (4):

(4)a.   John has *a sister* in the army.
   b.   #John has *the sister* in the army.

Secondly, in this construction the verb *have* does not have its normal possessive meaning – I call this de-thematicization: the verb phrase *have a sister* takes over the relational meaning from the determiner phrase (the property you have if someone stands in the sister relation to you). These two properties pattern together with *have*: if the determiner phrase is not a relation, definiteness effects do not show up, and neither does de-thematicization: both (5a) and (5b) are felicitous and possessive:

(5)a.   John has *a car*.
   b.   John has *the car*.

These two characteristics make the *have* constructions quite different from *there*-insertion constructions, and for that reason I argue that it is not attractive to try to reduce the analysis of *have* constructions to that for *there*-insertion contexts.

Nevertheless, my account relies crucially on the Adjectival Theory in which **relational** indefinites are generated at the type <d,<d,t>> of relations.

The analysis starts with the assumption that the possessive meaning of *have* can be de-thematicized: *have* loses its possessive meaning, and with that its thematic roles. As a consequence, it can no longer take a normal object noun phrase. In comes the Adjectival Theory. The relational indefinite is of type <d,<d,t>>, the type of relations between individuals. By the general process developed in Landman (2000), and already used in chapter 6, it can shift its interpretation to the Davidsonian type <d,<d,<e,t>>>, which is exactly the type of *have*. The two interpretations now combine through **semantic incorporation**, which is basically simply intersection (through which the complex receives the interpretation of the relational indefinite) and re-thematicization as a one-place predicate, meaning in essence that a thematic role for the subject is created.

I argue further that verbs of change of possession, like *buy* and *sell*, show systematic de-thematicized readings with relational indefinites as well, though not definiteness effects. These facts are accounted for if we assume that these verbs have as part of their meaning the same possession meaning that *have* has (basically, the notions of source and goal are reanalyzed along these lines). The facts discussed follow if we assume that this possession part can be similarly de-thematicized, and re-thematicized by the relational indefinite.

Chapters 10 and 11 deal with determiner phrases with *time* occurring in adverbial position. There are two types that pattern differently. In chapter 10, I argue that definite expressions like *every time the bell rang* are based on a maximalizing relative clause (in the sense of Grosu and Landman 1998) with a relativization gap based on the type of degrees.

I argue that this allows a derivation where the whole expression *every time the bell rang* denotes a degree on events (just as *three* is a degree on objects). I assume that the expression, though it looks like a determiner phrase (and hence shouldn't be able to occur in adverbial position), actually is syntactically formed with a null measure, so the full phrase is actually not a determiner phrase, but an adverbial measure phrase. The null adverbial measure I call CANTOR, and it relates to the (equally null) nominal measure CARDINALITY. Whereas CARDINALITY directly specifies the number of atoms of a sum, CANTOR measures the cardinality of a sum of events in terms of one–one mappings with a given sum of events. This account predicts (correctly) that adverbial definite *time* expressions count main-clause events indirectly (through one–one mappings), and it accounts for the "mapping" effects of these expressions, discussed in Rothstein (1995).

In chapter 11, I discuss adverbial indefinite *time* determiner phrases like *three times*. I argue that, unlike the definite cases discussed in chapter 10, these phrases count main-clause events directly. The simplest idea would be to assume that these phrases do in the adverbial domain what adjectival numerals, like *three*, do in the nominal domain. But I show, with some facts first discussed by Jenny Doetjes (Doetjes 1997), that such an account is too simple: the adverbial phrases introduce scopal relations that the nominal cases do not (meaning that the adverbial phrases are not simply intersective).

In my analysis, the scopal effects come in through the semantics of *time*. I argue that *time* is not a normal noun, but in fact a **classifier**. Classifiers shift between semantic domains (for instance, from mass to count). The classifier *time* shifts non-atomic sums of events to corresponding atomic group-events. This means that the scopal effect is actually a **gridding** effect.

Classifiers typically take complements, and I assume that in adverbial *three times*, *times* does takes a complement and that complement is a gap of the category PRED/PRED (in the sense of categorial grammar). This means, following standard assumptions in categorial grammar, that the expression *three times* is in fact not a DP, but a DP/PRED. In comes the Adjectival Theory again. For indefinite noun phrases (and only them), the type of this DP/PRED is a predicate modifier type, and I write this into the category as DP[PRED]/PRED. This is semantically a perfectly legitimate adverbial category, which combines with a predicate to give a predicate.

On the analysis developed, what looks like a determiner phrase in adverbial position is in fact not a determiner phrase, but a perfectly legitimate adverbial expression. This expression has indeed the semantics of a direct counter: it directly counts main clause events. At the same time, through the classifier, the counting is gridded, which means that the expression shows the correct scopal effects.

Chapter 1

Numerical Adjectives and the Type of Sets

In this chapter I discuss the analysis of numerical expressions inside noun phrases. More particularly, I will be interested in the semantics of noun phrases like *the three boys, the more than seven girls, the exactly ninety kids.* Let us go back in time to the period around 1980 when Generalized Qantifier Theory was established in the work of Barwise and Cooper and others (Barwise and Cooper 1981; Keenan and Faltz 1985; Keenan and Stavi 1986).

Barwise and Cooper provided a semantics for noun phrases of the form *the n NOUN,* with *n* a number expression. I will slightly generalize their analysis to noun phrases of the form *the r n NOUN,* with *r* an expression denoting a numerical relation, like *more than, less than, at least, at most, exactly,* or Ø (where *the n* is *the Ø n*). On Barwise and Cooper's analysis, *the r n* forms a partial determiner (of generalized quantifier type <d,<d,t>>, where d is the type of expressions denoting individuals), which gets its interpretation according to the following schema:

$$the\ r\ n \rightarrow \lambda Q.\begin{cases} \lambda P.\forall x[Q(x) \rightarrow P(x)] & \text{if } |Q|\ r\ n \\ \text{undefined} & \text{otherwise} \end{cases}$$

The function which takes a noun interpretation Q and gives the set of all properties that every Q has, if the cardinality of Q stands in relation r to n, and is undefined otherwise.

Thus, *the at most three boys* has the same interpretation as *every boy* if there are at most three boys ($|BOY| \leq 3$), and is undefined otherwise. In general, when defined, *the r n NOUN* has the same interpretation as *every NOUN.* The conditions under which it is defined are constrained by *r* and *n*.

With the above schema, we can define:

the boy = *the exactly one boys*
the boys = *the at least one boys*
both boys = *the exactly two boys*

This account is very successful in dealing with the partiality of definite noun phrases, the conditions under which definite noun phrases are defined: *the boy* is defined if and only if there is exactly one boy, *the boys* iff there are boys, *the at most three boys* iff there are at most three boys (which includes the possibility of no boys), etc. The pragmatic assumption that noun phrases should only be used when they are defined leads to the correct presuppositions for the use of these noun phrases: i.e. the felicitous use of *the at most three boys* presupposes that there are at most three boys.

The analysis is less successful in other respects. It does not incorporate a semantic singular–plural distinction, and does not deal with distinctions between distributive and collective readings: the above account only deals with distributive readings (*the*, when defined, is *every*). Also, and this is the aspect that concerns us most here, the analysis assumes that in *the r n NOUN*, *the r n* is a determiner which combines with the noun: we have a determiner schema which generates an infinite set of determiners. A similar assumption is dominant in the work of Keenan and his co-authors (Keenan and Faltz 1985, Keenan and Stavi 1986). This aspect of the analysis has been challenged, for instance by Rothstein (1988): there are several reasons to think that the constituent structure of these noun phrases is [[$_{DET}$ *the*] [$_{NP}$ *r n NOUN*]], and not [[$_{DET}$ *the r n*] [$_{NP}$ *NOUN*]] (see Rothstein 1988).

The first of these structures is supported by very strong evidence. While numerical phrases in predicate or argument indefinites must be initial in the noun phrase (i.e. they cannot mingle with adjectives), this is not so inside the nominal domain, i.e. not in the noun phrases that we are looking at here (a similar argument has been made by de Jong 1983):

(1)a. *Fifty ferocious lions* were shipped to Artis.
  b. #*Ferocious fifty lions* were shipped to Artis.

(2)a.   The animals in the shipment were *fifty ferocious lions*.
  b. #The animals in the shipment were *ferocious fifty lions*.

(3)a.   We shipped the *fifty ferocious lions* to Blijdorp, and the *thirty meek lions* to Artis.
  b.   We shipped the *ferocious fifty lions* to Blijdorp, and the *meek thirty lions* to Artis.

Of course, there are subtle and hard to pinpoint interpretation differences between the cases in (3a) and (3b). However, it seems that most of these can be attributed to contextual interpretation factors that we know are operative in the adjectival domain anyway, like focus, contrast, comparison set, etc. That is, we find such interpretation differences also when we consider strings of normal adjectives. The point about (3b) is the contrast with (1b) and (2b): (1b) and (2b) are crashingly bad, while (3b) is not.

A complex determiner analysis can only account for these facts if it not only allows numericals to be part of the complex determiners, but adjectives as well.

While Keenan (1987) seems prepared to make the latter assumption, it is not clear that this should be the default choice, if we can make the alternative analysis work. The alternative analysis assumes that numerical phrases (like *at most three*) are part of the noun phrase structure like adjectives. I will call the assumption that numerical phrases (and more generally, indefinites) are adjectives, at least semantically, the Adjectival Theory of Indefinites:

The Adjectival Theory of Indefinites:
Indefinites have the semantics of intersective adjectives.

To give form to the adjectival theory, we turn to the analysis of plurality originating in the work of Sharvy (1980) and Link (1983).

We assume that our interpretation domain for expressions of type d is a complete atomic Boolean algebra. I will be short here; for more details, see Landman (1991, 2000) (note that, for my purposes here, I use complete join and meet as the basic operations, instead of the standard two place operations).

Complete atomic Boolean algebras:
A **complete atomic Boolean algebra** is a structure $\mathbf{B} = \langle B,\sqcup,\sqsubseteq\rangle$, where B is a set, partially ordered by **part-of** relation $\sqsubseteq$, and for every $X \subseteq B$: $\sqcup X \in B$, where $\sqcup X$ is the **sum** of X, the smallest element of B such that for every $x \in X$: $x \sqsubseteq \sqcup X$.

Furthermore, the structure satisfies postulates (1)–(3) below, which use some of the following definitions:

Definitions:
Let $X \subseteq B$, $a,b \in B$:
$\sqcap X = \sqcup\{c \in B$: for every $x \in X$: $c \sqsubseteq x\}$
$a \sqcup b = \sqcup\{a,b\}$, $a \sqcap b = \sqcap\{a,b\}$
$0 = \sqcup\varnothing$; $1 = \sqcup B$
$\neg b = \sqcup\{c \in B$: $b \sqcap c = 0\}$
ATOM $= \{c \in B$: $c \neq 0$ and for no $d \in B-\{0,c\}$: $d \sqsubseteq c\}$
(the set of atoms, elements that have only themselves and 0 as part)
$(b] = \{c \in B$: $c \sqsubseteq b\}$, the ideal generated by b (the set of all b's parts)
$[b) = \{c \in B$: $b \sqsubseteq c\}$, the filter generated by b (the set of all elements that b is part of)
ATOM(b) $= (b] \cap$ ATOM
(the set of all b's atomic parts)
$|b| = |$ATOM(b)$|$
(the cardinality of element b is the cardinality of the set of its atomic parts)

Conditions:
1. **Distributivity**: if $a \sqsubseteq b \sqcup c$ then $a \sqsubseteq b$ or $a \sqsubseteq c$ or for some $b_1 \sqsubseteq b$ and some $c_1 \sqsubseteq c$: $a = b_1 \sqcup c_1$.
   (if a is part of a sum $b \sqcup c$, then it is either fully part of b or fully part of c, or the sum of some part of b and some part of c)

2. **Witness**: if a ⊑ b and a ≠ 0 and a ≠ b then for some c ⊑ b: c ≠ 0 and
    a ⊓ c = 0.
    (if a is a proper non-zero part of b, then there is another proper non-zero part c of b such that a and c have no non-zero part in common)
3. **Atomicity**: For every b ∈ B–{0}: ATOM(b) ≠ Ø
    (every non-zero element has atomic parts)

An atomic **mereology** is a complete atomic Boolean algebra with the bottom element 0 removed. It is good to point out that, while in the past I have been using atomic mereologies in the semantics of plurality, in this book it will be essential that the structures be full Boolean algebras.

Every complete atomic Boolean algebra has 2^α elements for some cardinality α, and per cardinality α there is, up to isomorphism, exactly one Boolean algebra with 2^α elements. One of the most instructive properties of these structures is their decomposition:

Decomposition Theorem:
Let **B** be a Boolean algebra and a an atom in B.
   [a) and (¬a] form non-overlapping isomorphic Boolean algebras (with the operations of **B** restricted to [a) and (¬a] respectively).
   Let h be an isomorphism from [a) into (¬a].
B = [a) ∪ (¬a], ordered by the transitive closure of relation:
⊑$_{[a)}$ ∪ ⊑$_{(¬a]}$ ∪ {<c,h(c)>:c ∈ [a)}.

Thus, every complete atomic Boolean algebra can be decomposed into two isomorphic Boolean algebras: for any atom a: the filter generated by a, and the ideal generated by dual atom ¬a. Since in a finite Boolean algebra of cardinality 2^{n+1} for atom a, the cardinality of [a) (and hence of (¬a]) is 2^n, this theorem gives us an instructive method for generating each finite Boolean algebra:

*   Two one-element Boolean algebras and an isomorphism give you the two-element Boolean algebra:

*   Two two-element Boolean algebras and an isomorphism give you the four-element Boolean algebra:

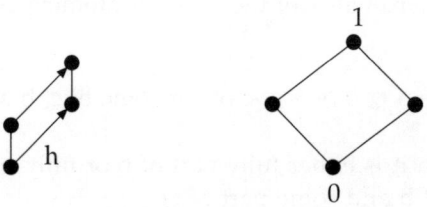

- Two four-element Boolean algebras and an isomorphism give you the eight-element Boolean algebra:

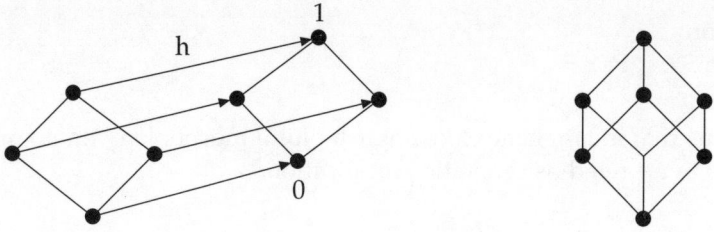

- Two eight-element Boolean algebras and an isomorphism give you the sixteen-element Boolean algebra:

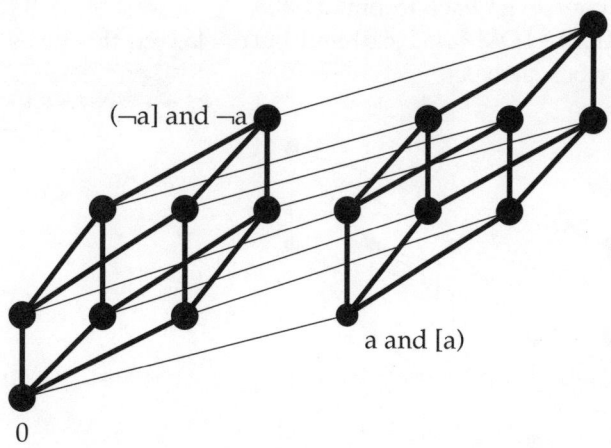

As you can see in the diagram, the eight-element Boolean algebra on the left provides the 0 and three of the atoms of the sixteen-element Boolean algebra, while its 1 becomes a dual atom ¬a. The eight-element Boolean algebra on the right provides the 1 and the remaining three dual atoms of the sixteen-element Boolean algebra, while its 0 becomes the fourth atom a of the sixteen-element structure. And this happens at every level: from two Boolean algebras with 2^α elements and α atoms, we form a Boolean algebra with $2^{\alpha+1}$ elements and $\alpha+1$ atoms: α atoms come from the Boolean algebra on the left, one more atom is the reinterpretation of the 0 element of the Boolean algebra on the right.

Thus the structure of type d of individuals is a complete atomic Boolean algebra of singular, atomic individuals and their plural sums. We now come to the interpretation of (count) nouns. Nouns are interpreted as expressions of type <d,t>, sets of individuals. We assume that in languages such as English singular nouns lexically select singular individuals, i.e. atoms – singular nouns denote sets of atoms:

Singular nouns:
boy → BOY   of type <d,t>   BOY ⊆ ATOM

We assume an operation of semantic pluralization (*) which we take to be closure under sum:

Pluralization:
$$*P = \{x \in D: \exists Z \subseteq P: x = \sqcup Z\}$$

And we assume that in languages like English plural morphology on nouns is (by and large) interpreted as semantic pluralization.

Plural nouns:
boys → *BOY

These assumptions, of course, go back to Link (1983).

Thus, if we assume that ATOM = {a,b,c,d} and BOY = {a,b,c}, this gives us: *BOY = {0,a,b,c,a⊔b,a⊔c,b⊔c,a⊔b⊔c}:

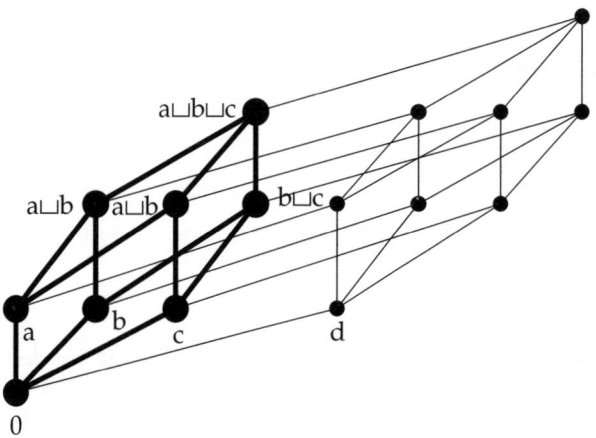

*P is the closure under sum of P. It is important to note that I use here the standard notion of closure for Boolean algebras (and not a notion modified for mereologies). On this notion, for each subset X of P, $\sqcup X \in *P$. Since one of these subsets is ∅, $\sqcup\emptyset \in *P$. Since $\sqcup\emptyset = 0$, $0 \in *P$. Thus, on the standard notion of closure under sum, $0 \in *P$.

Now, the standard assumption for intersective adjectives is that they intersect with the noun:

Intersective adjectives:
$[_{NP}$ ADJ NP] → ADJ ∩ NP   (λx.ADJ(x) ∧NP(x))

If we assume that an adjective like *young* also denotes a set of atoms, then we can make either one of two assumptions for a plural noun phrase like *young boys*: the adjective combines with the noun, and pluralization applies to the whole:

*(YOUNG ∩ BOY)

or the noun is pluralized and agreement triggers semantic pluralization of the adjective:

*YOUNG ∩ *BOY.

These are in essence alternative theories about where number takes its effect, but we do not at this point need to choose between them, since, by the Boolean structure,

*(YOUNG ∩ BOY) = *YOUNG ∩ *BOY

Thus, if YOUNG = {b,c,d}, *YOUNG = {0,b,c,d,b⊔c,b⊔d,c⊔d,b⊔c⊔d}, and *YOUNG ∩ *BOY = {0,b,c,b⊔c}. So *young boys* denotes the set of sums each of whose singular constituents is a young boy. All that this shows is that the standard account of intersective adjectival modification can straightforwardly be extended to the plural case.

Now we come to the adjectival theory of numericals. This theory is the assumption that numericals have the semantics of intersective adjectives. This means that they denote sets, like intersective adjectives, and that they combine with the noun through intersection. This gives us the following interpretation schema for numerical phrases:

r n → λx.|x| r n   of type <d,t>
the set of sums whose cardinality stands in relation r to number n.

With *at most* → ≤, *at least* → ≥, *exactly* → =, we get:

at most two → λx.|x| ≤ 2

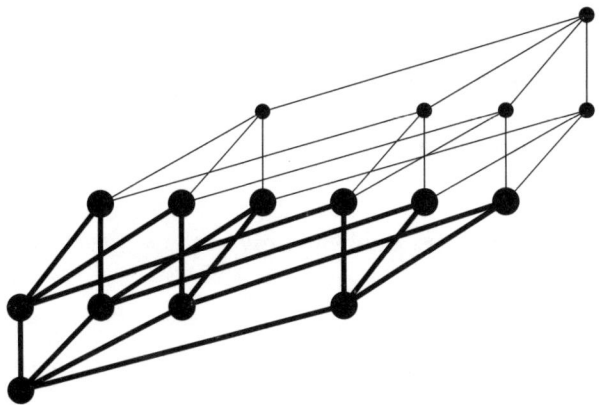

at least two → λx.|x| ≥ 2

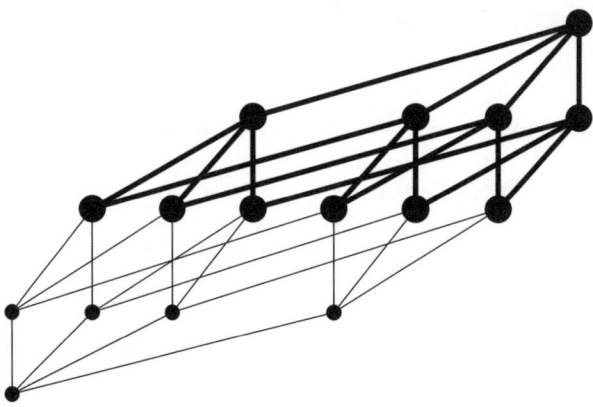

and *exactly two* → λx.|x| = 2

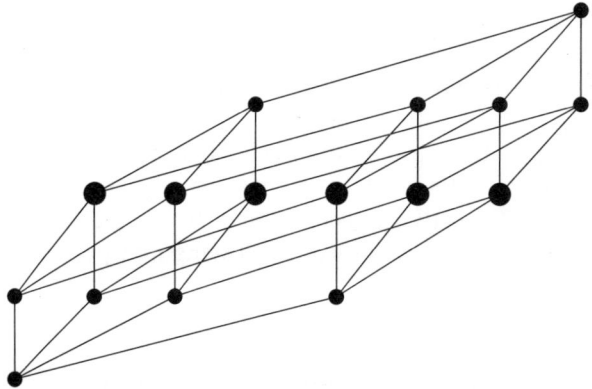

The diagrams illustrate that we can fruitfully define notions of upward and downward closure for sets of pluralities:

> Let **Y** be a Boolean algebra on a subset of **B** and let X ⊆ Y.
> X is **upward closed, UC** on **Y** iff
> if x ∈ X and y ∈ Y and x ⊑ y   then y ∈ X
> X is **downward closed, DC** on **Y** iff
> if x ∈ X and y ∈ Y and y ⊑ x then y ∈ X

Clearly, *at least two* is UC on D, *at most two* is DC on D, *exactly two* is neither. Intersecting these three numerical phrases with *BOY gives:

at most two boys → λx.*BOY(x) ∧ |x| ≤ 2

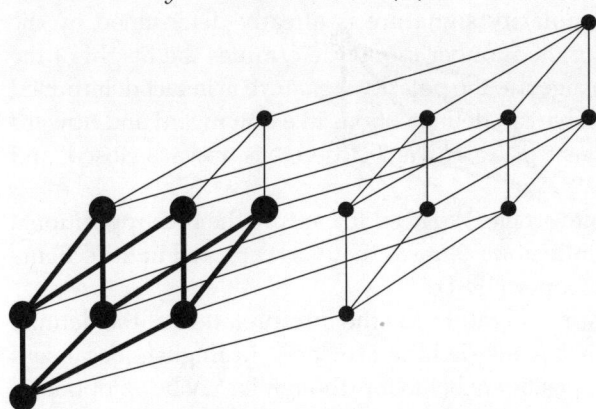

At most two boys is DC on D, and hence also on *BOY.

at least two boys → λx.*BOY(x) ∧ |x| ≥ 2

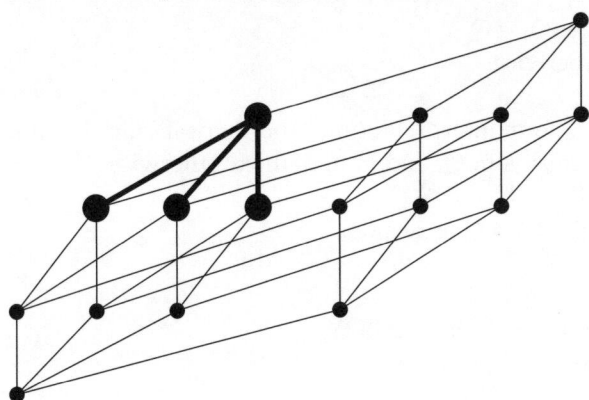

We see that *at least two boys* is not UC on D, but it is UC on *BOY. (Compare it with the diagram of the denotation of *BOY, given earlier.)

Finally, *exactly two boys* → λx.*BOY(x) ∧ |x| = 2

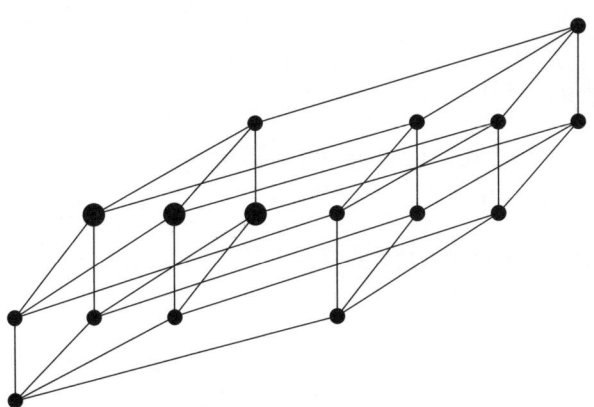

Exactly two boys is of course neither UC nor DC on D, or on *BOY.

So, what we can call the **polarity signature** is already determined by the numeral phrase. In fact, since the number n only determines the height of the interpretation in the Boolean algebra, the polarity signature is in fact determined by the numerical relation r. So we can define notions like downward and upward closure for numerical relations: $\leq$ is downward closed, $\geq$ is upward closed, and $=$ is neither.

We now come to the definite article. We need to capture the presuppositional behavior of the different definite noun phrases that was captured in the schema derived from Barwise and Cooper (1981).

Link (1983) proposes the sum operator $\sqcup$ as the interpretation of the definite article. This is not quite right for the definite article *the* in English, because it doesn't have the right presuppositional behavior (though it may be an option in certain cases where there is assumed to be an implicit definiteness operation). In later work, Link takes over the operation already proposed in Sharvy (1980), which is now usually notated as operation σ:

$$\sigma = \lambda Q.\begin{cases} \sqcup(Q) & \text{if } \sqcup(Q) \in Q \\ \text{undefined} & \text{otherwise} \end{cases}$$

The function which takes a noun interpretation Q and maps it onto the sum of the Qs if the sum of the Qs is in Q, and is undefined otherwise.

With this definition we get the following results:

the boy $\rightarrow \sigma(BOY)$
BOY = {a,b,c}, $\sqcup$BOY = a$\sqcup$b$\sqcup$c, a$\sqcup$b$\sqcup$c $\notin$ BOY,
Hence $\sigma(BOY)$ is undefined.

If we let GIRL = {d}, then $\sqcup$GIRL = $\sqcup${d} = d. d $\in$ {d}, hence σ(GIRL) = d. For singular predicate P, σ(P) is defined iff P is a singleton set. Thus, for singular predicates, σ coincides with the iota operator.

the boys $\rightarrow \sigma(*BOY)$
$\sqcup$(*BOY) = a$\sqcup$b$\sqcup$c, a$\sqcup$b$\sqcup$c $\in$ *BOY, hence σ(*BOY) = a$\sqcup$b$\sqcup$c.
In a full Boolean algebra, if P = $\emptyset$, *P = {0} and σ(*P) = 0.

We will discuss the meaning of this later, but it will have the consequence that felicitous use of *the boys* implicates that there are boys.

Let **Y** again be a sub-Boolean algebra of **B**, X $\subseteq$ B.
X shows **variety** on **Y** iff $\sqcup$(X $\cap$ Y) = $\sqcup$Y.

Equivalently, we can say that X shows variety on Y if each atom in Y is part of some element of X $\cap$ Y. (Because in a complete atomic Boolean algebra

$\sqcup(X \cap Y) = \sqcup(Y)$ iff $\cup \{ATOM(b): b \in X \cap Y\} = \cup \{ATOM(b): x \in Y\}$.) Variety is a consequence of a more general notion of **quantitativity** that I will not define here. But the intuition is as follows. Numerical phrases are quantitative restrictors. They restrict a set Y to a set $X \cap Y$ in which all the elements satisfy a certain quantitative profile, and this means that each element in $X \cap Y$ stands in a certain quantitative relation to its atoms. Quantitative means that the identity of the object and its atoms is irrelevant: any other object in Y that stands in the same quantitative relation to its atoms has the same quantitative profile and hence is in $X \cap Y$ as well.

Suppose that $b_1 \in X \cap Y$. $b_1 = \sqcup ATOM(b_1)$. Let $a_1 \in ATOM(b_1)$ and $a_2 \notin ATOM(b_1)$. Now look at $b_2 = \sqcup((ATOM(b_1) - \{a_1\}) \cup \{a_2\})$ (intuitively, the result of replacing in b_1 atomic part a_1 by atomic part a_2). Intuitively, b_2 has the same quantative profile as b_1, and hence b_2 is in $X \cap Y$ as well (if X is a quantitative restrictor). Since this argument can be made for any atom in Y, it follows that quantitative restrictors show variety on Y: while they kick out elements from the denotation of Y, the elements they leave in are built from the full variety of atoms in Y, since the restriction is quantitative and not qualitative.

It is easy to check that *at most one, at most two, at most three, at least one, at least two, at least three, exactly one, exactly two, exactly three* show variety on *BOY. This means that any of these noun phrases *the r n boys* will denote $\sqcup$*BOY ($= a \sqcup b \sqcup c$) if $a \sqcup b \sqcup c$ is in their denotation, and will be undefined otherwise. This means that in the model given, all of the following are undefined:

the at most one boy, the at most two boys, the exactly one boy, the exactly two boys.

And it means that in the model given, all of the following denote $a \sqcup b \sqcup c$, the sum of the boys:

the at most three boys, the at least one boy, the at least two boys, the at least three boys, the exactly three boys.

Thus we see that Link's theory of singular and plural predicates – with Sharvy's theory of the definite article as an operation with picks the maximal element out of a set, while presupposing that the set has a maximal element – and the Adjectival Theory of numericals provides the correct semantics for numerical definites.

This is an appealingly simple and conceptually elegant theory:

The Adjectival Theory as part of the theory of plurality:
Singularity on predicates is atomicity.
Plurality on predicates is closure under sum.
The definite article is a maximalization operator.
Numerical phrases are adjectives.

Let's look at the compositional structure of numerical definite noun phrases in a bit more detail. Up to now, I assume the following compositional analysis:

the → λQ.σ(Q)   Q a variable of type <d,t>
NOUN → N   N of type <d,t>
r n → λx.|x| r n   of type <d,t>

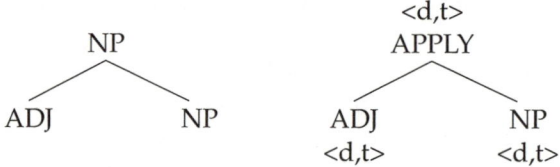

TYPE SHIFTING OPERATION ADJUNCT:
   ADJUNCT: <d,t> → <<d,t>,<d,t>>
   ADJUNCT[α] = λPλx.P(x) ∧ α(x)

(With ADJUNCT, the type mismatch in APPLY[ADJ,NP] is resolved as:

APPLY[ADJUNCT[ADJ], NP]) =
APPLY[λPλx.P(x) ∧ α(x), NP] =
((λPλx.P(x) ∧ α(x))(NP)) =
λx.NP(x) ∧ α(x)   of type <d,t>.

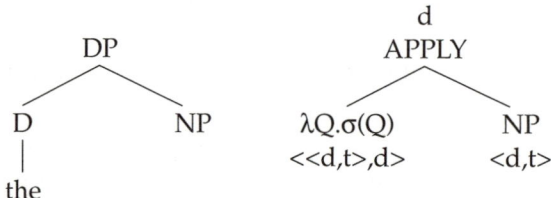

We haven't yet looked at the internal semantic structure of the numerical adjective. That is, we have treated *r n* as an unanalyzed whole.

In analyzing the numerical phrase as an adjective, we have tried to give the expressions involved – the determiner, the noun, and the adjective – the simplest and lowest possible interpretation. We now want to apply this same strategy of analysis to the internal analysis of the numerical phrase.

For that, I want to make the analysis a little bit more general. I have already suggested one way of doing that. Even though in a noun phrase like *the three boys* there is no numerical relation morphologically realized, I have given a general schema for noun phrases of the form *the r n boys*, subsuming *the three boys* under that case. This means that really I am assuming a morphologically null numerical relation Ø and a structure [*the* [[Ø *three*] [*boys*]]], with Ø interpreted as =.

I will now go one step further. Intersective plural numerical phrases like *at least three* in *the at least three boys* are part of a larger class of measure phrases like *at least three pounds (of)* in *the at least three pounds (of) sugar/boys*. Measure phrases pattern with the numerical phrases discussed here in that their semantics is **intersective**: *at least three pounds of sugar* denotes (sums of) sugar to the amount of at least three pounds. Intersective, here, means that it does in fact denote sugar. And this is, of course, true for *three boys* as well: *three boys* denotes (sums of) boys with three atoms. (While measures are intersective, classifiers in general are not. For a little more discussion, see chapter 11.)

This means that the more general form of the numerical phrase is:

r n m = numerical relation – number – measure
where the count measure Ø is again morphologically not realized.

Whether you want to represent these empty elements in the syntax is not so much the point. While for clarity that is what I will be assuming, you can just as well give a syntax in which these empty elements are just not there. The point is a semantic one:

The semantics of the numerical phrase is built from **three** semantic ingredients, even if only one is visible in *Ø three Ø*:
a numerical relation r, a number n, and a measure m.

Thus, I assume the following compositional structure:

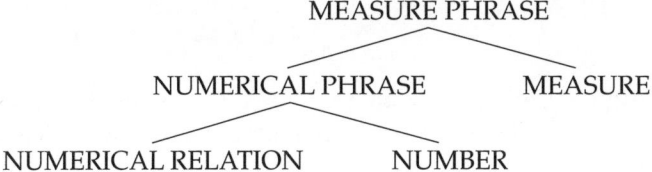

MEASURE PHRASE

NUMERICAL PHRASE   MEASURE

NUMERICAL RELATION   NUMBER

What I want to do now is provide as simple and natural as possible an interpretation for these structures.

We start with the category NUMBER. Let's assume we have a type n for numbers. Then the semantic interpretation is:

NUMBER	n
zero	0
one	1
two	2
. . .	. . .

Next, the category NUMERICAL RELATION. Obviously, as the name expresses, the simplest assumption is that expressions of this category denote relations between numbers, i.e. of type <n,<n,t>>.

NUMERICAL RELATION	<n,<n,t>>
at most	≤
less than	<
at least	≥
more than	>
exactly	=
Ø	=
. . .	. . .

So these are relations between numbers, nothing more: ≤ is the relation that 5 stands in to 7, but not to 4.

To combine the numerical relation and the number, we can follow the simplest assumption: since the types match for application, the semantics is just application:

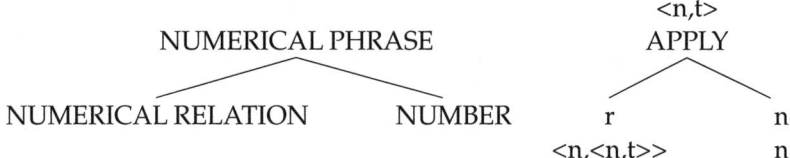

Thus, *at most five* → APPLY(≤,5) = (≤(5)) = λn.n ≤ 5 = {0,1,2,3,4,5} (on the domain of natural numbers, of course). Hence *at most five* is a number predicate, it denotes a set of numbers of type <n,t>.

Now we come to the measures. The simplest account of measures is, obviously, to assume that they are functions from objects to numbers: the objects may be mass objects for mass measures, the numbers may be numbers on a particular scale, but that's not so important for our present purposes. What is important is the type of measures: functions in type <d,n>:

MEASURES	<d,n>	
liter	LITER	
pound	POUND	
Ø	C	where C = λx.|x|
. . .		

This gives the following situation:

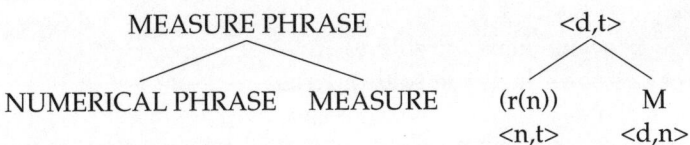

MEASURE PHRASE   <d,t>

NUMERICAL PHRASE   MEASURE   (r(n))   M
                                 <n,t>   <d,n>

In this case, the simplest operation that would give an interpretation at type <d,t> from inputs <n,t> and <d,n> is not functional application, but **function composition**, so we assume that the numerical phrase composes with the measure:

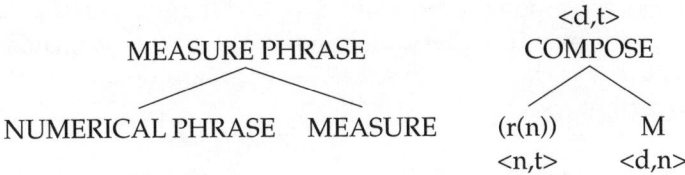

                                        <d,t>
        MEASURE PHRASE   COMPOSE

NUMERICAL PHRASE   MEASURE   (r(n))   M
                                 <n,t>   <d,n>

COMPOSE[(r(n)), M] = (r(n)) o M = λx.([r(n)]([M(x)]))

In this expression r is a relation between M(x) and n. Thus, in relational nota-tion, we could write this as λx.r(M(x),n). We will use, in fact, infix notation for this relation, and write: λx. M(x) r n.

Thus, the measure phrase Ø *three* Ø gets the semantics: (=(3)) o C = λn.n=3 o λx.|x|.

This is: λx.([λn.n=3] ([[λy.|y|](x)])) =
       λx. [λn.n=3 (|x|)] =
       λx.|x|=3   of type <d,t>.

In other words, the simplest assumptions give the correct results by the simplest means: the measure phrase is built by applying a numerical relation to a number, forming a numerical predicate, and composing the numerical pre-dicate with a measure.

The power of the adjectival theory is that it provides a simple and elegant analysis of numerical phrases in the nominal domain. And, as we will see at various points in this book, it provides a solid basis for simple compositional analyses of a variety of other nominal constructions.

I have defended the analysis [DET [NP NUM NOUN]] for numericals. I will end this chapter by discussing one case where I think the evidence goes the other way, and where we need to assume an analysis [[DET DET NUM] [NP NOUN]]. It concerns expressions like *every three* as in (4):

(4)   *Every three lions* are sold to Artis.

Note first that, unlike in the case of determiner *the*, the numerical cannot mingle with adjectives:

(5)a.   Every three ferocious lions are sold to Artis.
   b.   #Every ferocious three lions are sold to Artis.

A second peculiarity concerns the number. As is well known, *every* requires singular number on its head noun (6b), and triggers singular verb agreement (6c):

(6)a.   Every lion is sold to Artis.
   b.   #Every lions is sold to Artis
   c.   #Every lion are sold to Artis.

(4), on the other hand, has a plural head noun *lions*, and triggers plural agreement. Semantically, *every* quantifies over atomic individuals, *every lion* quantifies over singular lions; but *every three lions* quantifies over groups of lions. That is, (4) can be roughly paraphrased as (7):

(7)   The lions were sold to Artis in threes.

This means that, if we assume a structure [*every* [*three lions*]] we are going to violate just about everything we can think of about the syntax and semantics of *every*. On the other hand, if we assume a structure [*every three* [*lions*]] we can easily make all these facts fall into place.

First, obviously, the facts in (5) fall out: *three* cannot mingle with the adjectives. Secondly, we assume a standard semantics for *every*:

$$every \rightarrow \lambda Q\lambda P.Q \subseteq ATOM \wedge \forall x[Q(x) \rightarrow P(x)]$$

Every requires its head noun to be a set of atoms, hence singular, and triggers singular agreement. This means, that combining it with a noun *lions* is going to be infelicitous, and similarly, combining it with *three lions* is infelicitous. *Three* on the other hand is a plural predicate, a property of non-atomic sums:

$$three \rightarrow \lambda x.|x|=3$$

Let's now assume that we have a complex determiner *every three*. The natural assumption will be that it is formed by composition of *every* and *three*:

$$COMPOSE[\lambda Q\lambda P.Q \subseteq ATOM \wedge \forall x[Q(x) \rightarrow P(x)], \lambda x.|x|=3]$$

There is a mismatch here that needs to be resolved. One part is straightforward, we can shift $\lambda x.|x|=3$ with ADJUNCT to its modifier interpretation: $ADJUNCT[\lambda x.|x|=3]$

$$COMPOSE[\lambda Q\lambda P.Q \subseteq ATOM \wedge \forall x[Q(x) \rightarrow P(x)], \lambda Z\lambda x.Z(x) \wedge |x|=3]]$$

Now, if we apply Z to a variable U – as we do in composition – we get something that has the right type to apply the interpretation of *every* to, but not the right interpretation, because *every* requires a singular predicate, a predicate of atoms, and the predicate we get, $\lambda x.U(x) \wedge |x|=3$, is a plural predicate, a predicate of sums. So we need to shift this predicate to a predicate of atoms. The technique for doing this will be worked out in detail in chapter 11. Here I will only sketch the basic idea. Link 1984 introduces a **group-formation** operator $\uparrow$, which maps pluralities onto group-atoms: whereas a $\sqcup$ b denotes the sum of a and b, $\uparrow(a \sqcup b)$ denotes "a and b as a group", which is an atom in its own right. Landman (1989) also introduces an inverse operation of **membership specification** $\downarrow$, which maps a group atom like $\uparrow(a \sqcup b)$ onto the sum that makes up that group (i.e. onto a $\sqcup$ b). With this, we can introduce an operation that maps a set of sums onto a set of corresponding atoms:

$$^{\uparrow}P = \{\uparrow(x): x \in P\}$$

With this, we resolve the interpretation mismatch as follows:

COMPOSE[$\lambda Q \lambda P.Q \subseteq$ ATOM $\wedge \forall x[Q(x) \rightarrow P(x)]$, $\lambda Z \lambda x.Z(x) \wedge |x|=3$] =

$\lambda U.$APPLY[$\lambda Q \lambda P.Q \subseteq$ ATOM $\wedge \forall x[Q(x) \rightarrow P(x)]$, $^{\uparrow}(\lambda Z \lambda x.Z(x) \wedge |x|=3(U))$] =

$\lambda U.$ APPLY[$\lambda Q \lambda P.Q \subseteq$ ATOM $\wedge \forall x[Q(x) \rightarrow P(x)]$, $^{\uparrow}(\lambda x.U(x) \wedge |x|=3)$] =

$\lambda U \lambda P.$ $^{\uparrow}(\lambda x.U(x) \wedge |x|=3) \subseteq$ ATOM $\wedge \forall x[^{\uparrow}(\lambda y.U(y) \wedge |y|=3)(x) \rightarrow P(x)]$ =
(because indeed $^{\uparrow}(\lambda x.U(x) \wedge |x|=3) \subseteq$ ATOM)

$\lambda U \lambda P.$ $\forall x[^{\uparrow}(\lambda y.U(y) \wedge |y|=3)(x) \rightarrow P(x)]$.

Equivalently:

every three $\rightarrow \lambda U \lambda P.\forall a[$ATOM(a) $\wedge U(\downarrow(a)) \wedge |\downarrow(a)|=3 \rightarrow P(a)]$
The relation that holds between properties P and U if every group consisting of a sum of three Us has property P.

We see that this new determiner no longer has the requirement that the noun be singular, on the contrary, it maps a **plural noun** like *lions* onto the set of properties that every group correlate of sums of three lions has. Note that the universal quantification is over groups, not over sums, hence it can be contextually restricted to relevant groups (e.g. Landman 1989). Thus, the complex determiner *every three* takes as input semantically plural predicates, so it is not a surprise that it wants morphologically plural nouns:

every three lions $\rightarrow \lambda P.\forall a[*$LION($\downarrow$a) $\wedge |\downarrow a|=3 \rightarrow P(a)]$
The set of properties that every group consisting of a sum of three lions has.

The generalized quantifier *every three lions* denotes a set of properties of groups. This gives the correct semantics. Since the plural noun *lions* is the head noun, the whole noun phrase is morphologically plural, and it triggers plural agreement.

Thus, in this case, the assumption that we have a complex determiner *every three* makes perfect semantic and morphological sense. But, of course, that only strengthens the case against imposing the very same analysis onto the other noun phrases: when we have a complex determiner, as we do here, almost everything in the grammar jumps up and down to signal that we do, indicating that we can rest reasonably assured that in the other cases we don't. Thus the exceptional nature of this complex provides support for the adjectival analysis of the other cases.

Chapter 2

The Adjectival Theory of Indefinite Predicates and Arguments

2.1 Two Theories of Arguments and Predicates

In her influential paper (Partee 1987), Barbara Partee introduced the notions of argument type and predicate type for the interpretation of noun phrases, and she proposed that the types available for the interpretation of noun phrases in argument position (like *three girls* in (1a)) are type d of (singular (= atomic) and plural) individuals and <<d,t>,t> of generalized quantifiers, while the type available for the interpretation of noun phrases in predicative position (like *three girls* in (1b)) is type <d,t> of sets of individuals.

(1)a. *Three girls* walked
   b. The guests were *three girls*.

In this chapter, I will adopt this proposal and discuss the relative merits of two alternative ways of giving content to it.

The first theory I call Montague–Partee: it is (the core of) the proposal in Partee (1987), which consists of Partee's theory of predication, combined with the generalized quantifier theory of determiners, both of which ultimately derive from Montague (1970, 1973; the second through Barwise and Cooper 1981).

The other theory I call the Adjectival Theory of indefinite determiners. My causal chain for this name goes back to what I think is an initial baptism by Barbara Partee in her marginalia to a first draft of a paper by Godehard Link in the mid-1980s. I mention this, because the unpublished debate between Partee and Link forms the most direct inspiration for this chapter. In published work, versions or traces of the Adjectival Theory can be found in Bartsch (1973), Verkuyl (1981), Link (1987), Bowers (1991), and most explicitly in Bittner (1994), and in Krifka (1999); also related are van Geenhoven (1996), McNally (1998), and Dobrovie-Sorin and Laca (1996). This list is far from complete, and the authors on it shouldn't necessarily be expected to recognize their proposals in the version of the Adjectival Theory that I will develop here.

Both theories consist of a theory of determiners (A), and a type shifting theory (B).

Montague–Partee (MP):
MP-principle A – the Generalized Quantifier Theory of determiners:
All noun phrase interpretations are born at argument types.

An interpretation is born at a type if it is generated at that type without the help of the type shifting theory. The type of **quantificational** and **indefinite** determiners is the type of relations between sets of individuals: $<<d,t>,<<d,t>,t>>$.

every $\rightarrow \lambda Q\lambda P.Q \subseteq ATOM \wedge \forall x[Q(x) \rightarrow P(x)]$
The relation that holds between two sets P and Q iff Q is a set of atoms and every Q is a P.
three $\rightarrow \lambda Q\lambda P \exists x \in Q: |x|=3 \wedge P(x)$
The relation that holds between two sets P and Q iff some element of Q is a sum of three individuals having P.

This analysis of determiners implies that quantificational and indefinite **noun phrases** are born at the argument type $<<d,t>,t>$.

A large part of Partee's paper is concerned with the interpretation of the definite article. Since in the present chapter that will only be of marginal interest, I will assume only the lowest interpretation that Partee considers: the **definite** determiner is the sum operation of type $<<d,t>,d>$:

the $\rightarrow \lambda Q.\sigma(Q)$
The function that maps Q onto the sum of its elements if that is in Q, and is undefined if not.

This analysis of the definite determiner implies that definite noun phrases are born at the argument type of individuals, d.

MP-principle B – the Partee Triangle:
Predicate interpretations of noun phrases are derived from argument interpretations with type lowering operation BE.

ARGUMENTS PREDICATES

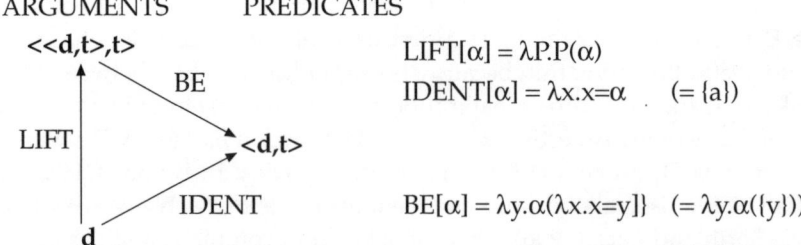

$<<d,t>,t>$

BE

LIFT

$<d,t>$

IDENT

d

$LIFT[\alpha] = \lambda P.P(\alpha)$
$IDENT[\alpha] = \lambda x.x=\alpha \quad (= \{a\})$

$BE[\alpha] = \lambda y.\alpha(\lambda x.x=y]\} \quad (= \lambda y.\alpha(\{y\}))$

In this triangle, d and $<<d,t>,t>$ are the argument types, and $<d,t>$ is the predicate type. Noun phrase interpretations can shift from type d to $<<d,t>,t>$ with type raising operation LIFT; they can shift from d to $<d,t>$ with type raising operation IDENT, and they can shift from <<d,t>,t> to <d,t> with type lowering operation BE.

The type shifting operation BE takes a generalized quantifier and maps it onto the set of individuals for which the property of being that individual is in that generalized quantifier.

The Adjectival Theory (AT):
AT-principle A – the adjectival semantics of indefinites:
Indefinite noun phrases are born at the predicate type.

Quantificational and definite determiners are interpreted as in MP (as relations between sets and functions from sets to individuals respectively). But indefinite determiners are interpreted at type <d,t>, the type of sets of individuals. This is the same type as that of adjectives, and semantically indefinite determiners combine with the noun through intersection:

three → $\lambda x.|x|{=}3$ of type <d,t>
The set of plural individuals consisting of three atoms.
girls → *GIRL   of type <d,t>
The set of all plural individuals that consist solely of girls.
three girls → $\lambda x.{}^*GIRL(x) \wedge |x|{=}3$
The set of all sums of girls each consisting of three individuals.

This means that quantificational and definite noun phrases are born at argument types, but that indefinite noun phrases are born at the predicate type <d,t>.

AT-principle B – the Existential Closure Triangle:
Argument interpretations of indefinite noun phrases are derived from predicative interpretations through type lifting with Existential Closure.

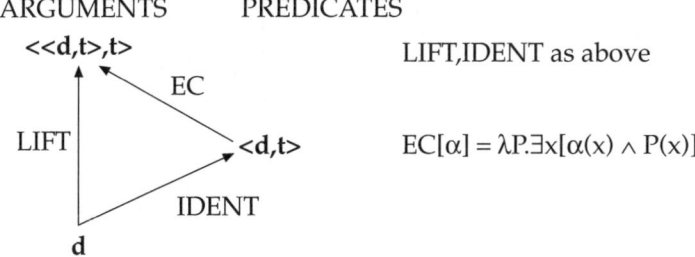

ARGUMENTS   PREDICATES

<<d,t>,t>   LIFT,IDENT as above

LIFT   <d,t> $EC[\alpha] = \lambda P.\exists x[\alpha(x) \wedge P(x)]$

d

In the Existential Closure Triangle, the relations between types d and <<d,t>,t> and between d and <d,t> are exactly as they are in the Partee Triangle. However, Partee's type lowering operation BE is replaced by a type lifting operation EC.

The type shifting operation EC takes a set α of individuals and maps it onto a generalized quantifier: the set of all sets that have a non-empty intersection with α.

The comparison between MP and AT will take the form of two matches and a play-off. The first match is a match played at high speed in the next section.

2.2   The First Match

2.2.1   The infelicity of quantificational predicates

As is well known, quantificational noun phrases in predicate position are infelicitous:

(2)   #Nirit is *every semantics professor at the party*.

This is a point in favor of the Adjectival Theory, because it predicts this: since in AT there is only **type lifting** and no **type lowering** and quantificational noun phrases start out at type <<d,t>,t>, they cannot be shifted to the predicate type.

Score board	MP	AT
Match one	0	1

However, Partee (1987) gives a semantic argument explaining why quantificational noun phrases are infelicitous as predicates (in terms of their meanings, rather than their type). I will discuss this argument below. For the moment, I will assume that the possibility of such a semantic explanation equals the score:

Score board	MP	AT
Match one	1	1

2.2.2   The first mismatch: *at least* and *exactly* interpretations

As is well known (see Horn 1972), in **argument position** numerical noun phrases like *three girls* have an *at least* interpretation, and an *exactly* implicature (which is shown by the felicity of (3a), where the *exactly* effect is canceled). As mentioned in Partee (1987), it has been observed that in **predicate position** these numerical noun phrases have an *exactly* interpretation (as shown by the infelicity of (3b), where the *exactly* effect cannot be canceled). (This observation seems to be due to Barbara Partee or Nirit Kadmon, or both.)

(3)a.   Three girls came in, in fact, four girls came in.
   b.   #The guests are three girls, in fact, they are four girls.

In Montague–Partee this can be readily accounted for. You generate at the argument type <<d,t>,t> distinct interpretations for *three girls* and *exactly three girls*, and make sure to choose them in such a way that type lowering operation BE maps them onto the very same set of individuals.

These facts are a problem, however, for the Adjectival Theory. In AT, indefinite noun phrases start out at the predicate type. But what the facts show is that at that type *three girls* and *exactly three girls* denote the same set:

$\lambda x.*GIRL(x) \wedge |x|=3$

Since the type lifting operation EC is a function, it cannot map this onto the two argument interpretations we want:

$$three\ girls \rightarrow \lambda P.\exists x[*GIRL(x) \wedge |x|=3 \wedge P(x)]$$
$$exactly\ three\ girls \rightarrow \lambda P.\exists x[*GIRL(x) \wedge |x|=3 \wedge P(x) \wedge$$
$$\forall y[*GIRL(y) \wedge P(y) \rightarrow y \sqsubseteq x]]$$

The conclusion is that AT must replace type shifting operation EC by an operation that is sensitive to more than just the predicate meaning. This is, of course, a disadvantage.

Score board	MP	AT
Match one	2	1

2.2.3   Downward entailing noun phrases: *at most three girls*

The Adjectival Theory predicts the wrong entailments for downward entailing noun phrases like *at most three girls*:

$EC[\lambda x.*GIRL(x) \wedge |x|\leq 3] = \lambda P.\exists x[*GIRL(x) \wedge |x|\leq 3 \wedge P(x)]$

With this interpretation, (4a) means: there is some sum of girls, consisting of at most three individuals, each of which walk. It can readily be seen that, on this interpretation, (4a) incorrectly entails (4b), and incorrectly does not entail (4c):

(4)a.   At most three girls walked.
   b.   Some girl walked.
   c.   Not more than three girls walked.

Score board	MP	AT
Match one	3	1

2.2.4   Negative noun phrases: *no girl*

The Adjectival Theory predicts the wrong meaning for negative noun phrases like *no girl*. As Partee (1987) points out, if, following MP, you take the standard (singular) interpretation of *no girl* at type <<d,t>,t>, and lower it to a predicate with BE, you get what seems to be the correct predicate interpretation:

BE[λP.¬∃x [GIRL(x) ∧ P(x)] = ATOM-GIRL
The set of singular individuals which are not girls.

On the other hand, if, in AT, you start out with that set as the interpretation for *no girl* at type <d,t>, and you lift it with EC to <<d,t>,t>, you obviously get the wrong interpretation:

EC[ATOM-GIRL] = λP.∃x[ATOM(x) ∧ ¬GIRL(x) ∧ P(x)]
The set of properties that some non-girl has.

Score board	MP	AT
Match one	4	1
Winner: Montague–Partee		

2.3   Whither the Adjectival Theory

If the prospective for the Adjectival Theory is this bad, one can quite reasonably wonder why anyone would be attracted to this theory in the first place, and why with rather great regularity it keeps being proposed as an alternative to Montague–Partee.

The key to the answer to this question was provided in chapter 1. There we saw that the adjectival theory in the nominal domain shows a lot of promise: it provides effortlessly and without stipulation the correct semantics for nominal numerical phrases: i.e., there are many arguments to show that inside a noun phrase like *the NUMERICAL PHRASE girls*, numerical phrases like *three, exactly three, at least three, at most three*, etc. behave semantically like intersective adjectives, intersecting with the interpretation of the plural head noun *girls*.

The point now is the following. If we look at the semantics of numerical noun phrases in **predicate position**, and we compare that with the semantics the Adjectival Theory provides in the nominal domain, we see that there is every reason to assume the very same semantics here. That is, the arguments for the Adjectival Theory in the nominal domain carry over straightforwardly to numerical noun phrases in predicate position: assuming the adjectival semantics gives us, without further ado, the correct semantics for numerical noun phrases in predicate position. As an indication, note that *the three girls* means *the exactly three girls*, and not *the at least three girls*. The adjectival semantics predicts this: *three girls* is interpreted as:

$$\lambda x.^*GIRL(x) \wedge |x|{=}3$$

The three girls is interpreted as:

$$\sigma(\lambda x.^*GIRL(x) \wedge |x|{=}3)$$

The latter expression is undefined if there aren't exactly three girls, hence indeed we have an *exactly* interpretation.

If we assume that also in predicate position *three girls* has exactly the same interpretation, then a sentence like *The guests are three girls* gets the following interpretation:

$$\lambda x.^*GIRL(x) \wedge |x|{=}3(\sigma(^*GUEST))$$

And this entails:

$$|\sigma(^*GUEST)|{=}3.$$

Hence, the same interpretation predicts the *exactly* interpretation of *three girls* in predicative position.

Now, of course, we saw in chapter 1 a difference between numerical nominals and numerical predicates: in the numerical nominal, numeral phrases can mingle with adjectives (as shown in (6)), while numerical predicates pattern with numerical arguments in that for them the numeral phrase must be initial (as shown in (5)).

(5)a.　　The animals in the shipment were *fifty ferocious lions*.
　　b.　#The animals in the shipment were *ferocious fifty lions*.

(6)a.　　We shipped the *fifty ferocious lions* to Blijdorp, and the *thirty meek lions* to Artis.
　　b.　　We shipped the *ferocious fifty lions* to Blijdorp, and the *meek thirty lions* to Artis.

This is, as far as I can tell, the only difference. But this difference is easily accounted for syntactically, for instance, by assuming an NP/DP distinction. We only need to make three simple assumptions, of which the first is in essence AT:

Assumption 1:
three girls in *the three girls* is an NP, with *three* a numerical adjective: [$_{NP}$ *three* [$_{NP}$ girls]]. This predicts that inside the NP mingling with other adjectives is in principle possible: *three* is adjoined to NP like other adjectives.

Assumption 2:
The **predicate noun phrase** *three girls* (and the argument noun phrase as well) has a DP-layer with an empty determiner D. This tells you that predicate and argument noun phrases are DPs and not NPs. Thus the initial structure of the predicate is: [$_{DP}$ Ø [$_{NP}$ *three* [$_{NP}$ girls]]].

Assumption 3:
In the DP with empty D, the numerical adjective must move into the DP-layer. This doesn't affect the semantics, which stays just λx.*GIRL(x) ∧ |x|=3.

For my purposes here, I can leave the actual syntax to be assumed at this point very much underspecified. I am not taking a stand on where the numerical lands in the DP-layer, or on why the movement takes place. This means that the assumption is still compatible with a wide range of syntactic implementations. But the ordering facts now follow straightforwardly: if the numerical is in the DP-layer in those noun phrases, it cannot mingle with adjectives which are in the NP-layer. (This account assumes that *every* and *the* are D-elements. It assumes an intersective semantics for the indefinite article *a* (e.g. *a* → ATOM). It does not take a stand on the syntax of *a*, i.e. on the question of whether or not it is a determiner.)

I am well aware that this is not a syntactic analysis, but rather an invitation to one. However, even at this level there is an important point to be made. The Adjectival Theory needs really only a very little bit of syntax (like the little movement in the sketched account) to get the facts right. Since this seems to be the only syntactic/semantic difference between numerical noun phrases in the nominal domain and predicates, the Adjectival Theory with only a little bit of syntax predicts the right syntax and semantics for numerical nominals and numerical predicates, without the stipulations that we commonly find in Generalized Quantifier Theory (and hence its descendant Montague–Partee). Thus, it is attractive to assume that numerical predicates pattern with numerical noun phrases inside the nominal domain, because they have the same adjectival semantics.

It seems that these considerations are strong enough to modify the score a bit: one more point for the Adjectival Theory:

Score board	MP	AT
Intermission	4	2

In the next two sections the second match is played. This match consists of playing the first match over, but more slowly now. The game is to re-evaluate the points assigned in the first match. For that reason, while in the first match we handed out points, in the second match we are going to take points away.

2.4   The Second Match: Predicate–Argument Mismatches

2.4.1   Mismatches for quantificational predicates

We come back to the infelicity of sentence (2):

(2)   #Nirit is every semantics professor at the party.

Partee (1987) points out the following fact about her type shifting operation BE: if you have a noun phrase of the form *every NOUN*, then applying BE to its generalized quantifier interpretation will give you a trivial interpretation (the empty set), unless the interpretation of the noun is a singleton set.

Partee argues that, while the determiner *every* does not contribute as part of its truth conditional semantics a restriction to non-singletons on its complement noun, there is reason to consider the possibility that the determiner *every* contributes a **presupposition** that its complement noun is restricted to non-singleton sets.

If so, we can explain why quantificational predicates like the one in (2) are infelicitous: *every* presupposes that *semantics professor at the party* is a non-singleton. Lowering this interpretation with BE to a predicate either violates the presupposition (leading to infelicity), or yields a systematically trivial predicate (which is also assumed to be infelicitous).

The problem with this account lies in the assumption that the restriction to non-singletons is a presupposition. Standardly, the restriction of the quantifier *every* on its complement noun is regarded as an implicature rather than a presupposition (e.g. a standard introduction text like Chierchia and McConnell-Ginet 1990). Winter (1998) discusses Partee's account directly, and provides strong evidence that the account doesn't work. Example (7) is modeled on Winter's example. A standard argument about canceling of implicatures shows that, when the quantificational noun phrase is in **argument position**, the non-singleton condition cannot be more than an implicature: (7a) is felicitous, showing that the effect is canceled. On the other hand – and this is the strength of Winter's argument – Winter shows that in the very same canceling context the quantificational **predicate** stays infelicitous: (7b) is infelicitous:

(7)a.   If Fred and Tanya weren't at the party, and Nirit was, then every semantics professor at the party danced.

   b.   #If Fred and Tanya weren't at the party, and Nirit was, then Nirit was every semantics professor at the party.

Example (7a) shows that the effect can be canceled, when the noun phrase is in argument position, arguing strongly that it is an implicature. But then, if in (7b) we lower the interpretation of the quantificational noun phrase to a predicate, the result should not be infelicity, but merely canceling of the implicature: that is, (7b) should be felicitous and should not have the implicature that there is more than one semantics professor at the party. But that prediction is wrong: (7b) is infelicitous.

What we see here is that we find a **mismatch** between the argument and the predicate interpretation of the quantificational noun phrase *every semantics professor at the party*: the argument interpretation is felicitous, but the predicate interpretation is not. This mismatch is not explained by Montague–Partee: the "more-than-one-element-in-the-domain-implicature" is too weak to explain the **robust** infelicity effect we find in predicative position.

In the Adjectival Theory, the default type shifting theory does not provide a lowering operation from <<d,t>,t> to <d,t>, and hence (2) and (7b) are infelicitous. The adjectival theory, hence does predict a robust effect. Thus, we take back the point that we assigned for this in match one to Montague–Partee:

Score board	MP	AT
Match two	3	2

2.4.2   Mismatches for downward entailing numerical noun phrases

For noun phrases like *at most three girls* we find a mismatch not of felicity, but of interpretation. The crucial mismatch that I want to draw attention to here is that while these noun phrases are (of course) downward entailing in argument position, they are not downward entailing in predicate position.

This can be seen by looking at the distribution of polarity sensitivity items. (8a), where the numerical noun phrase is in argument position, shows the standard fact about *at most three*: the polarity item *ever* is only felicitous in a downward entailing context; since (8a) is felicitous, this shows that the numerical noun phrase in argument position is downward entailing.

But in (8b) the numerical noun phrase is in predicate position, and (8b) is infelicitous. This shows that the numerical noun phrase in predicate position is not downward entailing:

(8)a.   At most three scientists who ever got the Nobel Prize were at the party.
  b.   #The guests were at most three scientists who ever got the Nobel Prize.

The observation can be shown directly as well. *At most three girls* in argument position, of course, passes the standard tests for downward "entailingness." But in predicate position it behaves like an intersective predicate, and that means that it is not downward entailing. Look at the examples in (9):

(9)a. The congregants are at most seven Jewish men.
   b. The congregants are men.

Suppose the congregants are 7 men and 15 women. An orthodox rabbi checks whether there is a minyan (for him, 10 Jewish men; for others, 10 Jewish persons), and sneeringly he says (9a). The reaction of my women informants to this set up is outrage, but importantly, not because the rabbi refuses to recognize non-orthodox minyans, but because he fails to count the presence of the women among the congregants in the first place: in the situation sketched (9a) is false, because the congregants actually include 15 women, and that shows that (9a) entails (9b). But this is an **upward** entailment, showing that *at most seven Jewish men* is not downward entailing in (9b).

The same facts can be replicated for numerical nominals as well: *at most three girls* in *the at most three girls* is not downward entailing, but is an intersective predicate (it denotes the set of sums of girls that consist of at most three atoms). These facts illustrate that indeed the adjectival semantics is correct for numerical predicates and numerical nominals. We see then that we have the following two interpretations:

at most three girls:
Argument interpretation: $\lambda P.\neg \exists x[*GIRL(x) \wedge |x|>3 \wedge P(x)]$
The set of properties that no sum of more than three girls has (downward entailing).

Predicate interpretation: $\lambda x.*GIRL(x) \wedge |x|\leq 3$
The set of sums of girls consisting of at most three singular individuals (intersective).

The problem for Montague–Partee is the following logical fact:

The problem for MP:
There is no type shifting operation which derives the correct predicate interpretation from the argument interpretation in all relevant cases.

This means that Partee's type shifting operation BE doesn't do it. It also means that the alternative operation MIN proposed in Winter (1998) doesn't do it either.

The problem is a problem of mismatch in polarity: because the argument interpretation is downward entailing and the predicate interpretation is not, there will be contexts where the argument interpretation is trivial, but the predicate interpretation is not trivial. But it is a fact of logic that you cannot derive with a type shifting operation a non-trivial predicate interpretation from a trivial argument interpretation. Look at (10):

(10)a.   At most 50 girls were at the party.
     b.   The guests were at most 50 girls.
     c.   The guests were girls.

Suppose that there are 20 girls. In that case, the downward entailing argument interpretation of *at most 50 girls* is trivial (the set of all sets). This predicts correctly that (10a) is trivially true. However, the predicate interpretation of *at most 50 girls* is *GIRL. This predicts correctly that (10b) is not trivial: in such contexts (10b) is equivalent to (10c).

There is a illuminating reformulation of the problem. Suppose that there are 20 girls and 20 boys. In that case, the argument interpretations of *at most 50 boys* and *at most 50 girls* are the same (the set of all sets), but the predicate interpretations are not (the set of all sums of boys and the set of all sums of girls respectively). But, of course, no function can map the same input onto two outputs, and since the type lowering operation is assumed to be a function, no type shifting operation can.

There is a solution readily available to Montague–Partee. Instead of assuming a simple type shifting operation, we can assume an only slightly more complex operation of Predicate Formation which takes as input the argument interpretation at type <<d,t>,t> and the noun interpretation that the argument is based on:

Predicate Formation:
Let α = (DET(NOUN)) of type <<d,t>,t>
PRED[α] = λx.NOUN(x) $\wedge$ BE[α](x)

If α is *at most fifty girls* then its <<d,t>,t> interpretation is, in the context given, the set of all sets, and BE[α] is D. Then PRED[α] = *GIRL $\cap$ D = *GIRL.

This works, but now we have equaled this particular score with the Adjectival Theory: we gave Montague–Partee a point because the mismatch between the *at least* and *exactly* interpretations forces the Adjectival Theory to make the type shifting operation sensitive to aspects of the interpretation not accessible to a standard type shifting operation (like the noun interpretation). We see now that we have to make exactly the same assumption if we adopt Montague–Partee. We take back the point:

Score board	MP	AT
Match two	2	2

2.4.3   Mismatches for negative noun phrases

There is a further problem for this reformulation of Montague–Partee. As argued above, for the generalized quantifier interpretation of *no girl*, Partee's operation BE gives an acceptable result. However, the new operation PRED does not give an acceptable result for *no girl*: the intersection of the set of non-girls with the interpretation of *girl* is, of course, empty. This means that, like the Adjectival Theory, Montague–Partee is forced into a theory which gives a **non-unified** account to different indefinite noun phrases (i.e. some shift with PRED and some shift with BE). Hence, Montague–Partee is not a more unified theory than the Adjectival Theory.

When it comes to negative noun phrases, I think that every theory will have to do something special. And this doesn't bother me much, because I think there is a lot of evidence that they actually are special. Let me in the briefest of ways sketch how the Adjectival Theory can deal with negative noun phrases. Details are given in chapter 8.

Assumption 1:
The interpretation of *no* is negation: ¬. The interpretation of the predicate *no girl* at type <d,t> is formed through **composition**: ¬ o GIRL, the set of non-girls.

Assumption 2:
The grammar treats the nominal negation as being **semantically separable**. This point has been made many times in the literature (e.g. Jacobs 1980), and I will discuss in chapter 8 lots of evidence from Dutch, and also from English, which shows that the nominal negation can take higher (often auxiliary) scope, while the remaining noun phrase material remains interpreted in situ.

Assumption 3:
This semantic separation takes place in the process that lifts the predicate interpretation to the argument interpretation: the type lifting operation (existential closure) does not apply to the composition of ¬ and the indefinite noun phrase; instead, the negation is separated: the type lifting operation applies to the interpretation of the indefinite noun phrase, and the negation is composed with the result; the argument interpretation is: ¬ o EC[GIRL]. This, of course, gives the correct argument interpretation for *no girl*.

The conclusion is: everybody needs to do something special for negative predicates, the Montague–Partee theory is no more unified here than the Adjectival Theory. Moreover, what the Adjectival Theory can do fits with a battery of facts about semantic separability of nominal negation. This means that one more Montague–Partee point goes:

Score board	MP	AT
Match two	1	2

2.5 Argument Formation

Let us now come to the mismatch in *exactly* effects and to the problems in getting the interpretation of *at most three girls* right.

The very same problems have been discussed in Landman (1998, 2000) in the context of the operation of Existential Closure over the event argument in neo-Davidsonian theories of events and plurality. What I claim is that these problems are general problems of existential closure operations, and the techniques developed in Landman (2000) can be adapted to the present case. In fact, the analysis here will be simpler than that in Landman (2000) for two reasons.

In the first place, I will be using a 0-object here, which allows me to simplify the general maximalization operation from Landman (2000) (but if you don't like the 0-object, you can take the more complex operation of Landman (2000) and get the correct semantics too).

Secondly, in this chapter I am only concerned with the problem of getting the meanings right in shifting from $<d,t>$ to $<<d,t>,t>$. This means that I am ignoring the complicated interactions between multiple noun phrase arguments of a verb that the theory in Landman (2000) addresses. Since it seemed didactic overkill to expose the reader to the ins and outs of the complex operation when only using it in a simple case, I have simplified it to fit the present case. The resulting simplification is close to a proposal in Kadmon (1987) (which derives partially from suggestions by Barbara Partee and Hans Kamp). This similarity is not surprising, because Kadmon (1987) was one of the main inspirations for my own work on maximalization. But the general theory is less similar to Kadmon (1987), and, as discussed in Landman (2000), more similar to work on maximalization in Krifka (1989a, 1989b) and Bonomi and Casalegno (1993). A more general version will be given in chapter 5.

I have argued above that, in the adjectival theory, in order to express the difference between the argument interpretations of *three girls* and *exactly three girls* the grammar must refer to more than just the predicate interpretation, since their predicative interpretation in the adjectival theory is the same. I will assume this extra thing to be a feature +R or –R, specified on the numerical relation, indicating whether or not the numerical relation is lexically realized. I assume further that this feature percolates up in the grammar, for the moment up to the DP.

+R: the numerical relation is **lexically realized**.
−R: the numerical relation is **not lexically realized**.

This means that the grammar given in chapter 1 generates the following syntactic and semantic representations of predicative DPs.

$$
\begin{array}{ll}
[\textit{Ø three girls}, & \lambda x.{}^*\text{GIRL}(x) \wedge |x|{=}3, -R] \\
[\textit{exactly three girls}, & \lambda x.{}^*\text{GIRL}(x) \wedge |x|{=}3, +R] \\
[\textit{at least three girls}, & \lambda x.{}^*\text{GIRL}(x) \wedge |x|{\geq}3, +R] \\
[\textit{at most three girls}, & \lambda x.{}^*\text{GIRL}(x) \wedge |x|{\leq}3, +R]
\end{array}
$$

We form the argument interpretation from the predicate semantics and **realization feature R**. I replace the type shifting operation of existential closure by an operation of **argument formation** which in general is the result of integrating two operations: **existential closure** and **maximalization**.

Existential closure:
EC: $<d,t> \rightarrow <<d,t>,t>$
$EC[\alpha] = \lambda P.\exists x[\alpha(x) \wedge P(x)]$

Maximalization:
MAX: $<d,t> \rightarrow <<d,t>,t>$
$MAX[\alpha] = \lambda P.\alpha(\sqcup(\lambda x.\alpha(x) \wedge P(x)))$ (i.e. $\lambda P.\sqcup(\lambda x.\alpha(x) \wedge P(x)) \in \alpha$)

In general Argument Formation is the conjunction of Existential Closure and Maximalization:

Argument Formation: general case
$AF[<\alpha,+R>] = \lambda P.EC[\alpha](P) \wedge MAX[\alpha](P)$

The exceptional case is the case where the numerical relation is realized as Ø. In this case maximalization is not integrated into the semantics, but forms the basis for an *exactly* implicature (see Landman 2000).

Argument Formation: special case
$AF[<\alpha,-R.] = EC[\alpha]$

In general, the idea is that both existential closure and maximalization are part of the semantics of indefinite argument DPs, unless the numerical relation is semantically present, but not lexically realized (in which case maximalization is only an implicature). We can extend the theory unproblematically to other indefinite noun phrases (but not negative ones), they will follow +R. Thus, the case of *three* is indeed special, it is something like a gap in the paradigm.

For simplicity, I will restrict myself to distributive cases: thus, in my expressions, λP will range over plural verbal interpretations which are Boolean algebras on subsets of D. Of course, I owe the reader an account of how the theory interacts with collectivity, but that goes beyond the discussion here. Let's look at what we get.

At least three girls

We start with the predicative DP interpretation:

[*at least three girls*, $\lambda x.{}^*GIRL(x) \wedge |x| \geq 3, +R$]

We apply Argument Formation:

$AF[<\lambda x.{}^*GIRL(x) \wedge |x| \geq 3, +R>] =$
$\lambda P.\exists x[{}^*GIRL(x) \wedge |x| \geq 3 \wedge P(x)] \wedge {}^*GIRL(\sqcup(\lambda x.{}^*GIRL(x) \wedge |x| \geq 3 \wedge P(x))) \wedge$
$|\sqcup(\lambda x.{}^*GIRL(x) \wedge |x| \geq 3 \wedge P(x))| \geq 3$

The second conjunct expresses that the sum of all sums of girls that have at least three atoms and that are sums of Ps is a sum of girls, and the third conjunct expresses that this sum has itself at least three atoms. Both of these statements are trivially true (and hence can be ignored). This means that the above can be reduced to:

$AF[<\lambda x.{}^*GIRL(x) \wedge |x| \geq 3, +R>] =$
$\lambda P.\exists x[{}^*GIRL(x) \wedge |x| \geq 3 \wedge P(x)]$

There is a general point here:

Argument formation for upward closed sets:
With the restriction of λP to distributive predicates, it holds that:
If for every P: $\lambda x.\alpha(x) \wedge P(x)$ is UC on P, then $AF[\alpha] = EC[\alpha]$

Hence we get as the argument interpretation:

at least three girls $\rightarrow \lambda P.\exists x[{}^*GIRL(x) \wedge |x| \geq 3 \wedge P(x)]$
The set of properties that some sum of at least three girls has.

Obviously, this is the correct interpretation: *At least three girls walk* is true if *WALK is one of these properties, and that means that there is a sum, which is a sum of girls, which consists of at least three individuals, and which is a sum of walking individuals.

At most three girls

We start with the predicative DP interpretation:

[*at most three girls*, $\lambda x.{}^*GIRL(x) \wedge |x| \leq 3, +R$]

We apply Argument Formation:

AF[<λx.*GIRL(x) ∧ |x|≤3,+R>] =
λP.∃x[*GIRL(x) ∧ |x|≤3 ∧ P(x)] ∧ *GIRL(⊔(λx.*GIRL(x) ∧ |x|≤3 ∧ P(x))) ∧
|⊔(λx.*GIRL(x) ∧ |x|≤3 ∧ P(x))|≤3

The first conjunct says that there is a sum in *GIRL with cardinality less or
equal to three and which is a sum of Ps. In order to simplify this, we use the
fact that we have a full Boolean algebra with a 0 element.

GIRL denotes a set of atoms, which means that 0 ∉ GIRL.
*GIRL = {x:∃Y ⊆ GIRL: x=⊔Y}

Since ∅ ⊆ GIRL, it follows that ⊔∅ ∈ *GIRL. Hence 0 ∈ *GIRL.
Since |0|=0, |0|≤3.

We have restricted λP to distributive predicates, hence to Boolean algebras
on subsets of the domain. Hence P will range over sets of the form *Q, for some
subset Q of the domain. By the same argument as before, 0 ∈ *Q, for each of
these Q's. This means that *GIRL(0) ∧ |0|≤3 ∧ P(0), hence that the first conjunct
is trivially true, for any value of P: ∃x[*GIRL(x) ∧ |x|≤3 ∧ P(x)].

The second conjunct is: *GIRL(⊔(λx.*GIRL(x) ∧ |x|≤3 ∧ P(x))). This says: the
sum of the sums of girls that have at most three atoms and that are Ps is itself
a sum of girls. As before, this is of course also true. This means that the result
of Argument Formation reduces to:

AF[<λx.*GIRL(x) ∧ |x|≤3,+R>] =
λP. |⊔(λx.*GIRL(x) ∧ |x|≤3 ∧ P(x))|≤3

We can simplify this even more, the sum of the set of all sums of girls that
have at most three atoms and that are Ps has at most three atoms iff the sum
of all sums of girls that are Ps has at most three atoms. Thus we get:

at most three girls → λP. |⊔(GIRL ∩ P)|≤3
The set of properties such that the sum of all girls having that property has
at most three atoms.

Again this is the correct interpretation. *At most three girls walk* is true if *WALK
is one of these properties, which means that the sum of all girls who are
walking individuals consists of at most three individuals. This does not entail
that there are girls who walk, but it does entail that there aren't more than
three girls who walk. Thus, including the 0 object gives us a very simple way
of dealing with the existential closure problems.

What we have used here is again a general fact:

Argument formation for downward closed sets:
With the restriction of λP to distributive predicates, it holds that:
If for every P: $\lambda x.\alpha(x) \wedge P(x)$ is DC on P, then $AF[\alpha] = MAX[\alpha]$

As we have argued, the reason is that if $\lambda x.\alpha(x) \wedge P(x)$ is DC on P, 0 is in its extension. This is the case for the relevant predicate in the argument interpretation of *at most three girls*, but not for the relevant predicate in the argument interpretation of *three girls*, *exactly three girls*, or *at least three girls*. Hence, 0 is able to neutralize the effect of the existential quantifier in the case of downward closed predicates like *at most three girls*, but not in the case of predicates that are not downward closed (all the others).

We see here that using full Boolean algebras (with 0), rather than mereologies (without 0), has more than cosmetic consequences. Earlier in this chapter we formulated one of the main logical problems for the Adjectival Theory: Existential Closure introduces an existential quantifier which produces the wrong readings for downward closed noun phrases in argument position (readings with existential import). We now see that, while this argument against the Adjectival Theory holds in theories in which the predicate interpretations never include 0, the argument doesn't hold once we regularize the theory to include 0: in such a theory existential closure over a downward closed predicate has no existential import.

The move to not only include 0 in the ontology, but to exploit it in the semantics is a major one, and we will see several more semantic applications of this move in the course of this book.

Exactly three girls

We start with the predicative DP interpretation:

[*exactly three girls*, $\lambda x.*GIRL(x) \wedge |x|=3, +R]$

We apply Argument Formation:

$AF[<\lambda x.*GIRL(x) \wedge |x|=3,+R>] =$
$\lambda P.\exists x[*GIRL(x) \wedge |x|=3 \wedge P(x)] \wedge *GIRL(\sqcup(\lambda x.*GIRL(x) \wedge |x|=3 \wedge P(x))) \wedge$
$|\sqcup(\lambda x.*GIRL(x) \wedge |x|=3 \wedge P(x))|=3$

$\lambda x.*GIRL(x) \wedge |x|=3 \wedge P(x)$ is neither DC nor UC. This means that the first and the third conjuncts cannot be neutralized. The second conjunct says that the sum of the set of sums of girls that have three atoms and that are sums of Ps is a sum of girls. This is clearly true, hence, we can simplify the above to:

$\lambda P.\exists x[*GIRL(x) \wedge |x|=3 \wedge P(x)] \wedge |\sqcup(\lambda x.*GIRL(x) \wedge |x|=3 \wedge P(x))|=3$

We can write this more simply as:

$$\lambda P.\exists x[\text{*GIRL}(x) \wedge |x|{=}3 \wedge P(x)] \wedge |\sqcup(\text{GIRL} \cap P)|{=}3$$

or even simpler, we get:

exactly three girls $\rightarrow \lambda P. |\sqcup(\text{GIRL} \cap P)|{=}3$
The set of all properties such that the sum of all girls that have that property has exactly three atoms.

On this analysis, *Exactly three girls walk* is true if *WALK is one of these properties, which means that the sum of all girls who are walking individuals consists of exactly three individuals. This is, of course, the required *exactly* reading.

Three girls

We start with the predicative DP interpretation:

[Ø *three girls,* $\lambda x.\text{*GIRL}(x) \wedge |x|{=}3, -R$]

In this case we have –R, and maximalization is not integrated into the semantics. The semantics, hence, is just existential closure:

three girls $\rightarrow \lambda P.\exists x[\text{*GIRL}(x) \wedge |x|{=}3 \wedge P(x)]$
The set of properties that some sum three girls has.

Three girls walk is true if *WALK is in this set, which holds iff there is a sum of girls which consists of three individuals and is a sum of walking individuals. This is an *at least* reading: the fact that there is a sum of three girls walking, is compatible with more girls walking (i.e. if there is a sum of five girls walking, there exist, of course, several sums of three girls walking).

In sum, we get the following results: We replace EC by AF, where AF = EC ⊓ MAX.

- For upward closed sets, like *at least three girls*, AF = EC (maximalization has no truth conditional effect).
- For downward closed sets, like *at most three girls*, AF = MAX (existential closure has no truth conditional effect).
- Non-upward, non-downward closed sets, like *exactly three girls*, express both an existence claim and a boundary claim: AF = EC ⊓ MAX.
- For Ø *three girls* maximalization is not integrated into the semantics, but forms the basis for a boundary implicature. Hence, here too AF = EC.

In conclusion: argument shift integrates existential closure and maximalization. Maximalization of the numerical relation is made part of the meaning if this relation is lexically realized. What we see is that while the Adjectival Theory runs into serious technical problems if it assumes Existential Closure as its type lifting operation, these problems are resolved elegantly if we replace Existential Closure by Argument Formation. And this means that we have actually solved the logical problems that have plagued the Adjectival Theory. This means that we take back the last point from Montague–Partee:

Score board	MP	AT
Match two	0	2
Winner: Adjectival Theory + Argument Formation		

2.6   Slugging It Out: Conjunctive Predicates

We are now concerned with conjunctive predicates, as in (11):

(11)   The guests are *three boys and four girls*.

While we are assuming that *three boys* and *four girls* denote sets at type <d,t>, it is quite clear that the predicate conjunction in (10) cannot be analyzed as intersection at the type of sets, because that obviously gives you only the empty set. The proper operation for conjoining sets of pluralities is an operation that I will call **Sum Pairing**:

Sum Pairing:
$\alpha \wedge \beta = \lambda x. \exists a \exists b [\alpha(a) \wedge \beta(b) \wedge x = a \sqcup b]$

Variants of this operation have been proposed by various authors (for a variety of linguistic phenomena); for instance, for a very explicit discussion of the problems of conjunction of sets of pluralities of events, see Lasersohn (1995).

Sum Pairing gives the right interpretation for the predicate in (10). (Note: if we replace in (10) *four girls* by *at most four girls*, we notice another argument for the 0-object: with a 0-object Sum Pairing will automatically give the correct interpretation; without a 0-object we have to complicate Sum Pairing considerably.)

As I have formulated it here, Sum Pairing involves Existential Closure on the conjuncts. If, as I have been arguing, maximalization effects are a general property of Existential Closure, then we might expect maximalization effects (which means, *at least* interpretations) here, not on the whole conjunctive noun phrase – that is just a predicate – but inside the conjunction on the conjuncts.

First we check that we do not find an *at least* interpretation for the whole predicate. Look at the board and example (12):

> 7, 11, 16, 18, 20, 22

(12) The numbers on the board are two prime numbers and three even numbers.   FALSE (#for that matter, four even numbers)

My informants judge that (12) is false, and they judge the continuation infelicitous. This shows that indeed we find normal *exactly* effects for the whole predicate: the predicate needs to cover the whole set of numbers on the board.

Now look at the next board and examples (13) and (14):

> 2, 3, 4, 6, 8

(13)a. The numbers on the board are exactly two prime numbers and exactly four even numbers.   TRUE
   b. The numbers on the board are exactly two prime numbers and exactly three even numbers.   FALSE

(14)a. The numbers on the board are two prime numbers and four even numbers.   TRUE
   b. The numbers on the board are two prime numbers and three even numbers.   TRUE (for that matter, four even numbers)

Unsurprisingly, my informants judge (13a) and (14a) true in this context (which shows that there is no semantic requirement that the conjuncts should be disjoint). The interesting thing is the contrast between (13b) and (14b). (13b), with *exactly* lexically realized, is judged false, because there are actually four even numbers. But my informants judge (14b) true, and find the continuation felicitous.

Thus, to be in the conjoined predicate denotation a sum must be a sum of two prime numbers and four even numbers and nothing else (that is the normal *exactly* effect on the whole predicate). But if one of the numbers is both prime and even, this sum cannot be described as a sum of exactly two prime numbers and exactly three even numbers, but it can be described as a sum of two prime numbers and three even numbers. This means that indeed we find maximalization effects on the conjuncts in Sum Pairing: inside the conjunction, *two prime numbers* and *three even numbers* have an *at least* reading.

These facts can be incorporated into Sum Pairing straightforwardly in analogy to maximalization in Argument Formation:

Sum Pairing with maximalization:

$<\alpha,-R> \wedge <\beta,-R> = \lambda x.\exists a \exists b[\alpha(a) \wedge \beta(b) \wedge x=a \sqcup b]$

$<\alpha,+R> \wedge <\beta,-R]> = \lambda x.\exists a \exists b[\alpha(a) \wedge \beta(b) \wedge x=a \sqcup b \wedge$
$$a = \sqcup(\lambda a.\alpha(a) \wedge a \sqsubseteq x)]$$

$<\alpha,-R> \wedge <\beta,+R> = \lambda x.\exists a \exists b[\alpha(a) \wedge \beta(b) \wedge x=a \sqcup b \wedge$
$$b = \sqcup(\lambda b.\beta(b) \wedge b \sqsubseteq x)]$$

$<\alpha,+R> \wedge <\beta,+R> = \lambda x.\exists a \exists b[\alpha(a) \wedge \beta(b) \wedge x=a \sqcup b \wedge$
$$a = \sqcup(\lambda a.\alpha(a) \wedge a \sqsubseteq x) \wedge b = \sqcup(\lambda b.\beta(b) \wedge b \sqsubseteq x)]$$

These facts are a problem for Montague–Partee. Montague–Partee distinguishes *exactly three girls* and *three girls* at the argument type, but not at the predicate type. Sum Pairing requires access to this very distinction at the predicate type. But if we access that distinction in a maximalization operation at the predicate type in Sum Pairing, we can just as well access it for maximalization in Argument Formation, and Montague–Partee becomes superfluous.

Have we clinched the case against Montague–Partee? Not yet. The rebuttal might go as follows: Montague–Partee can try to explain the maximalization effects in Sum Pairing by assuming that Sum Pairing involves not the predicate interpretation of the conjuncts, but the argument interpretations. In that case, you would expect maximalization effects. And this can be done easily: conjoin two argument DPs with conjunction at the type of generalized quantifiers, and lower the complex DP to a predicate. If that is the derivation, then indeed, you may well expect maximalization effects.

However, now look at (15)–(17):

(15)   The fighting ferocious three tigers and meek four panthers were giving us hair-raising problems.

(16)a.   The exactly two prime numbers and exactly four even numbers on the board illustrate a semantics problem.

   b.   #The exactly two prime numbers and exactly three even numbers on the board illustrate a semantics problem.

(17)a.   The two prime numbers and four even numbers on the board illustrate a semantics problem.

   b.   The two prime numbers and three even numbers on the board illustrate a semantics problem.

Example (15) shows that we are dealing with NP-conjunction: the numerical can mingle with the adjectives, and, importantly, the adjective *fighting* can naturally be interpreted as taking scope over the whole conjunctive NP, arguing against an account where a determiner *the* is deleted before the second conjunct.

Examples (16) and (17) show that, as expected, we find exactly the same maximalization facts inside the noun phrase here as in the predicative case in (13)–(14): (16b) is infelicitous, but (17b) is not, showing that *three even numbers* in (17b) has an *at least* interpretation.

Now, in order to deal with this, Montague–Partee would have to argue that in (17b) the interpretation of the **nominal**, the **NP** *two prime numbers and three even numbers*, inside the DP in (17b), is itself derived from the interpretation of the argument DP *two prime numbers and three even numbers*. This is unreasonable.

As argued, the Adjectival Theory with Maximalization can deal with all these facts unproblematically.

Score board	MP	AT
Final score	0	3
Winner: Adjectival Theory + Maximalization		

2.7 Who's the Winner?

The match is over, the winner has been declared. But who's the winner? As indicated by the list earlier in this chapter, over the last 30 years many people have proposed to analyze indefinite noun phrases as sets (or properties), and – I think – often with good arguments. But the bulk of these proposals do not even mention the problems with the Adjectival Theory as exposed in the first match (though these problems have been known for as long as the debate has raged). The whole purpose of me playing the first match in this chapter, was to argue that the bulk of proposals in the adjectival tradition actually lose the first match, and are in no way competition to the Montague–Partee analysis. I am completely in agreement with these proposals about the usefulness of the set (or property)-analysis of indefinites. But it just won't do to argue extensively that indefinites are sets, if you then just stick in an existential quantifier and hope for salvation, without addressing these problems. That is no competition for the Generalized Quantifier analyses, because the latter, though they may have problems, at least work. (By extension, the same is true in the analysis of *there*-insertion contexts, where the very same problems come up.)

McNally (1998) is one of the few papers that shows awareness of the problems and tries to do something about them. In fact, her analysis of the non-upward-entailing cases is similar to the analysis in Landman (2000) in that it involves a scalar component. But when the chips are down, McNally's analysis makes no real predictions, because she doesn't specify what the content of the scales is and how this content is derived. McNally seems to assume that this is just given in context. This may be plausible if you only look at arguments of one-place predicates, but, as argued in Landman (2000), no such simple scalar theory will extend to the case of arguments of two-place relations (e.g. in cumulative readings). While the theory discussed in the present chapter is a (didactic) reduction to the one-place case of a general theory of maximalization effects, McNally's analysis is tailored to the one-place case, and it isn't at all clear that it extends to the two-place case.

For the adjectival theory to be in the competition against Montague–Partee, it must minimally have an account of the downward entailing cases that works. Besides the theory presented here, the only adjectival theory (that I am aware of) that works is Krifka (1999). Krifka's proposal is in many respects similar to mine (it is also a scalar theory); he addresses a different set of problems to argue for the same conclusions. A comparison with Krifka's proposal must wait for another occasion.

As for the winner of the second match, rather than handing out prizes it is actually more appropriate to look at price tags. What the discussion shows, I think, is that any theory that wants to do full justice to the facts is going to be remarkably complex. Such a theory needs to replace the simple operation of Existential Closure by an operation which integrates, one way or other, but in a sufficiently general way, maximalization effects for scopal and non-scopal readings of arguments of relations, and accommodate both semantically integrated maximalization effects and maximalization implicatures. There doesn't seem to be a shortcut here: the winner will be complex.

2.8   Syntax–Semantics Mismatches

In the syntax of noun phrases, the central distinction that syntactic phenomena make reference to seems to be the NP/DP distinction. In the semantics of noun phrases, the central distinction seems to be the set/non-set distinction. Since I have argued that predicate noun phrases are DPs with a set interpretation, we see that there is a **mismatch** between the syntax and the semantics:

> **Syntax–semantic mismatch:**
> The syntax clusters arguments and predicates together.
> The semantics clusters predicates and nominals together.

What are the arguments that predicate noun phrases are DPs, and not NPs? I have two major arguments for that. The first argument concerns the mentioned difference in syntax between nominals and predicates, which is easily explained if nominals are NPs and predicates DPs.

The second argument concerns the existence of exceptional cases where quantificational noun phrases are reinterpreted at the set type, and hence can occur as predicates. (This fits with the central idea that type shifting is a mechanism that is available at no cost, but that the grammar may contain special mechanisms that provide something that the type shifting theory doesn't give you.) I am thinking here of two kinds of examples.

Case 1

I will propose in chapter 5 that noun phrases in *there* insertion contexts are semantic adjuncts with a set interpretation (involving a shift which is accessed from the predicate interpretation, and which can involve only noun phrases born at the predicate type), and I will show how this accounts for the standard definiteness effects. But, as is well known, there are exceptional cases, where quantificational noun phrases can occur in *there* insertion contexts:

(18)   There is *every reason* to distrust him.

I will argue that it is plausible to assume that what is involved here is a special **semantic reinterpretation** strategy which gives the quantificational noun phrase a set interpretation. But there is no evidence whatsoever for **syntactic restructuring** of a DP as an NP in cases like (18), and that is what a matching between the syntactic and the semantic distinctions would require. (I owe this argument to John Bowers, who convinced me of it.)

Case 2

I argued in Landman (1995, 2000) that quantificational noun phrases like *every girl*, but not *each girl*, can shift from a quantificational interpretation (at type <<d,t>,t>) to a collective definite (at type d, and hence shiftable into <d,t>). *Combine* in (19) is collective on its second argument: (19a) is felicitous, while (19b) is not:

(19)a.   In this class I try to combine *every theory of plurality*.
    b.   #In this class I try to combine *each theory of plurality*.

I do not assume that collective shift of *every NP* is part of the regular type shifting theory. While a collective reading for (19a) seems acceptable, in general, this shift seems to be a rather restricted phenomenon: for instance, it doesn't seem to be possible in subject position.

Now, what is relevant for our purposes here is the following. A quantificational noun phrase that has undergone collective shift has a collective interpretation at type d. From this type we can lift it with IDENT into the predicate type. This means that, while we do not get predicative interpretations of quantificational noun phrases in general, collective shifted interpretations might well occur as predicates. And this is indeed the case:

(20)a.   The press is *every person who writes about the news*.
    b.   #The press is *each person who writes about the news*.

Here again, we find under special circumstances a semantic shift from <<d,t>,t> to a type from which we can form a predicate. And again, it is completely implausible to assume that this must involve syntactic restructuring of a DP as an NP.

Moral

The assumption of the Perfect Matching between syntax and semantics derives, originally, from Montague's fixed type assumption. This assumption has frequently tempted both semanticists and syntacticians into imperialism (use the perfect match to import as much syntax as you can into the semantics, versus import as much semantics into the syntax as you can, presumably in the hope that the other will go away). But, as I have argued here for noun phrases, syntax and semantics are mismatched. The mismatch makes syntactic and semantic argumentation harder, because you actually need to determine very carefully which distinction (the syntactic or the semantic) your arguments apply to. It makes it also more interesting, because:

All perfect matchings are alike, each mismatch is interesting in its own way.

2.9   Sentence Adverbials inside Noun Phrase Conjunctions

This brief last section is concerned with a problem concerning the semantics of conjoined noun phrases which, to my knowledge, was first pointed out by Chris Collins in an unpublished seminar paper written for a seminar co-taught by Irene Heim and Jim Higginbotham at MIT in the early 1990s. It concerns the occurrence of sentence adverbials inside noun phrase conjunctions, as in (21):

(21)a.   The guests are *John, Bill, and Henry, and **maybe** Susan*.
   b.   The guests will be *three boys and **maybe** two girls*.
   c.   Mary invited *John, Bill, and Henry, and **maybe** Susan*.
   d.   Mary invited *three boys and **maybe** two girls*.
   e.   *Three boys and **maybe** two girls* met in the street.

The problem is: if such cases involve noun phrase conjunction, as I have been assuming, how can the adverb *maybe* occur at all? Secondly, if the semantics is sum formation, or more general, sum pairing, what can the semantics of *maybe* be?

At first sight, one may take this as an argument that the conjunction isn't really noun phrase conjunction, but a case of conjunction reduction. But there are two serious problems with that suggestion.

In the first place, as (21e) shows, *maybe* can occur inside the noun phrase also when the noun phrase argument has a collective reading. And, in that case, the sentence doesn't mean that three boys met in the street and maybe two girls met in the street, which is what conjunction reduction would give. The sentence means that a group met in the street which consisted of three boys, and maybe two more girls, but nothing else: that is, apart from the *maybe* effect, it behaves like a normal collective noun phrase.

The second problem, related to the first, is that it isn't clear at all that an analysis in terms of conjunction reduction gets the scope of the modal right. Look at (21a): you cannot give *maybe* scope over the whole sentence, because that gives a reading which is too weak: maybe the guests will be John, Bill and Henry and Susan. But when you separate, you get a reading which seems wrong: the guests are John, Bill, and Henry, and the guests are maybe Susan.

Yoad Winter mentions the problem in a footnote in Winter (1998), and makes the correct observation that the semantic effect of the modal *maybe* in these examples seems to be similar to a disjunction: (21a) does seem to be equivalent to (22):

(22)   The guests are *John, Bill, and Henry or John, Bill, Henry, and Susan.*

I think that this is, as far as it goes, a correct observation, but that leaves one ever more baffled about the compositional semantics of the cases in (21).

I think that the right way of approaching the problem in (21) is to look at other adverbials that have the same behavior, in particular temporal adverbials like *always, sometimes,* etc. Thus look at (23):

(23)   The guests are *John, Bill, and Henry, and **sometimes** Susan.*

The problem in (23) is, of course, exactly the same as in (21). But (23) readily suggests a solution to the problem. What does (23) mean? Well, it means that on some occasions the guests are John, Bill, Henry, and Susan, and on the other occasions, they are John, Bill, and Henry. Clearly, we are not talking here about the guests at a particular occasion, but about the guests at various occasions. But that means – and this is really the crux of the solution – that the proper analysis of (23) is not as a predication of a predicate of type $<d,t>$ to an individual (the guests) of type d, but as a predication of a predicate of type $<<s,d>,t>$ to an individual concept of type $<s,d>$: the function which maps every relevant occasion onto the guests at that occasion:

The guests → $\lambda s.\sigma(*GUEST,s)$ of type $<s,d>$.

This makes the predicate in (23) a predicate of type $<<s,d>,t>$. This means that (23) expresses that the guest-function $\lambda s.\sigma(*GUEST,s)$ of type $<s,d>$ is in the set of functions which is the interpretation of *John, Bill, and Henry, and sometimes Susan* at type $<<s,d>,t>$.

Now we follow standard compositional practice: the relevant interpretation of *John, Bill, and Henry, and sometimes Susan* at type $<<s,d>,t>$ can, and should, of course be derived from the interpretation of *John, Bill, and Henry* at type $<<s,d>,t>$ and the interpretation of *sometimes Susan* at type $<<s,d>,t>$, and the interpretation of *and* at this type. The default assumption is that conjunction would be the result of lifting sum pairing to type <<s,d>,t>:

Sum pairing for individual concepts:
Let α, β be of type <<s,d>,t>:
$\alpha \wedge \beta := \lambda f.\exists x \exists y[\alpha(x) \wedge \beta(y) \wedge f = \lambda s.x(s) \sqcup y(s)]$

We assume, of course, that the expression *John, Bill, and Henry* is rigid. That means that its interpretation at type <<s,d>,t> is going to be the singleton set containing the obvious constant function:

John, Bill, and Henry → {$\lambda s.$JOHN $\sqcup$ BILL $\sqcup$ HENRY} of type <<s,d>,t>.

This reduces the problem to finding the interpretation at type <s,d> of *sometimes Susan*. And, once we have this perspective, this is, of course, not very difficult:

The interpretation of *sometimes*: the idea
The adverbial *sometimes* as a noun phrase modifier is interpreted as a restriction on the domain of the functional interpretation of the noun phrase.

It is useful now to introduce a few useful concepts. As before, I take 0 to be the null object of type d.

$\lambda s.0$ is the constant function on 0 in type <s,d>.
Let α be a set in type <<s,d>,t>.
$\alpha(s) = \{f(s): f \in \alpha\}$

Let ADV stand for the interpretation of the adverbs *sometimes*, *always*, etc. I will assume that ADV is a function from <<s,d>,t> into <<s,d>,t>:

The interpretation of *sometimes*: the analysis
ADV[α] = {g: g differs at most from $\lambda s.0$ in that for **adv-many** s: g(s) $\in \alpha$(s)}

Let's see how this works.

Susan → {$\lambda s.$SUSAN} of type <<s,d>,t>.
Sometimes →
$\lambda \alpha.$ {g: g differs at most from $\lambda s.0$ in that for **some** s: g(s) $\in \alpha$(s)} of type <<<s,d>,t>,<<s,d>,t>>

Hence:

Sometimes Susan →
{g: g differs from $\lambda s.0$ in that for **some** s: g(s) = SUSAN}

We assumed before that:

John, Bill, and Henry → {$\lambda s.$JOHN $\sqcup$ BILL $\sqcup$ HENRY} of type <<s,d>,t>.

Hence:

> *John, Bill, and Henry, and sometimes Susan* →
> $\lambda f.\exists x \exists y [\alpha(x) \wedge \beta(y) \wedge f = \lambda s.x(s) \sqcup y(s)]$
> where:
> $\alpha = \{\lambda s.\text{JOHN} \sqcup \text{BILL} \sqcup \text{HENRY}\}$
> and:
> $\beta = \{g: g \text{ differs from } \lambda s.0 \text{ in that for } \textbf{some } s: g(s) = \text{SUSAN}\}$

This can be simplified to:

> λf: for some g differing from $\lambda s.0$ in that for some s: $g(s) = \text{SUSAN}$:
> $f = \lambda s.\text{JOHN} \sqcup \text{BILL} \sqcup \text{HENRY} \sqcup g(s)$

This means that the whole statement becomes:

> *The guests are John, Bill, and Henry, and sometimes Susan* →
> for some g differing from $\lambda s.0$ in that for some s: $g(s) = \text{SUSAN}$:
> $\lambda s.\sigma(\text{*GUEST},s) = \lambda s.\text{JOHN} \sqcup \text{BILL} \sqcup \text{HENRY} \sqcup g(s)$

Now, function g is a function that assigns SUSAN to some occasions, and 0, the null object, to the rest. Sum pairing will give us the required disjunction effect: the function $\lambda s.\text{JOHN} \sqcup \text{BILL} \sqcup \text{HENRY} \sqcup g(s)$ maps those occasions that g maps onto SUSAN onto JOHN $\sqcup$ BILL $\sqcup$ HENRY $\sqcup$ SUSAN, and the other occasions onto JOHN $\sqcup$ BILL $\sqcup$ HENRY $\sqcup$ 0, which is JOHN $\sqcup$ BILL $\sqcup$ HENRY.

Thus, (23) expresses that the guest function is identical to a function which maps some occasions onto the sum of John, Bill, Henry, and Susan, and the remaining occasions onto John, Bill, and Henry. This is the correct interpretation.

I think that this is an attractive analysis for (23), and it suggests, of course, an analysis for the cases in (21) as well: I assume that (21) involves also a functional reading, and that *maybe* restricts similarly the function domains. The only difference is the nature of the contextual functional arguments: occasions in the case of (23), modal alternatives in the case of (21).

Thus (21a), on its natural reading, asserts that the function which maps each epistemic alternative onto what the guests are according to that alternative is a function which maps alternatives either onto the sum of John, Bill, and Henry, or onto the sum of John, Bill, Henry, and Susan. We assert (21a) when we don't yet know what the actual set of guests is, but we have reduced the alternatives to alternatives of the above two kinds.

The analysis, of course, extends unproblematically to the other examples in (21a), including the collective cases.

Thus, rather than being problematic for the analysis of plurality and co-ordination, the cases discussed here turn out to fit into the analysis rather beautifully. The analysis will have a further application in chapter 8.

Chapter 3

The Variable Constraint
on Predicates and
There-Insertion Subjects

3.1 Predicates

3.1.1 Introducing the variable constraint

In chapter 2, I discussed the infelicity of quantificational noun phrases in predication contexts:

(1) #Nirit is every semantics professor.

I argued, following Winter (1998), that the infelicity cannot be attributed to a "presupposition" that the noun be non-singleton, as Partee has it. As Winter argues, in argument position, the "non-singleton effect" can easily be canceled, suggesting that what there is to it is more like an implicature. If so, it is by far too weak to explain the robust infelicity effects in (1): conflict between an implicature and the semantics of predication should not lead to infelicity, but to the disappearance of the implicature.

I proposed to derive the infelicity from the Existential Closure Triangle: quantificational noun phrases are generated at the type <<d,t>,t> of generalized quantifiers and cannot be lowered by the default type shifting theory into the type <d,t> of predicates. The default theory does not provide for interpretations of quantificational noun phrases at the type of sets, hence the infelicity.

So far so good? Not really. A major problem arises almost immediately. I claimed that this theory predicts the infelicity of (1), but it can easily be shown that this theory makes no such prediction. Neither does Partee's for that matter. The problem is that these theories are part of a more general semantic theory which includes mechanisms for variable binding, dealing with scope, relativization, and questions. And, of course, they should be. (Note: I talk here about variable binding mechanisms, but the discussion carries over straightforwardly to variable-free versions of those.) And the problem is that the scope mechanism neatly undoes what we have so carefully set up: on my account, the grammar can generate a reading for (1) after all; on Partee's account, it can generate a reading for (1) without going through the stage that would make it infelicitous. For exposition, I will use storage as my scope mechanism in the interpretation of (1):

1. $[_{DP}$ *every semantics professor*$] \rightarrow \lambda P.\forall x[SP(x) \rightarrow P(x)]$
    of type $<<d,t>,t>$

2. We store this interpretation. We use a variable x_n of type d, and store the quantificational interpretation under that index:

    $[_{DP}$ *every semantics professor*$] \rightarrow x_n$ STORE:$<n,\lambda P.\forall x[SP(x) \rightarrow P(x)]>$
    of type d

3. We lift variable x_n from type d to type $<d,t>$ with IDENT: IDENT$(x_n) = \lambda x.x=x_n$

    $[_{DP[PRED]}$ *every semantics professor*$] \rightarrow \lambda x.x=x_n$ STORE:$<n,\lambda P.\forall x[SP(x) \rightarrow P(x)]>$
    of type $<d,t>$

4. We combine this with copula *be*: $[_I$ *be*$] \rightarrow \lambda P.P$ of type $<<d,t>,<d,t>>$

    $[_{I'}$ *be every semantics professor*$] \rightarrow \lambda x.x=x_n$ STORE:$<n,\lambda P.\forall x[SP(x) \rightarrow P(x)]>$

5. We combine the result with subject *Nirit*, $[_{DP}$ *Nirit*$] \rightarrow$ NIRIT of type d

    $[_{IP}$ *Nirit is every semantics professor*$] \rightarrow$ NIRIT=x_n of type t
    STORE: $<n,\lambda P.\forall x[SP(x) \rightarrow P(x)]>$

6. Now we retrieve the stored interpretation, and get:

    $[_{IP}$ *Nirit is every semantics professor*$] \rightarrow \lambda P.\forall x[SP(x) \rightarrow P(x)]$ $(\lambda x_n.$NIRIT $= x_n) = \forall x[SP(x) \rightarrow$ NIRIT $= x]$

Thus, indeed, we have a felicitous derivation of (1) after all: the theory does not predict that (1) is infelicitous.

Clearly, then, the scope mechanism must be blocked in the above derivation. We need a stipulation, and, following age old practice, I will call it a constraint. There is more than one way in which such a stipulation can be imposed. I will formulate it as a constraint on type shifting:

The Variable Constraint:
Variables cannot be type shifted from argument types to corresponding predicate types (i.e. from a to $<a,t>$).

While formulated in terms of expressions, this should be understood as a semantic constraint. Thus, the constraint not only applies to a variable x_n, but also to expressions $\lambda x.x(x_n)$ or $^{\vee\wedge}x_n$, since these expressions are equivalent to x_n.

As is clear, the Variable Constraint directly blocks the above derivation for (1): the scope mechanism stores the interpretation of the quantificational noun phrase and uses a variable x_n of type d instead. But that variable was lifted to type <d,t> in step 3, which is now in violation of the Variable Constraint. Hence the scope mechanism no longer derives an interpretation for (1), and (1) is once again correctly predicted to be infelicitous.

3.1.2   Variable Constraint effects

The Variable Constraint is a restriction on variables of argument types, like type d, occurring in an environment that requires them to shift to non-argument types like <d,t>. The constraint does not concern expressions that are not variables: the interpretation of a definite like *the boys*, $\sigma(*BOY)$ of type d, can shift to $\lambda x.x=\sigma(*BOY)$ of the predicate type <d,t> without violating the constraint. Also, the constraint does not tell you that, say, predicate position is a scope island, forbidding quantifying into predicates:

(2)   Sue is *the mother of every boy.*

The noun phrase *every boy* is part of the predicate, but can take wide scope unproblematically. The Variable Constraint disallows resolving the type mismatch in (3a) as in (3b):

(3)a. $\lambda x_a \ldots [_{<a,t>} x] \ldots$
   b. $\lambda x_a \ldots \lambda y.y=x_a \ldots$ $(= \lambda x \ldots \{x\} \ldots)$

We expect Variable Constraint effects when we try to put a variable of type a in a context which requires an expression of type <a,t>. Operations that are standardly assumed to involve variable binding are scopal operations, relativization, and wh-movement. We will now look at what happens when the variable abstracted over by these operations is in predicate position.

Case 1: Wide scope readings

There once was a man in the land of Uz who, like many people in his region, believed that the heavenly body seen in the morning sky was a star called Phosphorus. The *de dicto* reading of (4) is true:

(4)   Job believes that Phosphorus is a star.

You may find him pointing at the planet Venus, exclaiming: "This, unbelievers, is a star." The *de re* reading (5b) of (5a) is true:

(5)a. Job believes that the planet Venus is a star.
   b. Job believes of the planet Venus that it is a star.

The question now is: does the situation sketched make the statement in (6) true?

(6) Job believes that Phosphorus is *a planet.*

Most will agree strongly that it doesn't. The Variable Constraint predicts this. Without the Variable Constraint, we could give the noun phrase *a planet* wide scope in the normal way: store the interpretation of *a planet*, use a variable x_n of type d instead, build up with it the interpretation of *Job believes that Phosphorus is a planet*, and retrieve the interpretation of *a planet*. Thus, the classical Montague–Partee analysis of noun phrases in predicative position predicts a *de re* reading for *a planet* in (6). The Variable Constraint prevents this reading: in order to derive a *de re* reading for the predicate, you must lift the variable x_n from type d to type <d,t>, which is precisely what the Variable Constraint disallows.

Thus, the Variable Constraint predicts, correctly it seems, that noun phrases which form predicates do not take wide scope.

Case 2: Relativization

Relativization involves abstraction over a semantic variable. In restrictive relativization in English, the semantic variable is the interpretation of the gap in the relative clause. English has four relevant relativizers:

(7)a. John is the wonderful doctor *who* Miriam recommended –.
   b. John is the wonderful doctor *which* Miriam recommended –.
   c. John is the wonderful doctor *that* Miriam recommended –.
   d. John is the wonderful doctor Ø Miriam recommended –.

For some speakers (7b) isn't perfect. The fact that (7a) is fine is good enough here. This is an animacy effect: with an inanimate subject, *who* is infelicitous, and *which* is fine, as can be seen in (8):

(8)a. #*Finnegans Wake* is the book *who* Fred likes – best.
   b. *Finnegans Wake* is the book *which* Fred likes – best.
   c. *Finnegans Wake* is the book *that* Fred likes – best.
   d. *Finnegans Wake* is the book Ø Fred likes – best.

What happens when the relativization gap is in predicative position? In that case we find a strong contrast:

(9)a.   #John isn't the actor *who his father was* –.
    b.   #John isn't the actor *which his father was* –.
    c.   John isn't the actor *that his father was* –.
    d.   John isn't the actor Ø *his father was* –.

(10)a.   #*Finnegans Wake* really is the wonderful book *who Fred considers it to be* –.
    b.   #*Finnegans Wake* really is the wonderful book *which Fred considers it to be* –.
    c.   *Finnegans Wake* really is the wonderful book *that Fred considers it to be* –.
    d.   *Finnegans Wake* really is the wonderful book Ø *Fred considers it to be* –.

Based on related data, Carlson (1977b) argues that relative pronouns in English are sorted in the following way:

which: sorted for abstraction over a variable of argument type d;
who: sorted for abstraction over a variable of argument type d, with further specification, like animacy;
that: unsorted;
Ø: unsorted.

With this assumption, the Variable Constraint predicts the infelicity of (9a,b) and (10a,b). In all cases in (9) and (10) we have a gap in predicate position which is arguably of type <d,t>. The restriction on *which*/*who* requires abstraction over a variable of type d, hence requires a variable of type d in this predicative position. The Variable Constraint does not allow lifting of this variable to type <d,t>, hence the derivation crashes.

    For (9c,d) and (10c,d) Carlson (1977b), Heim (1987), and Grosu and Landman (1998) suggest that the abstraction involves a variable not over individuals, but over degrees. While (9a,b) have a mismatch which cannot be resolved because of the Variable Constraint, i.e. they show configuration (11a), (9c,d) start with a different mismatch, the configuration (11b): Let F(j) be of type d, denoting the father of John:

(11)a. $\lambda x_d.$ $([_{<d,t>} x] (F(j)))$ violates the Variable Constraint.
    b. $\lambda z_{degree}.([_{<d,t>} z] (F(j)))$

The grammar does not allow the gap based on individual variable x to be reconstructed as predicate {x}. Grosu and Landman (1998) argue that the grammar has the option of reconstructing from a variable of type degree, a predicate of type <d,t> in (9c,d) by providing a different syntactic/semantic analysis for the relative clause, namely as a maximalizing relative. In maximalizing relatives the external head is semantically interpreted internal to the relative clause. Thus, the compositional semantics of these relative clauses is different from that of restrictive relatives, and the grammar can construct the following predicate as the interpretation of the gap in (9c,d):

(12) $\lambda x.\text{ACTOR}(x) \wedge \text{DEGREE}_{\text{ACTOR}}(x)=z$ of type $<d,t>$
       The property that you have if you are an actor to degree z.

Relativization can now felicitously abstract over degree variable z, giving a set, in fact a singleton set, of degrees.

(13) $\{\sqcup(\lambda z_{\text{degree}}.\ \text{ACTOR}(F(j)) \wedge \text{DEGREE}_{\text{ACTOR}}(F(j))=z)\}$
       The set consisting of the degree to which John's father was an actor.

Grosu and Landman (1998) assume that the fact that we have a singleton here is responsible for external definiteness effects: in the felicitous cases (9c,d) and (10c,d) the noun phrase that contains the relative has a definite determiner. Replacing this by an indefinite determiner is infelicitous:

(14)a.   #John isn't *an* actor that his father was –.
    b.   #Finnegans Wake is *a* wonderful book that Fred considers it to be –.

The same contrast shows up with other determiners as well:

(15)a.   His sons never became *the three presidents* that he had hoped they would –.
    b.   #His sons never became *three presidents* that he had hoped they would –.

On this analysis, the noun phrase *the actor that his father was* has interpretation (16) of type degree.

(16) $\sqcup(\lambda z_{\text{degree}}.\ \text{ACTOR}(F(j)) \wedge \text{DEGREE}_{\text{ACTOR}}(F(j))=z)$
       The degree to which John's father was an actor.

Indeed, the cases in question have, of course, a degree interpretation:

(17)   John isn't *half* the actor that his father was –.

From the interpretation in (16), interpretations at other types can be derived:

   IND: degree $\rightarrow <d,t>$
   $\text{IND}[\alpha] = \lambda x.\text{DEGREE}_p(x) \geq \alpha$

With IND we can interpret the noun phrase *the actor that his father was* – as a predicate of type <d,t>:

(18) $\lambda x.\text{DEGREE}_{\text{ACTOR}}(x) \geq \sqcup(\lambda z_{\text{degree}}.(\text{ACTOR}(F(j)) \wedge \text{DEGREE}_{\text{ACTOR}}(F(j))=z))$
The set of individuals that are actor at least to the degree that John's father was an actor.

Example (9c) expresses that John is not in the set in (18), i.e. the degree to which John is an actor is smaller than the degree to which his father was an actor. Obviously, which degree function is meant here is to some extent a matter of context (i.e. whether we're concerned with the quality of their acting, or how much their acting dominates their life, etc.).

The relevant point is as follows: the interpretation strategy of maximalizing relatives, which allows us to find a felicitous interpretation for (9c,d), does not involve shifting a variable of type d to type <d,t> (unlike the infelicitous (9a,b)), and hence does not violate the variable constraint.

Case 3: Wh-questions

I will postpone discussion of this case till later.

3.2   *There*-Insertion

Having shown Variable Constraint effects in predicate position, we will in this section show that the same interactions show up in the subject position of *there*-insertion contexts, that is, in the position that is open to the definiteness effects.

3.2.1   Quantificational noun phrases

I have been using traditional terminology to describe the three classes of noun phrases that the Partee Triangle gives us:

1. quantificational noun phrases are generated at type <<d,t>,t>
2. definite noun phrases are generated at type d
3. indefinite noun phrases are generated at type <d,t>.

But it is important to point out that on the current perspective these names are merely (in fact rather confusing) labels for classes of noun phrases that share a certain distribution. Thus, there is nothing particularly "quantificational" about quantificational noun phrases, since I don't have an independent definition of what "quantificational" means. Quantificational noun phrases are noun phrases that are infelicitous in predicative position, but not in argument position. The explanation for the infelicity is of a **typal** nature: they are compositionally generated with determiners of type <<d,t>,<<d,t>,t>>.

It is important to note that, while the type of generalized quantifiers $<<d,t>,t>$ is a crucially important semantic type – the unification type at which all noun phrases have derived argument interpretations – it doesn't have the same importance when we restrict our attention to the question of which types noun phrases are generated at (i.e. without shifting). Once we adopt a version of the Adjectival Theory, the real compositional work takes place at the types of sets, $<d,t>$, and of individuals d: that's where we find extensive compositional build-up (i.e. build-up of set interpretations from numbers, measures and sets), and that's where we find the bulk of the noun phrase interpretations. Most of the things that used to be classified as determiners of type $<<d,t>,<<d,t>,t>$ in Generalized Quantifier Theory are now reinterpreted as being of the types $<<d,t>,d>$ or $<<d,t>,<d,t>>$ (or shorter $<d,t>$) (i.e. all the definite and indefinite determiners).

In fact, the class of quantificational noun phrases is only based on a handful of determiners, and a heterogeneous lot, for that matter. For English and Dutch we basically get the following (ignoring negative ones, which is a story of its own):

English	**Dutch**
Each	Elk
Every	Ieder
Both	
Most	De meeste
	Sommige

All is not here, nor is Dutch *alle*. Following Dowty (1986), I assume that *all* is a noun phrase modifier, and that the noun phrases based on *all* are definites of type d. *Both* is here in English, but Dutch *(de) beide* is not. This is clearly related to the fact that English *both* is strictly distributive, like *each* – as argued by Roberts (1987) – while Dutch *(de) beide* allows collective interpretations. How heterogeneous the class is is shown by the inclusion of Dutch *sommige* (discussed by, among others, de Jong 1987).

(19)a.   The guests are *some friends of mine*.
   b.   #De gasten zijn *sommige vrienden van mij*.

The Dutch (19b) is robustly infelicitous, unlike, say, the result of replacing the indefinite with seemingly synonymous phrases, like *enige/een paar (a few) vrienden van mij*, which are fine. The inclusion of *sommige* among the determiners that build quantificational noun phrases shows that also the label "indefinite" is in essence an empty label. The proper terminology is obviously in the following ball park:

- quantifier denoting noun phrase – quantifier producing determiner
- individual denoting noun phrase – individual producing determiner
- set denoting noun phrase – set denoting determiner

Thus, while I will continue to use the traditional terminology, it is important to note that in the context of this book no significance should be assigned to those names.

3.2.2 *There*-insertion contexts

As is well known, *there*-insertion contexts show definiteness effects: quantificational noun phrases and definite noun phrases are infelicitous, while indefinite noun phrases are fine in *there*-insertion contexts:

(20)a.   #There were *most semantics professors* at the party.
    b.   #There were *the three semantics professors* at the party.
    c.   There were *three semantics professors* at the party.

It is important to point out that these infelicity facts are robust, as robust as the predication facts. This is so, despite the fact that various well-known kinds of exceptions exist. There is a considerable literature on these exceptions, definites or quantificational noun phrases occurring felicitously in *there*-insertion contexts (e.g. Prince 1981; Ward and Birner 1995). The interesting thing about these exceptions is their systematic nature: what we find is that there are rather well carved out "rescue" strategies that allow definites and quantification noun phrases in *there*-insertion contexts, strategies which involve either some form of semantic reinterpretation or rather special semantic settings.

    For instance, the cases in (21a) and (22a) are felicitous, but hardly on a literal interpretation: they seem to involve a scalar reinterpretation which is likely to be the key to their felicity:

(21)a.   There is *every reason to distrust him*.
    b.   #Every reason to distrust him exists.
    c.   There is good reason to distrust him,

(22)a.   There is the cutest little car you have ever seen in the shop.
    b.   There is a really cute car in the shop.

Other cases are the famous list interpretations, as in (23):

(23)   What do we need to buy? Well, there's *the cheese, and the butter* . . .

I will not develop an analysis of list readings here. I think that such an analysis requires us to think harder about the relation between lists and functions. As we will see in the next section, conflict with the variable constraint can sometimes be avoided by functional interpretations. That fact may be a fruitful starting point for an explanation for cases like (23).

    Despite this, the infelicity judgements are robust: the existence of rescue strategies does not affect the strength of our judgments concerning infelicity in *there*-insertion contexts: when these strategies fail, definites and quantificational noun phrases are robustly out, as in (24b):

(24)a.   There was *a boy* sick in my class today.
   b.   #There was *every boy* sick in my class today.

Classical accounts of definiteness effects in *there*-insertion contexts, starting with Milsark (1974), are along the following lines: try to find semantic properties that distinguish quantificational and definite noun phrases on the one hand from indefinite noun phrases on the other. A plethora of oppositions have been proposed here: old/new, specific/non-specific, presuppositional/non-presuppositional, strong/weak, non-existential/existential . . . and for many of these notions many different definitions have been proposed in the literature.

Not everybody bases their analysis on a single feature: de Jong (1987), for instance, uses combinations of two features. But what is salient in the tradition is the place where it locates the opposition: one property or cluster of properties carves out quantificational and definite noun phrases, while the other carves out indefinites.

To my knowledge, Higginbotham (1987) was the first to draw attention to the fact that the *there*-insertion facts are a strict subset of the predication facts. As we have seen, I basically define quantificational noun phrases as those noun phrases that are infelicitous in predicate position. As Higginbotham points out, all of these are infelicitous in *there*-insertion contexts as well. Besides them, of course, also definites are infelicitous in *there*-insertion. McNally (1998) argues that this connection between the predication facts and the *there*-insertion facts is not coincidental: not only are the *there*-insertion facts a subset of the predication facts, but *there*-insertion contexts interact with individual variables in the same way as predication contexts.

Case 1: Scope (Milsark 1974)

(25)a.   John believes that *a murderer* was hiding in the closet.
   b.   John believes that there was *a murderer* hiding in the closet.

In (25a) *a murderer* can have a *de dicto* or a *de re* reading. Milsark observed that a *de re* reading is basically unavailable for (25b), with *a murderer* in the *there*-insertion context. Carlson (1977a) discusses many of such scope facts in his analysis of bare plurals. Thus, predicate position and *there*-insertion pattern alike: noun phrases in these positions do not allow wide scope interpretations.

Case 2: Relativization
(Carlson 1977b, Heim 1987, Grosu and Landman 1998)

I discussed above the variable constraint effects of relativizing into predicate position. The discussion there was adapted from the literature, rather than straightforwardly taken over, because, while the relevant literature mentions predication contexts, it is actually about *there*-insertion contexts. When the relativization gap is in the *there*-insertion context, we find exactly the same facts as observed for predicative position: relativizers *which* and *who* are infelicitous, relativizers *that* and Ø are okay, but trigger external definiteness:

(26)a. #I took with me the three books *which there were – on the table.*
   b. I took with me the three books *that   there were – on the table.*
   c. #I took with me   three books *that   there were – on the table.*

Case 3: Wh-questions (Heim 1987)

Wh-questions is, of course, the third kind of variable binding construction where we should find Variable Constraint effects. Heim (1987) discusses the interaction of *there*-insertion contexts with wh-questions. Heim argues that the effects are there: she basically argues that question word *which* behaves the same as relativizer *which*, question word *what* behaves the same as relativizer *what*, but question word *who* patterns with *what* (hence is different from the relativizer *who*):

(27)a. #Which book was there – on the table?
   b. (?)Who was there – at the party?
   c. What was there – on the table?

The facts seem to be the same for predicate position:

(28)a. #Which professor are you –?
   b. Who are you –?
   c. What is that –?

Thus it seems that here too the effects are there. The case is more problematic, though. What is problematic is not so much the facts, as their interpretation. If we follow Carlson's story for relativization, then we should try to give an analysis in which *which* requires the gap to be interpreted as an individual variable, and let this be incompatible with the Variable Constraint. Then we should argue that the *what* cases do not involve abstraction over an individual variable, but, for instance, also a degree variable, and give an analysis along the lines of the one sketched for relativization. This is what Heim suggests for (27a) and (27c).

The problem is that this seems a rather problematic assumption for (27b) and (28b), the *who*-cases. One would think that, if any one of these cases involve abstraction over individual variables, it should be (27b) and (28b). What evidence is there that this isn't the case? While Heim notices actual degree interpretations for the relative clause cases, the degree strategy seems patently inappropriate for (27b) and (28b). I will discuss this problem further at the end of this chapter.

3.3   *There*-Insertion Contexts and Predication Contexts

There is a clear conclusion to be drawn from the above discussion, a conclusion which is also drawn by McNally (1998).

Not only is the distribution of noun phrases in *there*-insertion contexts a subset of that in predicative position, but *there*-insertion contexts interact with variable binding mechanisms in the same way as predicative contexts. Now, one can surely think of alternatives to the variable constraint to predict the distinctions between predicative position and argument position. But it seems clear that any such solution is crucially going to involve the set/non-set distinction, i.e. the fact that predicative position is set denoting, because that's precisely the aspect in which predicative position differs from argument position.

If so, then we should conclude that the very same set/non-set distinction lies at the heart of the *there*-insertion facts.

But this changes everything. If *there*-insertion subjects are set denoting like predicates, then whatever mechanism disallows quantificational noun phrases from predicative position, also disallows quantificational noun phrases from *there*-insertion position. But that means that the weak–strong tradition has been cutting up the class of noun phrases in the wrong way: the basic semantic distinction is not between definites and quantificational noun phrases on the one hand, and indefinites on the other, but between quantificational noun phrases and the rest: quantificational noun phrases cannot be default lowered into set-denoting interpretations, and hence they are infelicitous in set-denoting positions.

Hence there is no need for a unified semantic account of quantificational noun phrases and definites in order to explain their infelicity in *there*-insertion contexts. This is replaced by a unified semantic account of the infelicity of quantificational noun phrases in predicative position and *there*-insertion contexts. What is needed over and above that is an account of the infelicity of definites in *there*-insertion contexts.

I am proposing, with Higginbotham and others, that *there*-insertion subjects are set-denoting like predicates, and that the major distributional facts follow from this. Higginbotham (1987), McNally (1998), and also van Geenhoven (1998) go one step further. They assume that *there*-insertion subjects in fact are predicates.

On that account, what accounts for the infelicity of definites in *there*-insertion contexts? Well, there isn't much choice here. Obviously, from the noun phrases that are felicitous in predicative position, a further semantic filter needs to eliminate definites from the class of predicates allowed in *there*-insertion contexts. Enter, once more, a weak–strong distinction: both Higginbotham and McNally formulate a weak–strong distinction and restrict the noun phrases that can occur in *there*-insertion contexts to weak predicative noun phrases.

However, the assumption that *there*-insertion contexts are predicates is supported by the weakest arguments.

(29)a.   There are three girls in the garden.
   b.   There are presently three planes arriving from Paris.

McNally suggests that *three girls* in (29a) is a predicate, and *in the garden* is something like a backgrounded adjunct. Cases like (29b) she excludes from the discussion altogether as something which may be a different construction (since, clearly, it would be unattractive to assume that *presently . . . arriving from Paris* is a backgrounded adjunct).

For my purposes, such an analysis is just not good enough. I will be interested in the course of this book in developing a theory which will minimally account for the *there*-insertion facts in English – where we find *there*-insertion contexts with copulas and predicate codas (*are . . . in the garden*) and with, roughly, a class of unaccusative verbs (like *arrive*) – and in Dutch, where *there*-insertion contexts can be found with any predicate or verb:

(30)a. Netta zei dat   er   *drie meisjes* Dafna gekust hebben.
        Netta said that there three girls   Dafna kissed have
   b. #Netta zei dat   er   *de drie   meisjes* Dafna gekust hebben.
        Netta said that there the three girls   Dafna kissed have

I think that the predicate account of Higginbotham and McNally makes no sense for Dutch cases like (30a). For that reason it is, from my perspective, not very helpful.

Where I agree with Higginbotham and McNally, is that I too assume that *three girls* in (30a) has an interpretation derived from the predicate type of sets <d,t>. I do not assume, however, that *three girls* is in predicative position. I will outline my own proposal in the next chapter, and develop it in the rest of this book. In the remainder of the present chapter I will discuss the Variable Constraint in somewhat greater depth.

3.4   Role-value Predicates

3.4.1   Scope

Partee (1987) brings up the Williams' Puzzle as a potential problem for her account. The Williams' Puzzle concerns the examples in (31):

(31)a. This house has been *every color*.   (Williams 1983)
   b. Olivier has been *every Shakespearean king*.   (Partee 1987)
   c. In *Kind Hearts and Coronets*, several noble relatives stand between the hero and his title. Alec Guiness is every noble victim.   (Adapted from Landman 1986)

While, as we have seen, quantificational noun phrases are not supposed to be good in predicative position, the examples in (31) are fine. McNally (1998) proposes a constraint which says that quantificational noun phrases that quantify over individuals (type d) are not good in predicative position, but that quantificational noun phrases that quantify over other entities are allowed. She assumes that in the cases in (31) the quantificational noun phrases quantify over kinds, and that's why they are acceptable. Partee (1987) herself assumes that the quantificational noun phrase quantifies over properties. As I am taking (31b) as my model, I will assume that we can agree that the quantification noun phrase in (31b) quantifies over roles, whatever roles are.

McNally's assumption is an alternative to the Variable Constraint. However, it can be shown that McNally's assumption is not correct. While (31b) is alright, (32) is not:

(32)   #Richard III is every Shakespearean king on the program this year.

The contrast between (31b) and (32) is illustrative. In (31b) the predicate *has been every Shakespearean king* is a predicate of individuals, ascribed to the individual Laurence Olivier, and the sentence is acceptable. In (32) the pre- dicate *is every Shakespearean king on the program this year* is a predicate of roles, ascribed to the role Richard III, and the sentence is bad. (32) patterns with (1), where we have a predicate of **individuals** *is every semantics professor at the party* ascribed to the individual Nirit, where the sentence is bad. It is precisely this contrast which motivates the Variable Constraint: shifting a variable from type a to type <a,t> is not allowed, whether a is the type of individuals, or, say, the type of roles.

The same observation holds for *bona fide* kinds as well, (33) is also infelicitous.

(33)   #The Siberian tiger is every cat left in Mongolia.

The types of individuals (d), kinds (k), roles (r), properties (π), propositions (p), events (e) are all similar in that each of these types forms the bottom type a of a type shifting triangle [a,<<a,t>,t>,<a,t>]. This means that all these types are argument types. The Variable Constraint forbids shifting variables of these types from the argument type a to the corresponding predicate type <a,t>. This is the reason that I am not happy about analyses like the one in van Geenhoven (1998), that in essence identify the predicate type and the property type. van Geenhoven tries to connect the predication facts discussed here with the facts pointed out by Zimmermann (1993) concerning the object position of intensional verbs like *seek*. Zimmermann's observation is that quantificational noun phrases in the object position of *seek*, unlike definite or indefinite noun phrases, only allow *de re* interpretations:

(34)a.   John seeks every unicorn.   *de re* only
    b.   John seeks a unicorn/the unicorn   *de dicto/de re*

Zimmermann accounts for these facts by assuming that the object position of *seek* is of property type π (which he constructs as <s,<d,t>>). Indefinites and definites can have an interpretation at the property type π, quantificational noun phrases do not. The latter fact can, of course, be made to follow easily from the type shifting triangle that I assume: if the interpretation of definites and indefinites at type π is derived from their predicate interpretation at type <d,t>, through lifting with intensionalization operator ^, then quantificational noun phrases do not have an interpretation at type π, since they do not have a predicate interpretation at type <d,t>.

But, and this is where *seek* differs from predicate position, quantifying-in *every unicorn* **is** of course possible. This does not violate the Variable Constraint, because the type π of the object position of *seek* is **not** a predicate type in the first place, but an argument type. The fact that (34a) is in fact perfectly felicit-ous is one indication for that. Another indication is that numerical indefinites like *three unicorns* actually have an *at least* interpretation, and not an *exactly* interpretation:

(35)   John seeks three unicorns, in fact, he seeks five.

It is not difficult to strengthen this with more syntactic and semantic arguments, all showing that the property type π of the object position of *seek* may be an intensional type, but is not a predicate type.

The same holds for the type of roles r. The type of roles is an intensional type. This has been argued by Doron (1983), and can be shown neatly with the following examples.

(36)a.   Lewis Carroll is Charles Dodgson.
    b.   In the play, Derek Jacobi is Lewis Carroll.
    c.   In the play, Alec Guinness is Charles Dodgson.

While (36a) is naturally interpreted as an identity statement between expres-sions of type d, (36b) and (36c) have role interpretations similar to (31b). And on these interpretations, substitution is not valid. If the gimmick of the latest play about the life of Charles Dodgson is that Lewis Carroll and Charles Dodgson are played by different actors, then, of course, we cannot use (36) to conclude that Derek Jacobi is Alec Guinness. This suggests that what goes on with the role interpretations in (36b) and (36c) is nothing but another instance of the good old temperature paradox. And this is, when the chips are down, exactly Partee's analysis of why (31b) is alright.

The type of roles is an intensional type r, which we can reconstruct as type <s,d> of individual concepts. Noun phrases can have interpretations based on type r, in the noun phrase type triangle r,<<r,t>,t>,<r,t>:

$Richard\ III \rightarrow$ RICHARD III   of type r
$three\ Shakespearean\ kings \rightarrow \lambda r.{}^*SK(r) \wedge |r|=3$ of type <r,t>
$every\ Shakespearean\ king \rightarrow \lambda P.SK \subseteq ATOM \wedge \forall r[SK(r) \rightarrow P(r)]$
                                                  of type <<r,t>,t>

The definite and indefinite noun phrases at type r and $\langle r,t \rangle$ can form predicates of roles at type $\langle r,t \rangle$. Variables over roles cannot be lifted to that type, hence quantificational noun phrases of type $\langle\langle r,t\rangle,t\rangle$ do not have interpretations as role predicates.

But we're not interested in predicates of roles (type $\langle r,t \rangle$), but in predicates of individuals (type $\langle d,t \rangle$). The types of role expressions are of course the wrong types to form predicates of type $\langle d,t \rangle$. However, the bottom type of roles r is linked to the type of individuals d: individuals can play role, instantiate roles, in short, be the value of roles. The value operation from type r to type d can be an taken to be an extensionalization operation $^{\vee}$ (interpreted as the function that specifies the value of the role in the current relevant context).

Let's incorporate this as a shift operation:

$$\text{EXT: } r \to d$$
$$\text{EXT}[\alpha] = {}^{\vee}\alpha$$

(This isn't type lowering, but connecting the bottom of one triangle to the bottom of another.)

Now suppose we have a noun phrase α with a role interpretation of one of the types $r, \langle\langle r,t\rangle,t\rangle, \langle r,t\rangle$ in predicative position, where the target is a predicate of type $\langle d,t \rangle$. We can store the interpretation of α under a variable z_n of type r:

$$z_n \qquad \text{STORE: } \langle z_n, \alpha \rangle \qquad \text{with } z_n \text{ of type r}$$

Now we have a variable of type r in predicative position with target type $\langle d,t \rangle$. We can now **shift** z_n from type r to type d with EXT:

$$\text{EXT}[z_n] \qquad \text{STORE: } \langle z_n, \alpha \rangle \qquad \text{with } z_n \text{ of type r}$$

which is:

$$^{\vee}z_n \qquad \text{STORE: } \langle z_n, \alpha \rangle \qquad \text{with } z_n \text{ of type r}$$

$^{\vee}z_n$ is an expression of type d; crucially $^{\vee}z_n$ is not a variable of type d, hence IDENT can shift $^{\vee}z_n$ to type $\langle d,t \rangle$:

$$\text{IDENT}(^{\vee}z_n) \qquad \text{STORE: } \langle z_n, \alpha \rangle \qquad \text{with } z_n \text{ of type r}$$

which is:

$$\lambda x.x = {}^{\vee}z_n \qquad \text{STORE: } \langle z_n, \alpha \rangle \qquad \text{with } z_n \text{ of type r and } x \text{ of type d}$$

We now have a well formed predicate of type <d,t>, we can build up the sentence, take the stored noun phrase out of store by abstracting over role variable z_n and applying this to α in the usual way. We get:

(37)a.   Derek Jacobi is Richard III
         DEREK JACOBI = ᵛRICHARD III
         Derek Jacobi is the value of the Richard III role.
     b.   Derek Jacobi is three Shakespearean kings.
         $\exists r[*SK(r) \wedge |r|=3 \wedge \forall a \in ATOM(r): DEREK\ JACOBI = {}^\vee r]$
         There are three Shakespearean King roles that Derek Jacobi is the value of.
     c.   Derek Jacobi is every Shakespearean king.
         $\forall r[SK(r) \rightarrow DEREK\ JACOBI = {}^\vee r]$
         Derek Jacobi is the value of every Shakespearean King role.

Of course, the exact interpretation of the value operation ᵛ is dependent on what the the values of the role vary over. Thus, in (37a), this might mean: *in the current play*, in (37b), it could be, *in the current season*. This is, of course, contextually determined.

   The important point is this. This analysis of role-value interpretations – which is basically Partee's – is plausible, and perfectly compatible with the Variable Constraint: no variable gets lifted from type a to type <a,t>. Important too is that it predicts that noun phrases in predicate position with a role-value interpretation pattern completely with **argument interpretations** and not with predicate interpretations (in essence, because they are quantified in). And this is exactly what we see. One indication, again, is that the indefinite in (37b) is predicted to have an *at least* interpretation, and not an *exactly* interpretation.

   We can even go as far as to syntacticize the analysis:

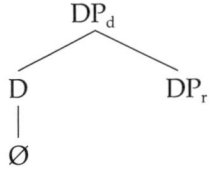

Here the empty D is interpreted as identity at type d, λx.x, triggering extensionalization, and taking an argument position with role interpretation as complement. Assuming that DP_r in this construction is an argument position, the scope mechanism applies to it as it does to normal argument positions, and the DP_r interpretation can be stored and quantified-in like other DP arguments. Whether or not we syntacticize the analysis in this way, clearly the grammar predicts correctly that role-value interpretations show scope like normal argument noun phrases and not like normal predicates.

   In the analysis, I have derived all interpretations in (37) with quantifying in. For (37a), there is also a direct interpretation: RICHARD III of type r can, of course, directly shift to a role-value interpretation. I mention here another possibility which does not use quantifying-in. The type shifting triangle does not include type lowerings like Partee's operation BE:

BE: $<<d,t>,t> \rightarrow <d,t>$
BE[α] = $\lambda x.\alpha(\lambda y.y=x)$

It would be compatible with the theory, though, to assume that role generalized quantifiers of type $<<r,t>,t>$ in the triangle based on r can be linked directly to the predicate type $<d,t>$ with an operation value:

VALUE: $<<r,t>,t> \rightarrow <d,t>$
VALUE[α] = $\lambda x.\alpha(\lambda z.^{v}z=x)$

That would allow for a direct derivation of all three cases in (37). I will not here explore the ramifications of this (but see below).

3.4.2 Relativization

We now expect that role-value interpretations should pattern with argument noun phrases also with respect to the other variable binding operations that we are looking at here, **relativization** and **wh-questions**. Thus, we predict that we should be able to form role-relative clauses and role-wh-questions with a **role gap** in predicative position. At least: what we predict is that such abstraction does not violate the Variable Constraint, for the same reason that the scope mechanism does not violate it. This means also that such abstraction should pattern with individual abstraction; that is, it should not show, for instance, the definiteness effects on the external head that we observed before for abstraction out of contexts of definiteness and predication.

We look at relativization first. (38) shows that we can relativize over a role gap in predicate position, and that it behaves like an argument gap: the relevant noun phrases in (38) have a role interpretation, and, as (38c) and (38d) show, there are no definiteness restrictions on the external head. The relative clause behaves like a normal restrictive relative clause, except that it restricts a role predicate, rather than an individual predicate.

(38)a. Every color that this house has been –, has been a pastel.
   b. Every Shakespearean king that Derek Jacobi has been –, has been a success.
   c. There are three Shakespearean kings that Derek Jacobi hasn't been –.
   d. There are many Shakespeakean kings that Derek Jacobi has been –.

All these cases involve the relativizer *that*. Earlier I mentioned Carlson's restriction on relativizer *which*, that requires the abstraction to be over a variable of argument type d. With this restriction, we expect that relativizing over a role variable with relativizers *which* and *who* should not be good. According to my informants, this is the case:

(39)a. #Every color which this house has been, has been a pastel.
　　b. #Every Shakespearean king which Derek Jacobi has been has been a success.
　　c. #There are three Shakespearean kings which Derek Jacobi hasn't been.
　　d. #There are three kings who Jacobi hasn't been.

It should be noted, though, that what the analysis of relativization required was that *which* and *who* do not allow a rescue strategy with a variable of a non-argument type, like degree. As for the question of whether *which* and *who* allow abstraction over variables of other **argument types**, like the type of roles r, there could well be some dialectical variation. For instance, the OED mentions some cases with *which* that are similar to the cases in (39), but describes them as "dialectical."

Note too, that I have not discussed free relatives here, nor relatives with prepositional relativizers (like *in which*), or functional relative clauses (Sharvit 1999). I am not claiming that the restrictions are uniform over all these cases.

3.4.3　Wh-questions

We already saw above that Heim argues that in the wh-case *which* patterns with the relativizer in that it seems to be restricted to type d, but *who* patterns with *what*, not seeming to have a sortal restriction. When it comes to abstraction over a role variable, it seems that even question word *which* is more liberal that relativizer *which*, in that it does seem to allow wh-questioning with a role variable:

(40)a. Mr Jacobi, which Shakespearean kings have you been –?
　　b. Mr Jacobi, which Shakespearean king are you this year –?
　　c. Mr Jacobi, in the new play, who are you –?
　　d. Mr Jacobi, what character are you –?

The conclusion is that, *pace* the sortal restrictions, also abstraction and relativization over role variables in role-value predicates behave like abstraction and relativization from argument position.

3.4.4　Some brief remarks on *there*-insertion contexts

Above I have given two options for deriving role-value predicates: through quantifying-in a role variable, and through linking the generalized quantifier role type $<<r,t>,t>$ with the individual predicate type $<d,t>$. Since I haven't even given the analysis of *there*-insertion contexts for individual level noun phrases, it is completely premature to start contemplating what predictions either of these role-value analyses would make in *there*-insertion contexts. That is, at this stage the theoretical options still vary between the following alternatives:

- role-value interpretations are not allowed in *there*-insertion at all (say, because role variables behave like definites);
- role-value interpretations are allowed in *there*-insertion contexts for all noun phrases (say, because all are generated with a set-interpretation of type <d,t> with linking <<r,t>,t> to <d,t>). But intermediate options are possible as well.

The problem is that the facts are very difficult to check. Obviously, there are **role interpretations** in *there*-insertion contexts as well, and they show normal definiteness effects:

(41)a.   There are *three kings* in this play.
   b.   #There is *every king* in this play.

There is nothing unexpected about those facts. The problem is that, in order to check the behavior of role-value interpretations, we need to set up our examples in such a way that we can be sure that the noun phrase in the *there*-insertion context has a **role-value interpretation**, and not a role interpretation. And this is very difficult to achieve.

   It seems that the contrast (with kinds, rather than roles) in felicity that McNally (1998) discusses is pertinent here:

(42)a.   #There is *every cat* in the garden.
   b.   There is *every kind of cat* in the garden.

But I will leave the discussion at this.

3.5   Wh-questions and Individual Variables

There is one remaining problem, that we mentioned above. (43) is felicitous:

(43)a.   Who are you –?

We claimed, with Heim, that, unlike *which*, question word *who* doesn't have the restriction to type d, and we can then assume that (43) does not violate the variable constraint, by invoking a variable not of type d.

   The problem is: how plausible is that? Isn't (43) a *locus classicus* of abstraction over a variable of type d?

   While there are many analyses of questions in existence that would analyze (43) as involving a variable of type d, not all analyses work this way. Engdahl

(1986), for instance, assumes that the individual reading of questions is a special case of the functional reading, and so does Chierchia (1993). As we know from the literature, functional readings are ubiquitous for questions, and in the worst case, we can say that it is practically impossible to show that a question must involve individual abstraction. Now, most of this literature concerns functional variables of type <d,d>. However, if we assume that the variables that questions abstract over are generally of type <a,d>, then we can assume that what looks at first sight like abstraction over variables of type d, really is to be construed as abstraction over type <s,d>, which is the role type.

The advantage of this is that it may address a well known problem in the analysis of questions with individual variables. Most theories of questions derive the question meaning from an abstract. Thus, the question interpretation of (43a) with an individual variable is derived from the abstract in (43b):

(43)b.   λx.you = x

For instance, Groenendijk and Stokhof (1982) derive this abstract, and derive from this question denotation (43c):

(43)c.   The set of worlds in which λx.you = x has the same denotation as in the real world.

The problem, and this is well known, is that the interpretation thus derived is **trivial**: (43b) denotes the set of individuals identical to you, which is the singleton set containing you (i.e. the predicate *being you*). And the set of worlds in which the predicate *being you* has the same denotation as it has in the real world is, in normal contexts, just the set of all (relevant) worlds. The question is not an informative question, because the answer is clear: you.

Now, one can try to tinkle with the rigidity of *you* (i.e. include less normal worlds), but that seems the wrong track to take for this problem: the intuition is that in a perfectly normal context, involving only perfectly normal alternatives, the question is informative, while the theory predicts that it is not.

This is where the functional reading comes in. If we put in predicate position a functional variable f of type <s,d> (or r), we can shift it with extensionalization to ˅f, and form the individual level predicate λx.x=˅f, without violating the variable constraint. We apply this predicate to the interpretation of *you* and get: you = ˅f. We abstract over variable f and get a functional interpretation for the question:

(43)d.   λf.you = ˅f
   e.   the set of worlds where the extension of λf.you = ˅f is the same as in the real world.

Thus, the question does not mean: *which individual is identical to you*, but it means: *which function takes you as a value?*

Now, the usual assumption about such questions is that the answer to such a question must be a function, i.e. an expression of the same type as the variable in the question. But given usual assumptions about type shifting, it would be surprising if one could straightforwardly read off the type of the variable in the question by looking at the answer, especially when it concerns two possible answers, one a DP of type d, the other a DP of type r. Such a theory would have to assume that a functional question cannot be answered with an individual answer, and that would mean that, in the context of the functional question, the individual answer cannot shift. This is just not very plausible.

Let me briefly expand on this. Let's make, for the purpose of the problems at hand (questions with short answers), a little toy question–answer theory. Let us assume that the question is an abstract, and that the answer turns the question into a new question: the question remaining after the answer. How does it do that? The simplest way of thinking about this is to shift the answer to a question in its own right and conjoining it, at the type of questions with the original question:

$$Q + A = \begin{cases} Q \cap \text{QLIFT}[A] & \text{if this is not empty} \\ \text{infelicitous} & \text{otherwise} \end{cases}$$

If the question is a functional question, like (43c), the type of the question is $<<s,d>,t>$. How do we lift an answer of type d or type $<s,d>$ to this type? Well, what about, in the standard way:

If $\alpha \in \text{EXP}_r$, then $\text{QLIFT}[\alpha] = \lambda r.\alpha = r$ $(= \text{IDENT}[\alpha])$
If $\alpha \in \text{EXP}_d$, then $\text{QLIFT}[\alpha] = \lambda r.\alpha = {}^\vee r$

Let's look at question (43a) and functional interpretation (43d):

(43)a.   Who are you?
      d. $\lambda f.\text{you} = {}^\vee f$

We can provide this question with a role answer of type r. This is the following situation:

(44)a.   *Question:*   Mr Heston, in the movie, who are you?
            Answer: Ben Gurion
      b.   Q: $\lambda f.\text{you} = {}^\vee f$
            A: BEN GURION$_r$

Assuming that the question–answering is felicitous, the result of answering the question is a singleton question (*which role is Ben Gurion$_r$?*)

$Q + A = (\lambda f.\text{you} = {}^\vee f) \cap (\lambda f.\text{BEN GURION}_r = f) =$
            $\lambda f.\text{BEN GURION}_r = f \wedge \text{you} = {}^\vee f$ $=$
            $\lambda f.f = \text{BEN GURION}_r$

In the context suggested, it is natural to assume that this question is not itself a question on the shared information. This means that we have reduced the original question to a question that is answered on the information, and in this way we can say that we have answered the original question.

Now let's look at an individual answer:

(45)a. *Question*: Who are you?
    Answer: The person you saw on the beach yesterday.
  b. Q: $\lambda f.you = {}^\vee f$
    A: $\sigma(\lambda x.I$ SAW x ON THE BEACH YESTERDAY$)_d$

$Q + A = (\lambda f.you = {}^\vee f) \cap (\lambda f. \sigma(\lambda x.I$ SAW x ON THE BEACH YESTERDAY$)$
$= {}^\vee f) = \lambda f.you = {}^\vee f \wedge \sigma(\lambda x.I$ SAW x ON THE BEACH YESTERDAY$) = {}^\vee f$

In this case the answer reduces the original question to the question:

Which natural function takes you as value for the present contextual index and the man I saw at the beach as value for some contextually salient index?

In a natural context, such an answer is felicitous, since it reduces the original question. Whether it is a complete answer on the shared information depends on whether it provides enough information to reduce the question to a question which is no longer a question on the shared information, and that is typically the case if enough information is provided to pick out a unique natural function.

The upshot for the present discussion is the following: with the Variable Constraint, we assume that the question (44a) only has a functional interpretation, and not an individual interpretation. This would be a problem if the type of the question and the type of the answer were required to match strictly. But the toy question–answer theory sketched here provides a natural way of analyzing both functional and individual answers to a functional question. This means that the answering data do not argue against the Variable Constraint.

Interestingly enough, when we put *you* in predicative position, we get only a role interpretation:

(46)a. *Question*: Who – is you?
  b. *Question*: Mr Ben Gurion, in this movie, who is you?
    Answer: Mr Heston.
  c. $\lambda x.x = YOU_d$
  d. Q: $\lambda x.x = {}^\vee YOU_r$
    A: $HESTON_d$

If we assume that *you* is like a variable in that it is subject to the Variable Constraint, then YOU_d cannot be lifted to the predicate type. This means that we do not get interpretation (46c), even though the gap of wh-extraction is in argument position. This means that we must interpret the predicate with YOU_r.

In this case the gap is in argument position, which means that it is naturally interpreted as being of type d. In this case, the question is Q in (46d):

Which individual is the value in the present context of the role YOU?

And this is a perfectly felicitous question. Answering the question Q with A gives:

Q + A = $\lambda x.x = {}^\lor YOU_r \land x = HESTON_d$
Which individual is the value in the present context of the role YOU and is identical to Mr Heston?

In a normal context, this no longer is a question on the background information, hence, in a normal context, it provides a felicitous complete answer to the question.

This last example, is of course, not really about questions, but about pronominal elements in predicative position. This is, of course, another area to look for effects of the Variable Constraint. The above initial discussion shows that the results are promising, but also that tests need to be carefully controlled for interpretations of pronominals at other types than type d. The discussion of pronominals goes beyond the scope of the present chapter, except for one more remark. Carlson (1991) notices the following curious facts about "introduction contexts" (see also Buering 1998):

(47)a.   Hi Fred, *this* is Mary.
   b.   #Hi Fred, Mary is *this*.

If we assume, as we should, that proper names can have an interpretation at type d and at type <s,d>, but that Carlson's *this* can only have an interpretation at type d, the facts in (47a) and (47b) follow from the Variable Constraint. (47a) is felicitous and expresses that the individual that I am pointing at is the value for the present context of the role MARY. (47b) is infelicitous.

One more remark. Doesn't this mean that the role interpretation of *Mary* in (47), and in play-contexts is exactly the same individual concept, and isn't that a problem? That is, aren't we talking about different things, when we talk about Mary as a normal individual concept, and the character Mary in a play?

I assume that this is a matter of finegrainedness of context indices and contextual restriction on the domains of functions from context indices to individuals. That is, we can assume that (47) and the play contexts involve the very same individual concept MARY, the same total function. However, in any particular context we will typically restrict ourselves to what we could call **natural stretches** of individual concepts, restrictions of these total functions to coherent sets of context indices. With finegrainedness of such context indices, the set of indices for which the play-stretch of the individual concept MARY is defined will be distinct from the set of indices from which the introductions-stretch is defined. For an analysis along these lines, and more pertinent discussion, see Sharvit (1999).

In sum: I proposed the Variable Constraint in order to explain peculiar facts about scope and relativization in predicate position and contexts of indefiniteness. Then I argued that this analysis is problematic if we must assume that question word *who* allows abstraction over an individual variable in predicate position. What I have argued now is that we do not need to make that assumption: these cases can be fruitfully reanalyzed as function-value predicates that do not violate the variable constraint.

Chapter 4

Problems for Weak–Strong Analyses of *There*-Insertion Subjects

---

4.1 The Proposal in a Nutshell

Let us recapitulate. The distribution of noun phrases in *there*-insertion contexts is a subset of that in predicative position, and *there*-insertion contexts interact with variable binding mechanisms in the same way as predicative contexts. We conclude from this that the very same set/non-set distinction lies at the heart of the *there*-insertion facts.

This means that whatever mechanism disallows quantificational noun phrases from predicative position, also disallows quantificational noun phrases from *there*-insertion position. Hence, the weak–strong tradition has been cutting up the class of noun phrases in the wrong way, at least as far as *there*-insertion contexts are concerned: the basic semantic distinction is not between definites and quantificational noun phrases on the one hand, and indefinites on the other, but between quantificational noun phrases and the rest. Hence there is no need for a unified semantic account of quantificational noun phrases and definites in order to explain their infelicity in *there*-insertion contexts.

The Adjectival Theory provides a unified semantic account of the infelicity of quantificational noun phrases in predicative position and *there*-insertion contexts: they cannot be lowered into the set type <d,t>.

What is needed over and above that is an account of the infelicity of definites in *there*-insertion contexts. As we have seen in chapter 3, Higginbotham and others assume that *there*-insertion contexts in fact are predicative positions, and they add the weak–strong distinction as a further semantic filter to eliminate definites from *there*-insertion predicates. However, as argued in the previous chapter, the assumption that the position of the indefinite in *there*-insertion contexts is a predicate position is untenable, as soon as we take verbal structures into account (like *arrive*).

I assume, with Higginbotham (1987) and McNally (1998), that the position open to the definiteness effect in *there*-insertion contexts has a type derived from the type of sets. But I do not accept that it is itself a predicate position.

What other salient category of expressions has an interpretation derived from the type of sets? Well, **intersective adjuncts**, like intersective adjectives and adverbs.

Predicative adjectives like *blond* are generated at the type of sets, BLOND of type $<d,t>$. As adjuncts, they shift to a modifier interpretation with the intersective type shifting operation ADJUNCT:

ADJUNCT: $<d,t> \rightarrow <<d,t>,<d,t>>$
ADJUNCT$[\alpha] = \lambda P \lambda x.P(x) \wedge \alpha(x)$ of type $<<d,t>,<d,t>>$

ADJUNCT itself is here, of course, nothing but conjunction (of type $<<d,t>, <<d,t>,<d,t>>>$) adapted as a type shifter. ADJUNCT is not just used for adjectives, but for all nominal adjuncts: prepositional phrases and relative clauses too get an intersective interpretation with ADJUNCT.

The same principle applies in the verbal domain. I assume a theory in which the category verb phrase VP is interpreted at type $<d,<e,t>>$, the type of functions from individuals into sets of events (see Landman 2000). Thus, *walk* is interpreted as:

$\lambda x \lambda e.\text{WALK}(e) \wedge \text{Agent}(e)=x$ of type $<d,<e,t>>$

Intersective adverbs like *quickly* are generated at the type of sets of events, e.g. QUICK of type $<e,t>$. When adjoined to VP, they shift with ADJUNCT into an intersective modifier of VPs of type $<<d,<e,t>>,<d,<e,t>>>$:

ADJUNCT: $<e,t> \rightarrow <<d,<e,t>>,<d,<e,t>>>$
ADJUNCT$[\alpha] = \lambda V \lambda x \lambda e.V(e,x) \wedge \alpha(e)$ of type $<<d,<e,t>>,<d,<e,t>>>$

When adverbs are transitive verb modifiers they shift with ADJUNCT from type $<e,t>$ to type $<<d,<d,<e,t>>>,<d,<d,<e,t>>>>$. We see the general form appearing:

Let $<a,t>$ stand for a set type, like $<d,t>$ or $<e,t>$.
I use the notation $<x^n,<a,t>>$ for $<x,<x, \ldots ,<x,<a,t>> \ldots >>$, with x occurring *n* times.
So, $<x^2,<a,t>> = <x,<x,<a,t>>>$.

Type shift operation ADJUNCT shifts sets to intersective modifiers:
ADJUNCT: $<a,t> \rightarrow <<x^n,<a,t>>,<x^n,<a,t>>>$
ADJUNCT$[\alpha] = \lambda R^n \lambda x_n \ldots \lambda x_1.R^n(x_1 \ldots x_n) \cap \alpha$

(This is, of course, the same as, $\lambda R^n \lambda x_n \ldots \lambda x_1 \lambda z.R^n(z,x_1 \ldots x_n) \wedge \alpha(z)$, with z a variable of type a.)

I will call the modifier types of the form $<<x^n,<a,t>>,<x^n,<a,t>>>$ the **adjunct domain** (based on $<a,t>$). What we see is that the adjunct domain of the type of sets of individuals <d,t> is accessed from the type of sets of individuals <d,t>. Similarly, the adjunct domain based on <e,t> is accessed from the type of sets of events <e,t>. Thus, the shift into the adjunct domain is accessed from the type of sets:

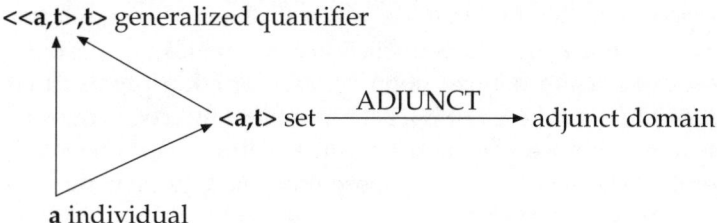

My proposal for the analysis of *there*-insertion contexts is now the following:

Proposal:
1. *There*-insertion position is an adjunct position.
2. Under certain conditions noun phrases can shift into the adjunction domain. This is what happens in *there*-insertion position.

Constraint:
In languages like English and Dutch such a shift into the adjunct domain is only possible for noun phrases that are generated at the set type, not for noun phrases that are shifted into the set type.

Thus, since adjunct interpretations are accessed from the type of sets, obviously noun phrases that do not have an interpretation at the type of sets, i.e. quantificational noun phrases, cannot be shifted into the adjunct domain, and hence are infelicitous in *there*-insertion position. Over and beyond this, the constraint in (3), above, says that a shift into the adjunct domain is somewhat special in that it applies only to noun phrases whose interpretation starts out as sets. Since definites are generated at the type d of individuals, and are only shifted into <d,t>, they cannot be shifted into the adjunction domain, and hence they are infelicitous in *there*-insertion position. In other words, definites can be lifted into predicate position, but not into adjunct position.

The idea then is that, under certain conditions, noun phrases can, so to say, hijack a type shift principle for adjectives (adjunction). But the shift is not fully **integrated** into the normal type shifting theory for noun phrases. This means that the type shifting theory at this place is not the transitive closure of the individual type shift operations. So, you can shift a noun phrase interpretation from d to <d,t> with IDENT, driven by the type of predicate position. We now allow a shift for noun phrase interpretations from <d,t> into the adjunct domain, driven by the type of the adjunct position. But the latter shift is kept separate from the normal type shifting theory: there is no shift from type d, through type <d,t> into the adjunct domain. (This means, by the way, that there could be languages in which the shift is integrated in the normal type shifting theory. In such languages you would find *there*-insertion contexts in which quantificational noun phrases are infelicitous, but definites are felicitous, i.e. the distribution of noun phrases in *there*-insertion contexts in such languages would be like the distribution in predicate position.)

I have, in the previous chapter, defined quantificational noun phrases extensionally as noun phrases that are infelicitous in predicative position. I will now define extensionally definite noun phrases as noun phrases that are felicitous in predicative position, but infelicitous in *there*-insertion contexts, whereas indefinite noun phrases are felicitous in predicative position and *there*-insertion position. The theory that I propose links these notions directly to the types at which they are generated: <<d,t>,t>, d, <d,t>.

The explanation I propose for the definiteness effects in *there*-insertion contexts has nothing whatsoever to do with a weak–strong distinction. In this sense, what I propose is radically different not just from the tradition, but also from more recent proposals like Higginbotham (1987), McNally (1998), or de Swart (2001). Those proposals go some way in linking definiteness effects to the type of sets, but do keep a place for weak–strong distinctions. Such approaches I will call **soft-set** approaches to definiteness effects. In this book, I will advocate a **hard-set** approach.

In this chapter, I will be concerned with outlining some arguments to prefer a hard-set approach over weak–strong or soft-set approaches. In the remainder of this book I will be concerned with developing a hard-set approach to *there*-insertion contexts (and other contexts that show definiteness effects). As we have seen, the crux of the analysis is going to be the assumption that noun phrases in *there*-insertion contexts are adjuncts. But the grammar doesn't normally allow noun phrases to be adjuncts, without some radical reinterpretation:

(1)   That is a very *Fred* thing to do.

That is, (1), with proper name *Fred* used as a prenominal adjective does not mean: that is a thing to do which is identical to Fred; i.e. its meaning is obviously not derived through shifting the interpretation of *Fred* with IDENT to <d,t> and intersecting the result with the interpretation of *thing*. Thus, the question that will be raised in the chapters to follow is a fundamental one: How can noun phrases be adjuncts? But first, in this chapter we discuss the weak–strong distinction.

4.2   Types versus Semantic Properties

In the literature that relates felicity in *there*-insertion contexts to a weak–strong distinction, two streams of thinking can be distinguished.

One stream starts with the definites and takes the partiality of definites as its guiding line. Definites are partial, hence presuppositional, indefinites are not. If we now argue that quantificational noun phrases are partial, or pre-suppositional as well, we have an opposition which fits the distribution in *there*-insertion contexts, moreover one that fits somewhat with the old–new distinction that is used elsewhere in the grammar. Proposals along these lines can be found in de Jong and Verkuyl (1985), de Jong (1987), Rullmann (1989), Diesing (1990), Zucchi (1995), and many others.

The other stream starts with indefinites and their salient property of symmetry:

DET(A,B) iff DET(B,A)

Here the task is to define the class of indefinites with the help of symmetry so as to exclude all definites and quantificational noun phrases. Well known examples of this stream are Barwise and Cooper (1981) and Keenan (1987).

Let me start by expressing right away that I am not denying that notions like presuppositionality and symmetry are important semantic concepts, nor even that they may be responsible for some kinds of definiteness effects. What I will be claiming is that the unification of definites and quantificational noun phrases that these theories strive for is misguided, and that the effect of pre-suppositionality or symmetry on felicity judgments is too weak to explain the robust judgments that we are dealing with here.

To avoid misunderstanding, let me sketch here the logic of my argument. The theories that I am concerned with here typically define a notion of pre-suppositionality or strength for determiners. They claim that *there*-insertion contexts are sensitive to this. Such a claim can take a weak form or a strong form.

In the **weak** form, the claim would be: the grammar is sensitive to the presuppositionality/strength of the determiners: noun phrases based on non-presuppositional/weak determiners are felicitous in *there*-insertion contexts, noun phrases based on presuppositional/strong determiners are infelicitous there.

The **strong** claim would be: presuppositional/strong determiners give the noun phrases that they head a property which is incompatible with something about the *there*-insertion context (say, their "existentiality" or "presentational meaning"), which non-presuppositional/weak noun phrases do not.

It is fair to say that what you find most commonly in the literature, is the weak claim, rather than the strong claim. Nevertheless, it is the strong claim that I find most interesting, and that I will discuss in detail, because it is the strong claim that really tries to give a purely semantic explanation of the definiteness effect. I will try to show here that the strong claim is untenable.

One can wonder what the point is of the exercise of showing the strong claim untenable if it is the weak claim, rather than the strong one, that we find in the literature. And the answer is that while the criticism doesn't directly affect the weak claim, it does so indirectly. This is because I think that the main reason that we find the weak claim (i.e. sensitivity of *there*-insertion to the strength of the determiner) exciting is that it seems to open the possibility that the strong claim is true, i.e. that it opens up the possibility for a semantic explanation of the felicity pattern in *there*-insertion contexts.

That is, a statement of the form:

α is infelicitous in C iff α's determiner has semantic property P

becomes a semantic explanation only when we can provide a semantic account of why α's determiner having this particular property P matters for felicity in C.

Now, maybe you will be able to show that in contexts of type C the gruesome strong determiner eating beast runs loose, and that's why having a strong determiner matters. But in the absence of the beast, it is more likely that a semantic explanation will run along the following lines. The strength of the noun phrase's determiner will carry some semantic property over into the interpretation which combines with the *there*-insertion context (i.e. the noun phrase interpretation, or the interpretation of the noun phrase-coda complex), a property which is incompatible with something about the semantics of *there*-insertion contexts, say, incompatible with the existential meaning of the construction. Thus, the main attraction of the weak claim is precisely that it opens up the possibility of explaining the distribution, which is the strong claim.

If we can argue that such a semantic account, i.e. the strong claim, is not tenable, the weak claim reduces to a grammatical stipulation like others. This is not a problem, there is nothing wrong with grammatical stipulations (we all make them). But it does mean that the weak claim doesn't have anything special to go for it: there is no a priori reason to think that it is a better stipulation than, say, my own stipulation that only noun phrases generated at the set type can shift into the adjunction domain. Which one is the better stipulation will need to be considered in the context of the role that they play in the whole theory.

This being said, let me now turn to the reasons why I think that theories that base the account of infelicity in *there*-insertion contexts on semantic distinctions like presuppositionality or strength are untenable.

4.3   Worry One: The Quantificational Class is Small and Heterogeneous

Quantificational noun phrases are noun phrases infelicitous in predicative position. I assume that they are generated at type $<<d,t>,t>$ by combining a noun with a determiner of type $<<d,t>,<<d,t>,t>>$, in the way Generalized Quantifier Theory assumes all noun phrases are generated. The first worry concerns the size and coherence of this class.

As mentioned above, for some elements there seems to be a coherent semantic reason why they occur in this class: English *both* is strictly distributive, like *each*, but Dutch *(de) beide* allows collective interpretations unproblematically:

(2)a.   #Both boys met in the park.
  b.   (De) beide jongens kwamen samen   in het park.
         Both   boys   came   together in the park

This patterns with their behavior in predicative position:

(3)a. #The guests were both boys.
   b. De gasten waren (de) beide jongens.

(The glosses of the Dutch examples can be read off straightforwardly from the corresponding English examples.)

Thus the reason for the exceptional nature of *every, each, both* and *iedere, elke* may be related to some peculiarity about how distributivity can be lexicalized in the nominal domain, i.e. through one of the operators:

$$\forall_{sing} = \lambda Q\lambda P.Q \subseteq ATOM \wedge \forall a[Q(a) \rightarrow P(a)]$$
$$\forall_{dist} = \lambda Q\lambda P.\forall a[a \in ATOM(\sqcup Q) \rightarrow P(a)]$$

(As argued in Landman (2000) and in chapter 2, *every* is different from *each, both* in that noun phrases of the form *every N*, but not *each N* can sometimes shift to type d and get a collective interpretation. Note that I assume that this is a special interpretation strategy, not part of the default type shifting theory.)

Such an explanation, however, isn't appropriate for *most*: both English *most* and Dutch *de meeste* are infelicitous in predicative position and *there*-insertion contexts:

(4)a. #The guests were most boys.
   b. #There were most boys at the party.
   c. #De gasten waren de meeste jongens.
   d. #Er waren de meeste jongens op het feest.

But there is no connection with distributivity (but see section 4.8 below). As argued above, the same is true for Dutch *sommige*, in contrast with *enige* (also meaning *some*) or *een paar* (*a couple*):

(5)a. #De gasten waren sommige jongens.
   b. #Er waren sommige jongens op het feest.
   c. De gasten waren enige/een paar jongens.
   d. Er waren enige/een paar jongens op het feest.

I repeat: the class of quantificational noun phrases is small (in terms of determiners that it is based on) and heterogeneous.

With this notion of size, the class of definites, noun phrases of type d can be regarded as very small too. Of the two definiteness operations, sum ⊔, and presuppositional sum σ, of type <<a,t>,a>, the latter lexicalizes as a nominal determiner of type <<d,t>,d>, and other definite determiners can be analyzed as compositions with σ.

The emerging picture is as follows: the type of sets, <d,t>, is where the action is; nominal definiteness and nominal distributivity can systematically bring you to different types, d or <<d,t>,t>; besides that, there are one or two elements like *most* and *sommige*, that, for reasons best known to themselves, tag on to distributive determiners in type, without being distributive semantically.

Thus, noun phrases that are not generated at the type of sets form a small class (in terms of the basic operators that they are based on), and not a homogenous class; moreover, the subclass of quantificational noun phrases seems to be heterogeneous itself. Given all this, it is not clear that we would want to semantically unify the class of non-set noun phrases (beyond them being non-set), unless, of course, the unifying feature is strikingly illuminating in the first place, which – if we think about weak–strong distinctions covering the whole class – it is not.

4.4   Worry Two: Quantificational Noun Phrases and Definites that are not Presuppositional

As mentioned, one major stream of literature that tries to unify semantically the class of non-set noun phrases uses a unifying property of presupposition-ality. The assumption here is that quantificational noun phrases of the form *Q Noun* presuppose that the noun interpretation is non-empty. In this, the assumption goes, they are like definite noun phrases of the form *DEF Noun*, but unlike indefinite noun phrases of the form *INDEF Noun*. A variant of this approach assumes that quantificational and definite noun phrases, unlike (weak) indefinites are discourse linked: the set denoted by their noun restriction is already contextually present. I will have more discussion of the discourse linkedness variant in chapter 7, when I discuss so-called strong indefinites. Here I will restrict myself to the obvious concern.

For quantificational noun phrases, the presuppositional effects are very weak, in fact, just as weak as Partee's non-singleton "presupposition" discussed above. That is, as we tend to show in our Introduction to Semantics or Logic classes, in argument position, such "presuppositions" can easily be canceled:

(6)   Every person who has come to me in the last two years with a winning lottery ticket has gotten a prize. Fortunately, I was on a polar expedition the whole time.

There is a ready counterargument to this observation. And that is that we find the same effects for certain *bona fide* definites, as in (7):

(7)a.   The persons who have come to me in the last two years with a winning lottery ticket have gotten a prize. Fortunately, I was on a polar expedition the whole time.

   b.   The at most three persons who have come to me in the last two years with a winning lottery ticket have gotten a prize. Fortunately, I was on a polar expedition the whole time.

The argument now is: the subject in (7) is a definite, hence on (almost) any-body's account presuppositional: that is, on most theories, the weakness of the effect in (7) is not a reason to deny that the definite in (7) is presuppositional. Apparently, local accommodation, or what have we, is readily available in (7). If it is in (7), why not in (6)? Hence there is no reason to think that (6) isn't presuppositional in the same sense.

I think that this argument is not valid. I think that the cases in (6) and (7) do not have a non-emptyness presupposition. And I think this can be shown by contrasting (6) and (7) with the cases in (8), all of which are clearly infelicitous.

(8)a. #The person who has come to me in the last two years with a winning lottery ticket has gotten a prize. Fortunately, I was on a polar expedi-tion the whole time.

b. #The three persons who have come to me in the last two years with a winning lottery ticket have gotten a prize. Fortunately, I was on a polar expedition the whole time.

I think that the facts in (6)–(8) can be described fruitfully with help of the zero-object 0 in the domain of singular and plural elements.

While a singular noun like *person* denotes a set of atoms and hence will not normally include the 0 object, the plural *persons* is the closure under sum: the set of all sums of subsets of the denotation of *person*. As we have seen, if we allow taking the sum of the empty set, this will include 0 in the denotation of the plural *persons*. The semantics of *at most three* will not exclude 0 from the denotation of *at most three persons*, but the semantics of *three* will exclude 0 from the denotation of *three persons*.

This means that the relevant nouns in (7) can be taken to include 0 in their denotation, while the nouns in (8) do not include 0.

What happens to the definite subjects in these examples when the denota-tion of the noun *person who has come to me with a winning lottery ticket* is empty? Call the denotation of this phrase P.

- For (8a), this means the following. The denotation of the subject is $\sigma(P)$, which is $\sqcup P$ if $\sqcup P \in P$. Since $P = \emptyset$, $\sqcup P = 0$ and $0 \notin P$. Hence $\sigma(P)$ is undefined.
- In (8b), the denotation of the subject is $\sigma(*P \cap \lambda x.|x|{=}3)$. $*P = \{0\}$, but $|0| \neq 3$, hence $*P \cap \{d: |d|{=}3\} = \emptyset$. Hence, also in (8b) the subject is undefined.
- In (7a), $*P = \{0\}$, and $\sqcup\{0\} \in \{0\}$, hence, the subject in (7a) denotes 0.
- Similarly, in (7b), the subject denotes 0.

What we see, then, is that if the denotation of the singular noun *person who has come to me in the last two years with a winning lottery ticket* is empty, then the subjects in (7) denote the null object, while the subjects in (8) are undefined. The undefinedness of the subjects in (8) means that the examples in (8) pre-suppose, as usual, that the singular noun *person who has come to me in the last two years with a winning lottery ticket* is non-empty, hence the infelicity of the examples in (8).

What about the examples in (7), where the subject is null-denoting? Well, that depends really on our analysis of verb denotations (i.e. the predicates), i.e. on whether they do or do not include 0. While I will give an event analysis of this – with a null event – in the next chapter, it is easiest here to simplify matters and think of verbal predicates as also denoting sets of type <d,t>.

The semantics for nouns that I have given tells us that some noun interpretations include 0, while others do not. This should, of course, not be taken as an absolute fact: contextual restriction and widening of predicates is a general phenomenon, and there is no reason to think that it could not affect the inclusion or exclusion of the null object in a noun denotation. But such contextual manipulation would be based on the default interpretations provided by the semantics. For verbs, I think that, since semantic plurality is not morphologically marked on them, there is less semantic pressure on them with respect to the inclusion or exclusion of the null object. This means that I assume that there isn't a default about inclusion or exclusion of the null object for verb denotations, and this means that the inclusion or exclusion of the null object for verb denotations can be freely pragmatically manipulated. This means that if the pragmatics tells us that it's better to assume that the verb interpretation does not contain a null object, we exclude it; while if the pragmatics wants a null object there, we equally readily include it. Why would the pragmatics tell us something about the inclusion or exclusion of a null object in a verb denotation? Because the Gricean maxims may force it to.

If the subject denotes the null object, as in the cases in (7) in the context sketched, the sentence is either **trivially true** or **trivially false**, depending on whether the verbal predicate contains a null object or not. This is quite simple: in this case the cases in (7) say: 0 ∈ *have got a prize.*

Obviously, the sentence is true if 0 is in the predicate denotation, false otherwise. The truth/falsity is trivial either way, since the inclusion or exclusion of 0 obviously does not depend on any facts about the world. The Maxim of Quality says the following:

Maxim of Quality:
Speak the truth.

In the present context, that means that the Maxim of Quality will prefer trivial truth over trivial falsehood. Thus, the Maxim of Quality will instruct us to include the null object in the predicate denotation, and hence, if the singular noun denotation is empty, the sentences in (7) will come out as trivially true.

Let's now look at the cases in (6) and (7) out of the blue, that is, in a context in which we do not make clear that the denotation of the singular predicate *person who has come to me with a winning lottery ticket* is empty (so, of course, we ignore the continuations about polar expeditions).

Out of the blue, the Maxim of Quantity will tell us:

Maxim of Quantity:
Avoid triviality.

Since, when the subject denotes the null object, the interpretation of the sentence is trivial, out of the blue, the Maxim of Quantity instructs us to avoid an interpretation where the subject denotes the null object. This means that, out of the blue, the sentences in (7) have an implicature that the singular noun denotation is not empty. Arguably, the same holds for (6).

It has been textbook wisdom, a wisdom we teach in our introduction classes, that a universal quantifier does not presuppose that the set it lives on is non-empty, but at most implicates this. The fact that (6) is felicitous has always been regarded as evidence for this: in (6) the implicature is canceled. What the examples in (7) show is that the same facts hold for certain kinds of definites: not all definites presuppose that the set they live on is non-empty: the cases in (7) implicate that, but do not presuppose it, because, as the examples show, the effect can easily be canceled. The infelicity of the cases in (8) shows that some definites do have a non-emptiness presupposition: for the definites in (8), the non-emptiness effect cannot be canceled, hence the infelicity.

What we see is that the simplest analysis (in a full Boolean algebra), dictated by the Adjectival Theory, with a simple assumption about verb denotations, straightforwardly predicts the facts in (7) and (8): the definites in (7) are predicted to have a non-emptiness implicature, while the definites in (8) are predicted to have a non-emptiness presupposition.

What these cases show is that not only shouldn't we try to force universal quantifiers into the mold of presuppositional expressions, but in fact, the assumption that definites are always presuppositional should be given up: this assumption is based on singular definites and, on the simplest analysis of plurality (which is the Boolean analysis) does not generalize to all plural definites. Hence the facts in (7) and (8).

I make a brief excursus here. While not fully worked out, I think this analysis is fruitful, not just for the cases at hand, but also because it provides a simple semantic/pragmatic mechanism to deal with a variety of phenomena that have been studied under the label "local accommodation." Thus the analysis extends straightforwardly to cases of dependent noun phrases like (9) and (10):

(9)a. In every family, the boys go into the army.
   b. In every family, the three boys go into the army.

(10)a. In some family, the girls go into the army.
   b. In no family do the girls go into the army.

Example (9b) presupposes that in every family there are three boys, but (9a) does not presuppose that in every family there are boys. If *the three boys* in (9b) denotes the function which maps every family onto the sum of the three boys in that family, the values of this function are either sums of three boys, or undefined. The presupposition is just that the function is fully defined: in every family there are three boys.

In (9a), *the boys* denotes the function which maps every family onto the sum of the boys in that family. In this case, the function can be fully defined, but assigning 0 to certain arguments. "Avoid triviality" instructs us, in this case, not to make the statement trivially false, because of one of those zeros. Allowing 0 in the predicate *go into the army* has the effect of making these instances trivially true, hence they no longer make the quantificational statement trivially false, i.e. the global effect is that these instances are ignored. Thus, there is at most an implicature that in every family there are boys, which is canceled by 0-manipulation.

Hence, due to the pragmatic manipulation of the zero object, which is possible in (9a), but not in (9b), these cases have very different presuppositions.

Example (10) is here to remind us that the pragmatic manipulation concerning "avoid triviality" may well go the other way: Including 0 in the predicate *go into the army* in (10) would trivialize the statements. So here, "avoid triviality" pressures us to exclude 0 from the predicates.

This is, of course, not a worked-out theory, but it's promising enough, since it explains intricate facts that, to my knowledge, are problematic for standard presupposition theories. End of excursus.

To return to the topic of this section: on this account, the definites in (7) are not presuppositional, their "presuppositional effects" concern the presence/ absence of the zero object in the denotation of the relevant predicates, which is pragmatically manipulated. Hence the reason why the effect is cancelable.

There is no reason to think that the "presuppositional" effects of the quantificational cases like those in (6) are any different from this. This means that we have countered the argument in favor of the presuppositionality in (6). Indeed, the effect in (6) is similar to what we find for the definites in (7). But, I have argued, it is not true that the effect in (7) is a presuppositional effect. The effect is an implicature in both quantificational noun phrases and these definites; we must distinguish between an **existence presupposition**, derived from **potential undefinedness** of a definite, and an **existence implicature**, derived from **potential triviality** of a definite.

Thus, the proper semantic analysis of definite noun phrases actually supports the conclusion that the non-emptiness effects in (6) and (7) are not presuppositional effects, but implicatures.

If so, then the problem that we posed for Partee's non-singleton presupposition arises with equal force in presuppositional theories of the definiteness effect: if the effects for quantificational noun phrases are not hardcore presuppositions, but zero-object implicatures, then it is a mystery why they would lead to infelicity in *there*-insertion contexts: they should just disappear like a good boy. But they don't.

Hence, the so-called presuppositional effects are too weak to explain the infelicity of quantificational noun phrases in *there*-insertion contexts. This argument applies *a fortiori* also to the definites in (7).

4.5   Worry Three: The Infelicity of Partitives

The previous concern was mainly about presuppositionality of quantificational noun phrases. The present concern is about presuppositionality of definites in general. I have claimed that the existence or non-emptiness implicatures of quantificational noun phrases are too weak to account for the infelicity in *there*-insertion contexts. I now want to argue that, in fact, the same is true for existence presuppositions of definites.

What I want to argue is the following: there actually is a detectable effect of presuppositionality on felicity in *there*-insertion contexts: i.e. presuppositionality of a noun phrase may well decrease the felicity of that noun phrase in *there*-insertion contexts. And if you want to attribute this to a weak–strong distinction to which the *there*-insertion context is sensitive, be my guest (although anybody's theory of topicality and topic positions is probably enough to explain the effects). But the presuppositionality effect is much weaker than the robust infelicity effects that we have been talking about. Hence, presuppositionality does not account for the robust infelicity effects.

What I am concerned with is partitives. It has been observed by many that there are infelicity effects associated with partitives in *there*-insertion contexts. For instance, Keenan (1987) states that, to the best of his judgment (11) isn't very good:

(11)   ?There are at least two of the ten students in the garden.

Similar judgments have been expressed about other partitives. It must be noted that there is considerable variation here. Some people have less problems with partitives than others; McNally, for instance, accepts several cases that others mark with a question mark, and so do my informants. I myself have very little problem with partitives in *there*-insertion contexts, but I have no reason to doubt that others do. However, it is important to note that already Keenan gives his judgment concerning (11) with some trepidation, and this, I think, is the most salient feature of the infelicity judgments we are concerned with here:

(12)a.   There are *three boys* in the garden.
    b.   ?There are *three of the boys* in the garden.
    c.   #There are *the three boys* in the garden.

The indefinite in (12a) is perfect, the partitive in (12b) is maybe slightly odd, somewhat infelicitous, but the definite in (12c) is strongly infelicitous.

Now, as I said above, I am quite willing to attribute the decrease in felicity in (12b), as compared to (12a), to a presuppositionality effect. But it's the contrast between (12b) and (12c) which is all important. If it's the presuppositionality of the partitive which is responsible for the judgment of (12b) as slightly infelicitous, then there is no explanation for why, in contrast to this, the infelicity judgment in (12c) is so strong and completely robust.

The case becomes even stronger when we look at (13):

(13)a.   *The three boys* have blue eyes/met in the park.
    b.   *Three of the three boys* have blue eyes/met in the park.

It seems that the two relevant noun phrases in (13) have exactly the same presuppositions: there is a sum of three boys, and this sum is the maximal sum of (contextually relevant) boys. They also have, it seems, the same truth conditions. That is, there may be an effect of Dowty's (1986) distributive subentailments in (13b) ("all of them are involved"), but, as Dowty argues, that effect is more an implicature.

That means that, quite independent of the details of your analysis of the partitive, at the generalized quantifier level <<d,t>,t>, the noun phrases in (13) should have the same interpretation. That is, one should be rather suspicious of an analysis that creates a real semantic difference between these two noun phrases at the type where they both denote sets of properties: i.e. an analysis that maps them onto different sets of properties, or an analysis that creates a difference between their undefinedness regions, because, I think, there is no independent evidence for such a move.

But, of course, these noun phrases do differ precisely in felicity in *there*-insertion contexts:

(14)a.   #There are *the three boys* in the garden.
    b.   ?There are *three of the three boys* in the garden.

In sum, then: the semantic and presuppositional difference between the noun phrases in the *there*-insertion context in (14a) and (14b) is too small to account for the major differences in infelicity. But that means that it isn't the presuppositionality of the definite in (14a) that is responsible for the robust infelicity judgment.

Note that I am not saying here that it isn't possible to come up with an analysis that creates a semantic difference between these two noun phrases (of course it is possible, since such analyses exist). Rather what I am saying is that we should not do so!

4.6   Worry Four: een mop van *some* en *most* (a joke about *some* and *most*)

This is in essence the same worry as worry three: the semantic difference between quantificational noun phrases and corresponding set expressions is so small as to make a distinction in terms of contentful semantic properties very dubious.

4.6.1 *Sommige*

The case of *sommige* has been discussed in the literature (e.g. de Jong 1987).
Sommige is not felicitous in predicative position and *there*-insertion contexts. In
fact, English *some* has tendencies in that direction too. That is, out of the blue,
for many speakers *some* can be rather questionable in these contexts. But *some*
can be rescued, for instance, stressed *some* is perfect in (15a). The corresponding Dutch case (15b) stays robustly infelicitous:

(15)a.   There are always SOME boys that will spoil the fun.
   b.   #Er   zijn altijd   sommige jongens die het moeten verpesten.
        There are always some   boys   that it   must   spoil

(I didn't put stress in (15b), because it is infelicitous with any stress pattern.)
    Now, it is quite clear that when we only look at truth conditions, there is
no detectable difference between *some* and other plural indefinites. *Sommige* is
clearly symmetric (no need to rewrite our logic textbooks); (16a) and (16b) are
equivalent:

(16)a.   Sommige jongens   zijn vegetariers.
       some   boys   are vegetarians
   b.   Sommige vegetariers zijn jongens.
       some   vegetarians are boys

That means that any account of the definiteness effect based on symmetry or
similar notions is in trouble: there just isn't a truth conditional difference between
sommige and, say, *enige* or *een paar*.
    What about presuppositionality? The conventional wisdom about *sommige*
is that it is used particularly when a contrast is implied (conventional here means
that books for learning Dutch are likely to tell you that, e.g. Fehringer (1999)).
So, utterance of (15a) is likely to imply that things might be different for other
boys. Now, we have that, of course, already as a conversational implicature
anyway, so the idea would be that in the case of *sommige* this is a bit more
than a conversational implicature, something conventionalized. If so, then the
denotation of *boys* must be assumed to be non-empty beyond the subset that
is asserted to be non-empty in (15a). This means that if the conventional wisdom
is correct, in many contexts *sommige* will come out looking presuppositional
in the required way.
    However, there is one important difference between contrast and presup-
positionality: in many contrast situations you know exactly where to look for
the non-empty remainder set: go to the contrasting element. If the element that
needs the contrast and the contrasting element are introduced in the same scope
environment, at the same discourse level, the net result is no presuppositionality. You do not need to rely on accommodation for that. Look at (17):

(17) Jan zal zijn hele   leven lang sommige vrienden anders behandelen
      Jan will his whole life   long some   friends   other   treat
      dan andere (vrienden).
      than others (friends)
      His life long, Jan will treat some friends differently from other (friends).

On the most natural interpretation, (17) means that at every future moment during Jan's life, among the friends that he will have then, there will be some that get preferential treatment. *Sommige vrienden* here has narrow scope with respect to *will his life long*, and the contrast, i.e. the requirement that the remainder set of friends is not empty, is satisfied within the predicate in the scope of the temporal operators. Thus, if you want to regard this as a presupposition, this presupposition is already satisfied locally, in the scope of the temporal operators. This means that there is, so to say, no "upward" presuppositionality: the net effect is that the statement compares per moment of time t, two subsets of the extension at t of *friends of Jan*, each of which is asserted to be non-empty.

   We can now try to give this the form of a *there*-insertion context, with *sommige vrienden* in the *there*-insertion context, and the contrast in the predicate, the coda. If the contrast is part of the coda, the presuppositionality is already satisfied in the indefinite+coda part, and hence that complex is not itself presuppositional. Thus, we have this kind of situation:

   there [(indefinite(coda))]

If presuppositionality is in conflict with something semantic about the *there*-insertion context, we would expect that *sommige vrienden* should improve here. But, to my ear, it does not. While (18a), with the bare plural *vrienden* has the same interpretation as (18), (18b) is still infelicitous:

(18)a. Zijn leven lang zullen er   vrienden zijn die   Jan anders
        His life   long will   there friends   be   than Jan other
        behandelt dan andere (vrienden).
        treats   than other   (friends)
   b. #Zijn leven lang zullen er   sommige vrienden zijn die Jan anders
        His life   long will   there some   friends   be   that Jan other
        behandelt dan andere (vrienden).
        treats   than others (friends)
        His life long will there be (some) friends that Jan treats differently from other friends.

Thus, the case of *sommige* is a problem both for the presuppositional interpretation of the weak–strong distinction, and for the interpretations that use symmetry.

The fact that Dutch *sommige* and English *some* differ in felicity is, of course, already a peculiarity, making *sommige* not quite the element that you want to base your whole theory on. *Sommige* is a problem for the symmetry approach, because it is not felicitous in *there*-insertion contexts, even though it seems perfectly symmetric. *Sommige* is a problem for the presuppositionality approach, since *sommige* is infelicitous, regardless of whether it contributes something presuppositional to the interpretation that combines with *there*, i.e. at the level where there ought to be a semantic conflict: in other words, when arguably there can't be a semantic conflict because no presupposition survives at that level, the sentence doesn't improve. Hence the "presuppositionality" of *sommige* does not explain its infelicity in *there*-insertion contexts.

4.6.2   *Most*

We are now concerned with the contrast in (19) and (20):

(19)a.   #The guests are most boys.
   b.   The guests are more than half of the boys.

(20)a.   #There were most boys at the party.
   b.   There were more than half of the boys at the party.

We observe a robust contrast here. As we have been assuming all along, *most boys* is a quantificational noun phrase, hence the infelicity of (19a) and (20a). On the other hand, (19b) and (20b) are felicitous, hence we assume that *more than half of the boys* has a set interpretation at type <d,t>, it patterns with indefinites.

It is not difficult to provide a semantics for *more than half of the boys*. Let's first extend the semantics of numerical noun phrases with partitives like *more than three of the boys*. I will call *the boys* the partitive head. In this analysis, I will not try to deal with one well known aspect of partitives, namely the restrictions on the partitive head. I will assume it to be just of type d. (One can attempt to get the restrictions out by assuming that it must actually be of the subtype of groups, and restrict access of noun phrases to that type. This can be done, but it has rather farfetched consequences that will lead us too far away here.)

My basic assumption is the following:

$of \rightarrow \sqsubseteq$ <d,<d,t>>   the part-of relation

We already gave an analysis of the measure phrase *more than three Ø* in chapter 1:

more than three Ø $\rightarrow$ (>(3)) o $\lambda x.|x| =$
                    $\lambda x.|x| > 3$ of type <d,t>

We have now two possibilities for continuing the analysis: we can either assume an analysis [[*more than three*] [*of the boys*]] or [[*more than three of*] [*the boys*]]. The first is the most straightforward one:

> *of the boys* → ⊑ (σ(*BOY))   of type <d,t> =
>   λx.x ⊑ σ(*BOY)

> *more than three of the boys* → λx.|x|>3 ∩ λx. x ⊑ σ(*BOY) =
>   λx.x ⊑ σ(*BOY)) ∧ |x|>3   of type <d,t>
> The set of sums of boys with more than three atoms.

The second analysis first combines *more than three* with *of*. For this we need an operation that conjoins a property and a relation:

> R ∧^{R} P = λyλx.R(x,y) ∧ P(x)

Then we assume the following analysis:

> *more than three of* → ⊑ ∧^{R} λx.|x|>3 =
>   λyλx.x ⊑ y ∧ |x|>3   of type <d,<d,t>>

This applies to *the boys*:

> *more than three of the boys* → [λyλx.x ⊑ y ∧ |x|>3] (σ(*BOY)) =
>   λx.x ⊑ σ(*BOY) ∧ |x|>3   of type <d,t>

While the first analysis is more straightforward than the second, the second fits better with the analysis of *more than half of the boys*. Let's turn to that now. The natural assumption about *half* is that it denotes a function from numbers to numbers, mapping every number onto half that number:

> *half* → λm. ½m   of type <n,n>

Thus *half* is a number expression of type <d,d>. In this case, we cannot apply the interpretation > of the numerical relation *more than* to it, but we can compose, and get a numerical phrase of type <n,<n,t>>, a relation between numbers (hence the same type as the numerical relation >):

> *more than half* → > o λm. ½m =
>   λnλm.n>½m   of type <n,<n,t>>
> The relation that holds between two numbers n and m if n is bigger than a half m.

We have seen count predicates before. Here we have a relation which is count on both arguments. The natural extension of the measure phrase analysis for numerical noun phrases given in chapter 1 is that the relational numerical phrase composes with the cardinality measure $\lambda x.|x|$ on both its arguments:

more than half Ø Ø → $\lambda n\lambda m.n>^1/_2m$ o $(\lambda x.|x|,\lambda x|x|)$

For clarity: the composition operation involved is:

R o (C,C) = $\lambda y\lambda x.((R(C(x)))(C(y)))$

Thus we get:

more than half Ø Ø → $\lambda y\lambda x.|x|>^1/_2|y|$ of type <d,<d,t>>
The relation that holds between two sums x and y if the cardinality of x is more than half of the cardinality of y.

This we can directly combine with the interpretation ⊑ of *of*:

more than half Ø Ø of → $\lambda y\lambda x.|x|>^1/_2|y| \cap \sqsubseteq =$
                    $\lambda y\lambda x.x \sqsubseteq y \wedge |x|>^1/_2|y|$ of type <d,<d,t>>
The relation that holds between two sums x and y if x is part of y and the cardinality of x is more than half of the cardinality of y.

This applies to the partitive head, and we get:

more than half Ø Ø of the boys → $\lambda x.x \sqsubseteq \sigma(\text{*BOY}) \wedge |x|>^1/_2|\sigma(\text{*BOY})|$
The set of sums of boys whose cardinality is more than half of the cardinality of the sum of the boys.

This is the correct set interpretation for *more than half of the boys*.
   In this case, we have assumed the constituent structure [[*more than half Ø Ø of*] [*the boys*]], for which we provided a simple interpretation. Had we chosen the constituent structure: [[*more than half Ø Ø*] [*of the boys*]] we would have to specify a complex semantic interpretation, following the following conjunction schema:

R $\wedge^{**}$ P = R($\sqcup$P) $\cap$ P

In argument position, Argument Formation derives from the set interpretation given the correct argument interpretation at type <<d,t>,t>:

more than half Ø Ø of the boys →
$\lambda P.\exists x.\ x \sqsubseteq \sigma(\text{*BOY}) \wedge |x|>^1/_2|\sigma(\text{*BOY})| \wedge P(x)\ \wedge$
   $\sqcup(\lambda x.x \sqsubseteq \sigma(\text{*BOY}) \wedge |x|>^1/_2|\sigma(\text{*BOY})| \wedge P(x)) \in$
                    $\lambda x.x \sqsubseteq \sigma(\text{*BOY}) \wedge |x|>^1/_2|\sigma(\text{*BOY})|$

Since the sum of sums of boys having P with cardinality more than half the sum of the boys has cardinality more than half of the boys and is a sum of boys, AF reduces to EC:

> *more than half Ø Ø of the boys* →
> $\lambda P.\exists x.\ x \sqsubseteq \sigma(*BOY) \wedge |x|>^1/_2|\sigma(*BOY)| \wedge P(x)$
> The set of all properties such that some sum of boys of cardinality more than half of the boys have that property.

The problem now is the following: this is not only the correct semantics for the argument noun phrase *more than half of the boys*, but it is obviously also the correct semantics for the argument interpretation of *most boys*: the set of properties that more than half of the boys have is of course the set of properties that more boys have than don't have, which is the standard semantics for *most boys*. That is, we can assume that *most* is a determiner of type $<<d,t>,<<d,t>,t>>$, with interpretation:

> $most \rightarrow \lambda Q \lambda P.\ \exists x.\ x \sqsubseteq \sigma(Q) \wedge |x|>^1/_2|\sigma(Q)| \wedge P(x)$

The noun phrase interpretation at type $<<d,t>,t>$ that will be derived for *most boys* is obviously going to be identical with what we derive for *more than half of the boys*. But that means that there is no semantic reason why *most boys* should be a quantificational noun phrase: as far as the truth conditions are concerned, things would work just as well if *most boys* were an indefinite with the same set interpretation as *more than half of the boys* which gets lifted to the argument type.

The case of *most boys/more than half of the boys* is problematic both for the presuppositional account and for the accounts based on symmetry. As far as can be detected, the only difference between *most boys* and *more than half of the boys* is the felicity in predicative position and *there*-insertion position (and phenomena related and reducible to that). There is no truth-conditional difference, and there is no presuppositional difference. Yet, *most boys* patterns with quantificational noun phrases, while *more than half of the boys* patterns with indefinites.

The semantic closeness between the two makes them similarly a problem for theories based on semantic properties like symmetry. One needs to be a little careful here. For instance, take partitives. Are partitives symmetric? Well, that depends on what notions like symmetry apply to here. Look at (21):

(21)a.   *Three of the* (boys, are dancers).
     b.   *Three of the* (dancers, are boys).

If we treat *three of the* as a constituent (as Keenan does), then clearly partitives are not symmetric, and are predicted to be infelicitous in *there*-insertion contexts (and this is problematic, because they only show very weak infelicity effects, if at all). However, this is not the only analysis one can give:

(22)a. *Three* (of the boys, are dancers).
   b. *Three* (dancers, are of the boys).

While (22b) is not a very good sentence of English, one could argue that the symmetry pattern that should be checked for partitives is that which relates the predicates *of the boys* and *are dancers*, semantically, the predicates: $\lambda x.x \sqsubseteq$ σ(*BOY) and *DANCER. (This analysis, hence, follows the interpretation of the first constituent structure.) If that is what we need to check for symmetry, then arguably, partitives with an indefinite numerical phrase count as symmetric, and hence they will count as felicitous in *there*-insertion. This is, it seems, a better story than making them non-symmetric.

   The problem is that even if you give a story that makes partitives symmetric, such a story is not going to make *more than half of the boys* symmetric. Because of the essential comparative nature of *most*, *most* is not symmetric: (19a) and (19b) are not equivalent:

(23)a. *Most* (boys, are dancers)
   b. *Most* (dancers, are boys)

Following the lead of the partitive, we might try an analogous analysis in (24):

(24)a. *More than half* (of the boys, are dancers)
   b. *More than half* (dancers, are of the boys)

This would be following the alternative constituent structure, with the complex semantics. But the point of the complex semantics is precisely to appropriately build in the comparison into the semantics, and (24a) and (24b) just will not come out as equivalent. And, of course, this is as it should be, because *more than half of the boys* and *most boys* have the same semantics. Thus, if we want to peel out *more than half* as a determiner-like element, it is not going to be symmetric. Hence, theories based on symmetry make the wrong predictions for noun phrases like *more than half of the boys*. Because of their essential non-symmetry, these expressions are predicted to be infelicitous in *there*-insertion contexts. But, of course, they are perfectly felicitous.

   There is, I think, a clear conclusion to be drawn: the semantic differences between *most boys* and *more than half of the boys* must by necessity be very small to non-existent. Such differences ought to be too finegrained and subtle to support the robust differences in judgments between the a and b cases in (19) and (20).

   There is no difference in presuppositions which is strong enough to support the robust difference in felicity. Symmetry doesn't support the difference (since *most boys* and *more than half of the boys* must be counted as non-symmetric). And in fact, there is no robust semantic property (that is, truth-conditionally robust) that distinguishes the interpretations of these noun phrases. This puts the strong, explanatory version of weak–strong theories in great doubt. Such a theory requires a semantic property to inherit up to the noun phrase inter-pretation (or even further up to the noun phrase-coda interpretation), in order to be incompatible with something about the semantics of the *there*-insertion construction (like its "existentiality," or "presentational meaning"). What we see is that no such semantic property can distinguish *most boys* from *more than half of the boys*. (But see section 4.8 for some modification of the discussion in this section.)

4.7   Worry Five: The Semantic Property of *There*-Insertion Contexts that Strong Noun Phrases are Supposed to be Incompatible with

If weak–strong effects derive from a conflict with a presentational meaning of the *there*-insertion construction, there has got to **be** a *there*-insertion construction, and the presentational meaning has got to come from somewhere. But it is not clear that there is a construction in this sense, i.e. that there is a *there*-insertion construction which has a meaning, let alone a presentational meaning. In fact, I will assume in the next chapter that in fact there isn't such a construction, and there isn't such a meaning (at least not grammatically encoded). A telling fact pointing in this direction (from Grosu and Landman 1998), is that we find similar definiteness patterns with **counting adverbs**:

(25)a.   Dafna jumped *three times/many times/no times*.
         There were three/many/no events of Dafna jumping.
    b.   Dafna jumped *every time/the three times*.
         For every contextually given event there is a jumping.
         The three contextually given events are each matched with an event of Dafna jumping.

Indefinite counting adverbs in (25a) count jumping events directly: (25a) counts events of Dafna jumping. Definite and quantificational event adverbs in (25b) count jumping events indirectly through matching (in the sense of Rothstein 1995): the cases in (25b) count jumpings indirectly through matching with events that are independently, contextually specified. I will analyze these cases in depth in chapters 10 and 11. What is important at this point is the observation that these cases show definiteness effects, not in terms of infelicity, but in terms of available interpretations: indefinite counting adverbs allow a direct counting interpretation, that quantificational and definite counting adverbs lack. Thus, we have definiteness effects, but no *there*-insertion construction to tag some-thing like a presentational meaning on. What we do have both here and in *there*-insertion constructions is a **typal distinction** between expressions that are born at the set type, and expressions that are not.

   That is, Rothstein (1995) gives a reanalysis of the cases in (25b) as preposi-tional phrases (with an empty preposition) (an analysis which I will criticize later). But the cases in (25a) are better analyzed as normal event adjuncts, that is as noun phrases which, exceptionally, can directly be analyzed as adverbials, hence as adjuncts.

The data in (25) were, in fact, my main reason (in 1997 when I started this work) to move away from explanations of definiteness effects in terms of weak–strong distinctions, and to an account which is based on typal distinctions and adjunction, because that way (and only that way, I think), it seems possible to come up with a unified account of the felicity patterns in *there*-insertion contexts, and the interpretation possibilities for counting adverbials.

If such a unification is a laudable aim – and I think it is – this makes a weak–strong account of *there*-insertion contexts even more problematic. My proposal, as mentioned before is the following:

Noun phrases born at the type of sets can shift under certain conditions into the adjunct domain.

I hope to show in this book that this proposal can explain a variety of definiteness effects, including felicity in *there*-insertion contexts and direct counting interpretations of *counting* noun phrases like *three times* (also, in fact, other cases discussed in the literature, like *measure* contexts, see for example de Jong (1987); I will not discuss these, though). I do not see that weak–strong distinctions show any hope of providing a unified explanation for definiteness effects in such diverse constructions.

4.8 A Note on Collective Interpretations

Barbara Partee (p.c.), following upon a remark in Partee (1987), raises the possibility that numerical noun phrases are only felicitous in predicative position on a collective interpretation. As I understand it, by this Partee does not mean that **as predicates** these predicates can only have a collective interpretation: distributive interpretations of these predicates can be forced in context as for all predicates: (26a) has a reading where it is equivalent to (26b).

(26)a. The guests in the upper room and the guests in the lower room are three girls.
  b. The guests in the upper room are three girls and the guests in the lower room are three girls.

What Partee means, I think, is that the simple predicate *are three girls* when applied to a plural subject ascribes a property to the plurality, and not to the atomic parts of the plurality. On Partee's view, this means that the noun phrase *three girls* in the predicate *are three girls* behaves more like a **collective** interpretation of *three girls* in argument position, than like a **distributive** interpretation of *three girls* in argument position.

This interpretation of the facts about predicates is driven, I think, by the view of Partee (1987) which derives predicate interpretations from argument interpretations; i.e. it is practically equivalent to the idea that only collective interpretations of indefinites at type <<d,t>,t> can be lowered to predicates.

On the Adjectival Theory, Partee's observation just follows from the basic interpretation of the indefinite predicates at type <d,t>: *are three girls* has interpretation:

$\lambda x.*GIRL(x) \wedge |x|=3$
The property that a sum has if it is a sum of girls, and it consists of three atoms

Applying this to a sum will always apply the cardinality predicate directly to the sum, and not to its atoms (because the cardinality predicate is not the pluralization of an atomic predicate (unlike *GIRL)). Thus we automatically get Partee's collectivity.

In the theory of plurality that I advocate there is a collective predicate that corresponds to the above predicate of sums:

$\lambda x.ATOM(x) \wedge *GIRL(\downarrow x) \wedge |\downarrow x|=3$
The property that a group has if it consists of a sum of three girls.

As I have argued in chapter 1, and will again in chapter 11, there are contexts that require a shift from the first predicate to the second with an operation like the following:

$$^{\uparrow}P = \lambda x.ATOM(x) \wedge P(\downarrow x)$$

But these predicates are almost synonymous: they only differ in what they apply to: sums, or corresponding group atoms.

Let us assume that predicates of type <d,t> can shift easily between a sum interpretation and the corresponding group interpretation, and, in fact, that for expressions at type <d,t> both interpretations are available. Then we expect that Argument Formation can in principle choose which of the two interpretations to operate on. And in fact, this will give us an ambiguity for the corresponding argument interpretations at type <<d,t>,t>:

three girls → $\lambda P.\exists x[*GIRL(x) \wedge |x|=3 \wedge P(x)]$ Distributive
$\lambda P.\exists x[ATOM(x) \wedge *GIRL(\downarrow(x)) \wedge |\downarrow(x)|=3 \wedge P(x)]$ Collective

These are, of course, precisely the two interpretations that I assumed in earlier work, e.g. Landman (2000). Thus, it is unproblematic to derive both collective and distributive argument interpretations in the Adjectival Theory.

This theory directly suggests a systematic perspective on the bulk of the expressions that I have retained as determiners, the elements involving the distributive operator (distributive *every*, *each*, English *both*). These expressions do not have collective interpretations, since their interpretation does not start out at type <d,t>, and hence cannot undergo group-atom shift (the above operation). They all build their meaning from the one true natural language quantifier in the nominal domain: the distributive determiner.

On this picture, using determiners of type <<d,t>,<<d,t>,t>> can be seen as a strategy for getting noun phrases that only have distributive interpretations. Edit Doron, Anita Mittwoch, and Arik Cohen pointed out (at a meeting where I presented this material) that on this picture there might be a semantic difference between *more than half of the boys* and *most boys* after all. Since *more than half of the boys* starts out at type <d,t>, we predict a distributive and a collective interpretation for this noun phrase. On the other hand, if *most boys* starts out at type <<d,t>,t>, it may only have a distributive interpretation.

Before saying more about this hypothesis, let me first point out that if there is a semantic difference between *most boys* and *more than half of the boys*, in that the latter can have a collective interpretation that the first cannot, it doesn't seem to be the case that this helps us in rescuing the weak–strong account of *there*-insertion contexts.

Indefinites in *there*-insertion contexts allow both collective and distributive interpretations: (27) has both a collective and a distributive interpretation:

(27) Er   droegen vier jongens een piano de trap   op.
      There carried   four boys   a   piano the stairs up
      Four boys carried a piano upstairs.

Thus, it will not do to assume that the position open to the definiteness effect only allows collective interpretations. Thus, even if there is a semantic difference after all, it doesn't seem to be the semantic difference that allows formulation of a weak–strong distinction.

That being said, I think it is still a quite attractive idea: *most* tags onto the distributive expressions, to get an expression which is unambiguously distributive. The question is: is it true?

It seems quite clear that *more than half of the boys* allows for collective interpretations (distributive interpretations we have already seen).

(28)a. More than half of the boys surrounded the teacher.
    b. More than half of the boys formed a long line.

Examples (28a,b) express that a group surrounded the teacher/formed a long line, and that group was constituted of boys, in total more than half of all the boys. These are the collective readings that we expect to get. The question is: are these readings absent for *most boys*. If so, then the following should be infelicitous:

(29)a. Most boys surrounded the teacher.
    b. Most boys formed a long line.

The problem is that the cases in (28) are really not bad enough. That is, we can agree that *most* prefers distributive readings. Now, there are people for whom the cases in (29) are straightforwardly infelicitous, they don't get collective readings; but other speakers find nothing really wrong with the cases in (29) (and that is the way my judgments for analogous cases in Dutch go).

The same is even more clearly true for *sommige* in Dutch. *Sommige* allows collective readings unproblematically:

(30) Sommige jongens vormden een cirkel/rij.
      Some   boys   formed a   circle/row

This means that the hypothesis – determiners are distributive, hence noun phrases generated from determiners are distributive – is problematic. The determiners *most* and *sommige* allow both distributive and collective interpretations. This means that ultimately also in distributivity/collectivity we do not find a semantic difference between the interpretations of *most boys* and of *more than half of the boys*; in particular a difference on which we can base a semantic, rather than typal, account of *there*-insertion constructions.

Chapter 5

There-Insertion Subjects
as Subjects Adjoined to
Verb Phrases

5.1 Thematic Constraints

As is well known, the syntactic distribution of noun phrases is restricted, meaning simply that they cannot occur in just any syntactic position. This is, of course, nothing special, because the syntactic distribution of other elements, like verbs, or adverbs, is similarly restricted. Most syntactic theories contain some syntactic characterization of the notions **argument position**, **predicate position**, and **adjunct position**. The simplest categorial restriction would go as follows:

Categorial Restriction:
- Noun phrases are restricted to argument positions.
- Verbs are restricted to predicate positions.
- Adverbs, adjectives, prepositional phrases and their ilk are restricted to adjunct positions.

Such a theory will need to say something special from the start about predicate position, because, as we know, noun phrases and adjuncts can occur as predicates. While this is a major issue, we will not be concerned with the question of how noun phrases are licensed in predicative position here; I assume that the theory of predication has adequate answers to the questions involved, and I will be concerned with the distribution of noun phrases in non-predicate position.

Whether the restriction of noun phrases to argument position characterizes the distribution of noun phrases (in non-predicative position) correctly depends here on the definition of argument position. It is standardly assumed that the syntactic definition of argument position is not enough to capture the distribution. Argument positions are standardly identified with complement positions or specifier positions of certain head elements (like specifier of I, specifier of V, complement of V, or complement of P). This puts the noun phrase in a formal relation to such head elements (here the elements I, V, P), and the standard wisdom is that this is not enough: there must be more than a formal relation between the noun phrase occurring in such positions and head elements, and this relation is usually given the form of a thematic constraint:

Thematic Restriction:
Noun phrases occurring in a tree must be thematically licensed by head elements.

In this, we again exclude predicate position from the discussion. The thematic restriction, as given here, is too strong. It is normally taken to apply to normal noun phrases, but not to certain exceptional elements called **pleonastics**. Let us distinguish these terminologically:

Thematic noun phrases are lexically contentful noun phrases.
Non-thematic noun phrases are special elements, like *it* in English which have a last-resort status: they fill a syntactic position which the grammar realizes, but which, for independent reasons, cannot be filled with a thematic noun phrase.

Thus, the thematic restriction becomes:

Theta Theory, principle 1 – Thematic Restriction:
Thematic noun phrases occurring in a tree must be thematically licensed by head elements.

I give this second formulation of thematic restriction for clarity. It is, of course, perfectly appropriate to stick to the first formulation as a default principle, and regard non-thematic noun phrases as a **rescue mechanism** to resolve a conflict.
   Thematic licensing is commonly expressed through a mechanism of thematic roles.

Theta Theory, principle 2 – Theta grid:
Head elements like verbs come lexically specified with a **theta grid**, an ordered list of thematic roles.

Theta Theory, principle 3 – Thematic Assignment:
Every role in a theta grid must be assigned to a thematic noun phrase in the tree.

What we have, so far, is that every role in a theta grid must be assigned to a thematic noun phrase in the tree, and every thematic noun phrase must receive a thematic role. What we know now is that, if a thematic role is assigned to a position, this position must be filled with a thematic noun phrase, meaning in particular, that it cannot be filled with a non-thematic pleonastic. This contrast concerns the subjects in (1):

(1)a.   *John* kissed Mary.   (thematic noun phrase *John*)
  b.   #*It/there* kissed Mary.   (non-thematic noun phrase *it/there*)

We also know that, if it is the case in a language that a position must be syntactically realized, cannot be empty, and is not assigned a thematic role, it can only be filled with a pleonastic. A common assumption is that raising verbs like *seem* assign a role to their complement position, but not to their subject position: thus the subject must be a pleonastic (in non-raising contexts):

(2)a.   #*John* seems that Mary is ill.   (thematic noun phrase *John*)
  b.   *It* seems that Mary is ill.   (non-thematic noun phrase *it*)

The next principles commonly assumed, concern constraints on thematic assignment:

Theta Theory, principle 4 – Uniqueness of Thematic Assignment:
Roles in a theta grid can be assigned only once.

Theta Theory, principle 5 – Assignment under Structural Relations:
Roles in the theta grid of a head are assigned to argument positions in certain structural domains. Most roles are internal roles, which are assigned inside the maximal projection of the head, the last one is an external role, which is assigned higher than that.

While principle 5 is the aspect of Theta Theory which has created the largest syntactic literature, most of it is going to be basically irrelevant for my concerns, except for one aspect which I will mention separately here:

Theta Theory, principle 5a – Assignment to Argument Positions:
Roles in the theta grid of a head are assigned to argument positions.

As David Dowty (1989, 1991) has argued, in a grammar which provides a semantically interpreted syntax, quite a few aspects of theta theory are redundant. For instance, if for a verb like *kiss* we specify the type as $<d,<d,<e,t>>$ (a function which maps two arguments onto a set of events), and its semantic interpretation as: $\lambda y \lambda x \lambda e.KISS(e,x,y)$), then we can assume that the principles of the grammar may well tell us that we must realize two syntactic arguments, which must have interpretations that fit with the semantic arguments x and y. Arguably, the verb *kiss* lexically constrains its arguments x and y. It is reasonable to assume that this by itself puts constraints on what noun phrases can realize the arguments: clearly, they must be noun phrases with an interpretation that can satisfy the lexical constraints imposed by *kiss*.

Thus it seems that the constraint that the argument must be a **thematic** noun phrase can made to follow from the semantics of **non-thematic** noun phrases: their interpretation is such that it cannot satisfy the lexical constraints imposed by the verb on the argument position. There are various semantic theories of such non-thematic noun phrases around in the literature, e.g. Sag (1982), Dowty (1985), Chierchia (1989), Rothstein (2001).

Similarly, the type theory has given rise to semantically based definitions of argument positions (like, the object is the first semantic argument in). Some such theories are purely semantic (like some versions of categorial grammar), others are mixed, and formulated as constraints on the syntax–semantic interface. Since Dowty's work, the question of whether you need to lexically specify theta grids and thematic roles at all is very much an open question. Dowty has cast strong doubts on the validity of many traditional arguments for the need of thematic roles in the grammar.

All this means that, in a semantically interpreted grammar principles (1)–(3) may well turn out to be rather redundant.

Principle (4), the uniqueness of thematic role assignment has a different status. I actually think that anybody's theory will need something here. However, I am not so sure that principle (4) is best formulated as a principle of thematic role assignment, rather than a more general principle of **lexical access**.

Principle (4) tells us that a thematic role like Goal cannot be assigned more than once by the same verb. This means that example (3), in which *Mary* and *to a girl* express the same role, is ungrammatical:

(3)   #John gives *Mary* a book *to a girl*.

Note that the example is chosen such that it is clear that a purely semantic explanation of the infelicity of (3) is not feasible: the goal is specified twice with semantically compatible expressions. There is no semantic reason why (3) isn't felicitous and means (4):

(4) $\exists e[\text{GIVE}(e) \wedge \text{Agent}(e)=\text{JOHN} \wedge \text{Theme}(e)\in\text{BOOK} \wedge \text{Goal}(e)=m \wedge \text{Goal}(e)\in\text{GIRL}]$

The reason that I am not happy about assuming that this is a principle of thematic role assignment is that we find the same phenomenon with **optional** adjuncts (which presumably are not assigned a role by the theta grid):

(5)   #*With a knife* John cut the salami *with a kitchen appliance*.

There seems to be a more general principle here, a principle that says that the semantic roles that can be specified as constraining a verb interpretation can be grammatically realized only once (unless the grammar allows a strategy to circumvent this). Even well known exceptions to this seem, at closer sight, to obey this principle. Thus, it is well known that a verb can be constrained by more than one temporal adverb:

(6)   *In 1990*, I had dinner with Susan *in January*.

But, as is also well known, these temporal adverbs must stand in a temporal inclusion relation to each other. In fact, temporal inclusion isn't quite good enough. The real observation, I think, is that the adverbs must be interpreted at different temporal grid levels. Thus, in the examples in (7), the adverb interpretations are semantically compatible, yet the examples are ungrammatical:

(7)a.   #*In January or February*, I had dinner with Susan *in January*.
   b.   #*Between Tuesday and Friday*, Dafna met Netta *between Wednesday and Sunday*.

If we assume that temporal adverbs do not denote one-place functions from events into times, but two-place functions from event-grid pairs into times, the data in (6) and (7) become compatible with the restriction on realizing roles more than once: the restriction says that relative to a certain temporal grid, the time role can be realized only once. Time roles can be realized more than once, if they differ in grid.

So, while I have formulated the principle as a principle concerning grammatical realization of roles defined for verb interpretations, I think the real principle is actually even wider than this. I think we find the same principle in the nominal domain with adjectives (again *pace* the possibilities of realizing more than one adjective of a certain sort by filling in implicit parameters, like grid, differently). The clearest case is that of measure adjectives which can be realized only once, even if the interpretations are compatible:

(8)   #*Between three and ten between five and twelve* girls sang.

Despite the misgivings of Dowty and others, I will actually assume a Theta Theory which incorporates principles (1)–(4), as part of a default grammar. This means that I assume that violation of (1)–(4) leads to infelicity, unless the grammar has special mechanisms to make up for it.

My main reason for making these assumptions precisely concerns the syntax and semantics of *there*-insertion contexts. I will be assuming that *there* is a non-thematic noun phrase, hence in the same ball park as *it* in the raising-verb construction we saw above. This means that the analysis will need to account for the fact that (9a) is grammatical, but (9b) is not:

(9)a.   *There* are *three girls* sick.
   b.   #*Mary, Sue and Jane* are *three girls* sick.

As it will turn out, on the analysis that I will develop, this is going to follow practically straightforwardly if I assume a mechanism of theta assignment along the lines of (1)–(4). As far as I can see, without such a mechanism (and in particular without principle (4)) it is going to be difficult to modify existing theories of pleonastics to get the facts in (9).

Now, as I mentioned, I have nothing to say about principle (5), but, obviously, I do have something to say about principle (5a). Principle (5a) restricts the distribution of noun phrases to argument position: since theta assignment is to argument position according to principle (5a), noun phrases to which a theta role is assigned can only occur in argument position. This aspect of theta theory I am not going to accept.

Since noun phrases are by and large restricted to argument position, I will need something else to make sure that my grammar doesn't wildly allow noun phrases in the wrong positions. My claim is the following: the effect of principle (5a) can be achieved, by and large, with a very natural constraint on semantic interpretation, a constraint that I will call **value restriction**. Note right away the "by and large": the claim is that value restriction will allow assignment of thematic roles to noun phrases in argument position, that it will disallow obvious cases of assignment of thematic roles to noun phrases in non-argument position, but that it may actually allow special situations where the latter assignment is actually acceptable (the *there*-insertion case being a case in point).

Theta Theory, principle 5a' – Value Restriction:
Let α be a syntactic expression which has a role R to assign, let β be a noun phrase and let T be the minimal syntactic tree containing both α and β.

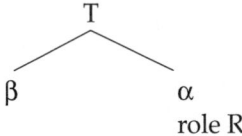

α can only assign role R to β if in the interpretation of T the interpretation of β constrains the value of role R in the appropriate way.
(In the simplest case: if β is a proper name, its interpretation should be the value of the role.)

Suppose that we have a verb like *kiss* and we want to assign its theme role to the noun phrase *Dafna* in the construction: [$_{V'}$ [$_V$ *kiss*] [$_{DP}$ *Dafna*]]. Can we do that, while satisfying the principle of value restriction? To answer this question we need to look at the semantic interpretation of the V':

Semantics: APPLY[λyλxλe.KISS(e) ∧ Ag(e)=x ∧ Th(e)=y, DAFNA]=
λxλe.KISS(e) ∧ Ag(e)=x ∧ Th(e)=DAFNA

In the interpretation of the V', the interpretation of noun phrase *Dafna* indeed constrains the value of the verb's role theme, hence indeed we satisfy value restriction. Hence we can indeed assign the theme role to the object in the complement position of the verb.

To give another example, suppose we replace in the above example noun phrase *Dafna* with [$_{DP}$ *the mother of* [$_{DP}$ *Dafna*]]. We ask the same question: can we assign the theme role to the noun phrase *Dafna* inside this noun phrase? The semantic interpretation of the V' in this case is going to be:

λxλe.KISS(e) ∧ Ag(e)=x ∧ Th(e)=σ(λx.MOTHER(x,DAFNA))

And in this interpretation, the interpretation of the noun phrase *Dafna* is not the value of the theme role. Hence we cannot assign the theme role of the verb to the noun phrase *Dafna* in this case.

Clearly, if we just put noun phrase *Dafna* in an adjectival position or an adverbial position, it is already not so clear that the semantic computation is going to give an output at all; but any way, if it does, it will normally not be an output that will make Dafna the value of the theme role in the interpretation of the structure that includes that adjectival or adverbial position and the verb *kiss*. This means that, in general, noun phrases are not going to be allowed in adjectival or adverbial position.

Value restriction is, of course, an incredibly plausible constraint (so much so that it seems reasonable that we may want to derive it from the way the grammar should work anyway, rather than impose it as an explicit principle). What I am trying to show here is that this plausible principle already does practically all the work that the original constraint (5a) – restricting role assignment to argument position – was supposed to do. Hence I assume that we can safely do without (5a), and use value restriction, (5a') instead.

5.2   Flip-flop

We will be concerned here with the analysis of the Dutch example (10):

(10)   (dat) er   een meisje zingt.
         that there a   girl   sings

Let me repeat my basic proposal:

Type shift operation ADJUNCT shifts sets to intersective modifiers:
ADJUNCT: $\langle a,t\rangle \rightarrow \langle\langle x^n,\langle a,t\rangle\rangle,\langle x^n,\langle a,t\rangle\rangle\rangle$
ADJUNCT[α] = $\lambda R^n\lambda x_n \ldots \lambda x_1.R^n(x_1 \ldots x_n) \cap \alpha$

The shift into the adjunct domain is accessed from the type of sets:

$\langle\langle a,t\rangle,t\rangle$ generalized quantifier

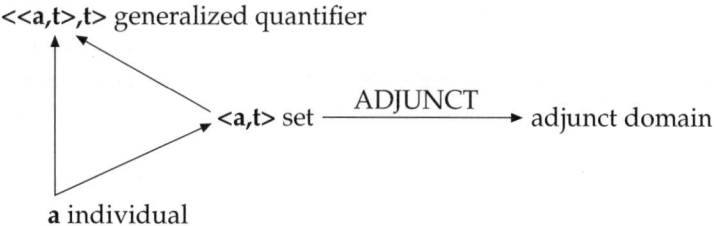

$\langle a,t\rangle$ set   ADJUNCT   adjunct domain

a individual

This shift is available for adjectives, prepositional phrases, relative clauses, and adverbial phrases. For noun phrases, this shift is not generally available. Noun phrases must be thematically licensed, and, as we have seen above, generally putting a noun phrase into an adjunct position and shifting its meaning into the adjunction domain, will not provide an interpretation for complex expressions where the noun phrase interpretation restricts the value of a role in the appropriate way. Hence noun phrases are not generally shiftable into the adjunct domain.

My proposal for the analysis of *there*-insertion contexts is the following:

Proposal:
1. *Een meisje* in (1) is in an adjunct position, adjoined to the verbal predicate.
2. The semantics given for combining this adjunct position with the predicate it is adjoined to will satisfy the value restriction.

Constraint:
In languages like English and Dutch such a shift into the adjunct domain is only possible for noun phrases that are *generated* at the set type, not for noun phrases that are shifted into the set type.

As we have seen in the previous chapter, the constraint gives us the definiteness effects. Assumption (1) tells us that we have the following situation (I use a simplified system of syntactic categories here, not distinguishing V and I, to focus on the semantics):

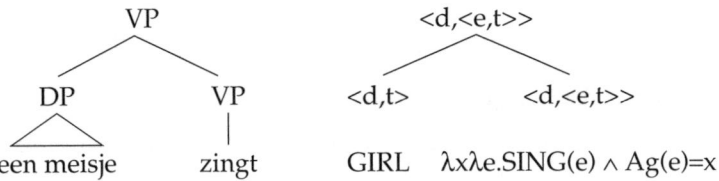

Thus, *een meisje* is a DP with set interpretation GIRL of type <d,t>. This is adjoined to verbal predicate *zingt* of type <d,<e,t>>. Adjunction being what it is, the complex VP must again have an interpretation of type <d,<e,t>>.

However, we cannot as it is provide an interpretation for the complex expression, since we have a type mismatch here. While the interpretation of expressions of type <d,t> can be shifted with ADJUNCT into the adjunction domain, ADJUNCT can only shift their interpretation to types of the form: <<a^n,<d,t>>,<a^n,<d,t>>>, and not types of the form <<a^n,<e,t>>,<a^n,<e,t>>>, while the verb interpretation is precisely of the latter form: <d,<e,t>>. This means that we have a type mismatch: as it is, we can in principle adjoin GIRL of type <d,t>, but not to the interpretation of *zingt* of type <d,<e,t>>.

This mismatch is resolved by a shifting operation. We have in principle two options for formulating such a shifting operation.

Solution one: semantic incorporation

The first strategy to resolve the type mismatch would be to shift the noun phrase interpretation from type <d,t> to type <e,t>, from a set of individuals to a set of events. Since <e,t> is the type at which adverbials start out, obviously it can shift into the adjunct domain from there, i.e., to type <<d,<e,t>,<d,<e,t>>>.

Such an operation can be formulated, and in fact, I will discuss a similar operation in chapter 9. This strategy is close to van Geenhoven's (1996) **semantic incorporation**.

I think semantic incorporation is the right approach to definiteness effects for relational nouns with *have*, as in (11):

(11)a.   John has a sister in the army.
    b.   #John has the sister in the army.

In chapter 9, I will provide an analysis for this case where the interpretation of *sister* is a relation of type <d,<d,t>> which can shift to type <d,<d,<e,t>>> and intersects with the meaning of *have*.

The fact that I will use semantic incorporation for definiteness effects with relational nouns in a way already indicates a problem for assuming this approach as the solution for definiteness effects in general (i.e. also in *there*-insertion contexts). The problem is that the approach works too well. If you can just shift a noun phrase from type <d,t> to type <e,t>, you will in fact be able to adjoin noun phrases wherever adverbials can be adjoined. But that means that you would expect adjunction and definiteness effects for any indefinite noun phrase, not just relational nouns, with *have*, and furthermore you would expect *there*-insertion contexts with direct objects, indirect objects, etc.

Now, there may well be languages where we find such phenomena across the board, and for those languages semantic incorporation may well be the right solution. But in the languages we are concerned with, definiteness effects in *there*-insertion contexts seem clearly to be a "top-of-tree" phenomenon, related to subject position. And semantic incorporation does not bring that out.

Solution two: flip–flop

The solution I will propose here involves a flip–flop mechanism. To introduce the idea, we go back to David Dowty's (1982) work on grammatical relations. Dowty proposed that the operation of **passive** involves a semantic operation which I call *P*, operating on relations with two nominal arguments (i.e. in my framework of type <d,<d,<e,t>>>), turning the nominal arguments around:

P: <d,<d,<e,t>>> → <d,<d,<e,t>>>
$P[\alpha] = \lambda x \lambda y \lambda e.\alpha(e,x,y)$

Thus, if we apply *P* to the relation KISS, *P* gives the BE KISSED relation:

$P[\lambda y \lambda x \lambda e.\text{KISS}(e) \wedge \text{Ag}(e)=x \wedge \text{Th}(e)=y] =$
$\lambda x \lambda y \lambda e.\text{KISS}(e) \wedge \text{Ag}(e)=x \wedge \text{Th}(e)=y$

Normal passive is the composition of Existential Closure and P, EC o P, where EC is as usual:

$\text{EC}[R] = \text{APPLY}[R, \lambda P.\exists x[P(x)]]$

$\text{EC o } P[\lambda y \lambda x \lambda e.\text{KISS}(e) \wedge \text{Ag}(e)=x \wedge \text{Th}(e)=y] =$
$\lambda y \lambda e.\exists x[\text{KISS}(e) \wedge \text{Ag}(e)=x \wedge \text{Th}(e)=y]$

Dowty uses operation P in particular to deal with the semantics of passives with a *by*-phrase, but the perspective of passive as the composition of EC and P is, of course, independently a fruitful perspective.

Now, operation P turns the two nominal arguments in a relation of type $<d,<d,<e,t>>>$ around. My proposal is:

Proposal:
Type shift operation FLIP is just operation P, but one level higher at type $<d,<e,t>>$, thus it flips the nominal and the event argument around:

Operation FLIP:
FLIP: $<d,<e,t>> \rightarrow <e,<d,t>>$
$\text{FLIP}[\alpha] = \lambda e \lambda x.\alpha(e,x)$

Hence,

$\text{FLIP}[\ \lambda x \lambda e.\text{SING}(e) \wedge \text{Ag}(e)=x\ ] = \lambda e \lambda x.\text{SING}(e) \wedge \text{Ag}(e)=x$
of type $<e,<d,t>>$

Operation FLOP is just the same operation as FLIP, except that it flops the relation from type $<e,<d,t>>$ back to type $<d,<e,t>>$:

Operation FLOP:
FLOP: $<e,<d,t>> \rightarrow <d,<e,t>>$
$\text{FLOP}[\alpha] = \lambda x \lambda e.\alpha(e,x)$

Hence,

$\text{FLOP}[\ \lambda e \lambda x.\text{SING}(e) \wedge \text{Ag}(e)=x\ ] = \lambda x \lambda e.\text{SING}(e) \wedge \text{Ag}(e)=x$
of type $<d,<e,t>>$

With the FLIP–FLOP mechanism we can resolve the type mismatch.

We want to adjoin the interpretation of *girl*, GIRL of type $<d,t>$ to the interpretation of *zingt*, $\lambda x \lambda e.\text{SING}(e) \wedge \text{Ag}(e)=x$ of type $<d,<e,t>>$, and, as we have seen, we have a type mismatch. So, the situation is:

ADJOIN[GIRL, λxλe.SING(e) ∧ Ag(e)=x] must resolve as a predicate of type <d,<e,t>>.

1.   FLIP the verb phrase meaning λxλe.SING(e) ∧ Ag(e)=x of *zingt* of type <d,<e,t>> to λeλx.SING(e) ∧ Ag(e)=x of type <e,<d,t>>. Thus, we reduce the problem to:

ADJOIN[GIRL, FLIP[λxλe.SING(e) ∧ Ag(e)=x]] must resolve as a predicate of type <d,<e,t>>.

that is:

ADJOIN[GIRL, λeλx.SING(e) ∧ Ag(e)=x] must resolve as a predicate of type <d,<e,t>>.

2.   Adjunction resolves this as follows:

ADJOIN[GIRL, λeλx.SING(e) ∧ Ag(e)=x] =
APPLY[ADJUNCT[GIRL], λeλx.SING(e) ∧ Ag(e)=x]

where in this context ADJUNCT[GIRL] resolves as:

ADJUNCT[GIRL] =
λZλeλx.Z(x,e) ∧ GIRL(x)   with Z a variable of type <e,<d,t>>.

Thus,

ADJOIN[GIRL, λeλx.SING(e) ∧ Ag(e)=x] =
APPLY[λZλeλx.Z(x,e) ∧ GIRL(x), λeλx.SING(e) ∧ Ag(e)=x] =
λeλx.SING(e) ∧ Ag(e)=x ∧ GIRL(x)   of type <e,<d,t>>

This means that we have reduced the problem to:

λeλx.SING(e) ∧ Ag(e)=x ∧ GIRL(x) of type <e,<d,t>> must resolve as a predicate of type <d,<e,t>>.

3.   The last mismatch is resolved with FLOP:

FLOP[λeλx.SING(e) ∧ Ag(e)=x ∧ GIRL(x)] =
λxλe.SING(e) ∧ Ag(e)=x ∧ GIRL(x)   of type <d,<e,t>>

In short:

Type mismatch:
ADJOIN[GIRL, λxλe.SING(e) ∧ Ag(e)=x] must resolve as a predicate of type <d,<e,t>>.

Resolution:
FLOP[ADJOIN[GIRL,**FLIP**[λxλe.SING(e) ∧ Ag(e)=x]]] =
λxλe.SING(e) ∧ Ag(e)=x ∧ GIRL(x)   of type <d,<e,t>>.

The idea, thus, is the following. The FLIP–FLOP mechanism *hijacks* a grammatical operation *P* to allow the adjunction: you flip the d and e variable around, then you can do the adjunction, and you flop the e and d variable back.

We have resolved the mismatch and successfully adjoined the indefinite noun phrase *een meisje* to the verb phrase *zingt*. The noun phrase is a thematic noun phrase, hence, by the thematic constraints, it must receive a thematic role. So let us assume that the verb *zing* assigns it the agent role. The fact that it is in adjunct position is not a problem for this, because we have not restricted assignment of thematic roles to argument positions. The value restriction says that we can assign the agent role to *een meisje* if in the semantic interpretation of the tree in which *een meisje* is adjoined the interpretation of *een meisje* constrains the agent role in the appropriate way.

This means that in this interpretation the value of the agent role in the event type should be restricted to girls. And this is, of course, the case. Hence:

Value restriction for adjoined subjects:
Resolving the adjunction type mismatch with FLIP–FLOP has the consequence that the value restriction of the assignment of the agent role to *een meisje* is satisfied. Hence, the agent role of the verb *zingt* is assigned felicitously to the adjunct noun phrase.

In other words, while in general assigning a thematic role to a noun phrase in adjunct position will violate the value restriction, due to the particular semantic mechanism of FLIP–FLOP proposed here, assigning the role to the adjunct noun phrase does not violate value restriction. Since the noun phrase must receive a role, and the only role available is the agent role, the adjunct must receive the agent role.

This means that while *een meisje* is syntactically and semantically an adjunct, it is like an argument as far as thematic role assignment is concerned (and this means that there may well be various respects in which it patterns with real arguments).

The analysis predicts that we find adjunct noun phrases (and hence *there*-insertion contexts) as a "top of tree" phenomenon. Operation *P* as applied to an n-place relation of type <d^n,<e,t>>, is an operation which flips the outer two arguments in the type around. To resolve the type mismatch for the adjunction we need to derive a type that ends in <d,t>, rather than <e,t>. Only in the type of one-place predicates (<d,<e,t>>) does *P* give you a type that ends in <d,t>, namely <e,<d,t>>. Since that is the type we need to resolve adjunction, it follows that we can do this form of adjunction only to one-place predicates, i.e.

FLIP–FLOP as a top-of-tree phenomenon:
We only have adjoined indefinite subjects, not adjoined direct objects, nor adjoined indirect objects, etc.

As I mentioned, FLIP–FLOP hijacks a grammatical operation for passive. This is an attractive assumption, because there is a relation between *there*-insertion constructions and passives. French, and marginally also English, passives allow *there*-insertion; more directly, Dutch and German allow what are called impersonal passives: passives of intransitive verbs with a pleonastic subject, which, surprise, surprise, in Dutch is also *there*:

(12)   Er   werd gedanst.
       There was   danced (Dancing went on)

While I will not go into the ins and outs of the semantics of impersonal passives here (a rich topic in itself), the connection is tantalizing.

5.3   The Semantics from the Adjoined Indefinite Upwards

This is where we are. We have derived a VP with an adjoined indefinite subject [$_{VP}$ [$_{DP}$ *een meisje*] [$_{VP}$ *zingt*]], with the interpretation of a one-place predicate of type <d,<e,t>>:

$\lambda x\lambda e.\text{SING}(e) \wedge \text{Ag}(e)=x \wedge \text{GIRL}(x)$
The relation that holds between an individual and an event if that event is a singing and the individual is a girl which is the agent of that event.

VPs are not sentences. The grammar needs to derive a sentence. Sentences do not have the meanings of one-place predicates. The grammar needs to derive a sentence with a sentence meaning, which is (at least initially) a meaning of type <e,t>, an event type. Hence, the predicate meaning of type <d,<e,t>> – derived at the VP level – must be reduced to a sentence meaning of type <e,t>. The way the grammar does this is by realizing syntactically a **subject position**, and the predicate interpretation will have to apply to the interpretation of the subject. These are just standard grammatical assumptions.

But the verb *zingt* has only one thematic role to assign, the agent role, and it was forced to assign this to the adjoined indefinite noun phrase *een meisje*. More precisely, we showed that the verb can assign the agent role to *een meisje*, even though it is an adjunct. We assume that principle (1) of the Theta Theory applies to *een meisje*: *een meisje* is a thematic noun phrase which must be thematically licensed. This means that in order to thematically license *een meisje*, we must assign the agent role to it. Since thematic roles cannot be assigned more than once, we now derive the conclusion that the grammar forces there to be a subject position (in order to do the reduction from type <d,<e,t>> to type <e,t>), but cannot assign a thematic role to it. Hence the subject position is a non-thematic position. This means that thematic noun phrases cannot fill it, only non-thematic noun phrases, pleonastics can. We will say more about the syntax of the non-thematic subjects in the next subsection. In this subsection I want to finish the semantic discussion of example (10).

Let us call the pleonastic element in the subject position of *there*-insertion contexts pl_{there}. I will assume that the semantics of pl_{there} is simply **existential closure**:

$$[_{DP} \; pl_{there} \;] \rightarrow \lambda P.\exists x[P(x)] \qquad \text{of type} <<d,t>,t>$$

This means that application derives the following interpretation at type <e,t> for (10):

APPLY$[\lambda x \lambda e.SING(e) \wedge Ag(e)=x \wedge GIRL(x), \lambda P.\exists x[P(x)]] =$
$\lambda e.SING(e) \wedge \exists x[Ag(e)=x \wedge GIRL(x)] =$
$\lambda e.SING(e) \wedge GIRL(Ag(e)) \qquad \text{of type} <e,t>$
The set of singing events with a girl as agent.

We need to derive from this an interpretation at type t. In the Davidsonian theory this is traditionally done by an operation of **event existential closure**:

EEC: <e,t> $\rightarrow$ t
EEC$[\alpha] = \exists e[\alpha(e)]$

For the case at hand, this will derive the correct interpretation:

$\exists e[SING(e) \wedge GIRL(Ag(e))]$
There is an event of singing with a girl as agent.

So far so good, but now we will need to address once more the problems of non-upward entailing noun phrases. On the present analysis, it is as if we break the meaning of an argument indefinite DP in two: the indefinite bit we add as an adjunct, the existential quantification we add in the subject position as the interpretation of the pleonastic. But then we need to be concerned about maximalization effects.

In the analysis presented in chapter 2, I made maximalization part of the type shifting operation ARGUMENT FORMATION, which shifts the indefinite from type <d,t> to type <<d,t>,t>. But, in the present construction, the indefinite doesn't shift to the argument type, it gets adjoined from type <d,t>, and the existential closure is brought in by the pleonastic. But, obviously, the *there*-insertion constructions have the maximalization effects that arguments do:

(13)a. There are three girls in the garden.
   b. There are exactly three girls in the garden.
   c. There are at most three girls in the garden.

In (13a) *three girls* has an *at least* reading and an *exactly* implicature, and we need to make sure that we get the semantics of (13b) and (13c) right.

Now, I mentioned in chapter 2 that the theory I developed there was tailored to solve a particular problem: how can we get the standard generalized quantifier interpretations of type <<d,t>t> for indefinites from their interpretations at type <d,t>? I pointed out there that in the context of this specific problem, I could simplify the general analysis of maximalization that I gave in Landman (2000). We have now reached the point where the simplification leads to problems, and we need to present the general approach.

The first step towards the general approach is a regressive step. I spent all of chapter 2 arguing against the type shifting operation EC of existential closure, as an operation from <d,t> to <<d,t>,t>, carefully replacing it by Argument Formation. My first step towards the general theory is to go back to existential closure, in the type shifting theory for argument interpretations.

This means, of course, that we get back the blatantly wrong results, if nothing more is done. And in fact I will continue to assume that it is maximalization that needs to take place. It's just that maximalization does not take place at the level of argument formation, but later, at the level of the event type.

I discussed in Landman (2000) the case of maximalization effects in cumulative readings, and I argued that these effects cannot be analyzed at the level where the noun phrases involved combine with the verbal structure (which is the place where indefinites shift to argument interpretations), but must be analyzed at the level where the noun phrases involved take their scope. And I argued with cumulative readings, that this is the level of the event type <e,t> which results when the verb is combined with its arguments:

Maximalization at the event type:
Maximalization is an operation which maximalizes an event type of type <e,t> relative to the information constraining the thematic roles on that event type.

You may notice that I say thematic role and not argument role here. This is not carelessness: it is precisely what will bring the maximalization effects in *there*-insertion under the same mechanism that deals with maximalization effects of indefinite arguments. This means that the derivation of indefinite argument DPs in chapter 2 gets modified in the following way.

We build up the interpretation of the indefinite at type <d,t> exactly as in chapter 2:

[$_{DP}$ *r n girls*] → <λx.*GIRL(x) ∧ |x| r n, ±R> of type <d,t>

In fact, it will be convenient for our present purposes to store the set interpretation under the feature ±R: we will call the latter a maximalization trigger:

[$_{DP}$ *r n girls*] → λx.*GIRL(x) ∧ |x| r n   of type <d,t>
          Maximalization trigger: <±R, λx.*GIRL(x) ∧ |x| r n >

For argument interpretations, we apply EC, but keep track of the maximalization trigger:

[$_{DP}$ *r n girls*] → $\lambda x.\exists x[*GIRL(x) \wedge |x|\ r\ n]$ of type $<<d,t>,t>$
                    Maximalization trigger: $<\pm R, \lambda x.*GIRL(x) \wedge |x|\ r\ n >$

My next assumption follows Landman (2000), but extends the analysis given there directly to the case which is relevant here. When the DP combines with the verbal structure, a thematic role T is assigned to it. In this process role T is combined with the maximalization trigger. The combination works as follows:

COMBINE[T,$< \pm R,\alpha>$] = $<\pm R,\lambda e.\alpha(T(e))>$

For example, if the thematic role is *Ag, and the maximalization trigger of the DP is $<+R,\lambda x.*GIRL(x) \wedge |x|=3>$, then COMBINE gives:

$<+R,\lambda e.[\lambda x.*GIRL(x) \wedge |x|=3](*Ag(e)) > =$
$<+R,\lambda e.*GIRL(*Ag(e)) \wedge |*Ag(e)|=3>$

This means that what the maximalization trigger now stores under +R is an event type: the set of events whose (plural) agent is a sum of girls and whose (plural) agent is a sum of three atoms.

As said, this takes place when the argument DP or, for that matter, the adjoined DP combines with the verbal predicate and is assigned a thematic role. The resulting maximalization trigger is stored in what I call in Landman (2000) a **maximalization set**, which is associated with the verbal predicate and inherited upwards. Thus, one by one, maximalization triggers for the arguments or adjuncts that receive a thematic role are collected in the maximalization set. The semantic combination of the predicate with its argument or adjunct stays the same. We will end up with an interpretation of the sentence at type $<e,t>$, and a maximalization set, containing the maximalization triggers collected in the derivation.

At this point, we follow the analysis in Landman (2000, ch. 7). I will only sketch the analysis here, the details are in Landman (2000). In that analysis, for a sentence like *r n girls danced* we have available at the sentence level:

- **The event type**: α
  $\lambda e.*DANCE(e) \wedge *GIRL(*Ag(e)) \wedge |*Ag(e)|\ r\ n$
  The set of sums of dancing events whose plural agent is a sum of girls with cardinality standing in relation r to n.
- A scale with **scalar endpoint**: $\sqcup(\cup SC_\alpha)$ (See Landman 2000 for discussion.)
  $\sqcup(\lambda e.*DANCE(e) \wedge *GIRL(*Ag(e)))$
  The sum of all events of girls dancing.

- **Maximalization triggers** relative to the noun phrase arguments: $\langle \pm R, \beta_i \rangle$:
  For *r n girls*: $\langle \pm R, \lambda e.*GIRL(*Ag(e)) \wedge |*Ag(e)| \ r \ n \rangle$
  > The set of all events whose plural agent is a sum of girls with cardinality standing in relation r to n.

At this level, the operation of maximalization builds two kinds of information:

Existential information (ex):
$\exists e[\alpha(e)]$
The event type is non-empty.

$\exists e[*DANCE(e) \wedge *GIRL(*Ag(e)) \wedge |*Ag(e)| \ r \ n]$
There is a dancing event with a sum of girls as agent whose cardinality stands in relation r to n.

Maximalization information (max$_i$):
For each trigger, $\langle \pm R, \beta_i \rangle$: $\sqcup(\cup SC_\alpha) \in \beta_i$
For each trigger, the scalar endpoint is in the trigger.

$*GIRL(*Ag(\sqcup(\lambda e.*DANCE(e) \wedge *GIRL(*Ag(e))))) \wedge$
$|*Ag(\sqcup(\lambda e.*DANCE(e) \wedge *GIRL(*Ag(e))))| \ r \ n$
The agent of the sum of all dancing events with girls as agent is a sum of girls with cardinality standing in relation r to n.

This information is integrated into a statement of type t, much in the way maximalization was in chapter 2:

Maximalization creates an output at type t:
$ex \wedge max_1 \wedge \ldots \wedge max_n$
Except: if max_i derives from a non-lexically realized trigger (Ø *three girls*)
         max_i is made an implicature core.

We assume that in the case that all triggers derive from downward closed arguments, the null event, 0_e is in the event type α. In that case, **ex** is trivial for the same reason as before, and there is no existential entailment. To illustrate, we get:

At most three girls danced.
$\exists e[*DANCE(e) \wedge *GIRL(*Ag(e)) \wedge |*Ag(e)| \leq 3] \wedge$
$|*Ag(\sqcup(\lambda e.*DANCE(e) \wedge *GIRL(*Ag(e))))| \leq 3$

We assume that the first conjunct trivially holds because $0_e \in *DANCE$, $0_d \in *GIRL$, $*Ag(0_e)=0_d$, and $|0_e|=0_d$. The second conjunct can be simplified to:

$|*Ag(\sqcup(\lambda e.DANCE(e) \wedge GIRL(Ag(e))))| \leq 3$

which is equivalent to:

$|\sqcup(\lambda x.\text{GIRL}(x) \wedge \exists e[\text{DANCE}(e) \wedge \text{Ag}(e)=x])| \leq 3$
The sum of dancing girls has cardinality at most three.

It is not hard to see that indeed in upward closed cases maximalization reduces to existential closure:

At least three girls danced.
$\exists e[*\text{DANCE}(e) \wedge *\text{GIRL}(*\text{Ag}(e)) \wedge |*\text{Ag}(e)| \geq 3]$
There is a sum of dancing events with as plural agent a sum of girls of cardinality at least three.

As argued in Landman (2000), the maximalization theory provides a unified account to scopal problems stemming from the interaction between the event argument and non-upward entailing noun phrase arguments that extends to cumulative readings and *exactly* implicatures.

It is simple to see that the theory accounts for the readings of non-upward entailing noun phrases in *there*-insertion contexts as well, like the cases in (13b,c):

(13)a.   There are three girls in the garden.
    b.   There are exactly three girls in the garden.
    c.   There are at most three girls in the garden.

This is, because these cases are given exactly the same semantics as the cases in (14):

(14)a.   Three girls are in the garden.
    b.   Exactly three girls are in the garden.
    c.   At most three girls are in the garden.

The cases in (14) only differ from the cases whose semantics I have just illustrated in that they have a stative predicate *are in the garden* instead of an eventive one like *danced*. That is irrelevant for this aspect of the semantics, hence the theory assigns the correct interpretations to the examples in (14), and hence too to the examples in (13).

I want to address one more problem here. Look at (15):

(15)a.   Er   dansten meisjes.
        There danced girls
    b. $\exists e[*\text{DANCE}(e) \wedge *\text{GIRL}(*\text{Ag}(e))\,]$
    c.   Er   danste een meisje
        There danced a   girl
    d. $\exists e[\text{DANCE}(e) \wedge \text{GIRL}(\text{Ag}(e))\,]$

Here is the problem: the plural noun *meisjes* has interpretation *GIRL. Hence, along the line of the previous discussion, one would think that (15a) should come out as having interpretation (15b): there is a sum of dancing events with some sum of girls as agent. But as we have seen, *GIRL contains 0_d, and *DANCE may well contain 0_e, $*Ag(0_e)=0_d$, which means that (15b) has no existential import. And this is rather dramatic, because it means that (15a) does not entail (15c). This is because (15c) does have existential import: (15d) says that there is a (non-null) dancing event with a (non-null) girl as agent. But, of course, (15a) should entail (15c), hence something has gone wrong.

The flaw in the argument is the following. While it is true that the **noun** *meisjes* has interpretation *GIRL, containing 0_d, we are not forced to assume that (15a) has interpretation (15b). The reason is that *meisjes* in (15a) is not simply a bare noun, but a **bare plural noun phrase**. This means, given the assumptions in chapter 2, that *meisjes* in (15a) is actually a **DP** with an empty determiner $[_D \emptyset]$.

Now, in chapter 2 I assumed for numerical DPs like *at least three girls* that the DP starts out with an empty determiner, and that the numerical phrase moves into the DP layer. For DPs where that movement takes place, I assumed that the empty determiner interpretation is trivial: $[_D \emptyset] \rightarrow \lambda P.P$. I will now assume that for DPs where that movement from the NP layer to the DP layer does not take place, the interpretation of the empty determiner is almost, but not quite trivial: $[_D \emptyset] \rightarrow \lambda P.(P-\{0_d\})$. This, I assume, is the interpretation of the empty determiner that we find in bare plural DPs. The same interpretation will be assumed in chapter 8 inside negative DPs.

Thus, in bare plural DPs, the empty determiner has existential import, and the interpretation derived for (15a) is (15e):

(15)e. $\exists e[*DANCE(e) \wedge [*GIRL-\{0_d\}](*Ag(e))]$

Example (15e) says that there is a sum of dancing events with a sum of girls as agent, but this time the sum of girls is required to be a sum of real girls (it can't be 0_d). This means that (15e) does entail (15d), and hence (15a) entails (15c).

The conclusion of the present discussion about maximalization is as follows: Landman (2000) argues for replacing the operation of event existential closure by the more elaborate operation of event maximalization, which integrates existential and maximalization information at the level of the event type. While the motivation for the theory was the analysis of cumulative readings, the theory, together with the null-objects of the Boolean domains, actually also solves the logical problems of the Adjectival Theory of indefinites (the problems of generating indefinites at the type of sets) and the adjunct (set-based) analysis of *there*-insertion constructions.

5.4   Non-thematic Subjects

In this section, I will give a halfway theoretical description of the distribution of non-thematic subjects in German (G), English (E), French (F), and Dutch (D).

I choose these languages, because they show interesting cross distinctions. Note that, in this chapter, I am only interested in the distribution of the non-thematic subjects: getting the distribution and syntax of the predicates in *there*-insertion right will be a topic for the next chapter.

I say "halfway theoretic description," and not "syntactic analysis," because, as will become clear, what I will present is more a rationalization of the syntactic distribution than a syntactic analysis; in fact, it requires a syntactic analysis, rather than presents one.

A remark on terminology, what I call here non-thematic elements, are usually called pleonastics. Not only does "non-thematic elements" describe better what I am talking about, but I will include a null non-thematic element Ø, and I personally find "null pleonastics" terminologically embarrassing.

I will assume that the pronominal system of these languages contains a set of non-thematic elements, which are elements that can in principle occur in non-thematic DP-positions (and only there). This set consists of two elements, which I will call "Ø" and "lr."

Ø is, of course, an empty element, while lr is short for **last resort element**:

Non-thematic elements:	{[$_{DP}$Ø], [$_{DP}$lr]}			
	German	Dutch	French	English
Last resort element:	*es*	*het*	*il*	*it*

Note that the elements *there* in English, or *er* in Dutch are not (initially) part of this set. I will discuss them later.

As the name, "last resort element" already indicates, I assume that the set of non-thematic elements is ordered:

Last resort:
lr can only occur in a non-thematic DP position if Ø cannot.

I already made the assumption in the last subsection that the semantic interpretation of non-thematic elements is existential closure. I will refine this assumption here:

Typing and interpretation of non-thematic elements:
[$_{DP}$ Ø] → λP.∃x[P(x)]   of type <<d,t>,t>.
[$_{DP}$ lr] → λP.∃x[P(x)]   of type <<a,t>,t>.

Thus, Ø is sorted for type <<d,t>,t>, based on the type of individuals d, while lr is not sorted.

We find non-thematic positions with raising-predicates (without raising), like the subject position of *seems that John is an idiot*; with weather-predicates, like the subject position of *rains*; and, of course, with the subject position of *there*-insertion constructions. I will make the following assumptions:

- *seem* is a transitive verb which assigns a thematic role to its complement position, but not to its subject position. Clearly, the complement position of *seem* is of type p of **proposition**. The subject position is, as said, non-thematic, but we can still ask: what is its type? I will assume that its type is also type p of propositions (or possibly type e of events, but not type d of individuals). Thus the type of *seem* is <p,<p,<e,t>>>, and it requires a non-thematic subject of type <<p,t>,t>.
- *rain* is an intransitive verb which does not assign a thematic role to its subject position. I assume that the type of its subject position is type e of **events** (and again, not type d of individuals). Hence the type of *rain* is <e,<e,t>>, and it requires a non-thematic subject of type <<e,t>,t>.
- The type of the subject of *there*-insertion constructions is just the type of individuals d. This is what we assumed all along: the VP we derived requires a non-thematic subject, but is of type <d,<e,t>>; hence it requires a non-thematic subject of type <<d,t>,t>.

From this typing we can now derive a first consequence:

Non-thematic subjects of raising and weather predicates:
In all four languages, D,G,F,E, non-thematic subjects of raising predicates and weather predicates cannot be realized as Ø, and hence must be realized as lr.

This is because Ø is of type <<d,t>,t>, which is the wrong type to combine with the raising predicate or the weather predicate. As we will see below, the typing of *there* and *er* follows that of Ø. Thus we find:

(16)a.   Es/#Ø scheint dass der Hans ein idiot ist. (G)
         lr   seems that the Hans an idiot is
   b.   Het/#Ø/#er   schijnt dat Hans een idioot is. (D)
        lr   there seems that Hans an   idiot   is
   c.   Il/#Ø semble que Hans est un cretin. (F)
        lr   seems that Hans is   an idiot
   d.   It/#Ø/#there seems that Hans is an idiot. (E)
        lr

(17)a.   Es/#Ø regnet. (G)
         lr   rains
   b.   Het/#Ø/#er   regent. (D)
        lr   there rains
   c.   Il/#Ø pleut. (F)
        lr   rains
   d.   It/#Ø/#there rains. (E)
        lr

In what remains we will be concerned with the distribution of non-thematic elements in the subject position of *there*-insertion contexts.

My next assumption is the main assumption which requires, rather than presents, a syntactic theory:

Distribution of non-thematic element Ø:
Ø can occur in non-thematic positions of type d if it is **licensed**.

Given the last-resort nature of lr, this means directly that if Ø is not licensed, lr must occur. Now, I don't have a syntactic theory of the licensing of Ø, but I will assume that such a theory must support the following crosslinguistic division:

Parameter one: Licensing of Ø:
German, Dutch: Ø is licensed in non-thematic DP position of type d.
French, English: Ø is not licensed in non-thematic DP position of type d.

Licensing should be understood as a default principle. In Dutch and German, Ø is licensed in non-thematic DP position of type d; this means that Ø will occur there, unless there is an independent principle that forbids it to occur. Such an independent principle is the verb second restriction:

Verb second restriction in Dutch and German:
If the verb is in second position (in C), the first position (spec of C) must be **lexically** realized (if the CP is not a yes–no question).

Since Ø is not lexically realized, the verb second restriction tells us that even if Ø were to be licensed in position SPEC of C with verb second, it cannot occur there (but see below).

In French and English, Ø is not licensed, and this should be taken to mean that it is not automatically licensed. For it to be licensed after all, there would have to be something special actually licensing it.

Again, a syntactic theory of such licensing is required. (It seems plausible that such a theory will relate the licensing of Ø in G,D versus F,E to differences in the verbal system of these languages. I do not have such a theory, but, since I am not requiring it to do a vast amount, it doesn't appear to be a syntactic impossibility to come up with something which is syntactically reasonable here. Thus, I think that up to now I haven't really strayed outside what is syntactically reasonable.)

I will now make a more dramatic gesture. I have above introduced non-thematic DPs, I will now introduce a non-thematic adverbial, which I will call "pl."

Non-thematic adverbial pl:
[$_{ADV}$ pl] is a non-thematic adverbial.
[$_{ADV}$ pl] → λT.T   of type $<<<d,t>,t>,<d,t>,t>>$
(Hence pl is interpreted as identity on the domain $<<d,t>,t>$.)

The sense in which pl is a non-thematic adverbial is given by the following constraints:

Syntax of non-thematic adverbial pl:
pl can adjoin to DP (Hence pl is similar to elements like *only* and *all*.)
pl licenses Ø in the construction [$_{DP}$ [$_{ADV}$ pl] [$_{DP}$ Ø]], where this complex is in a non-thematic DP position.

I take this description to exhaust the distribution of pl: pl only occurs in non-thematic DP positions, adjoined to non-thematic element Ø.

Now we get to the second crosslinguistic division:

Parameter two: Realization of pl:
English, Dutch: pl is realized (E: *there*, D: *er*).
French, German: pl is not realized.

Thus, while German has adverb *da* which shares several uses and readings with Dutch adverb *er* and English adverb *there*, German *da* is not a realization of pl (i.e. *da* does not adjoin to non-thematic DP Ø). Similarly, French *y* is not a realization of pl (*y* is a clitic on the verb, and not an adjunct to non-thematic DP Ø).

In sum, I assume that Ø and lr are non-thematic DPs. pl (*there/er*) is not itself a non-thematic DP, but [$_{DP}$ pl [$_{DP}$ Ø]] is a non-thematic DP (*there* Ø, *er* Ø). Since pl Ø contains Ø, lr will be a last resort element with respect to pl Ø as well.

This completes the theory. Let us now look at the predictions that it makes for non-thematic subjects of *there*-insertion contexts in the four languages.

German

Since German does not have pl realized, there are only two ways in which non-thematic DPs of type d can be realized in principle: Ø and lr, which is *es*. As we saw, in German, Ø is always licensed in non-thematic DP positions of type d, except in first position in verb second constructions (because it is lexically empty). Since lr occurs if Ø is not licensed, it follows that lr must occur if the non-thematic DP of type d is first position in a verb second construction:

(18)a. Es/#Ø sind drei Mädchen im   Garten
        lr   are   three girls   in-the garden
  b. Es/#Ø wurde getanzt.
        lr   was   danced

If the non-thematic DP position of type d is not first position under verb second, Ø is licensed, and hence Ø occurs, and not lr:

(19)a. Im   Garten laufen Ø/#es (ja doch) drei Mädchen.
        In-the garden walk   lr (indeed) three girls

   b.   In Amsterdam wurde Ø/#es getanzt
        In Amsterdam was   lr danced

French

Like German, French does not realize pl, so here too there are two elements we need to consider: Ø and lr, which is *il*. But unlike in German, Ø is not licensed in non-thematic DP position of type d, and (unlike in English, as we will see), there is nothing in French to license it. Hence, in French, non-thematic subjects of type d are, just like non-thematic subjects of other types, realized as the last resort element *il*:

(20)a.   Il/#Ø est arrivé deux filles de   Paris.
         lr   is arrived two   girls from Paris
    b.   Il/#Ø est mangé trois pommes.
         lr   is eaten   three apples

Note that, as I remarked before, we are not here dealing with the peculiarities of the French word-order in the predicate, nor with the fact that in French, unlike German, Dutch and English, agreement is with the non-thematic subject, and not with the adjoined thematic subject. I will come back to these issues in the next chapter.

English

English is like French in that Ø is not licensed in non-thematic DP position of type d. This means that non-thematic DP positions of type d cannot be realized as [$_{DP}$ Ø].

But English has pl, realized as *there*. This means that Ø is licensed in non-thematic DP position of type d in the construction: [$_{DP}$ [$_{ADV}$ *there*] [$_{DP}$ Ø]]. Since lr *it* is a last resort element, *it* only occurs if Ø is not licensed at all. But Ø is licensed, if the non-thematic DP position is realized as [$_{DP}$ [$_{ADV}$ *there*] [$_{DP}$ Ø]]. This means that *it* cannot occur in non-thematic DP position of type d, and that non-thematic DP positions of type d are obligatorily realized as [$_{DP}$ [$_{ADV}$ *there*] [$_{DP}$ Ø]]:

(21)a.   There/#Ø/#it arrived three girls from Paris.
    b.   There/#Ø/#it are three boys in the garden.

Dutch

Dutch is like German in that Ø is always licensed in non-thematic DP position of type d, except when this position is first position under verb second. This means that, like German, non-thematic DP positions of type d which are not first position under verb second can always be realized as Ø. This means that the latter positions cannot be realized as lr *het* (like in German).

But Dutch is like English in that it realizes pl, *er*. Since Ø is also realized in [DP [ADV *er*] [DP Ø]] it follows that, like English, in Dutch non-thematic DP position of type d can also always be realized as [DP [ADV *er*] [DP Ø]]. This means that in Dutch, non-thematic DP positions of type d which are not first position under verb second are optionally realized as [DP Ø] or [DP [ADV *er*] [DP Ø]] (and never as *het*). If the non-thematic DP position of type d is first position under verb second, it cannot be realized as Ø (like in German). But since [DP [ADV *er*] [DP Ø]] is lexically contentful, realizing this position as [DP [ADV *er*] [DP Ø]] is compatible with the verb second restriction. It follows that if the non-thematic DP position of type d is first position under verb second it is obligatorily realized as [DP [ADV *er*] [DP Ø]]:

(22)a.   Er/#Ø/#het zijn drie   meisjes in de tuin.
         pl   lr   are three girls   in the garden
   b.   Er/#Ø/#het werd gedanst.
         pl   lr   was   danced

(23)a.   In de tuin   lopen Ø/er/#het drie   meisjes.
         In the garden walk   pl lr   three girls
   b.   In Amsterdam werd Ø/er/#het gedanst.
         In Amsterdam was   pl lr   danced

This system seems to rationalize the main facts about non-thematic DP positions in these four languages adequately, and, I think, elegantly.

Note that when we think about the syntax and semantics of *there*-insertion constructions along these general lines, part of the motivation for analyses based on weak-strong distinctions falls by the wayside. On the analysis given, *there*-insertion constructions do not have a "presentational" meaning: my grammar assigns them the same meaning as you would get if you were to put the indefinite in subject argument position. And I think this is what the grammar should do. I will discuss this further in chapter 7. Secondly, as I mentioned in the previous chapter, there isn't really such a thing as a *there*-insertion construction. There is an adjoined thematic subject, and there is a non-thematic subject. This really isn't enough to hang something like a "presentational meaning" on. Such a meaning cannot come from *there*, say, stemming from the "locative origin" of *there*, because, as we see, closely related languages realize the non-thematic subject without the help of something like *there*. Such a meaning cannot plausibly come from the semantics of the non-thematic subject itself, since the most plausible assumption about non-thematic subjects is obviously that they have as little meaning as possible, preferably none, because that is precisely what makes them non-thematic.

Thus the construction does not plausibly provide anything for strong determiners to be semantically incompatible with. That should make one think twice, I think, about the plausibility of the weak–strong approach to definiteness effects.

Chapter 6

There-Insertion Subjects Adjoined to Saturated Predicates

We have, in chapter 5, developed an account of *there*-insertion subjects adjoined to VPs. This account was tailored to Dutch, where we find *there*-insertion with any kind of verb. As is well known, in English, *there*-insertion contexts are restricted to copular constructions, and a small set of verbs (like *arrive*). The current chapter will compare the Dutch and the English data. I will analyze the differences between the languages in terms of a difference between two kinds of predicates that the subject can adjoin to. The two kinds of predicates are saturated and unsaturated one-place predicates. So I will start with a discussion of those.

6.1   Saturated and Unsaturated One-Place Predicates

Frege (1892) introduced a distinction between saturated and unsaturated one-place predicates. The distinction basically concerns two ways of thinking about properties.

In the unsaturated form, a property is thought of as something essentially incomplete (unsaturated), something which needs to apply to an object to become complete (it needs to be saturated by an object). In the saturated form, a property is thought of as a complete entity in its own right.

Chierchia (1989) and Rothstein (1983, 2001) import this distinction into the grammar (i.e. into the semantic composition). Both Chierchia and Rothstein assume that VPs are interpreted as saturated one-place predicates (properties, in Chierchia's ontology), that there is a grammatical requirement that the complement of inflection I must be interpreted as an unsaturated one-place predicate, and hence that an operation of predication must take place, an operation which turns a saturated predicate into an unsaturated predicate.

Both Chierchia and Rothstein then derive the effects of the extended projection principle (that there be a subject) from a grammatical constraint that the IP must have a complete (or saturated) interpretation, hence that reduction must take place, and that the grammar must realize a subject in order to do that reduction.

The latter assumption is, of course, a standard assumption in semantically interpreted grammars with interpretations in typed domains, and I have made the same assumption in the previous chapter. That is, the standard assumption is the same as Chierchia and Rothstein's assumption, if you identify interpretations at type <d,<e,t>> with unsaturated one-place predicates. This is exactly what I will assume:

Unsaturated predicates:
Type <d,<e,t>> is the type of unsaturated one-place predicates.

Thus, unsaturated predicates are functions from individuals to sets of events. They are unsaturated in that they are typally specified as predicates that must apply to an argument (of type d).

Chierchia assumes that saturated one-place predicates are entities in a primitive type of properties. His reasons for this have to do with the interpretation of nominalization constructions, like those where infinitives or gerunds become arguments (as in *Thinking isn't fun*). These concerns are not relevant for my present purposes. Rothstein (2001) assumes that unsaturated one-place predicates are predicates of type <e,t> which have a distinguished variable free for abstraction. I will assume with Rothstein that:

Saturated predicates:
Type <e,t> is the type of saturated one-place predicates (as well as of sentential interpretations).

Thus saturated one-place predicates denote sets of events. How are unsaturated and saturated one-place predicates related?

For Rothstein, they are related through abstraction: you get an unsaturated predicate from a saturated predicate by abstracting over the distinguished free variable. You get a saturated predicate from an unsaturated predicate by applying it to the distinguished free variable.

For Chierchia, they are related through operations linking the domains of one-place predicates <d,t> and properties: nominalization and predication.

Rather than following Rothstein's distinguished variable approach, I will imitate Chierchia's operations as operations between Rothstein's domains <d,<e,t>> and <e,t>.

The assumption is that one-place predicates have both a saturated and an unsaturated form. The intuition is that these are different grammatical ways of encoding the same information.

Not every expression with an interpretation at type <e,t> will be a one-place predicate: IP interpretations, for one thing, will not. What is the difference between a saturated one-place predicate and an IP interpretation? This will be characterized in terms of the theta grid: a one-place predicate has one role present in the theta grid (hence the theta grid can be identified with that one role), while an IP interpretation has an empty theta grid.

One-place predicates: (logical expressions)
A **one-place predicate** is a pair <α,R>, consisting of an expression of type <a,<e,t>> or <e,t>, and a role R.

One-place predicate <α,R> is **saturated** if the type of α is <e,t>, **unsaturated** if the type of α is <a,<e,t>>.

With this, we can define the notion of one-place predicates also for syntactic expressions:

One-place predicates: (syntactic expressions)
Expression α is a **one-place predicate** if its interpretation is α and its theta grid is R and <α,R> is a one-place predicate.
α is **(un)saturated** iff <α,R> is (un)saturated.

We can now introduce operations linking the saturated and unsaturated version of a predicate. They are linked by the operations of EXPRESS and SUPPRESS:

Express:
EXPRESS: <e,t> × <e,d> → <d,<e,t>> × <e,d>
EXPRESS[<α,R>] = <λxλe.α(e) ∧ R(e)=x, R>

Suppress:
SUPPRESS: <d,<e,t>> × <e,d> → <e,t> × <e,d>
SUPPRESS[<α,R>] = <APPLY[α,λP.∃x[P(x)]], R>

Example: Take the following unsaturated one-place predicate:

<λxλe.SING(e) ∧ Ag(e)=x, Ag>

SUPPRESS[<λxλe.SING(e) ∧ Ag(e)=x, Ag>] =
          <λe.SING(e) ∧ ∃x[Ag(e)=x], Ag> =
          <SING, Ag>, where SING is of type <e,t>.

Thus, we turn the unsaturated one-place predicate consisting of the function that maps every individual onto the set of singing events with that individual as agent and the agent role, into the saturated one-place predicate consisting of the set of singing events and the agent role. Indeed, we **suppress** the explicit argument-applying-nature of the predicate.

EXPRESS[<SING,Ag>] = <λxλe.SING(e) ∧ Ag(e)=x, Ag>

By **expressing** the argument, we get the original unsaturated predicate back. I will be using these operations later. With Rothstein and Chierchia, I will assume:

The type requirement on the complement of inflection:
The complement of inflection I must be an unsaturated one-place predicate.

This means that I will assume that the complement of inflection must be a one-place predicate. I do not follow Chierchia and Rothstein's assumption that the VP must be a **saturated** one-place predicate which is turned into an unsaturated predicate by predication. Indeed, for verbs like *sing* I assumed in previous chapters that they start out lexically as **unsaturated** one-place predicates, and I will not change that assumption. So what I will assume is:

Predication:
If the complement of inflection is a saturated predicate, it is turned into an unsaturated predicate with EXPRESS.

The type requirement on IP:
The interpretation type for IP is $<e,t>$ with an empty theta grid.

Let me make a brief digression now about verbs that do not assign a thematic role to their subject. I have assumed the types $<p,<p<e,t>>>$ for *seem* and $<e,<e,t>>$ for *rain*, but I haven't yet given their semantic interpretations. For this, I will now introduce a **non-thematic role** $0: e \rightarrow a$:

$0:e \rightarrow a$
For every $e \in E$: $0(e) = 0_a$

I will assume that this non-thematic role is listed in the theta-grid. We have the following interpretations:

seem $\rightarrow \lambda q \lambda p \lambda s.\text{SEEM}(s) \wedge 0(s)=p \wedge \text{Th}(s)=q$ of type $<p,<p,<e,t>>>$ $<\text{Th},0>$
rain $\rightarrow \lambda f \lambda e.\text{RAIN}(e) \wedge 0(e)=f$ of type $<e,<e,t>>$ $<0>$

Assuming that *that John is an idiot* is interpreted as $^\wedge\text{IDIOT}(\text{JOHN})$, this will give the following interpretations for the examples in (1):

(1)a. It seems that John is an idiot.
   b. It rains.

For (1a) we get:

$\exists s[\text{SEEM}(s) \wedge \exists p[0(s)=p] \wedge \text{Th}(s)=^\wedge\text{IDIOT}(\text{JOHN})]$
$< >$

Since for every e (and hence for every state s) 0(e)=0, ∃p[0(e)=p] is trivially true. So we get:

∃s[SEEM(s) ∧ Th(s)=^IDIOT(JOHN)]
< >
There is a semblance state with the proposition that John is an idiot as theme.

Similarly, for (1b) we get:

∃e[RAIN(e) ∧ ∃f[0(e)=f]]
< >

which, by the same argument, reduces to:

∃e[RAIN(e)]
< >
There is a raining event.

The advantage of the assumption that non-thematic role 0 is represented in the theta grid (and gets removed in the semantic interpretation at the IP level), is that the VPs *seem that John is an idiot* and *rain* now count as one-place predicates.

For VPs with an adjoined subject like *een meisje zing*, where the agent role is assigned to the adjunct, I will assume that in the adjunction step the role Ag in the theta grid is replaced by the non-thematic role 0 (which gets removed at the level of the IP interpretation). This non-thematic role has no semantic role to play (as we will make sure below), and is solely there so that here too the VP with the adjoined subject counts as a one-place predicate. With these assumptions it now follows that:

VPs are one-place predicates:
VPs are uniformly interpreted as one-place predicates, hence they can be the complement of inflection.

6.2   Predicate Formation

In English (and in Dutch), we find *there*-insertion in copular constructions, i.e. with copular predicates. In this section we discuss such predicates. (Note: the predicates, not yet the adjunction to them!)

I discussed noun phrases in predicate position in chapter 2. There I assumed, with Partee, that the predicate type is <d,t>. That is, I assumed that in these constructions the type of the complement of inflection can be <d,t>. But, in the previous section I have assumed that the type of the complement of inflection is uniformly <d,<e,t>>, the type of an unsaturated one-place predicate. This means that we have a conflict to resolve here. The conflict should be resolved, of course, without giving up the theory of DPs in predicate position defended in chapter 2.

I will assume that what we need is an operation which in predicate position uniformly shifts DPs with a set interpretation at type <d,t> to predicative DPs of category DP[PRED] with an interpretation at type <d,<e,t>>. Similarly, adjectives, prepositional phrases, and adverbs should shift their interpretation at their respective set types to the uniform predicate type <d,<e,t>>. I will develop the theory here for expressions that are assumed to start out at set type <d,t>.

Fortunately, I don't have to develop something new here, since the basic techniques for this shift were developed in chapter 8 of Landman (2000). There I discussed the problem of adding a scope mechanism to a Davidsonian theory. The problem can be briefly explained as follows. Look at (2a) with interpretation (2b):

(2)a. Three girls didn't kiss a boy.
   b. $\exists x[*GIRL(x) \wedge |x|=3 \wedge$
       $\forall a \in ATOM(x): \neg \exists e[KISS(e) \wedge Ag(e)=a \wedge BOY(Th(e))]$
       There is a sum of three girls, each of which didn't kiss a boy.

In the Davidsonian theory, negation needs to take scope over the event quantifier. This means that we need to build the natural interpretation of (2) from the interpretation $\lambda P.\exists x[*GIRL(x) \wedge |x|=3 \wedge P(x)]$ of type <<d,t>,t> and the **scopal predicate**:

   $\lambda x.\forall a \in ATOM(x): \neg \exists e[KISS(e) \wedge Ag(e)=a \wedge BOY(Th(e))]$ of type <d,t>
   The property that a sum has if all its atomic elements don't kiss any boys.

The problem we have here is that this involves a scopal predicate of type <d,t>, rather than a Davidsonian predicate of type <d,<e,t>>. But that means that at this level of the derivation, we have lost access to the Davidsonian structure, and hence our semantic operations can, from this level onward, not be formulated on Davidsonian structure. I argued in chapter 8 of Landman (2000) that this is a serious problem, because the semantics must access Davidsonian structure also at this level (for reasons of maximalization). And I argued for a mechanism that can bring scopal predicates of type <d,t>, and more generally, scopal relations of type <d^n,t>, into a Davidsonian form of type <d^n,<e,t>>. This mechanism allows us to shift the scopal predicate of type <d,t> to a Davidsonian predicate of type <d,<e,t>>, encoding the same information, and allow the grammar, including the theory of maximalization to operate on the result.

The mechanism I developed for this was called a **scope shift** mechanism. I will describe it briefly. I assume that the domain of eventualities E contains as a subdomain a domain S of what I call **argument states**. An argument state is really nothing but a Davidsonian encoding of a structured meaning or situation: it corresponds to an n-place relation between individuals, and n individuals standing in that relation. The argument states have roles defined on them, and the only function of the latter is to encode the arguments. Thus, I assume a set of argument roles $A_1, A_2, \ldots$ and let an **n-place argument state** be a state in S for which the roles $A_1, \ldots, A_n$ are defined (for some further constraints, see Landman (2000)).

The idea is that we can create a correspondence between a property and the set of one-place argument states of having that property, and between a relation and the set of two-place argument states of standing in that relation.

For certain (stative) properties these argument roles can be identified with real thematic roles, but since there will be property states corresponding to arbitrarily complex properties, often they will be non-thematic roles, whose function is mainly or solely to encode argument structure in a Davidsonian interpretation.

The whole purpose of introducing this structure is to be able to switch between properties and corresponding sets of argument states. I do this by adding to the models a scope linking operation, [ ], mapping each n-place property (of type $<d^n,t>$) into a set of n-place argument states (in S) of type $<e,t>$. The main constraint on this function is that it satisfies the following correspondence principle:

Scope linking operation [ ]:
[ ]: $<d^n,t> \rightarrow <e,t>$

Correspondence principle:
for every n-place relation R, and individuals $d_1, \ldots, d_n$:
$R(d_1, \ldots, d_n)$ iff $\exists s \in [R]$: $A_1(s)=d_1 \wedge \ldots \wedge A_n(s)=d_n$

To see how this works, let α be the property of type $<d,t>$ introduced above:

$\alpha = \lambda x. \forall a \in ATOM(x); \neg \exists e[KISS(e) \wedge Ag(e)=a \wedge BOY(Th(e))]$ of type $<d,t>$
The property that a sum has if all its atomic elements don't kiss any boys.

We can shift this, using scope linking to a one-place predicate of type $<d<e,t>>$ (with theta grid $<A_1>$, containing argument role A_1):

$\lambda x \lambda s.s \in [\alpha] \wedge A_1(s)=x$ of type $<d,<e,t>>$
$<A_1>$

This operation, from $<d,t>$ to $<d,<e,t>>$ I will call **scope shift**. With this predicate, the grammar is able to derive the following interpretation for (2a):

(2)c. $\exists s[s \in [\alpha] \wedge *GIRL(A_1(s)) \wedge |A_1(s)|=3]$
There is a state of having the property that all your atoms don't kiss a boy and a sum of three girls is in that state.

With the correspondence principle we are able to switch back from this Davidsonian interpretation to a property interpretation: such a state exists iff that sum of girls has the property α, hence, by the correspondence principle (2c) is actually equivalent to the desired interpretation (2a). Hence, the scope shift operation allows us to get the right interpretation for (2a), but also for cases that crucially involve maximalization. (See Landman 2000 for details.)

It is good to point out from the start that I do not assume that this switch is a type shifting principle which can be freely accessed to resolve type mismatching. In Landman 2000, I introduced it as part of the operation of derived predicate formation in the scope mechanism. I will generalize that here by assuming that it is accessed by predicate formation in general. That is, for an expression of category XP with interpretation at type $<d,t>$, I propose to derive its predicate interpretations of category XP[PRED] and interpretation at type $<d,<e,t>>$ through the scope shift mechanism. Let me give an example:

(3)   The guests are three boys.

We start where we ended in chapter 2:

   $[_{DP}$ *three boys* $] \rightarrow \lambda x.{}^{*}BOY(x) \wedge |x|=3$ of type $<d,t>$

[ ] associates with the property a set of one-place argument states:

   $[\lambda x.{}^{*}BOY(x) \wedge |x|=3]$ of type $<e,t>$
   The states of being a sum of three boys.

Scope shift uses this set, in order to associate with the DP *three boys* a one-place predicate *three boys* of category DP[PRED] and type $<d,<e,t>>$, and role A_1 on the theta grid:

   Scope Shift:
   $[_{DP[PRED]}$ *three boys*$] \rightarrow$
   $\lambda x \lambda s.s \in [\lambda x.{}^{*}BOY(x) \wedge |x|=3] \wedge A_1(s)=x$ of type $<d,<e,t>>$
   $<A_1>$
   the function that maps each sum of individuals onto the set of states of that sum of individuals being a sum of three boys.

Thus, the DP[PRED] is now indeed a one-place unsaturated predicate according to the definition given in the last subsection, and hence, it can be the complement of I.

Auxiliary *be* denotes, as usual, the identity function $\lambda P.P$ – in this theory at type $<<d,<e,t>>,<d,<e,t>>>$ – this gives the same interpretation for the I' as for the DP[PRED]:

[$_{I'}$ *be three boys*] →
$\lambda x \lambda s.s \in [\lambda x.^*BOY(x) \wedge |x|=3] \wedge A_1(s)=x$ of type <d,<e,t>>
<A$_1$>

Now the subject *the guests*, with interpretation σ(*GUEST) combines with the
I' in the normal way, we apply the predicate interpretation to the subject interpretation, the role disappears from the theta grid, and we get for the IP:

[$_{IP}$ *the guests are three boys*] →
$\lambda s.s \in [\lambda x.^*BOY(x) \wedge |x|=3] \wedge A_1(s)=σ(^*GUEST)$ of type <e,t>
< >
The set of states of the guests being a sum of three boys.

Maximalization applies to this in the normal way, and we get, as the interpretation of (3):

$\exists s[s \in [\lambda x.^*BOY(x) \wedge |x|=3] \wedge A_1(s)=σ(^*GUEST)]$
There is a state of the guests being a sum of three boys.

With the correspondence principle, this is equivalent to:

$((\lambda x.^*BOY(x) \wedge |x|=3) (σ(^*GUEST)))$

which is:

$^*BOY(σ(^*GUEST)) \wedge |σ(^*GUEST)|=3$
Every guest is a boy, and the total number of guests is three.

Thus, the analysis of predicative DPs in chapter 2 now fits with the general
perspective of the complement of I being an unsaturated one-place predicate
of type <d,<e,t>>. This means, then, that the earlier discussion about the place
of the predicative type in the type shifting triangle for noun phrases isn't affected
at all: we still assume that indefinite DPs, and only they, are born at the type
<d,t>. The only thing we add is that predicate formation makes them into unsat-
urated one-place predicates of type <d,<e,t>>. In sum, the operation of predicate formation can be given as follows:

Predicate Formation PF:
Let α be an expression of category XP with interpretation α of type <d,t>.
The operation PF of predicate formation turns α into a predicative XP of
category XP[PRED], with an interpretation of type <d,<e,t>> and theta grid
<A$_1$>:

PF[< [$_{XP}$ α], α > = < [$_{XP[PRED]}$ α], $\lambda x \lambda s.s \in [α] \wedge A_1(s)=x$, <A$_1$> >

6.3 Episodic Predicates, Passive Verbs, and Unaccusative Verbs

Since Carlson (1977a), predicates like *be available, be in the garden* have been called "stage level predicates," and predicates like *be intelligent* "individual level predicates." Since this terminology is grounded in the specifics of Carlson's ontology, Krifka et. al. (1995) proposed a maybe more neutral terminology, by calling them "episodic" and "non-episodic" predicates, respectively. I will follow their terminology here.

Carlson, and others since (in particular Stump (1985), and more recently Kratzer (1995)) have introduced a battery of semantic distributional tests showing differences between these two kinds of predicates. One of these tests actually predates Carlson, and goes back to Milsark (1974). Milsark observed that episodic predicates are felicitous as codas in *there*-insertion contexts, while non-episodic predicates are not:

(4)a.   There is a boy *in the garden/available.*
  b.   #There is a boy *intelligent.*

Attempts have been made, in particular by Chierchia (1995), to fine tune the semantics of *there*-insertion contexts so as to directly predict this distribution from the difference in meaning between episodic predicates and non-episodic predicates. Such accounts are doomed to failure, because, while the semantic distinction between episodic and non-episodic predicates seems to be cross-linguistically robust, the interaction with contexts of indefiniteness is not. More precisely, when we look at the distributional tests discussed in the literature, we find that the facts in Dutch are much the same as they are in English: there is every reason to believe that the meanings of episodic and non-episodic predicates in Dutch are much the same as they are in English. But, it turns out, there is a clear difference between Dutch and English, when it comes to the interaction of these predicates with contexts of indefiniteness. While English examples like (4b) are robustly judged to be seriously infelicitous, the judgments concerning corresponding examples in Dutch range from mildly unnatural to perfectly fine (5b).

(5)a.   Er   is een jongen in de tuin.
        There is a   boy   in the garden
  b. (?)Er   is een jongen intelligent.
        pl   is a   boy   intelligent

Out of the blue, (5b) is maybe a bit unnatural, but a bit of context makes it perfectly acceptable. Importantly, the same bit of context does not improve the English examples:

(6)a.   In mijn klas zijn er twee jongens intelligent, en   de rest is oliedom.
         In my   class are pl two   boys   intelligent and the rest is dumb
   b.   #In my class, there are two boys intelligent, and the others are dumb.

The distinction can be shown in Dutch with verbs as well. *Weten* (know) and *geloven* (believe) are prime examples of non-episodic verbs, like their English counterparts, but they are perfectly felicitous in contexts of indefiniteness, the same for *kennen* (the other counterpart of *know*):

(7)a.   In Amerika, weten er veel   mensen niet dat Texel een eiland is.
         In America know pl many people not that Texel an island is
         In America, many people don't know that Texel is an island.
   b.   In Nederland, geloven er veel   mensen dat Cape Cod een eiland is.
         In Holland,   believe pl many people that Cape Cod an   island is
         In Holland, many people believe that Cape Cod is an island.
   c.   Er kennen maar heel weinig mensen Linear B.
         pl know   only very few   people Linear B
         Only very few people know Linear B.

The facts in German seem to be the same as the Dutch facts, while French patterns with English:

(8)a.   Es sind nur wenig Leute intelligent.
         lr are only few   people intelligent
   b.   Es kennen nur sehn wenig Leute   Linear B.
         lr know   only very few   people Linear B
   c.   Weil   ja   doch nur sehr wenig Leute   Linear B kennen.
         Because yes still only very few   people Linear B know
         Because after all only very few people know Linear B.

(9)a.   Il y a   trois filles dans le   Jardin.
         lr clit aux three girls in   the garden
   b.   #Il y   a   trois filles intelligentes.
         lr clit aux three girls intelligent

Since, as I mentioned, Dutch patterns like English with respect to many other tests for the episodic/non-episodic distinction, these facts suggest that it is a mistake to try to attempt a purely semantic explanation of the English facts directly in terms of the semantics of the episodic/non-episodic contrast, since such an explanation ought to carry over directly to Dutch.

So far we see that in English and French only episodic predicates occur felicitously as the coda in *there*-insertion constructions, while in Dutch and German, all predicates are allowed.

I have already mentioned in previous chapters, that something similar holds for verbs. The examples in (7) show that there is no semantic restriction concerning episodicity for verbs in *there*-insertion constructions in Dutch: verbs that pattern with non-episodic predicates are felicitous. Secondly, what the examples show is that there is no restriction concerning adicity of verbs: transitive and intransitive verbs are both allowed in *there*-insertion constructions. To give an example with a normal transitive verb:

(10)   Er hebben drie meisjes Dafna gekust.
       pl have   three girls   Dafna kissed
       Three girls kissed Dafna.

The examples in the *Oxford English Dictionary* present the following situation for English. Examples with transitive verbs can be found with modal auxiliaries in medieval times:

(11)   **There** *could* no man it *aquenche* with no craft.   [1387]

But no examples are cited dating from after the mid sixteenth century. Exactly around that time the first examples with passive verbs are found. *There*-insertion contexts with passive verbs are by no means common in English, but they do exist, even in contemporary English:

(12)a.   **There** *coulde* not *be founde* a more goodlyer man.   [*c*.1533]
   b.   **There** *were* no plenipotentiaries *sent* to the East and back again. [1877]
   c.   Here, **there** *were found* many relics of Franklin's expedition. [modern]

The remaining cases that the *OED* cites are with intransitive verbs. Most examples cited, from the earliest times to modern days, are with *come, arise* or *result*:

(13)a.   Tha *com* **thaer** gan in to me heofencund Wisdom.   [*c*.888]
   b.   **There** *shall come* a starre out of Iacob, and a Sceptre shall rise out of Israel.   [1611]
   c.   Then **came** *there* a voice, Soon *shall* **there** *arise* a prophet.   [undated]
   d.   And **ther** *ros* wrethe and strif anon Ayzen moysen and aron.   [*c*.1250]
   e.   From all these things **there** *resulted* consequences of vast importance. [1857]

A second class concerns verbs like *stand, peak up* and archaic modals like *behove, chance, want*:

(14)a.   In thulke therwolke feire tour **ther** *stont* a tron with muche honour. [*c*.1320]
   b.   For to sle a man . . . **there** *behoueth* but one stroke well sette.   [1477]

    c.   **There** *chaunced* to the Princehand to rize An auncient booke.   [1590]
    d.   In these Cottian Alps . . . **there** *peaketh up* a mightie high mount.   [1609]
    e.   **There** *want* not sufficient materials on which to form a true judgement.
        [1761–2]

To complete the picture, notice (15), which doesn't seem to be allowed any longer in modern English:

(15)   **There** *died* an infinite number of people.   [1566]

The interesting thing about the list in (14)–(15) is, of course, its consistency: all the verbs involved are **unaccusatives**, intransitive verbs that, among others, make their subject a theme rather than an agent. Thus the English facts show that in English the verbs that are allowed in *there*-insertion are (somewhat marginally) passives and (some, but not, or no longer all) unaccusatives. In this, English again patterns with French:

(16)a.   *Il *dansent* trois filles.
        lr dance   three girls
    b.   Il est arrivé une fille de   Paris.   UNACCUSATIVE
        lr cop arrived a   girl from Paris
        There has arrived a girl from Paris.
    c.   Il est mangé trois pommes.   PASSIVE
        lr cop eaten   three apples
        There were eaten three apples.

(Examples like (16c) are called "impersonal passives" in the Romance literature, to be distinguished from what is called "impersonal passives" in the Germanic literature, which are passives of intransitive verbs.)

    In sum, then, the key parametric difference between Dutch and German on the one hand, and English and French on the other, is that Dutch and German allow *there*-insertion constructions with any verb and any predicate, while English and French only allow *there*-insertion with episodic predicates, passive verbs, and unaccusative verbs.

    For Dutch and German this means that the analysis I have given so far suffices to get all the facts discussed right. I gave the analysis of flip-flop and adjunction for verbs in the previous chapter. With the analysis of predicate formation introduced in this chapter, the very same analysis will derive the interpretations of adjoined subjects with predicates. As an example, let's look at the derivation of (17a):

(17)a.   (dat) er een meisje intelligent is.
         that pl a   girl   intelligent is

        [$_{ADJ}$ *intelligent*] → INTELLIGENT   of type <d,t>

Predicate formation forms a predicative adjective of type <d,<e,t>>:

$[_{ADJ[PRED]}$ *intelligent* $] \rightarrow \lambda x \lambda s.s \in [$ INTELLIGENT$] \wedge A_1(s)=x$
$\quad\quad$ <A_1>$\quad\quad$ of type <d,<e,t>:

The DP *een meisje* with interpretation GIRL of type <d,t> adjoines to this.

ADJOIN[GIRL, $\lambda x \lambda s.s \in$ [INTELLIGENT] $\wedge$ A$_1$(s)=x]

gets resolved as:

FLOP[APPLY[ADJUNCT[GIRL], FLIP[$\lambda x \lambda s.s \in$ [INTELLIGENT] $\wedge$ A$_1$(s)=x]]]

which is:

$\lambda x \lambda s.s \in$ [INTELLIGENT] $\wedge$ A$_1$(s)=x $\wedge$ GIRL(x)

The role A$_1$ is assigned to *een meisje*, and replaced by 0, and we get:

$[_{ADJ[PRED]}$ *een meisje intelligent* $] \rightarrow$
$\quad\quad \lambda x \lambda s.s \in$ [INTELLIGENT] $\wedge$ A$_1$(s)=x $\wedge$ GIRL(x)$\quad\quad$ of type <d,<e,t>>
$\quad\quad$ <0>

This combines with the copula *is*, interpreted as identity (and, of course, in Dutch the I position is sitting on the right):

$[_{I'}$ *een meisje intelligent is* $] \rightarrow$
$\quad\quad \lambda x \lambda s.s \in$ [INTELLIGENT] $\wedge$ A$_1$(s)=x $\wedge$ GIRL(x)$\quad\quad$ of type <d,<e,t>>
$\quad\quad$ <0>

This applies to the non-thematic subject $[_{DP}$ *er* Ø $]$ with interpretation $\lambda P.\exists x[P(x)]$, and we get:

$[_{IP}$ *er een meisje intelligent is* $] \rightarrow$
$\quad\quad \lambda s.\exists x[s \in$ [INTELLIGENT] $\wedge$ A$_1$(s)=x $\wedge$ GIRL(x)]$\quad\quad$ of type <e,t>
$\quad\quad$ < >

Maximalization derives an interpretation of type t:

$[_{IP}$ *er een meisje intelligent is* $] \rightarrow$
$\quad\quad \exists s \exists x[s \in$ [INTELLIGENT] $\wedge$ A$_1$(s)=x $\wedge$ GIRL(x)]$\quad\quad$ of type t
$\quad\quad$ < >

This interpretation is equivalent to:

$\exists x[GIRL(x) \wedge \exists s[s \in [INTELLIGENT] \wedge A_1(s)=x]]$

With the Correspondence Principle, this is equivalent to:

$\exists x[GIRL(x) \wedge INTELLIGENT(x)]$

So we derive (17a) with interpretation (17b):

(17)a.   (dat) er een meisje intelligent is.
        that pl a   girl   intelligent is
   b. $\exists x[GIRL(x) \wedge INTELLIGENT(x)]$
        There is a girl which is intelligent.

Our task, then, is to account for the English and French facts.

6.4   Saturated One-Place Predicates

What I will assume is the following:

Episodic predicates as saturated predicates:
Episodic predicates, passives and unaccusatives optionally allow a second
derivation as saturated one-place predicates.

For an episodic predicate, like *available*, the simplest way to give form to this
is the following. We start with its interpretation as an episodic adjective of type
<d,t>:

$[_{ADJ}$ *available* $] \rightarrow$ AVAILABLE   of type <d,t>.

And we formulate the following operation of saturated predicate formation for
episodic predicates:

Saturated Predicate Formation SPF:
Let α be an expression of category XP with interpretation α of type <d,t>,
where α is an episodic predicate.
The operation SPF of saturated predicate formation turns α into a predicative XP of category XP[PRED], with an interpretation of type <e,t>, and theta
grid <A_1>:

PF$[< [_{XP} \alpha], \alpha >] = < [_{XP[PRED]} \alpha], [\alpha], <A_1> >$

$[\alpha]$ is, of course, the set of one-place argument states corresponding to α. For
available this gives:

[$_{\text{ADJ[PRED]}}$ *available*] → [AVAILABLE]   of type <e,t>.
          <A$_1$>
          The set of states of being available.

This is a saturated one-place predicate. This saturated predicate is the complement of inflection I, which imposes the requirement on the interpretation of its complement that it be an unsaturated one-place predicate of type <d,<e,t>>. There is a type mismatch, which is resolved through the operation of EXPRESS (i.e. Chierchia and Rothstein's predication):

[$_{\text{ADJ[PRED]}}$ *available*] → EXPRESS[[AVAILABLE],A$_1$]   of type <d,<e,t>>.
          <A$_1$>

which is:

[$_{\text{ADJ[PRED]}}$ *available*] → λxλs.s ∈[AVAILABLE] ∧ A$_1$(s)=x
          <A$_1$>   of type <d,<e,t>>

This means that, after predication, we have derived an unsaturated one-place predicate, and the interpretation now looks just like what we got with predicate formation PF for *intelligent* in one step. This is, technically, the simplest analysis. It is possible to try a slightly different route, and motivate the possibility of deriving a saturated interpretation from the semantics of the episodic predicate as an **episodic predicate**.

For instance, we can make the episodic nature of the adjective *available* perspicuous in its interpretation, say, as:

[$_{\text{ADJ}}$ *available*] → λx.∃s[AVAILABILITY STATE(s) ∧ In(s)=x]   of type <d,t>.
The set of individuals which are in an availability state, where availability states can be thought of as being **situated**, and hence episodic.

This can be thought of as deriving from, or contextually related to a semantic relation between individuals and situated states:

λxλs.AVAILABILITY STATE(s) ∧ In(s)=x   of type <d,<e,t>>

The grammatical or contextual availability of this relation, may well facilitate the grammatical or contextual availability of a **shifted interpretation** of *available* to type <e,t> (where you existentially close the individual argument, rather than the event argument of the relation):

λs.∃x[AVAILABILITY STATE(s) ∧ In(s)=x]   of type <e,t>

The assumption, then, would be that saturated predicate formation shifts the <d,t> interpretation of *available* to this <e,t> interpretation:

[$_{\text{ADJ[PRED]}}$ *available*] → λs.∃x[AVAILABILITY STATE(s) ∧ In(s)=x]
<In>   of type <e,t>

From there on, the story would be the same.

For my purposes here, the only thing that is important is that episodic predicates allow a second interpretation as a saturated one-place predicate, so I do not here need to choose.

I will make a similar assumption for **passives**. Standardly, passivization derives from a transitive verb like *kiss* a passive verb or VP *kissed* of type <d,<e,t>:

[$_{\text{VP[PASS]}}$ *kissed*] → λyλe.KISS(e) ∧ ∃x[Ag(e)=x] ∧ Th(e)=y
<Th>

which (given the semantic constraint that the agent role is defined on all kissing events) is the same as:

[$_{\text{VP[PASS]}}$ *kissed*] → λyλe.KISS(e) ∧ Th(e)=y
<Th>   of type <d,<e,t>>

Thus, passivization derives an unsaturated one-place passive predicate. What I will assume is that optionally we can also derive a saturated one-place passive predicate:

[$_{\text{VP[PASS]}}$ *kissed*] → KISS
                <Th>   of type <e,t>

Here too, since the complement of I needs to be of type <d,<e,t>>, predication with EXPRESS will derive an unsaturated one-place passive predicate of type <d,<e,t>>:

[$_{\text{VP[PASS]}}$ *kissed*] → EXPRESS[KISS,Th]
                <Th>   of type <e,t>

which is indeed the same unsaturated one-place predicate we derived before:

[$_{\text{VP[PASS]}}$ *kissed*] → λyλe.KISS(e) ∧ Th(e)=y
                <Th>   of type <d,<e,t>>

I make the same assumption for unaccusatives like *arrive*. I assume that, like all intransitive verbs, *arrive* has an interpretation as an unsaturated one-place predicate at type <d,<e,t>>:

[$_{\text{V}}$ *arrive*] → λxλe.ARRIVE(e) ∧ Th(e)=x
                <Th>   of type <d,<e,t>>

But, I assume that the grammar optionally also allows an interpretation as a saturated one-place predicate at type <e,t>:

   [$_V$ *arrive*] → ARRIVE
                    <Th>   of type <e,t>

As before, when this becomes the complement of I, predication with EXPRESS must turn this into an unsaturated one-place predicate of type <d,<e,t>:

   [$_{VP}$ *arrive*] → EXPRESS[ARRIVE,Th]
                     <Th>   of type <d,<e,t>>

which is:

   [$_{VP}$ *arrive*] → λxλe.ARRIVE(e) ∧ Th(e)=x
                     <Th>   of type <d,<e,t>>

As in the case of the episodic predicates, there is ample room for trying to relate the possibility of deriving saturated predicates for passives and unaccusatives to the special properties of these constructions, their object, theme relatedness, etc. As before, I am not at all opposed to pursuing this line (on the contrary). But, as before, the only thing I need here is the assumption that unaccussatives and passives allow a derivation as a saturated one-place predicate.

Note that I haven't assumed that they must be analyzed as saturated predicates, rather than unsaturated ones. I am going to relate the occurrence of these predicates in *there*-insertion constructions to the availability of the saturated interpretation. Given that in English, passives occur in such constructions only grudgingly, and that certainly not all unaccusatives occur, I prefer to assume that the saturated predicate interpretation is an option for these predicates, but an option that the language can choose to use only sparsely.

6.5   Adjunction to Saturated One-Place Predicates

We now come to adjunction of the indefinite subject. The FLIP–FLOP mechanism allows for adjunction of indefinite subjects to unsaturated one-place predicates. I will now assume that adjunction of indefinite subjects is actually possible for one-place predicates in general, hence also for saturated one-place predicates.

With adjunction to unsaturated one-place predicates we had to resolve the following type mismatch:

   ADJOIN[α,β] where α is of type <d,t> and <β,R> is a one-place predicate of type <d,<e,t>>.

and this was resolved as:

FLOP[APPLY[ADJUNCT[α], FLIP[β]]]

If we allow adjunction to saturated predicates, we need to resolve:

ADJOIN[α,β] where α is of type <d,t> and <β,R> is a one-place predicate of type <e,t>.

Resolving this in exactly the same way:

FLOP[APPLY[ADJUNCT[α], FLIP[β]]]

leaves one type mismatch unresolved: FLIP requires an input of type <d,<e,t>>, but β is only of type <e,t>. But this mismatch is, of course, resolved with predication operation EXPRESS:

FLOP[APPLY[ADJUNCT[α], FLIP[**EXPRESS[β,R]**]]]

Thus, adjoining the indefinite subject to a one-place predicate creates an unsaturated one-place predicate as follows:

Adjoining DPs to one-place predicates:
Let [$_{DP}$ α] be a DP with interpretation α of type <d,t>, and
[$_{PRED}$ β] a one-place predicate with interpretation β and role R.

[$_{PRED}$ [$_{DP}$ α] [$_{PRED}$ β]] is an unsaturated one-place predicate with interpretation ADJOIN[α,β] and role 0.

If β is of type <d,<e,t>>,
ADJOIN[α,β] = FLOP[APPLY[ADJUNCT[α], FLIP[β]]]
If β is of type <e,t>,
ADJOIN[α,β] = FLOP[APPLY[ADJUNCT[α], FLIP[EXPRESS[β,R]]]]

We take stock by asking what the additions in this chapter contribute to the analysis of the Dutch examples? The answer is, nothing whatsoever! I have shown the derivations of the examples in (18):

(18)a.   Dafna is intelligent.
    b.   Er is een meisje intelligent.
        pl is a   girl   intelligent

Intelligent shifts with predicate formation to an unsaturated one-place predicate of type <d,<e,t>>. We apply inflection to that, and the result applies to the subject *Dafna*, and we get (18a). We adjoin *een meisje* to the unsaturated predicate, apply inflection to it, and apply the result to the non-thematic subject, and we get (18b). In both cases we get the right interpretation with the correspondence principle.

Now let's think about the cases in (19):

(19)a.   Dafna is beschikbaar (om de lerares te helpen)
         Dafna is available   for the teacher to help
         Dafna is available to help the teacher.
    b.   Er is een meisje beschikbaar.
         pl is a   girl   available

For (19a), we get, of course, exactly the same derivation as for (18a): shift *beschikbaar* with predicate formation from type <d,t> to an unsaturated predicate of type <d,<e,t>>, apply inflection to this, and apply the result to *Dafna*. But we get a second derivation for (19a): shift *beschikbaar* with saturated predicate formation from type <d,t> to a saturated predicate of type <e,t>. Shift this with predication with EXPRESS to an unsaturated predicate of type <d,<e,t>> and join the first derivation from there. This second derivation derives, obviously, the same interpretation as the first.

For (19b) we have three derivations. The first is the same as for (18b): shift *beschikbaar* to an unsaturated predicate of type <d,<e,t>>, adjoin *een meisje*, apply inflection to it, and apply the result to the non-thematic subject.

In the second derivation, we shift *beschikbaar* to a saturated predicate of type <d,<e,t>>, shift this with predication with EXPRESS to an unsaturated predicate of type <d,<e,t>>, and join the first derivation. Again, obviously, this derivation gives the same interpretation as the first derivation.

In the third derivation, we also shift *beschikbaar* to a saturated predicate of type <e,t>. But this time we adjoin *een meisje* to the saturated predicate. We get as interpretation:

ADJOIN[GIRL, [AVAILABLE]], where the role of the saturated predicate *available* is A_1.

which resolves as:

FLOP[ADJUNCT[GIRL], FLIP[EXPRESS[[AVAILABLE,A_1]]]]

Since EXPRESS[AVAILABLE,A_1] is precisely the interpretation that predicate formation to type<d,<e,t>> derives for *beschikbaar*, we have at this stage derived the very same unsaturated one-place predicate as we got in the first derivation for (19b). Hence the interpretation we derive with this derivation is once more the same. So, indeed, for Dutch and German, adding saturated interpretations for episodic predicates, passives, and unaccusatives and allowing adjunction to saturated predicates gives you more derivations, but not more interpretations.

So we come to English and French. We are now in a position to express the parametric difference between Dutch and German on the one side, and French and English on the other:

Adjunction Parameter:
Dutch and German: DPs with an interpretation born at type <d,t> can adjoin to one-place predicates.
English and French: DP's with an interpretation born at type <d,t> can adjoin to saturated one-place predicates.

For Dutch and German nothing changes. For English and French the facts discussed now follow. English and French do not allow adjunction of an indefinite DP adjunct to unsaturated predicates. Non-episodic predicates, like *intelligent*, transitive verbs, and intransitive verbs that are not unaccusative do not support derivations of saturated predicates, hence they do not support adjunction of an indefinite DP adjunct, and hence, one-place predicates derived from them they cannot occur in *there*-insertion contexts. Episodic predicates like *available*, passives, and unaccussatives optionally support a derivation as saturated one-place predicates. In as much as the language allows itself to make use of this option, adjunction of an indefinite DP adjunct is possible, and one-place predicates derived from them can occur in *there*-insertion contexts.

Thus the parameter given successfully predicts the facts in the languages under discussion. The interesting thing about this parameter is that it is a semantic parameter, in that the generalization about adjunction is not stated in terms of syntactic category, but in terms of the associated semantic type.

Of course, we can always syntacticize the distinction by introducing a unifying syntactic category for unsaturated predicates and a unifying syntactic category for saturated predicates. But that seems besides the point. For one thing, there is no reason to think that acquiring the correct settings for this semantic parameter, is more complicated than acquiring the correct setting of its syntacticization: as parameters go, this semantic parameter seems to be an eminently learnable one.

I started off this chapter with a brief introduction to the predication theories of Chierchia and Rothstein. Clearly, the present theory owes much to those theories. I mentioned before that the present theory differs from theirs in one crucial respect: while I assume with Chierchia and Rothstein that the derivation of every sentence must go through a stage where you have an unsaturated one-place predicate (i.e. the complement of I), I do not accept their assumption that the derivations always get to the stage where you have an unsaturated one-place predicate from a stage where you have a saturated predicate. We are now in a position to appreciate the importance of this difference between their theories and mine: it is crucial for the explanation of the English and French facts about *there*-insertion contexts that only some unsaturated one-place predicates derive (and derive optionally) from an earlier stage as saturated predicates.

6.6   The Predication Head

In Dutch and German adjunction of the indefinite subject is to one-place predicates, saturated or unsaturated. In fact, as we have seen, as far as the data we have discussed is concerned, a more specific parameter, namely the assumption that adjunction is to unsaturated one-place predicates only would make the same predictions. Following customary practice when parameters are concerned, I have assumed the more general parameter, so that the two settings stand in a subset relation.

This means that I assume that in Dutch and German the indefinite subject can be adjoined to the saturated or unsaturated complement of I. In fact, since I′ itself is also an unsaturated one-place predicate, as far as the facts that I have discussed here are concerned the adjunction could even be to I′. Since I make the standard assumption that in Dutch and German the heads in the verbal domain (like V and I) are sitting on the right side, and anyway verb cluster-collapse on the right side takes place in these languages, it's very hard to argue in these languages that the adjunction must be to one of these positions rather than the others.

Since in English and French the heads in the verbal heads are assumed to be sitting on the left side, the place of the adjunction site may be visible in the surface syntax. Since in these languages there is only adjunction to saturated one-place predicates, the adjunction must be lower than I, but higher than V.

And here we have a problem, because the data of unaccusative verbs suggests that what I have called the adjoined indefinite subject is actually sitting **to the right of V**, which suggests that it actually might be in object position. That has in fact been a standard assumption in the French literature. Look at the following data:

(20)a.   There **is** *a girl* in the garden.
   b.   There **arrived** *a girl* from Paris.
   c.   Il y **a**   *une fille* dans le   jardin.
       lr cl aux a   girl in   the garden

These data are compatible with my analysis so far. We assume that the copula *is* in (20a) and the inflected verb *arrived* in (20b) have moved to I, and *a girl* is just adjoined to the one-place predicate in (20a) and (20c), and to the VP with one-place predicate interpretation in (20b). But the data are problematic as soon as we get **perfective cases**:

(21)a.   There has **been** *a girl* in the garden.
   b.   Il y a   **eu**   *une fille* dans le   jardin.
       lr cl aux had a   girl in   the garden
   c.   There has **arrived** *a girl* from Paris.
   d.   Il est **arrivé** *une fille* de   Paris.
       lr aux arrived a   girl from Paris

    e.   There was **sent** *a letter* to the king.

    f.   Il est **mangé** *trois* pommes.

        lr aux eaten   three apples

In all these cases the I position is filled by the auxiliary, and there is a perfective or passive participle present. If this participle is in the V position, then clearly my analysis of the English cases is in trouble, and the classical French wisdom, that the indefinite is in object position is, at least as far as the word order is concerned, a more plausible analysis. (Clearly I am not going to assume that the indefinite subject can be right adjoined!)

    Fortunately, English comes to my help here. The data are actually more complex than the cases in (21) suggest. While it is true that the indefinite occurs to the right of perfective and passive participles, it actually must occur to the left of progressive participles:

(22)a.   There is *a visitor* **arriving** from Paris tonight.

    b.   #There is **arriving** *a visitor* from Paris tonight.

    c.   There have been *planes* **leaving** from this airport since the thirties.

    d.   #There have been **leaving** *planes* from this airport since the thirties.

The data in (22) are, I think, completely detrimental to the alternative suggestion that the indefinite is in object position. The facts in (22) again fit perfectly with my analysis of the indefinite as being adjoined to the saturated one-place predicate, lower than I, but higher than V, on the assumption that the progressive participle is in V.

    Let's pause for a second to consider (and reject) two alternative analyses of the data in (22), analyses which would make the data in (22) irrelevant. In the first place, we need to consider the possibility that *arriving from Paris tonight* in (22a) is an adjunct on *visitor* and hence we have a DP *a visitor arriving from Paris tonight*. Secondly, we need to consider the possibility that *arriving from Paris tonight* in (22a) is a secondary predicate on the structure *there is a visitor*. That neither of these analyses is tenable can best be seen by regarding example (22c) with a perfective and a progressive participle. Compare (22c) with the examples in (23):

(23)a.   *Three girls leaving from the airport* have kissed Mary.

    b.   I have met John *leaving from the airport*.

Both in (23a), where *leaving from the airport* is an adjunct inside the subject noun phrase, and in (23b), where *leaving from the airport* is a secondary predicate, the perfective in the main clause is a perfective on the main verb *kiss/meet* and not on the progressive in the adjunct *leaving*. The adjunct nature is shown by the fact that we conclude readily (24a) from (23a) and (24b) from (23b) (simple adjunct-drop):

(24)a.   Three girls have kissed Mary.
  b.   I have met John.

This is, of course, not the case in a normal progressive construction, as in (25a).

(25)a.   The plane has been *leaving from the airport* for an hour now.
  b.   The plane has been for an hour now.

In (25a), the perfective is a perfective on *be leaving*, and since semantically, the copula is identity, the perfective is semantically a perfective on *leaving*. And, of course, nobody would claim that in (25a) *leaving from the airport* is an adjunct, which is also shown by the fact that (25b), though probably true, is not a conclusion that we arrive at by an adjunct-drop inference from (25a), unlike in the cases in (23/24). Now look again at (22c):

(22)c.   There have been *planes* **leaving** from this airport since the thirties.

It seems clear that (22c) patterns with (25a), and not with the adjunct examples in (23). The perfective in (22c) is a perfective on *be leaving*, and hence on *leaving*, and dropping *leaving from this airport* or *leaving from this airport since the thirties*, given statements that, though probably true, are also not derived naturally through adjunct-drop inferences (22c):

(26)a.   There have been planes.
  b.   There have been planes since the thirties.

Thus it seems justified to assume, as I have, that *leaving* in the examples in (22) is a progressive participle which is part of the main verbal structure of the sentence, and not part of an adjunct.

   But then, what about the cases in (21), where the perfective participle seems to be sitting in the wrong place? These data can be accounted for if we make, with Bowers (1993), the assumption that in English and French predication is realized as a syntactic projection in between the V and the I projection (with the predication head position, like the other head positions in the verbal domain on the left). This gives the following structure:

$$[_{I'} \text{ I } [_{PredP} [_{P'} \text{ P XP[PRED] }]]]$$

where XP[PRED] is required to be a one-place predicate (saturated or unsaturated), and P′ an unsaturated one-place predicate. The semantics stays just as I have given it. The only difference, then, is that the requirement of there being an unsaturated one-place predicate is not imposed on the complement of I, but one level lower on the complement of the predication head P. Since it is the complement of P, the XP[PRED] which can be saturated, we predict, on this analysis, that the adjoined indefinite subject is adjoined to the complement of P, hence that it occurs right of P, but left of V.

For our present purposes this has the advantage that it gives us a head position P between I and the adjoined indefinite. We now make the following assumption:

The position of verbal elements:
- The auxiliaries and inflected verbs occur in I.
- The perfective participle occurs in P.
- The progressive participle occurs in V.

With this assumption, we account for the English and French word order facts in (20)–(22).

Needless to say, the assumption needs further syntactic motivation. Nevertheless it is fair to state that in order to account for the word order facts, the adjunction theory needs to rely mainly on something which has been defended in the syntactic literature independently (the P head), while the indefinite-in-object-position theory has real problems explaining how the indefinite – which on that theory should be in object position – seems to occur to the left of V in English progressives.

We get the word order facts for English (and French, where you cannot tell, because French does not have the progressive participle): as (22c) shows, the indefinite will appear sandwiched between the perfective and the progressive participle.

Obviously, since in Dutch and German the predicate head, if there were one, would be sitting on the right side, there is no comparable data that could tell whether predication is syntactically realized in these languages.

6.7   Subject–Verb Agreement and Theology

The grammatical theory of predication developed here allows for two distinct semantically based notions of subject, which will usually, but not always, coincide.

Two notions of subject:
The **thematic subject** of a one-place predicate is the noun phrase which receives the thematic role in the theta grid of the predicate.

The **reduction subject** of an unsaturated one-place predicate is the noun phrase that does the semantic reduction from type $<d,<e,t>>$ to type $<e,t>$.

If these are the two grammatically relevant notions of subject, it need not come as a surprise that subject–verb agreement has, in principle, two options: agreement can be with the thematic subject, or with the reduction subject. And, of course, we find both kinds:

Subject–verb agreement:
- German, English, Dutch have agreement with the thematic subject.
- French has agreement with the reduction subject.

Now, all four languages that we are dealing with are non-prodrop languages. As is well known, there is a connection between being a prodrop language and having rich agreement morphology. If so, it is natural to assume that the non-prodrop requirement takes the following form:

Non-prodrop:
The subject that the verb agrees with must be lexically realized.

This does not have any particularly interesting consequences for non-thematic subjects in German, English, and Dutch, since the agreement is with a thematic subject anyway, and not with a non-thematic subject. For French, on the other hand, it implies independently that the non-thematic subject must be lexically realized, and hence it must be realized as *il*.

There is another interesting consequence of this for German. German has one exceptional verb, the verb *geben*, for which subject–verb agreement patterns with French:

German *geben*:
Geben agrees with the reduction subject, and not with the thematic subject.

This is shown in (27):

(27)a. Es gibt   ein Gott.
     Ir gives a   god
   b. Es gibt/# geben viele Götter
     Ir gives/#give   many gods

So *geben* is a special case in German, where the agreement is not with the thematic subject, but with the reduction subject. But now the non-prodrop assumption, as formulated above, makes a prediction about *geben*: the non-prodrop requirement says that the subject that the verb agrees with must be lexically realized. In the case of *geben* this is the non-thematic subject. But that means that we predict that, while the non-thematic subject in German in general can be empty, the non-thematic subject of *geben* cannot be empty, and hence must be realized as *es*, even if it is not in first position under verb second. And this prediction is correct:

(28)a. In Hinduism gibt es viele Götter.
     In Hinduism gives Ir many gods
     In Hinduism, there are many gods.
   b. In Hinduism gibt's   viele Götter.
     In Hinduism gives-Ir many gods

    c.   #In Hinduisim gibt Ø viele Götter.
         In Hinduism gives Ø many gods

We now turn to final questions, such as those raised by the previous examples and those in (29):

(29)a.   There is a God.
    b.   There is a benevolent God.
    c.   #There is God.
    d.   There are angels.

In (29a) we have only a noun phrase in the position open to the definiteness effect of *there*-insertion constructions and no predicate. The DPs in (29) behave in the same way as the adjoined DPs in (30a):

(30)a.   There is a benevolent God in heaven.
    b.   #There is a benevolent God intelligent.

We have, of course, the non-thematic subject, we have the definiteness effects (29c), and we have agreement with the thematic subject (29d). All these things would be very hard to account for, if the DP *a God* in (29a) were the predicate: it wouldn't be adjoined, and we would expect effects of predicate position, but not of adjoined position. Normal predicates need a thematic subject, allow definites, and even nominal predicates show normal agreement with the external subject, as in (31):

(31)   Hesperus and Phospherus are/#is the same planet.

So, if we were to pursue that analysis, we would have to make some rather special assumptions about the interpretation of this construction. The alternative is to assume that the DP is an adjoined indefinite subject also here. This means that it must be adjoined to a saturated predicate.

    Should we follow the lead of the verb *exist*, which is an unaccusative verb, and assume that *be* in (29a) is an unaccusative main verb? This is problematic, because *be* really is not a main verb:

(32)a.   Does there exist a God?
    b.   #Does there be a God?
    c.   Is there a God?

I will take *exist* as my lead, though not in its verbal form, but in its nominal (or prepositional phrase form) *in existence*, as in (33a).

(33)a.   There is a God in existence.
    b.   There is a God Ø.

We start with the PP *in existence*:

[$_{PP}$ *in existence*] → EXIST   of type <d,t>
                     The set of objects actually existing.

This gives us a saturated one-place predicate:

[$_{PRED}$ *in existence*] → [EXIST] of type <e,t>.
                <A$_1$>
The set of states of objects existing.

I assume that this predicate has a null-variant:

[$_{PRED}$ Ø] → [EXIST] of type <e,t>.
        <A$_1$>

This means that (29a) is analyzed as (33b), and has in essence the same structure and semantics as (33a): in (33a), the indefinite *a god* is adjoined to the saturated predicate *in existence*, in (33b) to the null-variant of the latter. For both we derive the following interpretation:

∃s ∈ [EXIST]: GOD(A$_1$(s))

And with the Correspondence Principle this is equivalent to:

∃x[EXIST(x) ∧ GOD(x)]
A god is among the existing things.

Chapter 7

Some Questions about *There*-Insertion in Dutch

Question One
How do you know that the adjoined subject is in an adjunct position, and not in, say, the VP-internal subject position, specifier of VP?

Answer
You don't. The theory I have presented is neutral about there being a VP-internal subject position. Further, the adjoined subject is an adjunct, but also a thematic subject. This means that we may well expect it to show dual behavior. (For instance, Manfred Krifka (personal communication) points out that there are accenting differences between typical adjuncts and typical arguments, and that what I have called the adjoined subject patterns with arguments in this way. I don't find this surprising, since the adjoined subject is the thematic subject, and it doesn't surprise me that the thematic subject patterns with arguments for the purpose of accenting.)

In general, in Dutch it is already practically impossible to determine convincingly that an adjunct is an I' adjunct rather than a VP adjunct, or vice versa (since the heads are sitting on the right side). Whether the expression is adjoined to VP or in the specifier position of VP is *a fortiori* impossible to determine. But then, I have no a priori theory of the specifier position of VP, that is, of the internal subject position of VP.

The main problem with the assumption that the indefinite is in an internal subject position is that this position is a specifier position, which is an argument position. The problem then is that you don't expect definiteness effects. Thus, if you insist that the indefinite is in an internal subject position, you must make the theory of argument positions less unified by assuming that this particular argument position is **semantically** an adjoined position, i.e., that it has the semantics of adjunction. And I am not sure that this move is worth the effort, given that I showed in chapter 5 that we can come up with a perfectly coherent theory which allows the indefinite noun phrase as a thematic subject in adjunct position. Hence, I prefer to stay agnostic on the question of whether there is a VP internal subject position.

Question Two
How do you know that the adjoined subject is inside the I′ and *er* outside (and not, say, the adjoined subject in the IP subject position, and *er* in a higher adverbial position)?

Answer
A first indication are facts about adverb placement in Dutch. The unmarked placement of adverbs is as left adjuncts to I′ or VP. (Since the verbal elements are sitting either at the right side of the tree, or higher up in second position, it is practically impossible to distinguish I′-adjunction from VP-adjunction. I will assume that both are possible.) Indefinite objects can occur to the left of these adverbs, but there is something marked about that order. Similarly, adverbs can occur to the left of the IP subject, but this too is marked.

I use "marked" as a neutral term here, it doesn't mean ungrammatical, infelicitous, nor does it mean that the interpretation is necessarily different. Marked order is an order that feels clearly special, but for which it is often hard to pinpoint exactly why.

(1)a. Netta zei dat Dafna **gisteren**   *een meisje* kuste.   **Unmarked**
        Netta said that Dafna yesterday a   girl   kissed   SUB < **ADV** < OBJ
   b.   Netta zei dat Dafna *een meisje* **gisteren**   kuste.   **Marked**
        Netta said that Dafna a   girl   yesterday kissed   SUB < OBJ < **ADV**
   c.   Netta zei dat **gisteren**   *Dafna* een meisje kuste.   **Marked**
        Netta said that yesterday Dafna a   girl   kissed   **ADV** < SUBJ < OBJ
        Netta said that Dafna kissed a girl yesterday.

We find exactly the same facts for the indefinite adjoined subject (AS is the adjoined subject):

(2)a. Netta zei dat er **gisteren**   *een meisje* op straat   **Unmarked**
        Netta said that pl yesterday a   girl   at street   *er* < **ADV** < AS
        liep.
        walked
   b.   Netta zei dat er *een meisje* **gisteren**   op straat   **Marked**
        Netta said that pl a   girl   yesterday at street   *er* < AS < **ADV**
        liep
        walked
   c.   Netta zei dat **gisteren**   *er* een meisje op straat   **Marked**
        Netta said that yesterday pl a   girl   at street   **ADV** < *er* < AS
        liep
        walked
        Netta said that there was a girl walking in the street yesterday.

We see that with respect to markedness of adverb placement, *er* patterns with the IP subject, while the adjoined subject patterns with the object. The most reasonable explanation for this is that the adjoined subject is inside the I' layer, while *er* is outside.

A second, rather reliable test comes from verb second. In verb second, the inflected verb occurs in second position (standardly taken to be C). The first position must be realized, but there isn't much constraint on what can occupy the first position. Basically, anything can occur there, as long as it is a constituent, and moving it there doesn't violate syntax. Take the following starting structure:

> XP C Fred Dafna een boek gegeven heeft
>   Fred Dafna a   book given   has

The auxiliary moves to C:

> XP *heeft*$_i$ Fred Dafna een boek gegeven Ø$_i$

All of the following are felicitous, and they all involve movement of a constituent:

> Fred *heeft*$_i$ Ø Dafna een boek gegeven Ø$_i$
> Dafna *heeft*$_i$ Fred Ø een boek gegeven Ø$_i$
> Een boek *heeft*$_i$ Fred Dafna Ø gegeven Ø$_i$
> Gegeven *heeft*$_i$ Fred Dafna een boek Ø Ø$_i$
> Een boek gegeven *heeft*$_i$ Fred Dafna Ø Ø$_i$
> Dafna een boek gegeven *heeft*$_i$ Fred Ø Ø$_i$
> Fred has given Dafna a book.

Ungrammatical is, for instance, the following case, where a non-constituent is moved:

> #Dafna gegeven *heeft*$_i$ Fred Ø een boek Ø Ø$_i$

Also ungrammatical, and this is the important case here, is the following:

> #Fred Dafna een boek gegeven Ø$_i$ *heeft*$_i$ Ø

This is strongly ungrammatical, even though we are moving a constituent. The above representation indicates already one major reason why this is ungrammatical. If you want to move a constituent that includes VP-material and the IP subject, you will move the trace in I of the inflected verb in C, and in fact, you will move it over the inflected verb in C. This, anybody will assume, violates syntax, hence the above case is unacceptable.

Now look at the following case:

XP C er drie meisjes op straat gespeeld hebben.
      pl three girls   at street played   have

We move the auxiliary to C:

XP *hebben*$_i$ er drie meisjes op straat gespeeld Ø$_i$

We find the following facts:

er *hebben*$_i$ Ø drie meisjes op straat gespeeld Ø$_i$
drie meisjes *hebben*$_i$ er Ø op straat gespeeld Ø$_i$
op straat *hebben*$_i$ er drie meisjes Ø gespeeld Ø$_i$
gespeeld *hebben*$_i$ er drie meisjes op straat Ø Ø$_i$
op straat gespeeld *hebben*$_i$ er drie meisjes Ø Ø$_i$
drie meisjes op straat gespeeld *hebben*$_i$ er Ø Ø$_i$
#er drie meisjes op straat gespeeld *hebben*$_i$ Ø Ø$_i$
There were three girls playing in the street.

It is the contrast between the last two cases which is crucial here. Moving the adjoined subject along with VP material to first position (as a constituent) is grammatical (with the right intonation), but moving *er* along with VP-material to first position is strongly ungrammatical. This shows convincingly that the adjoined subject is (or can be) part of the VP (hence lower than the trace in I), while *er* must be higher than the trace in I: the adjoined subject is inside the I' layer, while *er* is outside.

Question Three
Is *er* really optional? Couldn't we say that the cases where *er* is not there are really cases where the indefinite is in the IP-subject position?

Answer
The strongest evidence for the optionality of *er* comes from impersonal passives. What we find for impersonal passives is that *er* is optional, although there are cases where it seems obligatory, or virtually obligatory. Let's start with a case like that:

(3)a.   Boven   wordt   er gedanst
         Upstairs is[imperf] pl danced
         Upstairs they do dancing
  b.   ?Boven   wordt   Ø gedanst.

To my ear, out of the blue, (3a) is a lot better than (3b). Nevertheless, I would hesitate to call (3b) really infelicitous or ungrammatical, even out of the blue.

The fact is that how good leaving out *er* is in impersonal passives depends on contextual factors. If you increase the "weight" of the predicate, the example without *er* becomes just as good as the example with *er* (the example relates to a scene downstairs in a flamenco bar. I can't for the life of me remember from which movie):

(4)a. Boven   wordt er voor veel   geld   topless gedanst.
      Upstairs is   pl for   much money topless danced
      Upstairs they do topless dancing for a lot of money
   b. Boven   wordt Ø voor veel   geld   topless gedanst.
      Upstairs is   for   much money topless danced

There really is no difference between the cases in (4a) and (4b), neither in felicity, nor in interpretation. Similar cases (where leaving out *er* is not as good for a less weighty predicate, and becomes fine if you make the predicate more weighty) are easy to find.

Er is of course obligatory in impersonal passives in first position under verb second (we saw that in the last chapter). There is one other case, also related to verb second where *er* seems to be obligatory. As I explained above, since the requirements on what can be in first position under verb second are very minimal, you can raid the VP with verb second, i.e. leave nothing in it. There is nothing dramatic about this: this is, of course, what happens with simple inflected intransitive verbs:

(5) Jan *loopt*$_i$ Ø Ø$_i$
    Jan walks

Let's raid the cases in (3) and (4) (leaving out *boven* to make the first constituent slightly less topheavy):

   XP *wordt*$_i$ er gedanst Ø$_i$
   XP *wordt* er voor veel geld topless gedanst Ø$_i$

We have seen that we cannot move *er* along with the VP material, so leave it in place, but move everything else to first position. You get:

(6)a. Gedanst *wordt* er Ø Ø$_i$
   b. Voor veel geld topless gedanst *wordt* er Ø Ø$_i$

And these cases are perfectly felicitous. Now do the same for the cases without *er*, and the result is strongly ungrammatical:

(7)a. #Gedanst *wordt* Ø Ø Ø$_i$
   b. #Voor veel geld topless gedanst *wordt* Ø Ø Ø$_i$

Thus, as far as non-thematic subjects go, we see that a non-thematic CP-subject must always be lexically realized (for independent reasons), while a non-thematic IP-subject must be lexically realized if the VP is empty. I do not have an explanation to offer, but it seems that this is the way the facts are.

What is so convincing about the comparison with impersonal subjects is that the distribution of *er* really seems to be exactly the same for adjoined subject cases:

(8)a.   Boven   hebben er meisjes gedanst
            Upstairs have   pl girls   danced
    b.   (?)Boven hebben Ø meisjes gedanst

Example (8a) is, of course, fine. While I personally think (8b) is fine too (with the same interpretation as (8a)), other speakers may regard it as questionable, or assign a different interpretation to it (due to, say, the influence of genericity). But, when we make the predicate heavy in exactly the same way as in the impersonal passive cases, then the **minimal pair** (9a) and (9b) no longer differ in felicity, or in interpretation:

(9)a.   Boven   hebben er voor veel   geld   meisjes topless gedanst.
            Upstairs have   pl for   much money girls   topless danced
    b.   Boven   hebben Ø voor veel   geld   meisjes topless gedanst.

Finally, when we raid the VP in verb second we get exactly the same facts as for impersonal passives:

(10)a.   Meisjes gedanst *hebben*$_i$ er Ø Ø$_i$
      b.   Voor veel geld meisjes topless gedanst *hebben*$_i$ er Ø Ø$_i$

(11)a.   #Meisjes gedanst *hebben*$_i$ Ø Ø Ø$_i$
      b.   #Voor veel geld meisjes topless gedanst *hebben*$_i$ Ø Ø Ø$_i$

All in all, the facts suggest that *er* is optional with adjoined subjects in the same way as in impersonal passives.

If we need to assume that in the case *er* is not there, the indefinite is in the IP subject position, we need to reanalyze (9b). The element Ø disappears, since *meisjes* now would be sitting in the IP-subject position, and the prepositional phrase *voor veel geld* must be reanalyzed as an IP-adverb. The problem is that this isn't brought out by the intuitions about markedness of order. As we saw before, the order ADV(PP) < SUB is marked, and that is the order we are supposed to find in (9a). But the order in (9a) is perfectly unmarked.

The position that in Dutch, in the cases without *er*, the indefinite is sitting in the IP subject position is actually taken by Reuland (1988) and, following him, Diesing (1990). They use this assumption to account for the contrast between (12a) and (12b):

(12)a. dat koeien op het dak liggen.
         that cows   on the roof lie
     b. dat er koeien op het dak liggen.
         that pl cows   on the roof lie

Reuland claims that (12a) is infelicitous, while (12b) gets only an existential read-ing. The explanation is that in (12b) *koeien* is inside the VP, and is interpreted existentially there, while in (12a) *koeien* is in the IP subject position, where it cannot get an existential interpretation, but only a generic interpretation. The latter interpretation is not naturally compatible with the locative predicate *op het dak*, hence the infelicity of (12a).

    Diesing argues, following Rullmann (1989), that there is a similar contrast between cases like (13a) and (13b).

(13)a. dat er drie meisjes uit   Parijs aangekomen zijn.
         that pl three girls   from Paris arrived   are
     b. dat drie meisjes uit   Parijs aangekomen zijn.
         that three girls   from Paris arrived   are

The claim is that in (13a) *drie meisjes* has only an existential reading, while in (13b) *drie meisjes* has only an presuppositional reading. By following Reuland in assum-ing that the Dutch IP subject cannot be empty, unlike the German IP subject, Diesing commits herself to a theory which makes much stronger predictions for Dutch than it does for German. Unnecessarily strong predictions, because they are obviously wrong for Dutch. Existential readings without *er* obviously do exist in Dutch as well. (9b) is a case in point, and so are the cases in (14):

(14)a. Ik vind het schokkend dat Ø om twaalf uur   nog kinderen in het
         I think it shocking   that   at twelve o'clock still children in the
         winkelcentrum rondhangen.
         shopping mall hang around
         I find it shocking that at twelve o'clock there are still children hanging
         around in the shopping mall.
     b. Molly zei dat ze de zaal uitgelopen was toen Ø tegen   haar
         Molly said that she the hall walked out was when   against her
         verwachting in zestien altviolisten   op het podium verschenen om
         expectation in sixteen viola players at the stage   appeared   for
         Beethoven's Grosse Fuge uit te voeren.
         Beethoven's Grosse Fuge   to perform
         Molly said that she had walked out of the hall when, against her expecta-
         tion, there appeared sixteen viola players on the stage to perform
         Beethoven's Grosse Fuge.

These cases have perfectly fine existential readings, which you would expect, also on Diesing's theory, if you assume that the IP subject can be empty, and hence the indefinite VP internal.

If you accept that – and I think you should – you do need, of course, a different account of the contrasts in (12) and (13), if you believe that these contrasts are real.

Question Four
How do you know that *er* is in subject position?

Answer
Bennis (1986) raised this question. *Er* has many functions, including, of course, that of a locative adverbial. Bennis argued that these different functions are not unrelated, because he showed that conflation of functions can take place: one *er* that can do two functions simultaneously. If we follow the standard assumption that the *er* that we're concerned with is a subject pleonastic it would be rather a mystery how a DP *er* and an adverbial *er* can be conflated: on the standard assumption, they are unrelated. If, on the other hand *er* is systematically an adverb, how can it occur in subject position? The subject position is a DP argument position, and, as we know, adverbs do not occur in argument position, except when specially licensed.

My analysis is meant to allow us to have our cake and eat it. With Bennis I assume that the *er* of *er*-insertion is an adverb, but unlike him I assume that it is adjoined to Ø in argument position. Thus, *er* is in the subject position, but it isn't the subject, *er* Ø is the subject. But why is it in subject position?

Bennis (1986) assumes, against the standard theory, that *er* is actually an adverb sitting in normal adverbial position. But Bennis puts constraints on the adverb *er* that *de facto* force it to sit right next to the empty IP subject position (except when it occurs in first position in verb second). See Bennis (1986) for details.

Can we distinguish an analysis in which *er* is in subject position from analysis where it is cleverly forced to sit in adverbial position next to an empty subject position?

I think we can, and I think the distinguishing argument shows that *er* really is in argument position. Again, we come back to verb second effects. As we have seen several times, the verb second effect in Dutch requires one constituent to be in first position if the inflected verb is in the second position. The verb second effect is, in general, very strong. Thus, if the inflected verb is in second position, and we try to put both the IP subject and an adverb in first position, the result is crashingly bad:

(15)a. *#Morgen   Netta* zal Dafna kussen.
       Tomorrow Netta will Dafna kiss
       Tomorrow Netta will kiss Dafna.
  b. *#Netta morgen* zal Dafna kussen.

Now, when we violate the verb second condition by putting two adverbs in first position, that is, two expressions that without verb second would occur in adverbial position in the sentence, the sentence is also not good, but by far not as crashingly bad as (15):

(16)a.   ?*Morgen   buiten* zal Netta Dafna kussen.
         Tomorrow outside will Netta Dafna kiss
         Tomorrow Netta will kiss Dafna outside.
    b.   ?*Buiten morgen* zal Netta Dafna kussen.

Presumably, when the two expressions are both adverbs, the processor makes a heroic (but not completely successful) attempt at reconstructing them as a single (stacked) adverbial phrase.

The question now is what happens if we violate the verb second condition by putting an adverb and *er* in first position?

(17)a.   #*Morgen   er*   zal een meisje Dafna kussen.
         Tomorrow there will a   girl   Dafna kiss
         Tomorrow there will be a girl kissing Dafna.
    b.   #*Er morgen* zal een meisje Dafna kussen

The answer is that the cases in (17) are crashingly bad, as crashingly bad as those in (15). This is expected if *er* is sitting in the subject position, but not if it is an adverb in adverbial position generated right next to an empty subject position.

It seems, then, that *er* does really pattern with subjects, and not with expressions in normal adverbial position.

Question Five
Is there any semantic difference between sentences with *er* and the indefinite adjoined to VP, and the same sentences without *er* and the indefinite in IP subject position?

Answer
None whatsoever. That's a major attraction of the analysis.

This answer may be a bit too short, so I will reformulate the question in the form of three more detailed questions.

Question Six
What semantic differences between the *er*-insertion construction and the construction with the indefinite in subject position do we expect, due to independent factors?

Answer
In the first place, I have ignored **genericity** completely. Now this is a topic that I want to stay away from here as much as possible. But, of course, I will assume,

with everybody else, that the generic interpretation mechanism can apply to indefinites in subject position, while the same mechanism cannot apply to the adjoined subject. This will predict that sentence (18a) has a generic interpretation that (18b) lacks.

(18)a.   (dat) een meisje danst.
      that a   girl   dances
   b.   (dat) er een meisje danst.
      that pl a   girl   dances

So there is no problem with predicting generic interpretations.

At the same time, I am not restricting the interpretation possibilities for IP subject position. While generic interpretations are possible, the analysis I have developed also generates sentences with indefinites in subject position with an existential interpretation: the standard derivation of (18a) (which does not invoke a generic operator or anything) will derive the very same existential reading for (18a) as it does for (18b). In this respect, the theory of the IP subject follows Montague's standard analysis.

Of course, the analysis of genericity will need to have something to say about cases where non-generic interpretations of indefinite IP subjects range from problematic to marginal (e.g. with non-episodic predicates). This discussion, important as it is, I want to stay out of here.

Secondly, as explained in chapter 3, the theory of definiteness effects that I have given here does not rely on positions being marked as part of the syntax–semantic interface for an opposition weak–strong. Indefiniteness effects come in as a consequence of adjunction involving type <d,t>. There is no grammatical restriction which says that DPs generated inside the VP must (or can) be weak, while DPs generated in the IP subject position must be strong. This means too that the theory does not rely on any notion of strong indefinite.

Again, let me be clear about what I think you get for free from independent assumptions about the grammar and its interfaces. I assume that anybody's grammatical theory will need to assume an interface level which has access to syntax, semantics, intonational structure, and discourse structure including topic/focus articulation. The latter arguably involves some pragmatic notion of old and new information, and I assume that there is no reason to ignore the abundant research on this topic, showing, with all due qualifications, a connection between the higher regions of the syntactic tree (including the IP subject position) and the discourse notion of topic, old information, on the one hand, and the lower regions of the syntactic tree (including the adjoined positions) and the discourse notion of focus, new information, on the other.

This means that, on anybody's theory, we can expect the IP subject position to be a natural position for definites, and not so natural a position for non-generic indefinites. It means, on anybody's theory, that, when non-generic indefinites do occur in IP subject position, we can expect some markedness, and we can expect some discourse linking effects, stemming from the natural tendency to interpret what occurs in this position as topic.

But since we're relying here on discourse structure and pragmatics, we expect these effects to be quite weak. This holds the other way round too: DPs in adjoined position may have a tendency to be interpreted as providing non-discourse linked information, but we expect this effect to be weak as well. In this, my analysis differs from theories in which the grammar links the positions IP-subject and adjoined DP (or internal subject as it may be in other theories) to a semantic strong–weak distinction.

In sum then, I do accept that there is something "presentational" to *there*-insertion contexts, and something "non-presentational" to indefinites in the IP subject position. But I assume that this just follows from what anybody assumes about the pragmatics of topic–focus articulation anyway: the *there*-insertion construction provides a way of putting the subject in a position which is not biased towards topic interpretation, and that's where the presentational effects stem from.

Thus I do not assume that *there*-insertion constructions have, semantically, a "presentational meaning," let alone that this is something brought in by the meaning of *there*.

Thus, there is in the analysis of indefinites a role for pragmatic notions of discourse linking, but I assume that these effects are weak (or, more appropriately, when we think about mechanisms for assigning and reassigning discourse structure, avoidable). What I mean by "weak" is that, even though I assume with everybody else that there is a tendency for IP subjects to be discourse linked, indefinite IP subjects are not forced to be either generic or discourse linked by the grammar. Hence, one would expect that discourse linking in IP subject position can be overruled in appropriate contexts.

Similarly, even if one takes a functional perspective and thinks of the *there*-insertion construction as a strategy to avoid the subject being in topic position, indefinite adjoined DPs are not made non-discourse linked by the grammar (though, for independent reasons, they cannot be generic), and again, we expect that their general tendency to be non-discourse linked can be overruled in context.

Thus, I assume that differences in meaning, in the broad sense, between the two types of indefinite constructions come in as a consequence of the interaction with the theory of genericity and topic–focus interaction. But I assume that there is no semantic difference, over and above the weak interactional effects mentioned.

Question Seven
What about the assumption that the adjoined subject position (or VP internal subject position) must be weak?

Answer
There are two main reasons why one would expect the adjoined indefinite to rather strongly favor a weak, existential, non-discourse linked interpretation.

One is, as mentioned, its occurrence in a region of the syntactic tree which is readily interpreted as part of the focus and not the topic area. From a pragmatic point of view, one would expect this effect to be rather pervasive, because of the existence of a minimal alternative (the case without *er*), which doesn't put the indefinite in this area.

The other reason follows from the Variable Constraint. The Variable Constraint tells us that the adjoined indefinite cannot take wide scope. Now, I am not assuming that the scope mechanism as applied to indefinites forces grammatically the wide scope indefinite to be discourse linked. That is, my position here is similar to my position on the association of these effects with grammatical position: independent considerations about the interface already make you expect the effects found, so that there is no need to derive them from the grammar. But one doesn't need to swing to the other extreme either. There is no need to deny that discourse linking is a time honored device to bring out wide scope interpretations, which means, of course, that by assigning wide scope to an indefinite, one doesn't have to do much work at the interface to get a discourse linked interpretation for it.

That option is not available in the adjoined position, hence if you insist on avoiding the default pragmatics for the adjoined indefinite, you will need to rely on other methods to bring out the interpretation. This means that, ceteris paribus, you would expect adjoined subjects to be more frequently and more readily interpreted as non-discourse linked than direct objects, because the latter do have the option of the scope mechanism.

How would you override the course of nature for adjoined indefinites? Well, for instance, by indicating that the focus isn't the indefinite itself, but some aspect of it. If we want to put focus on part of the indefinite, we may well choose to put the whole indefinite in the region where we naturally expect to find the focus, but without forcing the whole indefinite noun phrase to be discourse "new." In such a case, we would find precisely the kind of interpretation that the theory that links the weak–strong distinction to grammatical position claims to be impossible. Such is the case in (19). Since the examples are long, I give the paraphrase first, and a gloss of the relevant part separately.

(19) Er gingen acht kinderen mee op reis. Vier hadden brood bij zich, twee hadden geld bij zich, en er hadden *twee kinderen* helemaal niets bij zich.

Eight children came along on the trip. Four had bread with them, two had money with them, and two of them had absolutely nothing with them.

. . . er hadden *twee kinderen* helemaal   niets   bij   zich.
. . . pl had   two children completely nothing with SELF

In (19), we set up a context which includes a set of eight children. And then we specify, for subgroups, what they had taken along. The focus in the last sentence in the discourse is naturally on the numerical part *twee* of the adjoined indefinite *twee kinderen*, and on *niets* (*nothing*), and not on the full indefinite. The full indefinite is obviously discourse linked to the set of children introduced before. That is, it is **presuppositional** in the sense of Rullmann and Diesing. But (19) is fine.

The effect of this end of the discourse is not semantic, not even discourse semantic (i.e. in terms of old–new structure), but purely pragmatic: there is an **implicature**: "isn't it outrageous, to send your children on a trip without anything?" Similar cases can be produced readily:

(20)   Ik denk dat je de koeien van boer Jansen nog maar eens moet tellen, want Erik heeft me net verteld dat er *twee koeien* op het dak liggen.

I think that you should recount the cows of farmer Jansen, because Erik has just told me that two of them are lying on the roof.

... dat er *twee koeien* op het dak liggen.
... that pl two cows on the roof lie

Again, (20) is fine on the interpretation where *twee koeien* is discourse linked to the set of cows of farmer Jansen. In this case, the idea of cows lying on the roof is so outrageous, that *roof* naturally attracts the focus. The indefinite needs not be focused at all, and the sentence is still good.

I take it to be very clear, then, that the hypothesis that the grammar tells us that the adjoined indefinite must be discourse new, non-presuppositional is untenable.

Question Eight
What about the assumption that indefinites in the IP subject position must be strong?

Answer
I want to start with setting the stage with example (21) from *De Uitvreter* by Nescio (pretty randomly chosen, similar examples abound). As we will see, this example does not prove anything about the IP subject position, but it does, I think, say something about the notion of topic.

(21)   Overal hoorde je op de waranda's deuren opengaan, **de menschen** kwamen buiten. *Sommigen* applaudisseerden mee; *een kind* begon te huilen; *een hond* jankte alsof binnen een maand 't heele blok zou komen uit te sterven.

All around, you could hear doors opening on the balconies, **people** coming outside. *Some* applauded along; *a child* started to cry; *a dog* howled as if within a month the whole block would die out.

The domain of quantification is given here by *de menschen*, which is interpreted as the people living in the neighborhood. The first indefinite *sommigen* (*some*) is obviously linked directly to this set. It is not so clear that the second indefinite *een kind* is linked to this set (the scene is set in Holland, at the beginning of the twentieth century, in the late evening, which induces a natural contextual restriction to grown-ups, which does not get canceled: the whole discourse implies that the grown-ups came outside on their balconies.) The third indefinite, *een hond* is, for biological reasons beyond our control, not linked to this set. In fact, if we need to regard this indefinite as linked, then only in the weakest of senses, in that we might reasonably assume that in a populated neighborhood some people might keep dogs, and that the set of dogs kept by people in the neighborhood can be activated contextually. But, arguably, any indefinite can be discourse linked in this weak sense (which can be seen when we replace in the above discourse *een hond jankte* by *er jankte een hond*, which makes no difference for discourse linking.)

The stylistic effect of the sequence of initial indefinites here is not discourse linking in the way it is standardly understood. Rather the effect is the auditory equivalent of a panoramic nightview in which a spot light lights up different bits in turn. I think that this is a topic effect, and it shows, I think, that the stronger notion of discourse linking as linking to a set presupposed in the discourse is only one of a range of topic effects.

On this view, we expect a difference between what we could call focus effects and topic effects for indefinites. I have argued before that there are a variety of factors that conspire to strengthen presentational effects for indefinite adjuncts. While I argued that the effects can be circumvented, I do agree with everybody else that there really are such effects and that they are usually quite clear.

When it comes to discourse linking as a topic effect, I think that topic can play too many different discourse functions to expect any clear effects here. As a consequence, I expect to find what in fact we do seem to find: distinctions and effects that are too weak to seriously base a semantic theory on.

In all this discussion, I am, of course, not denying that there are genericity effects associated with subject indefinites, nor that genericity affects episodic predicates and non-episodic predicates in different ways. I am focusing here on claims concerning obligatory discourse linking of non-generic indefinites in IP subject position. What I am claiming is that the facts are so subtle, the effects so weak, and what we find so much expected for independent reasons, that it isn't reasonable to invent a semantic notion of "strong indefinite" to cover them.

The example in (21) should not be taken as a counterexample to the claim that indefinites in IP subject position must be strong. Since the indefinites are all in first position under verb second, we do not need to assume that they come from the IP subject position: they could come from the position adjoined to VP. With excuses to Nescio, we can undo the verb second effect, this makes no difference, except in literary quality:

(22) Overal hoorde je op de waranda's deuren opengaan, je hoorde hoe **de menschen** buiten kwamen. Je hoorde hoe *sommigen* mee applaudisseerden: je hoorde hoe *een kind* begon te huilen; je hoorde hoe *een hond* jankte alsof binnen een maand 't heele blok zou komen uit te sterven.

All around, you could hear doors opening on the balconies, you heard how **people** came outside. You heard how *some* applauded along; you heard how *a child* started to cry; you heard how *a dog* howled as if within a month the whole block would die out.

As I argued before, if we were to accept Reuland and Diesing's theory – which assumes that the indefinites must be in the IP subject position in (22) and cannot be semantically reconstructed as being lower down – then cases like (22) are counterexamples to the claim that indefinites in IP subject position must be strong (and in fact it is very easy to find counterexamples of all sorts).

There are two ways out. In the first place, one can maintain that the relevant indefinites must be in IP subject position, but that Dutch is like Diesing assumes English to be: Dutch allows semantic reconstruction of the IP subject lower down.

I have already indicated above that I do not find this way out very plausible (since you must tinkle considerably with markedness assumptions about adverb placement). The analysis would predict that the position of the indefinite as the IP subject does not, in the end, make a semantic difference at all.

In English, you at least still get a difference with episodic versus non-episodic predicates, but as we have seen, there is no such distinction in Dutch. And indeed, both (23a) and (23b), with a non-episodic predicate, differing only in the presence of *er*, allow non-discourse linked interpretations:

(23)a. De leraar Klassieke Talen voorspelt somber dat in twintig
The teacher Classical Languages predicts somberly that in twenty
jaar nog maar heel weinig mensen Latijn en Grieks kennen.
years still only very few people Latin and Greek know

b. De leraar Klassieke Talen voorspelt somber dat in twintig
The teacher Classical Languages predicts somberly that in twenty
jaar er nog maar heel weinig mensen Latijn en Grieks kennen.
years pl still only very few people Latin and Greek know

The classics teacher predicts somberly that in twenty years time only very few people will know Latin and Greek.

This means that the proposal is no longer that indefinites in the IP subject position are interpreted as strong, but only, that they are interpreted as strong, if they are not semantically reconstructed in a position where they are interpreted as weak. This means that, effectively, it predicts nothing, and we can just as well not link strength to the IP subject position, and still get the facts right.

The second way out is what I have been assuming: Dutch is like German in that the IP subject position can be empty. This means that cases without *er* have in principle two structural analyses, one, where the IP subject is empty, and the indefinite is VP-internal, and one, where the indefinite is in the IP subject position. In this case, we could test the theory about strong IP subjects, if we had a reliable test for telling when a (non-generic) indefinite is in either position. The problem is that I don't think that there is such a test.

For German, Diesing proposes that interpolation adverbials like *ja doch* provide such a test. She assumes that a DP which occurs (in embedded sentences) to the left from *ja doch* must be in the IP subject position, because the adverbials like *ja doch* are generated at the VP-boundary (or the I'-boundary, that makes no difference for the present discussion).

While Diesing initially suggests that it works the other way round too – what is right of *ja doch* is VP internal, and hence predicted to be weak – she does not maintain the latter suggestion all the way through. As Diesing shows, indefinites can have generic interpretations while occurring right of *ja doch* or *denn*, and, consequently, Diesing assumes that *ja doch* can occur adjoined to IP.

Diesing supports her assumption about these adverbials with facts about generic interpretation and extraction. Bare plurals occurring left of *ja doch* must be interpreted generically, and *was für* split and numerical split are ungrammatical from indefinites left of *ja doch* (the extraction facts she attributes to Angelika Kratzer). Diesing provides an account on which *was für* split from IP subjects (but not VP internal subjects) is ungrammatical, and uses this to motivate her assumption that *denn* marks the VP boundary.

I cannot here pass judgment on the strength of the contrasts that are cited in Diesing (1990) for German. The corresponding Dutch facts are as follows:

(24)a. Wat   hebben *toch*   voor mieren jou gebeten?
        What have   I-ASK-YOU for   ants   you bitten
        What kind of ants were they, I ask you, that bit you?
   b.   Wat hebben *toch* jou voor mieren gebeten?
   c.   Wat hebben jou *toch* voor mieren gebeten?
   d.   Wat hebben jou voor mieren *toch* gebeten?
   e.   Wat hebben voor mieren *toch* jou gebeten?
   f.   Wat hebben voor mieren jou *toch* gebeten?

The pattern of markedness that we find here is, I think, the standard pattern for markedness in the middle field. Definite noun phrases and adverbials do not show a strong ordering preference – definites are leaning slightly to the left; indefinites are less marked when they occur right of definites and when they occur right of adverbials. This makes (24c) the most unmarked order, and

(24e) the most marked order, and the others somewhere in between. This agrees with my intuitions.

But it would be strongly incorrect to call the marked cases ungrammatical or infelicitous. For each of these cases you can find various intonation patterns that make them quite acceptable (for instance, stress on the finite verb and the perfective participle improves all of them), and these patterns may suggest different information structures, but it is actually very difficult to pinpoint what the differences actually are.

Importantly, in (24c), (24d), and (24f) *toch* obviously does not mark the VP boundary, because the direct object is to the left of it. But this means that the discussion of where the adverbial is cannot be seen separately from the discussion about the middle field and issues of scrambling. And since the data concerning order in the middle field, and its interpretation – except for unstressed definite pronouns – is incredibly complicated and non-robust, it would be unwise to accept leftness of indefinites with respect to adverbials like *toch* as a robust test for them being in IP subject position.

The middle field data are, I think, of extreme delicacy. Consider the following examples (a take-off on Wagner's attitude towards Hermann Levi):

(25)a. Richard brieste dat hij net binnen was, toen *er*, **ja toch speciaal om HEM te beledigen**, een JOOD de dirigeerstok opnam om ZIJN Idyll te spelen.

  b. Richard brieste dat hij net binnen was, toen Ø, **ja toch speciaal om HEM te beledigen**, een JOOD de dirigeerstok opnam om ZIJN Idyll te spelen.

  c. Richard brieste dat hij net binnen was, toen *er* een JOOD, **ja toch speciaal om HEM te beledigen**, de dirigeerstok opnam om ZIJN Idyll te spelen.

  d. Richard brieste dat hij net binnen was, toen Ø een JOOD, **ja toch speciaal om HEM te beledigen**, de dirigeerstok opnam om ZIJN Idyll te spelen.

  Richard fumed that he had just come in, when a JEW, indeed just to offend HIM, took up the baton to play HIS Idyll.

There are ever so subtle differences between these examples. The order of the indefinite *een jood* and the adverbial phrase *ja toch om HEM te beledigen* is unmarked in (25a) and (25b), but marked in (25c) and (25d). Because of the natural connection between the adverbial phrase as a comment on the stressed part of the indefinite, the markedness effect is present, but very weak: all cases in (25) are clearly acceptable (even though (25a) is slightly smoother than (25c), and (25b) slightly smoother than (25d)).

Let us consider (25c) now. Since *er* is present, the indefinite is the adjoined subject. But then the indefinite adjoined subject can occur right of the adverbial phrase, which means that Diesing's test breaks down for these Dutch examples.

Clearly it need not be the case that what occurs right of the adverbial phrase can only be the external subject. In fact, when the appropriate pragmatic connections and intonation are provided, even **indefinite objects** can occur right of these adverbials, with only weak markedness:

(26)a.   Richard brieste dat de koning, ja toch speciaal om HEM te beledigen, een JOOD tot hofdirigent had benoemd.
   b.   Richard brieste dat de koning een JOOD, ja toch speciaal om HEM te beledigen, tot hofdirigent had benoemd.

     Richard fumed that the king, indeed especially to offend HIM, had appointed a JEW as court conductor.

In the examples given here, I have indicated a stress pattern that makes the examples particularly easy. A standard reaction to this is: Ah yes, but if you assign the sentence "neutral focus," then the adverbial does pick out the external subject reliably, and then the examples are ungrammatical.

However, there is actually a wide variety of stress patterns (and contexts) on which the examples are acceptable, and not all of them require focus on the indefinite. As is well known from focus theory, what interpretations a particular focus assignment will pick out is strongly influenced by information structure, in particular the question–answer structure in discourse (see e.g. Kadmon and Roberts 1986, Roberts 1996, Kadmon 2001). This means that I think that it is advisable to be rather skeptical about the concept of "ungrammaticality on neutral focus." And this means that we cannot accept the placement of sentence adverbials as a reliable test for IP subject position. (Diesing has some discussion of focus issues, but it seems that the questions she discusses are really tangential to the questions discussed here.)

This means, then, that the assumption that non-generic indefinites in the IP subject position are obligatorily discourse linked or presuppositional is in effect untestable, because you cannot show for any counterexample where an indefinite has a non-presuppositional reading, that the indefinite in question must be analyzed as being in the IP subject position.

What we have seen in the answers to the last two questions is that basically in any of the relevant surface string positions you can get discourse linked or non-discourse linked interpretations for indefinites (as you would expect, if you believe, as I do, that this notion is a pragmatic notion). And this means that, with respect to this relatively well defined notion of discourse linking, which we find in the work of de Jong and Verkuyl (1985), Rullmann (1989), and Diesing (1990), the grammatical hypothesis linking strength to IP subject position, and weakness to VP-internal subject position is either false or untestable. This obviously means that, for theories that use weaker (or less well defined notions of discourse linkedness) the prospects are worse: they cannot avoid being completely untestable. Thus, at the current stage of the available theories, I advise agnosticism about the usefulness in grammatical theory of notions of strong indefinites.

Question Nine
Then what about theories that assume that marked orders of indefinites and adverbials are due to scrambling, and scrambled indefinites must be interpreted as strong?

Answer
The cases in (25c) and (25d) are also relevant here. What I have argued is that, while there may be subtle differences between the examples in (25), there is no clear difference in discourse-linkedness or presuppositionality: all the examples in (25) clearly allow non-discourse linked, non-presuppositional interpretations for the indefinite.

If we assume, as is commonly done, that in (25c) and (25d) the indefinite is **scrambled** over the adverbial phrase, then the assumption that indefinites scrambled over adverbials are strong is also untenable.

Again, I am not denying that there are weak–strong effects associated with scrambling structures, meaning that there is some sort of connection between the order of definites, indefinites, and adverbials in the middle field and weak–strong effects. For instance, it is true, I think, is that if the construction involves an indefinite and a scopal adverb, then the marked order is not scopally ambiguous in the way that the unmarked scope order is (when you think about it, this is not really surprising). And, of course, as is well known, ordering facts about adverbs and unstressed pronouns are very strong:

(27)a.   Ik heb *'m* **gisteren** gezien.
       I   have him yesterday seen
       I saw him yesterday.
   b.   #Ik heb **gisteren** *'m* gezien

But there is good reason to assume that the facts in (27) are a separate story. Schaeffer (1998) shows that the facts in (27) are acquired sharply and practically instantaneously around age three, while acceptability facts concerning ordering facts involving full definites, indefinites, and adverbs are acquired in a long and slow process up to age 11 or beyond, if it ever stops. If it ever stops, because Schaeffer's comparison adult data show remarkable deviation from the theoretical standard, much more than you would expect, if the weak–strong distinction is grammaticized as the theory proposes. In short, these data are much too complex and subtle to be simply and neatly tied to a grammatical weak–strong distinction.

It never fails to surprise me when time and again in presentations the markedness facts are presented as clear grammaticality judgments, whether the claim is of the form "indefinites to the left of adverbials are ungrammatical" or of the form "**weak** indefinites to the left of adverbials are ungrammatical." I wish people would stop making these claims.

Chapter 8

The Problem of Negative
Noun Phrases

8.1 Negative Noun Phrases in Argument Position

I discussed the analysis of downward entailing noun phrases like *at most three girls* in earlier chapters.

(1) At most three girls danced.

On the maximalization account (1) is analyzed as follows:

> **Existence:** There is a sum of events in the set of all sums of dancing events (including the null event), whose agent is in the set of all sums of girls (including the null object) and has at most three atoms below it.
>
> **Maximality:** The sum of the agents of all dancing events with girls as agent has at most three atoms below it.

The idea is, here, that the plural noun *girls* has, by default, the null object in it, and the downward closed modifier does not eliminate it. Secondly, the verbal predicate is assumed to contain, by default, the null event. Consequently, the existence statement, by its semantics, is simply a tautology, and can be ignored.

Of course, the use of *at most three* may easily in context bring in an implicature: not null. And the semantics of the verbal part may eliminate null by itself. In that case, the existence statement does have existential import, as an existence implicature or entailment. While this makes the semantics of (1) dependent on the pragmatic manipulation of the null object (and this may have many ramifications that need to be considered), I have argued that it is a fruitful way of dealing with cases like (1).

In Landman (2000), I presented various arguments for assuming that negative noun phrases are different, and do not fall under the maximalization strategy. At this point it is useful, though, to see what the maximalization analysis would predict for negative noun phrases, like the one in (2):

(2)   No girls danced.

The obvious way to do this is by analyzing *no* as *exactly zero*. This gives the following semantics:

> **Existence:**   There is a sum of events in the set of all sums of dancing events (including the null event), whose agent is in the set of all sums of girls (including the null object) and has no atoms below it.
>
> **Maximality:** The sum of all agents of dancing events with girls as agent has no atoms below it.

The existence statement is, once again, trivial, and the maximality statement gives the correct semantics for (2): the maximality statement is equivalent to the statement that the sum of dancing events with girls as agent is the null event, which means, of course, that there are no girls dancing.

Thus, the analysis of *no* as *exactly zero* seems to have a lot going for it. Despite this, in Landman (2000), I argued against this analysis. My reasons had to do with cumulative readings. While downward entailing numerical noun phrases engage in scopeless, cumulative readings, *no* doesn't seem to. Look at the examples in (3):

(3)a.   At most two girls kissed at most six boys.
  b.   No girls kissed at most six boys.
  c.   At most two girls kissed no boys.

Example (3a) has a natural cumulative interpretation: the total number of girls kissing a boy is at most two and the total number of boys kissed by a girl is at most six. Such a scopeless reading is non-existent in (3b) and (3c), the only readings that we get are scopal.

The problem is, that if *no girls* is analyzed as *exactly zero girls*, and with that interpretation subject to the maximalization theory, we predict that there is a scopeless reading after all, and in fact, we predict, that (3b) and (3c) have a reading on which they are equivalent to the most natural reading of (4):

(4)   No girl kissed any boy.

For (3b) we get: the sum of the set of kissing events with girls as agent and boys as theme has the null object as agent; for (3c) we get that this sum has the null object as theme. In either case, it will denote the null event, hence the equivalence with (4). But, of course, (3b) and (3c) do not have that reading!

This means, then, that it won't do to analyze negative noun phrases as the borderline case of downward closed numerical noun phrases. (On the contrary, I argued in Landman (2000), that the inverse seems to happen: while *zero boys*

looks like a numerical noun phrase with a borderline number, it is semantically **reanalyzed** as a negative noun phrase.) One reason is that the cases in (5)
are not equivalent to (4) either:

(5)a.   Zero girls kissed at most six boys.
   b.   At most two girls kissed zero boys.

Another reason (given in Landman 2000) is that the number zero doesn't
pattern with other numbers. Unlike *three girls*, *zero girls* only has an *exactly-*
interpretation in argument position.

Thus, for negative noun phrases in argument position I assume, following
Landman (2000), that they have their normal interpretation at the type of generalized quantifiers <d,<d,t>>, that their interpretation is not added in situ
to the event type (where they would fall under the maximalization theory),
but that negative noun phrases in argument position must take scope over the
event type.

8.2   Negative Noun Phrases in Predicate and Adjunct Position

Negative noun phrases pattern with indefinites, and they are allowed in predicative position and in contexts of indefiniteness:

(6)a.   De gasten zijn *geen meisjes*.
        The guests are no   girls
        The guests aren't girls.
   b.   Er zit *geen spek*   in de val.
        pl sits no   bacon in the trap.
        There isn't any bacon in the mouse trap.
   c.   Er speelt *geen meisje* in de tuin.
        pl plays no   girl   in the garden
        There isn't any girl playing in the garden.

We have seen in chapter 2 that Partee (1987) assumes that at type <d,t>, *geen
meisje* (*no girl*) denotes ATOM – GIRL. The problem of deriving the correct interpretation for negative noun phrases is even more acute in *there*-insertion contexts, than in argument position.

The analysis of *there*-insertion contexts that I have given separated the
semantic contribution of the adjoined subject and the non-thematic subject:
the interpretation of the adjoined subject is added intersectively to the VP interpretation as a one-place predicate; in particular, as a restriction on the value
of the relevant **role** of the one-place predicate.

Existential closure over the value of this role comes in as part of the semantic
reduction from type <d,<e,t>> to <e,t>, i.e. through the interpretation of the

non-thematic subject. This means that, if we choose, with Partee, ATOM – GIRL as the interpretation of *no girl*, and we just follow the analysis of *there*-insertion given in previous chapters, we cannot but derive (6c) with the incorrect interpretation (6d):

(6)c.   Er speelt geen meisje in de tuin.
    d.   ∃e[PLAY(e) ∧ Ag(e) ∈ ATOM-GIRL ∧ IN(e)=σ(GARDEN)]
         Some non-girl plays in the garden.

The diagnosis of what goes wrong is straightforward. The standard assumption in event theories (see Landman 2000) is that negation needs to take scope over the event type. What we see in the cases in (6) is that that holds also for nominal negation, and that it holds regardless of whether the negative noun phrase is an argument, a predicate, or an adjunct.

   This is not a problem for negative noun phrases in argument position, because we can give them wide scope with the scope mechanism. But it is a problem for negative noun phrases in predicative or adjoined position, because the variable constraint prevents us from giving them wide scope.

8.3   Semantic Break-up

What we have seen for negative noun phrases in argument position holds for auxiliary negation as well: auxiliary negation must take scope over the event type. I will start by providing a simple mechanism that does that. First, I will assume that while auxiliary negation is sitting under I, its semantics is that of a sentence operator of type <t,t>:

Auxiliary negation
niet (not) → ¬   of type <t,t>

Since the complement of I is of type <d,<e,t>> this obviously gives a type mismatch. I will assume – against standard assumptions – that negation cannot type shift, and hence the mismatch must be resolved in a different way. The resolution mechanism is a **type-driven scope mechanism**. It consists of a type-driven storage mechanism:

Storage of negation by type mismatch:
Negation gets stored if there is a type mismatch with its complement.

As usual, the stored element is carried along in the derivation in a store. And there is a type-driven retrieval mechanism:

Retrieval of negation by type matching:
Negation gets retrieved from store **as soon as** the input type matches.

We can show that this mechanism indeed does what it is supposed to do: give auxiliary negation scope over the event type. Consider example (7):

(7) Dafna zwemt niet.
     Dafna swims not

The VP *zwem* has type <d,<e,t>>. The auxiliary negation has type <t,t>; there is a type mismatch, hence it is stored:

$\lambda x \lambda e.$SWIM(e) $\wedge$ Ag(e)=x   STORE: ¬
of type <d,<e,t>>

This combines with the subject, we get an interpretation of type <e,t>, maximalization derives an interpretation of type t:

$\exists e$[SWIM(e) $\wedge$ Ag(e)=DAFNA]   STORE: ¬
of type t

We have reached the correct input type for ¬, hence ¬ must come out of store, and we get:

¬$\exists e$[SWIM(e) $\wedge$ Ag(e)=DAFNA]   of type t

(Obviously, when there is more than one element that can be retrieved at this point (in particular, a subject), there is room for some variation, including cross-linguistic variation, as to what "retrieve **as soon as** the types match" exactly means in this case.)

This is a very simple mechanism that gives you, semantically, Montague's semantics for negation – nothing more, nothing less (Montague 1973). Of course, I am well aware that there is a lot more to be said about negation, its interaction with scope, etc. I am keeping things as simple as I can here, because I am really concerned with fitting my problematic cases into a relatively standard account with as little effort as possible. So, for my purposes here, Montague's analysis, which gives negation sentential scope (and hence will have to give the subject wide scope to derive a reading where it has scope over negation, or where it distributes over negation) works well enough.

We now come to the proposal for nominal negation. For the derivation of argument interpretations, I have already discussed the strategy in chapter 2: a strategy of semantic break-up:

Semantic break-up:
Semantically, negative noun phrases of the form *no girl* can be broken up into a negation and an indefinite noun phrase.
The negation can take scope independently from the remainder indefinite noun phrase.

In fact, I need to add only one more assumption to the analysis already given, namely the specification of the semantics of nominal negation. I will assume that nominal negation has two interpretation possibilities:

Nominal negation

$geen$ (no) $\rightarrow \neg_n$ where n is $<t,t>$ or $<<<d,t>,t>,<<d,t>,t>>$

Thus nominal negation is interpreted either as $\neg$ of type $<t,t>$, or as $\lambda T \lambda P. \neg T(P)$ of type $<<<d,t>,t>,<<d,t>,t>>$. On the first interpretation, nominal negation is incorporated auxiliary negation. On the second interpretation, nominal negation is a noun phrase modifier (like *only, all,* and, as we have seen, *er*). So, on this analysis, nominal negation is not a determiner.

Thus, we have the following situation: the semantic interpretation of the noun phrase *geen meisje* needs to combine nominal negation $\neg$ and the noun phrase interpretation GIRL of type $<d,t>$. Since $\neg_n$ requires either type t or $<<d,t>,t>$ as input, there is a type mismatch, and negation is stored. So we derive:

> *geen meisje* $\rightarrow$ GIRL   STORE: $\neg_n$
>   of type $<d,t>$

The negative noun phrase can occur in argument position, predicative position, or adjoined position in *there*-insertion.

In argument position, we apply existential closure to derive an argument interpretation of type $<<d,t>,t>$. As usual with storage, we apply this to the non-stored part of the interpretation. This gives the following argument interpretation for *geen meisje*:

> $\lambda P. \exists x[GIRL(x) \wedge P(x)]$ STORE: $\neg_n$
> of type $<<d,t>,t>$

$<<d,t>,t>$ is one of the input types for nominal negation, hence $\neg_n$ must be retrieved at this point and we get the correct interpretation of the noun phrase in argument position (which then will be sensitive to the scopal requirements for argument noun phrases):

> $\lambda P. \neg \exists x[GIRL(x) \wedge P(x)]$ of type $<<d,t>,t>$

The non-stored part of the interpretation of *geen meisje* is of set type $<d,t>$, hence *geen meisje* can occur in predicative and adjoined position, and the semantic composition just follows the semantic composition of *a girl* in predicative and adjoined position, with $\neg_n$ stored. Such derivations do not go through type $<<d,t>,t>$, but will, after maximalization reach type t. So we get for predicative position

(8)   Avrum is geen meisje.

$\exists s[s \in [GIRL] \wedge A_1(s)=AVRUM]$ STORE: $\neg_n$
of type t

which is equivalent to:

GIRL(AVRUM)   STORE: $\neg_n$
of type t

The negation must come out of store here, hence we derive:

$\neg$GIRL(AVRUM)   of type t

The story is exactly the same for *there*-insertion contexts. The first time in the derivation you will come across a type at which the negation can (and hence has to be) retrieved, is after maximalization has brought you to type t. We get for (6c):

(6)c.   Er speelt geen meisje in de tuin.
        $\exists e[PLAY(e) \wedge GIRL(Ag(e)) \wedge IN(e)=\sigma(GARDEN)]$ STORE: $\neg_n$
        of type t

Negation comes out of store, and we derive the correct interpretation:

$\neg\exists e[PLAY(e) \wedge GIRL(Ag(e)) \wedge IN(e)=\sigma(GARDEN)]$ of type t.

The moral is: if we allow ourselves to break-up the negative noun phrase, and we allow the negative to take its natural scope independently of the nominal material (at the first type t or <<d,t>,t>> you come across), negative noun phrases fit into the analysis unproblematically (at least for the cases discussed).

I do not blame the reader who, at this point, is disappointed by the break-up solution. Let's face it, I get the wrong interpretation, and my solution is to simply break-up the noun phrase interpretation and put the negation in the right place. *Ad hoc*, brute force, choose your own epithets. I quite understand such a reaction.

Well, let me be a bit more precise. Maybe you already do not like the storage mechanism for auxiliary negation. There my answer is that, given Davidsonian considerations (which also apply in theories that don't look Davidsonian, like, say, Discourse Representation Theory), you need some mechanism or other anyway. As a scope mechanism, it is a local mechanism, since retrieval is triggered as soon as you reach type t, which, of course, every derivation goes through. If you prefer an alternative mechanism, that is acceptable to me.

For instance, the mechanism as it is, is practically identical with the structured meaning mechanism used in Krifka (1991), so, instead of a storage mechanism, we can shift the negative noun phrase to a structured meaning,

which is the pair consisting of the noun phrase interpretation and the negation, and, at the right type shift it back to an interpretation which is not a pair.
Thus, if you're already disappointed about the scope mechanism, I will not be
sympathetic.

But break-up is another matter. Such a mechanism should not be invoked
without strong supporting evidence. I want to argue now that the evidence for
"break-up" is actually overwhelming.

8.4   The Evidence for Semantic Break-up

There is a long literature on the topic of semantic break-up, mainly from German
(e.g. Jacobs 1980, Kratzer 1995, Krifka 1999, Rullmann 1995, de Swart 2000). I
will discuss some arguments here which I think should appeal particularly to
semanticists. I will first discussed several Dutch cases, and after that talk about
English. In all the cases discussed below, we find a negative noun phrase, where,
arguably, the noun part can or must be interpreted in situ, while simultaneously, the negation can or must take higher scope.

8.4.1   Negative noun phrases in intensional contexts

Look at the examples in (9):

(9)a.   Dafna zoekt geen griffioens.
         Dafna seeks no   griffins.
         Dafna doesn't seek any griffins.
    b.   Griffioenen zoekt Dafna niet.
         Griffins   seeks Dafna not
         Griffins, Dafna doesn't seek.

Example (9a) has a *de re* reading, on which it expresses that Dafna does not
stand in the SEEK relation to any actual griffin:

$\neg\exists x[GRIFFIN(x) \wedge SEEK(DAFNA,x)]$

But (9a) has also a *de dicto* reading, in which no relation between Dafna and
actual griffins is expressed. This reading can be paraphrased as in (9b) in which
griffioenen is topicalized, and the negation is auxiliary negation.

How should we derive this *de dicto* reading? In Montague's classical analysis,
the *de dicto* reading would be analyzed as a relation SEEK between Dafna and
the intension of a generalized quantifier:

$SEEK(DAFNA,^{\wedge}\lambda P.\neg\exists x[GRIFFIN(x) \wedge P(x)])$

This expresses that Dafna stands in the SEEK relation to the function which assigns to every possible world the set of properties that no griffin has. That this analysis is untenable for the *de dicto* reading of (9a) becomes clear when we try to formulate what it means for Dafna to stand in the SEEK relation to an intensional entity of this type. Let's look at the *de dicto* reading of (10a):

(10)a. Dafna seeks a griffin.
    b. SEEK(DAFNA,^λP.∃x[GRIFFIN(x) ∧ P(x)])
    c. SEEK(DAFNA, T)

What does (10a) mean? Well, the story goes, the meaning postulate for SEEK will tell us something like the following:

> SEEK(DAFNA,T) holds iff Dafna is engaged in a particular kind of result oriented behavior, which is successful if she manages to bring herself into a world where she has found T.

The problem is that such a meaning postulate is fine for the *de dicto* reading (10b) of example (10a), but it is wrong for the *de dicto* reading (9b) of example (9a): (9a) does not express that Dafna tries to bring herself into a world where she has not found any griffins. It expresses that she isn't trying to bring herself into a world where she has found any griffins.

Thus, on Montague's analysis of the *de dicto* reading, the negation is sitting in the wrong place. For Montague, the only alternative is to scope it out. But that gives the *de re* reading, which is also wrong.

Zimmermann (1993) argues against Montague's analysis, in favor of an analysis where the complement of SEEK is an intensional property, rather than the intension of a generalized quantifier. His analysis of the *de dicto* reading of (10a) relates Dafna to an intensional property:

> SEEK(DAFNA,^GRIFFIN)

But if we try to analyze the *de dicto* reading of (9a) along these lines, we get the same problems as before: at the level of properties, the only plausible analysis of negation is as complementation. So the *de dicto* reading of (9a) would become:

> SEEK(DAFNA,^(ATOM − GRIFFIN))

which means that Dafna seeks non-griffins, and not that Dafna doesn't seek griffins. Again, the negation would be sitting in the wrong place.

The conclusion is clear. (9a) has a *de dicto* reading. This reading is not the *de re* reading. (9a) doesn't have the *de dicto* reading that Montague's theory generates. Neither does it have the *de dicto* reading that we just tried to generate on Zimmermann's theory (nor does Zimmermann assume that it has that reading).

On the reading that we are after, *griffioenen* is in the intensional context, but the negation is not: the negation takes auxiliary scope, as is clear from the paraphrase in (9b).

It seems that we don't have an alternative but to take this completely literally. The negative noun phrase *geen griffioenen* can semantically be broken up. The negative determiner *geen*, though syntactically inside the noun phrase and in the intensional context, can take scope independently of its complement *griffioenen*, and be interpreted as auxiliary negation. *Griffioenen* itself can stay in situ, hence *de dicto*.

Assuming a Zimmermann-style analysis, break-up now gives the following interpretation for (9a), which is the correct one:

¬SEEK(DAFNA,^GRIFFIN)

The case can be made even stronger, when we look at *try to find*:

(11)a.   Dafna probeert geen imitatie schildpadden te vinden.
         Dafna tries   no   mock   turtles   to find.
     b. Imitatie schildpadden probeert Dafna niet te vinden.
         Mock   turtles   tries   Dafna not to find
         Dafna doesn't try to find mock turtles.

Example (11a) has the same kind of *de dicto* reading as (9a), the reading which can be paraphrased as (11b). Thus, while the negation is part of the object of the infinitive complement of the intensional verb *proberen* (*try*), semantically, it takes scope over the intensional verb, and it can do so, while leaving *imitatie schildpadden* (*mock turtles*) in the intensional context.

Unsurprisingly, we see the same facts with other modals:

(12)a.   We kunnen hier **geen** dingen voor jou **meer**   laten liggen
         We can   here **no**   things for   you **longer** let   lie
     b. We kunnen dingen hier voor jou **niet meer**   laten liggen
         We can   things here for   you **no**   **longer** let   lie
         Leaving things lying around here is because of you **no longer possible**.

On the salient reading of (12), *dingen* (*things*) is in the scope of the modal operator, but the negation *geen* is not. The modal verb negation-polarity item *kunnen . . . geen . . . meer* means the same as the English **not possible any longer**. Again, this is expected if there is break-up, and hard to explain without.

There is an alternative account for these facts which does not rely on semantic break-up, and maintains the lexical integrity of negative noun phrases. This strategy is pursued in de Swart (2000). Instead of assuming semantic break-up, we can assume that nominal negation takes the interpretation of its complement noun and maps it onto an **argument reducer** interpretation: a function from n+1-place relations into n-place relations, encoding the scope of the negation. For instance, for the negative noun phrase as the object of an intensional verb, we could assign the following interpretation to the nominal negation:

$no \rightarrow \lambda Q \lambda R \lambda x. \neg R(x, Q)$ with Q a variable of the type $\langle s, \langle e, t \rangle \rangle$.

This strategy maintains the lexical integrity of the negative noun phrases, but at the cost of introducing a new interpretation type schema for such noun phrases. A type schema, since we need a different instance of the schema for different relations (i.e. the interpretations of transitive verb, di-transitive verbs, etc.).

Since I think that the objections that de Swart raises to the break-up strategy do not apply to the version of it developed in this chapter, I think the issue is really: do we want to maintain lexical integrity at the cost of introducing argument-reduction types for noun phrases, or do we want to give up lexical integrity? I think that the cases discussed in the next subsection show that it is lexical integrity that has to go.

8.4.2 Negative noun phrases in idioms

Look at the following idiom:

(13)   Spijkers op laag water zoeken
       Nails   at low tide   seek
       "seeking nails at low tide"
       Meaning: trying to find nit-picking things to criticize.

The object noun phrase *spijkers* is part of the idiom. As such it is frozen, and cannot, for instance, take wide scope:

(14)   Dafna denkt dat Abba   spijkers op laag water zoekt.
       Dafna thinks that Daddy nails   at low tide   seeks
       Dafna thinks that Daddy is just trying to find nit-picking things to criticize.

Example (14) does have a wide scope reading of *spijkers* as well: there are actual nails such that Dafna thinks Abba is looking for them at low tide. But this reading is about actual nails, and looking for things at the seaside, that is, it is no longer idiomatic.

Secondly, it is the bare plural *spijkers* which is part of the idiom. It is the **semantic unit** *spijkers op laag water zoeken* which gets the idiomatic reading. And in this semantic unit, *spijkers* cannot be replaced by other noun phrases without loss of idiomatic meaning:

(15)a.   Jij   zoekt alleen maar spijkers op laag water.
         You seek only   nails   at low tide

b.   ?Jij   zoekt enige/drie spijkers op laag water.   UNIDIOMATIC
You seek   a few/three nails   at low tide

That is, the cases in (15b) are no longer idiomatic.

Now we look at negative noun phrases in (16a), and we see that there is no problem with having a negative noun phrase: (16a), with a negative noun phrase, is perfectly fine and idiomatic, and it means the same as (16b):

(16)a.   Ik zoek geen spijkers op laag water.
I seek no   nails   at low tide
b.   Spijkers op laag water zoek ik niet.
Nails   at low tide   seek I   not
I do not want to find nit-picking things to criticize.

But this is a problem. Should we assume a second idiom, *geen spijkers op laag water zoeken*? That seems wrong as *geen* is not part of the idiom. But then, if we assume lexical integrity of the negative noun phrase, we would have to assume that in (16a) the idiomatic interpretation is tagged upon a **semantic non-unit**: the noun in the negative noun phrase plus the verbal predicate. This is because if we assume lexical integrity, the derivation of (16a) contains a semantic unit corresponding to *geen spijkers op laag water zoeken*, but not corresponding to *spijkers op laag water zoeken*. The problem is that the latter is what we are looking for.

Break-up provides the natural explanation. The negation can take auxiliary scope, leaving the indefinite part of the negative noun phrase *spijkers* in situ. Thus, with break-up, (16a) is indeed derived with a semantic unit corresponding to *spijkers op laag water zoeken*. Hence the facts about idioms providing an argument against de Swart's argument reduction strategy, and in favor of semantic break-up.

Just to have an example without an intensional verb, we see the same for the idiom in (17):

(17)   Een slecht figuur slaan.
A   bad   figure hit
"To hit a bad figure"
Meaning: make a bad impression

Look at the following dialogue:

(18)a.   Ik sloeg een slecht figuur daar!
I hit   a   bad   figure there
I made a bad impression there!

b.   Nee hoor, je   sloeg helemaal   geen slecht figuur.
Not at all you hit   completely no   bad   figure
Not at all, you didn't make a bad impression at all.

Again, this is perfectly idiomatic, and that only makes sense if the negation is interpreted as auxiliary negation, like it is in the English paraphrase.

8.4.3   Negative noun phrases in cognate objects

Mittwoch (1998) argues that sentences with cognate objects present the event argument as an object, i.e. the cognate object. Alternatively, we can say that a cognate object is an object which is semantically interpreted as directly modifying the event argument. Mittwoch mainly discusses Hebrew examples, since cognate objects are productive in Hebrew. Here I will be concerned with a colloquial construction in Dutch (or at least, in my Dutch), whereby a transitive verb is made a di-transitive verb, where the direct object of the transitive verb is made into the indirect object, and the new direct object is a cognate object:

(19)a. Ik douche Dafna.
        I shower Dafna
   b.   Ik douche Dafna **een warme douche**.
        I shower Dafna a   warm shower
        I am giving Dafna a warm shower.

Mittwoch argues that cognate objects cannot take wide scope; they are interpreted in situ. And the reason is that cognate objects directly express restrictions on the event argument. A *de re* reading would express something like: there is a warm shower such that I shower Dafna it. I agree with Mittwoch that this is practically incoherent, and it is not what the sentence means. The sentence means just that I am showering Dafna with warm water. That is, the cognate object is interpreted in situ, under the scope of the event quantifier introduced by maximalization. Since negation must take scope over this event quantifier, negative noun phrases should not occur as cognate objects, if the only possibilities are in situ or scoped out. But they do: (20a) is fine and means the same as (20b):

(20)a. Ik douche Dafna geen koude douche
        I shower Dafna no   cold shower
   b.   Een koude douche douche ik Dafna niet.
        A   cold   shower shower I Dafna not
        I am not giving Dafna a cold shower.

Again, break-up – and it seems only break-up – can explain this.

8.4.4   Negative noun phrases in metalinguistic discourse

Look at the following scene (which took place when Dafna was not yet very verbal):

(21)   *Enter* Abba *and* Dafna.
    Abba: Zal   ik je   een broodstok geven?
            Shall I   you a   breadstick give
            Shall I give you a breadstick?
    Dafna: Ba!
            Ba
            Yes!
    Abba: Dat heet   helemaal   geen broodstok, dat heet   soepstengel!
            That is called completely no   breadstick that is called soupstem
            That isn't called "breadstick" at all, that is called "soupstem"!
                                                    [*Exeunt*

We're concerned with the noun phrase *geen broodstok* in Abba's last statement. If we give *geen broodstok* a *de re* interpretation, we obviously get the wrong reading:

   There is no breadstick such that this is called "it."

If we give *geen broodstok* a *de dicto* interpretation, the reading is also obviously wrong:

   This is called "no breadstick."

Obviously, this is neither called "it" nor "no breadstick." The correct interpretation we derive with semantic break-up:

   It isn't called "breadstick."

The cases that I have discussed here were all cases where we have a negative noun phrase in object position, and the negative element *geen* can take scope in the same way as the auxiliary negation *niet* does, leaving the remainder part of the negative noun phrase in situ.

   If we can do break-up for negative noun phrases in object position, it is reasonable to assume that this break-up strategy is also available for negative noun phrases as predicates or adjoined subjects. As we have seen, with this assumption, we allow negative noun phrases as predicates and adjoined subjects, and derive the correct interpretation with the break-up.

8.4.5   Semantic break-up in English

I have argued that in Dutch we find very strong evidence for break-up. The obvious next question is: what about English? (The present section was written in reaction to a discussion with Hans Kamp, who raised this question.)

English too allows negative noun phrases in contexts of indefiniteness, so it ought to follow that in English, too, break-up is possible. But what is the evidence for break-up in English? I would argue that in English break-up is available, but, for independent reasons, this much harder to show.

What makes it so difficult to show that break-up exists in English is that English does not greatly like negative noun phrases in object position. Negative noun phrases are, of course, fine in subject position, as in (22a), but, unlike Dutch, for object position, English strongly prefers to express the negation through auxiliary negation (22b), rather than through a negative noun phrase object (22c):

(22)a.   No girl danced.
   b.   Dafna didn't kiss any girls.
   c.   #Dafna kissed no girls.

This makes testing break-up difficult in English, because all the pieces of evidence that I mentioned for Dutch are cases with the negative noun phrase in object position.

Nevertheless, English doesn't completely disallow negative noun phrases in object position: they are allowed in very stilted and in very colloquial speech. And when we look for the effects of break-up, we see that they do show up. Negative objects occur in stilted, motto-like language, as in (23):

(23)   Seek no evil!

Let me set up some context. Suppose your father spent his life trying to prove that unicorns exist, by trying to find one. However, he has never found one, and, moreover, he knows it: he has never believed of any actual object that it was a unicorn, he has never looked for any actual object, believing that it was a unicorn. His life is a failure. You visit him on his deathbed. He sighs and says to you with some forgivable pompousness;

(24)   Child, I have always lived by the motto: Seek no unicorns.

It seems to me that, in the context sketched, what your father says in (24) is blatantly false. There doesn't seem to be an interpretation on which, in this context, (24) is true. This means that in this context the statement *seek no unicorns* does not have a *de re* interpretation, because on that interpretation, in this context (24) would be true, but it is not.

It seems that the only way we can make sense of the fact that (24) is acceptable but false in the context sketched, is by assuming break-up: *seek no unicorns* is interpreted by break-up as *Don't seek unicorns*.

This is an example of stilted language. An example of colloquial language is the following. We come out of a meeting and I say to you:

(25)   Wow, when that guy started to talk about your work, you really blew a
          fuse there.

In a very irritated voice, you say to me:

(26)   Oh come off it, I blew no bloody fuse.

This is, of course, very colloquial but perfectly idiomatic. This suggests that
here too the nominal negation can take auxiliary scope, while the remainder
of the noun phrase stays in situ, and hence stays part of the idiom.

   So, English does seem to allow break-up as well. I do not know why English
so strongly prefers auxiliary negation over putting a negative noun phrase in
object position. But what the examples discussed here show is that there are
language usages in English where the prohibition against negative objects is
relaxed, and there we do find break-up. The conclusion we should draw, then,
is not that break-up does not exist in English, but that English does not like
negative objects.

   This is a fact about object position in English. As we all know, there is no
such restriction for subject position in English. When we now think about the
adjoined subject (and predicate position), there is actually no reason to expect
that it should pattern with object position rather than subject position, in this
respect. Thus, there is no reason to expect that negative noun phrases can't
naturally occur as adjoined subjects in English, and hence in *there*-insertion
contexts (or as predicates).

   As I argued above, when negative noun phrases do occur in object position,
break-up is available. Hence, there is, once again, no reason to expect that
break-up should not be a natural possibility for positions (lower than I)
where negative noun phrases do naturally occur, like adjoined to VP in *there*-
insertion contexts. This means that the break-up analysis of negative noun phrases
in *there*-insertion contexts that I have given for Dutch carries over to English
unproblematically.

8.5   The Problem of Negative Noun Phrases
inside Conjunctions

The discussion in this section was written in reaction to a discussion with Gennaro
Chierchia, who raised the question.

8.5.1   Distributive readings of conjunctive
noun phrases with negative conjuncts

I have given an analysis of negative noun phrases which relies on a break-
up strategy. This analysis could deal with negative noun phrases in argument

position, predicate position, and adjunct position. The question now is: what happens when a negative noun phrase is **inside** a conjunction which is in one of these positions, in particular, in a *there*-insertion context, as in (27a)?

(27)a. Er dansten drie jongens en   geen meisjes.
        pl danced   three boys   and no   girls
        Three boys were dancing and no girls.
   b. Er dansten drie jongens en er dansten geen meisjes.

The natural interpretation of (27a) is a reading where the predicate **distributes** over the **conjunction**, i.e. where (27a) is equivalent to (27b). This is the reading that I will be interested in here.

Let me, before I continue, make one side remark. While before I have used the singular *geen meisje*, I am now using the plural, *geen meisjes*. Following the semantics for the singular, one would expect the semantics for the plural to be:

$$geen\ meisjes \rightarrow \text{COMBINE}[\neg_n, {}^*\text{GIRL}]$$

However, I am assuming that in the DP *geen meisjes*, *geen* is a DP modifier, and hence *meisjes* in *geen meisjes* is a bare plural DP. This means that I assume for *meisjes* the same semantics that I have assumed for bare plural DPs, which is ${}^*\text{GIRL}-\{0\}$. So, the semantics for the plural *geen meisjes* is:

$$geen\ meisjes \rightarrow \text{COMBINE}[\neg_n, {}^*\text{GIRL}-\{0\}]$$

As we have seen, the type mismatch is resolved through storage (introducing a bit of bracket notation which will be useful below):

$$geen\ meisjes \rightarrow <{}^*\text{GIRL}-\{0\}], \text{STORE}:\neg_n>$$
$$\text{of type} <d,t>$$

For (27a), the obvious question now is: how does the analysis continue from here? Passing on the stored negation from the negative conjunct to the whole conjunctive noun phrase not only violates what we standardly assume about such passing-on mechanisms (i.e. a coordinate structure constraint), but will derive a wrong interpretation as well: obviously, the negation should not have scope over the whole conjunctive noun phrase. That is, the sentence does not mean:

It's not the case that there were three boys and some girls dancing.

It seems, then, that the analysis is stuck. Let us show the point where we are stuck. We assume that nominal negation *and* is interpreted as $\wedge_n$, which needs to combine with two set-denoting expressions:

drie jongens en geen meisjes →
COMBINE[$\wedge_n$, $\lambda x.*BOY(x) \wedge |x|=3$, <*GIRL–{0},STORE:$\neg_n$>]

and we don't know how to resolve this combination.

I assume that the analysis indeed is stuck, and gets unstuck by a special rescue strategy.

Rescue strategy:
$\wedge_n$ can be interpreted as $\wedge_{<t,<t,t>>}$ (Wenn der Not am Höchsten ist, which is, as far as we're concerned when one of the conjuncts has a stored negation).

Now the problem reduces to the resolution of a type mismatch of the very same sort as what we had for negation $\neg_n$. This can be resolved in exactly the same way: through storage of $\wedge_n$:

Resolution:
drie jongens en geen meisjes →
<[$\lambda x.*BOY(x) \wedge |x|=3$, <*GIRL–{0},STORE:$\neg_n$>], STORE:$\wedge_n$>

This means that we get a **parallel semantic derivation**: the semantic derivation applies all following operations in parallel to each conjunct.

We adjoin in parallel to the interpretation of *dansen*:

<[$\lambda x \lambda e.*DANCE(e) \wedge *Ag(e)=x \wedge *BOY(x) \wedge |x|=3$,
<$\lambda x \lambda e.*DANCE(e) \wedge *Ag(e)=x \wedge *GIRL–{0}(x)$, STORE:$\neg_n$>], STORE:$\wedge_n$>

We apply in parallel to the non-thematic subject, and get, after reduction:

<[$\lambda e.*DANCE(e) \wedge *BOY(*Ag(e)) \wedge |*Ag(e)|=3$,
<$\lambda e.*DANCE(e) \wedge *GIRL–{0}(*Ag(e))$, STORE:$\neg_n$>], STORE:$\wedge_n$>

We do maximalization in parallel:

<[$\exists e[*DANCE(e) \wedge *BOY(*Ag(e)) \wedge |*Ag(e)|=3]$,
<$\exists e[*DANCE(e) \wedge *GIRL–{0}(*Ag(e))]$, STORE:$\neg_n$>], STORE:$\wedge_n$>

Now we can retrieve the stored $\neg_n$:

<[$\exists e[*DANCE(e) \wedge *BOY(*Ag(e)) \wedge |*Ag(e)|=3]$,
$\neg \exists e[*DANCE(e) \wedge *GIRL–{0}(*Ag(e))]]$, STORE:$\wedge_n$>

And we finally retrieve the stored $\wedge_n$, and get:

$\exists e[*DANCE(e) \wedge *BOY(*Ag(e)) \wedge |*Ag(e)|=3] \wedge$
$\neg \exists e[*DANCE(e) \wedge *GIRL–{0}(*Ag(e))]$

This is equivalent to the following interpretation for (27a):

(27)a.   Er dansten drie jongens en geen meisjes.
$\exists e[*DANCE(e) \wedge *BOY(*Ag(e)) \wedge |*Ag(e)|=3] \wedge$
$\neg\exists e[DANCE(e) \wedge GIRL(Ag(e))]$

There is a sum of dancing events with a sum of three boys as agent and there isn't a dancing event with a girl as agent.

I take interpretation of $\wedge_n$ as $\wedge_{<t,<t,t>>}$ to be a special mechanism that isn't readily available. I assume that it is triggered by a very special situation: a stored negative element which must be interpreted as a sentence connective at the next t-stage. I assume that this can force the connective *and* to be also stored as a sentence connective to be retrieved at the next t-level.

The analysis predicts that a stored negation inside a conjunction can only be resolved in a mechanism that forces a distributive interpretation for the nominal conjunction (i.e. that forces "conjunction reduction"). This brings us to the next problem.

8.5.2   Collective readings of conjunctive noun phrases with negative conjuncts

The next problem is that in a conjunction where one of the conjuncts is a negative noun phrase, the conjunction can be interpreted as non-distributive. This we find in the natural reading of (28a).

(28)a.   Er kwamen drie jongens en   geen meisjes samen.
          pl came   three boys   and no   girls   together
          Three boys and no girls gathered.
    b.   Er kwamen drie jongens samen.

The reading of (28a) that we are interested in is a collective reading, in particular with respect to *en* (*and*): a group gathered which consisted of three boys, and which didn't include any girls. Interestingly, on this interpretation, *geen meisjes* doesn't really have a semantic effect: (28a) is equivalent to (28b) (the effect, of the negative noun phrase, then, is like a pragmatic comment).

The analysis that I developed in the previous subsection makes a clear prediction:

In the derivation of the collective reading in (28a), *geen meisjes* cannot have its standard interpretation with a stored negation.

The reason is that in that case the rescue strategy will store the conjunction, and a distributive reading is forced. (28a) does have such a reading, but it's not the one we are interested in here. This means that we are forced to provide a special interpretation strategy for the negative noun phrase.

Fortunately, we have already provided the basis for the solution of this problem in chapter 2, section 2.9. There I was concerned with the semantics of modals inside conjunctive noun phrases, like *John, Bill, and Henry, and maybe Susan*. I assumed there that modals allow an interpretation as quantificational modifiers of sets of individual concepts, i.e. at type $<<<s,d>,t>,<<s,d>,t>>$. Since modals and negation are in the same auxiliary ball park, it is not unreasonable to assume that this interpretation strategy is available for the resolution of nominal negation inside conjunctions as well.

Rescue strategy:
geen $\rightarrow \lambda\alpha.\{g_{<s,d>}$: g differs at most from $\lambda s.0$ in that for no s: $g(s) \in \alpha\}$

This combines with the interpretation of the bare plural DP *meisjes*: $*GIRL-\{0\}$. This gives:

geen meisjes $\rightarrow \{g_{<s,d>}$: g differs at most from $\lambda s.0$ in that for no s: $g(s) \in$
$*GIRL-\{0\}\}$
The set of individual concepts that differ at most from $\lambda s.0$ in that for no s: the value of the function for s is a real sum of girls.

Since for every s: $\lambda s.0(s)$ is itself a function such that for no s: $\lambda s.0(s) \in$ $*GIRL-\{0\}$, functions which at most differ from $\lambda s.0$ in that they do not assign a real sum of girls to any argument are identical to $\lambda s.0$. This means that we get the following result:

geen meisjes $\rightarrow \{\lambda s.0\}$ of type $<<s,d>,t>$

This is, of course, exactly what we want!
The interpretation of *drie jongens* at type $<<s,d>,t>$ is, along the lines of the analysis of *John,Bill and Henry* in chapter 2, section 2.9:

drie jongens $\rightarrow \{f_{<s,d>}$:every s: $*BOY(f(s)) \wedge |f(s)|=3\}$
The set of individual concepts that map every argument onto a sum of three boys.

These two interpretations form the input for Sum Pairing at type $<<s,d>,t>$, which (unsurprisingly) will give you as the interpretation for *drie jongens en geen meisjes* just the interpretation of *drie jongens*:

drie jongens en geen meisjes $\rightarrow$
$\lambda f.\exists x \exists y[\forall s[*BOY(x(s)) \wedge |x(s)|=3] \wedge y = \lambda s.0 \wedge f = \lambda s.x(s) \sqcup y(s)] =$
$\lambda f.\exists x \forall s[*BOY(x(s)) \wedge |x(s)|=3 \wedge f = \lambda s.x(s) \sqcup 0] =$
$\lambda f.\exists x \forall s[*BOY(x(s)) \wedge |x(s)|=3 \wedge f = x] =$
$\{f_{<s,d>}$: $\forall s[*BOY(f(s)) \wedge |f(s)|=3]\}$
(the interpretation of *three boys*)   of type $<<s,d>,t>$

The rest of the derivation of (28a) consists of working out the details of how the adjunction should go from here, since the interpretation is of type <<s,d>,t>, and we have defined the adjunction for type <d,t>. One can work out various strategies here. To complete the example here, I will just do the simplest here:

Lower α from type <<s,d>,t> to type <d,t>:
LOWER[α] = λx.∃f ∈ α ∃s[f(s)=x]

(Note that it is not automatically clear that this is type lowering in the sense in which I am not allowing it. I do not allow default lowering within a Partee triangle, but the present operation could be interpreted as **linking** two triangles, rather than lowering within one triangle.)

This lowering gives:

drie jongens en geen meisjes → λx.*BOY(x) ∧ |x|=3

And we derive (with the assumptions about collectivity from Landman 2000):

(28)a. Er kwamen drie jongens en geen meisjes samen.
∃x[*BOY(x) ∧ |x|=3 ∧ GATHER(↑(x))]
There is a sum of three boys which, as a group, gathers.

Alternatively, we can extend access to the adjunction domain from type <d,t> to type <<s,d>,t>. In the long run, this may be the better option, but it is more work than I am willing to put in at this point.

In sum, we derive an interpretation on which the conjunction is not distributive, and on this interpretation, *geen meisjes* does not have a semantic effect: the collective interpretation of (28a) is semantically equivalent to that of (28c):

(28)c. Drie jongens kwamen samen.

The point is, of course, that the collective interpretation of (28b) already disallows the possibility of including girls in the group. Thus, the negative conjunct in (28a) adds no further restriction, and is more like a discourse comment, or a clarifying afterthought.

8.6 The Problem of Exception Phrases Modifying Nominal Negation

The break-up strategy for nominal negation stores the negation, and treats it semantically like auxiliary negation. This analysis raises obvious problems for the semantics of *almost*, for instance in examples like (29):

(29)   There are *almost no girls* in the garden.

The problem is straightforward: semantically, *almost no* in (29) lives on the interpretation of the noun *girls*. If *no* is semantically just standard negation, and not a determiner which lives on its complement, then how do you get the semantics of *almost no* right? That is, it seems that you don't have a choice of treating *almost* as an adverb. But normally, when *almost* occurs adverbially, it doesn't live on a nominal argument:

(30)   I almost shook hands with every delegate.

On its most prominent reading, (30) means that my shaking hands with every delegate almost took place, not that there were a few delegates that I didn't shake hands with. If this is so, it is a real problem for the analysis of (29): how can we get *almost no* to live on the noun if *no* is semantically normal negation, which doesn't live on a noun, and *almost* is semantically normal adverbial *almost* which doesn't live on a noun either?

The crucial observation is that, despite the above claim about adverbial *almost*, there is solid evidence from Dutch and English to show that when the negation is uncontroversially auxiliary negation, and *almost* is adverbial, *almost* can live on a noun.

Look at the Dutch examples in (31) and (32):

(31)a.   Ik heb daar *geen gieren*   gezien.
         I   have there no   vultures seen
         I didn't see any vultures there.
     b. *Gieren*   heb ik daar *niet* gezien.
         Vultures have I   there not seen

(32)a.   Ik heb daar *bijna   geen gieren*   gezien
         I   have there almost no   vultures seen
         I saw almost no vultures there.
     b. *Gieren*   heb ik daar *bijna   niet* gezien.
         Vultures have I   there almost not seen

Just as (31a) and (31b) are equivalent apart from focusing effects, (32a) and (32b) (on the most prominent reading) are equivalent. But this means that *almost* in (32b) lives on the noun vultures, just as it does in (32a), even though the negation in (32b) is **auxiliary**, non-nominal negation. We see the same in English:

(33)a.   *Airplanes* you *almost didn't* see in those days.
     b. You *almost didn't* see *any airplanes* in those days.

While in these cases *almost*, of course, allows an irrelevant reading, expressing that airplane-seeing almost did not take place, it clearly allows another reading: in those days you saw very few airplanes. This is an interpretation where *almost* lives on the noun *airplanes*. I will call this interpretation of adverbial *almost* an **associated interpretation**.

The fact that we can get associated interpretations for adverbial *almost* with auxiliary negation means that in any case we will need a strategy for interpreting adverbial *almost* as associated, also when there is an auxiliary negation. I propose that, since that strategy is available anyway, it can be used in the adjunct cases, where the negation (and hence the *almost*) is separated.

Rather than providing a general theory, I will here just sketch how an analysis of *there*-insertion cases like (29) might go. I'll be concerned with a derivation for the following cases:

(34)a. Er dansten *bijna   geen meisjes*.
    pl danced almost no   girls
   b. Er dansten *geen meisjes behalve Dafna*.
    pl danced no   girls   except Dafna

Both *bijna* and *behalve Dafna* are semantically exception phrases. To have a name available we represent them as:

bijna → **bijna$_n$**
behalve Dafna → **behalve$_n$(DAFNA)**

A natural type for n is that of determiner modifiers, but in the present cases, where we assume that the negation is $\neg_t$ which must be stored, the determiner modifier type is not available. Both *bijna* and *behalve Dafna* can have adverbial interpretations, where they would be of type <<e,t>,<e,t>>. We assume:

In **bijna$_n$**, n can be specified as <<e,t>,<e,t>>. I will call this **bijna$_R$** (and I discuss R below)
In **behalve$_n$**, n can be specified as <d, <<e,t>,<e,t>>>.
(Hence **behalve$_n$(DAFNA)** will also be of type <<e,t>,<e,t>>. Let's call this **behalve$_R$(DAFNA)**.)

If we choose these interpretations for the interpretation of the relevant noun phrases in (34), we have no choice but to assume that, like the interpretation $\neg_t$ of the nominal negation, the interpretations **bijna$_R$** of nominal *bijna* and **behalve$_R$(DAFNA)** of nominal *behalve Dafna* must be stored. Thus, we get for the noun phrase interpretations:

bijna geen meisjes → <*GIRL–{0}, STORE: $\neg_{<t,t>,}$ **bijna$_R$**>

geen meisjes behalve Dafna → <*GIRL–{0}, STORE: $\neg_{<t,t>,}$ **behalve$_R$(DAFNA)**>

Now, index R is not arbitrary here. It is the name of a role, in particular, the role that is assigned to the adjoined noun phrases, in (34a) and (34b) this is the agent role. Hence, what we have so far is:

bijna geen meisjes → <*GIRL–{0}, STORE: $\neg_{<t,t>}$, **bijna**$_{*Ag}$>

geen meisjes behalve Dafna → <*GIRL–{0},STORE: $\neg_{<t,t>}$, **behalve**$_{*Ag}$(DAFNA)>

Now, since the semantic derivation gets to type <e,t> before it gets to type t, the exception phrases will come out of store before negation does. We can now do the derivation of (34a) and (34b) up to the event type:

er dansen bijna geen meisjes →
<λe.*DANCE(e) $\wedge$ *GIRL–{0}(*Ag(e)), STORE: $\neg_{<t,t>}$, **bijna**$_{*Ag}$>

er dansen geen meisjes behalve Dafna →
<λe.*DANCE(e) $\wedge$ *GIRL–{0}(*Ag(e)), STORE: $\neg_{<t,t>}$, **behalve**$_{*Ag}$(DAFNA)>

At this level, the exception phrases come out of store:

er dansen bijna geen meisjes →
<**bijna**$_{*Ag}$(λe.*DANCE(e) $\wedge$ *GIRL–{0}(*Ag(e))), STORE: $\neg_{<t,t>}$>

er dansen geen meisjes behalve Dafna →
<**behalve**$_{*Ag}$(DAFNA)(λe.*DANCE(e) $\wedge$ *GIRL–{0}(*Ag(e))), STORE: $\neg_{<t,t>}$>

Just to work the story to the end, let's assume that maximalization is just event existential closure. We get to type t, and the negation will come out of store:

er dansen bijna geen meisjes →
$\neg\exists$e[e $\in$ **bijna**$_{*Ag}$(λe.*DANCE(e) $\wedge$ *GIRL–{0}(*Ag(e)))]

er dansen geen meisjes behalve Dafna →
$\neg\exists$e[e $\in$ **behalve**$_{*Ag}$(DAFNA)(λe.*DANCE(e) $\wedge$ *GIRL–{0}(*Ag(e)))]

What is left to specify is the semantics of **bijna**$_{*Ag}$ and **behalve**$_{*Ag}$.

bijna$_R$: type <<e,t>,<e,t>>
Let c be the contextual value such that cardinalities bigger or equal to c are too big for *bijna* to be appropriate.
bijna$_R$(α) = α – {e $\in$ E: |R(e)|< c}

behalve$_R$: type <d,<<e,t>,<e,t>>
(**behalve**$_R$(DAFNA))(α) = α – {e $\in$ E: DAFNA $\sqsubseteq$ R(e)}

To these interpretations I add a semantic constraint which I will call the **Input Constraint**:

The Input Constraint:
bijna$_R$ and **behalve**$_R$(DAFNA) require their input set of type <e,t> to be non-empty.

The input constraint will have the consequence that (34a) implies (34c), and that (34b) implies (34d):

(34)a. Er dansten *bijna geen meisjes.*
        Almost no girls danced.
   c.   Er dansen meisjes.
        Some girl danced.

(34)b. Er dansten *geen meisjes behalve Dafna.*
        No girls danced except Dafna.
   d.   Dafna danste.
        Dafna danced.

The input event type in both cases is the set of evens of (real) girls dancing. Since this is, by the input constraint non-empty, the implication in (34c) follows in the case of (34a). The same implication follows from (34b). In this case, by the semantics, it also follows that it can only be Dafna who does the dancing, hence (34d) follows from (34b). I will not speculate here on the nature of that implication, i.e. whether it should be a presupposition or an entailment (see Sevi (1998) for discussion for *almost*, von Fintel (1993) for exception phrases). Let us work out the semantics:

bijna$_{*Ag}$(λe.*DANCE(e) $\wedge$ *GIRL–{0}(*Ag(e))) =
{e $\in$ E: *DANCE(e) $\wedge$ *GIRL–{0}(*Ag(e))} – {e $\in$ E: |*Ag(e)|< c} =
{e $\in$ E: *DANCE(e) $\wedge$ *GIRL–{0}(*Ag(e)) $\wedge$ |*Ag(e)|≥c}
The set of dancing events whose agent is a sum of (real) girls of cardinality **bigger** than is appropriate for *bijna*.

Hence we get:

(34)a. Er dansten *bijna geen meisjes.*
        ¬∃e[*DANCE(e) $\wedge$ *GIRL–{0}(*Ag(e)) $\wedge$ |*Ag(e)|≥ c]
        There is **no** sum of dancing events whose agent is a sum of (real) girls of cardinality **bigger** than is appropriate for *bijna*.

behalve$_{*Ag}$(DAFNA)(λe.*DANCE(e) $\wedge$ *GIRL–{0}(*Ag(e)))] =
{e $\in$ E: *DANCE(e) $\wedge$ *GIRL–{0}(*Ag(e))} – {e $\in$ E: DAFNA $\sqsubseteq$ *Ag(e)} =
{e $\in$ E: *DANCE(e) $\wedge$ *GIRL–{0}(*Ag(e)) $\wedge$ ¬(DAFNA $\sqsubseteq$ *Ag(e))}
The set of dancing events with sums of (real) girls as agent where the agent does not have Dafna as part.

Hence we get:

(34)b. Er dansten *geen meisjes behalve Dafna.*
        ¬∃e[*DANCE(e) $\wedge$ *GIRL–{0}(*Ag(e)) $\wedge$ ¬(DAFNA $\sqsubseteq$ *Ag(e))]
        There is no sum of dancing events with (real) girls as agent that doesn't have Dafna as part.

In this case, we can simplify this to:

¬∃e[DANCE(e) ∧ GIRL(Ag(e)) ∧ Ag(e)≠DAFNA]
There is no dancing event with a girl other than Dafna as agent.

In sum, the point is this. I have shown that, just as there is independent evidence for the break-up strategy of nominal negation, there is independent evidence for the existence of an associated analysis of adverbial *almost*. This opens the possibility to assign **nominal** *almost* the semantics of **adverbial** *almost*, **associated** with the role that the noun phrase it is part of receives (something analogous must be designed for assiociatedness, when it is in predicative position).

If so, the type mismatch will require us to store in the noun phrase both the sentential negation, and the adverbial associated interpretation of *almost*. The retrieval mechanism will retrieve the adverbial interpretation of *almost* before the negation, and the semantics of *almost* as an exception phrase will derive the correct interpretation.

The same analysis is assumed for the exception phrase *behalve Dafna*. There is another fact about exception phrases which shows the need for allowing such an analysis for exception phrases. As is well known, *almost* and *exception phrases* modify naturally positive and negative universals, but not naturally existential noun phrases. Larry Horn (1972) pointed out, as evidence for polarity sensitive *any* having an existential rather than universal interpretation, that *almost* can modify free choice *any* but not polarity sensitive *any*. However, it has also been pointed out that exception phrases do seem to be able to modify polarity sensitive *any*:

(35)   I *don't* lend this book to **anyone** *except John*.

(These cases were pointed out to me by Kai von Fintel, and to him by Irene Heim.) In this case, *anyone* is polarity sensitive *any*, and not free choice *any*, yet the exception phrase is allowed. The natural explanation is that the exception phrase is somehow able to scramble together the auxiliary negation and the polarity item and be licensed by the combination.

Now you could try to do this by reinterpreting the auxiliary negation as a nominal negation. What I am suggesting is that it may be more natural to leave the negation in (35) auxiliary negation, but assume that in this case the exception phrase can have an adverbial associated interpretation, associated with *anyone*.

In that case, we can get the correct interpretation of (35) without having to give up the assumption that *anyone* in (35) is polarity sensitive *any*. As argued in Kadmon and Landman (1993), this is as it should be.

Chapter 9

Relational Indefinites and Semantic Incorporation

9.1 The Data

While most nouns have their basic interpretation in type <d,t>, the type of sets of individuals, **relational nouns** have their basic interpretation in type <d,<d,t>>, the type of relations between individuals. Prime examples are nouns expressing **kinship relations**, like *sister* and *daughter*. A first observation about these nouns is the following:

Observation 1

In most environments, **relational indefinites**, that is indefinites based on relational nouns, are out of the blue slightly infelicitous. This holds too for *there*-insertion contexts. On the other hand, **relational definites**, definites based on relational nouns are better (except, obviously, in *there*-insertion contexts), and get a normal contextual interpretation:

(1)a. #*A sister* came to the party.
   b. *The sister* came to the party.

(2)a. #Bill kissed *three daughters*.
   b. Bill kissed *the three daughters*.

(3)a. #There is *a brother* in the garden.
   b. #There is *the brother* in the garden.

These distinctions are not very robust: it is easy to create contexts in which the (a)-examples are fine. These facts are easily explained, if we assume that relational nouns start out at type <d,<d,t>>. If they start out at this type, the relational argument needs to be supplied to get a normal NP or DP meaning. In the case of the indefinite, this needs to be done as an independent process; in the case of the definite, this process can be a natural part of the presuppositional interpretation we associate with the definite anyway.

I will now be concerned with a class of verbs that I will call **possessive verbs**. These are **verbs of possession** like *have* and *keep*, and verbs of change of possession like *buy* and *sell*. I call these verbs possessive verbs because they imply a possessive relation between their subject and object. (Matters are, of course, always more complex, the paraphrases are very approximate and are meant to contrast with cases discussed below.)

(4)a.   John **has** *a dog.*
       John possesses a dog.
   b.   John **has** *a dog* in the garden.
       John possesses a dog and it is in the garden.

(5)a.   John **keeps** a dog.
       John possesses a dog and he keeps it.
   b.   John **keeps** *a dog* in the garden.
       John possesses a dog and he keeps it in the garden.

(6)   John **bought** *a dog* in Thailand.
       As a consequence of a buying action by John in Thailand, he possessed a dog.

(7)   John **sold** *a dog* to the collector.
       John possessed a dog and sold it to the collector.

We come to the next two observations.

Observation 2

While in most environments relational indefinites are somewhat infelicitous, relational indefinites are perfectly felicitous in the object position of possessive verbs.

Observation 3

While with normal indefinites in their object position, possessive verbs imply a possessive relation between the subject and the object, with **relational indefinites** they do not imply a possessive relation between object and subject, instead they imply just the relation expressed by the relational indefinite. (I apologize for the objectionable practices expressed in some of the following examples; it's what you get when you combine more fancy possession verbs with relational nouns.)

(8)a.   John **has** *a sister.*
       ≠ John possesses a sister.
       = Someone is sister to John.

b.   John **has** *a sister* in Paris.
Someone is sister to John and is in Paris.

(9)a.   John **keeps** *a mistress*.
Someone is mistress to John and John keeps her.
b.   John **keeps** *a mistress* in Paris.
Someone is mistress to John and John keeps her in Paris.

(10)   John **bought** *a wife* in Thailand.
As a consequence of a buying action by John in Thailand, someone was wife to John.

(11)   John **sold** *a son* to the monastery.
Someone was son to John and John sold him to the monastery.

Observation 4

In the case of *have* and noun phrases based on relational nouns we actually observe definiteness effects: definites based on relational nouns are infelicitous in the object position of *have*. We do not observe such effects with non-relational noun phrases, nor with relational noun phrases for the other possessive verbs (though *keep* looks a bit like a borderline case):

(12)a.   #John **has** *every sister*.
b.   #John **has** *every sister* in Paris.

(13)a.   John **has** *every dog*.
b.   John **has** *every dog* in the garden.

(14)a.   #John **keeps** *every mistress*.
b.   ?John **keeps** *every mistress* in Paris.

(15)   The sheik **bought** *every wife* in Thailand.

(16)   John **sold** *every son* to the monastery.

A final observation concerns **episodic predicates**:

Observation 5

Have and *keep* allow episodic predicates, but not non-episodic predicates. *Buy* and *sell* allow neither. These facts hold in English as well as in Dutch.

(17)a.   John has a mistress *within reach*.
b.   #John has a mistress *intelligent*.

   c.   Jan heeft een minnares *onder   handbereik*.
        Jan has   a   mistress under handreach
   d.   #Jan heeft een minnares *intelligent*.
        Jan has   a   minnares intelligent

(18)a.   John keeps a mistress *within reach*.
    b.   #John keeps a mistress *intelligent*.

(19)a.   #John bought a mistress *within reach*.
    b.   #John bought a mistress *intelligent*.

(20)a.   #John sold a mistress *within reach*.
    b.   #John sold a mistress *intelligent*.

The last set of data is not particular to the cases of relational noun phrases. We find the same contrast for possessive verbs and normal noun phrases:

(21)a.   John has a dog *within reach*.
    b.   #John has a dog *intelligent*.
    c.   Jan heeft een hond *onder   handbereik*.
        Jan has   a   dog   under handreach
    d.   #Jan heeft een hond *intelligent*.
        Jan has   a   dog   intelligent

(22)a.   John keeps a dog *within reach*.
    b.   #John keeps a dog *intelligent*.

(23)a.   #John bought a dog *within reach*.
    b.   #John bought a dog *intelligent*.

(24)a.   #John sold a dog *within reach*.
    b.   #John sold a dog *intelligent*.

Nevertheless, these data are diagnostically useful. The contrast between the episodic and non-episodic cases in (17), (18), (21), and (22) is related to the well known contrasts discussed by Stump (1985). Stump argues that (25a), with an episodic adjunct, is ambiguous between a causative and a non-causative interpretation, while (25b), with a non-episodic adjunct, only has a causative reading:

(25)a. *Lying on the couch*, John got very burned.
       Non-causative: while he was lying on the couch, John got very burned.
       Causative: because he was lying on the couch, John got very burned.
    b. *Having a very sensitive skin*, John got very burned.
       #**Non-causative**: while he had a very sensitive skin, John got very burned.
       Causative: because he had a very sensitive skin, John got very burned.

Now, we know that *have* and *keep* can have both a possessive interpretation, and a causative interpretation. The causative interpretation is found for instance in (26):

(26)   We had the dog neutered.

The examples in (27) and (28) indicate that causative *have* is similar to small clause predicate *consider*:

(27)a.   The witch doctor had John available in a week.
   b.   The witch doctor had John intelligent in a week.

(28)a.   I considered John unavailable.
   b.   I considered John intelligent.

We see that for these small-clause interpretations of *have* (and *keep*), the predicate can be episodic or non-episodic. Not so for the possessive interpretations of *have* and *keep* in (21) and (22). The crucial observation is that the cases in (17) and (18), with the **relational noun phrases** as the objects of *have* and *keep*, pattern completely with the possessive interpretation of *have* and *keep* in (21) and (22).

Conclusions

- The cases of *have* and *keep* with **relational objects** differ from normal transitive verbs in that **indefinite relational objects** are perfectly felicitous. In fact, *have* shows definiteness effects.
- These cases differ from possessive *have* and *keep* (with non-relational objects) in that they do not imply a possessive relation between subject and object; instead they imply that the relation expressed by the relational object holds between subject and object. Further, possessive *have* and *keep* do not show definiteness effects with non-relational objects.
- But *have* and *keep* with relational objects pattern with possessive interpretations of *have* and *keep*, and not with causative small clause interpretations, as shown by the episodic/non-episodic predicates.

In this chapter, I want to provide an account of the non-possessive interpretations of these verbs with relational indefinites and of the definiteness effects with *have*.

Let me start by setting some parameters for such an analysis. At first sight, one might want to try to take the episodic/non-episodic contrast as a starting point for an analysis of (29):

(29)   John has a sister *in the army*.

We might be tempted to assume a small clause analysis for *a sister in the army* which requires an episodic predicate and imposes some indefiniteness constraint on the small clause subject.

But the facts that we have discussed do not favor such an analysis. The restriction to episodic predicates is not restricted to the cases that show definiteness effects (i.e. we find it for the normal possessive cases as well). The restriction does not cross-linguistically pattern with the restriction to episodic predicates in *there*-insertion contexts: while Dutch allows non-episodic predicates in *there*-insertion, it does not allow them here. And, as we have seen, the most likely candidates for a small clause analysis, the causative cases in (27), do not show the restriction to episodic predicates. All in all, there is no particularly good reason to think that a small clause analysis will solve our problems.

Secondly, we might want to take the *there*-insertion analysis that I have developed as our model. In that case, we might assume that *a sister* in (29) is **adjoined** to the episodic predicate. But this is problematic for three reasons.

In the first place, again, we would not expect, in Dutch, the restriction to episodic predicates, since adjunction to non-episodic predicates is acceptable in Dutch.

Secondly, if the *have* cases are really modeled directly on the *there*-insertion cases, we would expect **object pleonastics**, non-thematic object DPs. But I assume with Rothstein (2001) (and many others) that there are no object pleonastics (see the arguments in Rothstein 2001).

Thirdly, if the indefinite is simply adjoined, we would expect the object position of *have* to show definiteness effects for all noun phrases, not just relational ones. Now, it is possible to maintain that that is indeed the case: you could try to argue that while relational noun phrases only allow an adjoined analysis, other noun phrases allow an adjoined or argument analysis. In that case, the definiteness effects would only be visible with the relational indefinites.

Such an analysis (if worked out properly) is very hard to refute. Nevertheless, I am inclined to take the **differences** between the *have* cases and the *there*-insertion cases as a guideline here. If we are successful in modeling the felicity of relational indefinites in the *have* cases on the *there*-insertion cases, why aren't relational indefinites perfectly felicitous in *there*-insertion cases to start with?

In the next section I will develop an analysis for the simple case of *John has a sister*, not for the case in (29). The reason for not discussing (29) is not that the analysis doesn't extend to it (it does), but that working out the details of the cases that involve the episodic predicate brings in various complex issues that are independent of my concerns here. I assume that whether or not you want to analyze the construction with the episodic predicate **syntactically** as a small clause, **semantically** a complex predicate is formed: *have in the army*. (That is, *in the army* is, semantically, a secondary predicate.) I make the same assumption for cases of real possession cases such as (30):

(30)   John has a dog in the garden.

Semantically, the complex predicate, *have in the garden*, is interpreted as a relation between a possession state, a possessor x, and a possessed theme y, such that some state of y being in the garden relates appropriately to that possession state. And it must be specified in context what "relates appropriately" means. Since working this out really is an issue in the theory of complex predicate formation and secondary predication, I will refrain from doing so here. Nevertheless, the analysis that I will develop for *have* below extends unproblematically to cases like *have in the army* in (29).

9.2   Dethematicization and Rethematicization through Semantic Incorporation

Let us start with (31):

(31)   John has a dog.

Let us call a **possession state** a state for which the roles Po for **possessor** and Th$_P$, for **possessed theme** are defined. I will assign the following interpretation to possessive *have*:

$have \rightarrow \lambda y \lambda x \lambda s.Po(s)=x \land Th_P(s)=y$ of type <d,<d,<e,t>>
          <Th$_P$,Po>

With this we derive the following interpretation for (31):

$\exists s[Po(s)=JOHN \land DOG(Th_P(s))]$
There is a possession state with John as possessor and a dog as possessed theme.

We move to (32):

(32)   John has a sister.

sister is a relational noun with interpretation:

$sister \rightarrow \lambda y \lambda x.SISTER(x,y)$ of type <d,<d,t>>
          "x is sister to y"

This doesn't fit the above interpretation of *have*. As a first try, we could assume that it is contextually lowered to type <d,t>:

$sister \rightarrow \lambda x[SISTER(x,c)]$ of type <d,t>

and that this is made the object of *have* in the normal way, giving:

$\exists s[Po(s)=JOHN \land SISTER(Th_P(s),c)]$

Assuming, finally, that contextual variable c is specified as JOHN, this gives:

∃s[Po(s)=JOHN ∧ SISTER(Th$_p$(s),JOHN)]
There is a possession state with John as possessor and the sister-of relation holding between the possessed theme and John.

While there is no reason to assume that this derivation is blocked in the grammar, it doesn't seem to be readily available at all. There are two problems with this derivation. In the first place, it imposes a possession relation on John and his sister, which seems unwarranted. Secondly, the mechanism that specifies John as the brother is contextual, and could hence just as well be specified otherwise. Thus, if the king is a contextually relevant individual, we could specify c as the king, and (32) would mean that John has a sister of the king in his possession.

In fact, I think, in context, (32) allows such a reading, where John, the bad knight has taken a sister of the king hostage. But that is, of course, not the interpretation of (32) that we are looking for, and that means that this interpretation strategy, hence, this derivation, should be a distant second choice. How then should the natural, intended interpretation of (32) be derived?

My proposal is to take the facts discussed in the last section completely seriously: *have* in (32) patterns with possessive *have*. I assume that this is so, because it is derived from possessive *have*. But it does not have the possessive meaning. I assume that this is so, because it has lost its possessive meaning.

Now, the possessive meaning of possessive *have* is completely expressed in terms of the **thematic possessive roles** of possessor Po and possessed theme Th$_p$. Thus, if we assume that *have* loses its possessive interpretation, this means in essence that it loses its thematic possessor roles. In this, it becomes a "super-light-verb." This is what I assume happens:

Dethematicization of *have*:
Dethematicized *have* is interpreted as:
have → λyλxλs.s ∈ S ∧ x ∈ D ∧ y ∈ D   of type <d,<d,<e,t>> (S the set of
        <–,–>   all states)

Thus *have* becomes a trivial relation which does not have roles to assign.

At this point, something must happen in the grammar, since *have* is semantically still a two-place relation, but it cannot assign a role to its object position, which means (since I assume with Rothstein (2001) and others that there are no object-pleonastics) that it cannot have an object at all. Hence, the grammar gets stuck.

What happens at this point is that **semantic incorporation** of the indefinite relational noun takes place. The indefinite relational noun phrase *a sister* has an interpretation born at type <d,<d,t>>. This type is input to the operation of **scope shift**, which shifts its interpretation from type <d,<d,t>> to an interpretation of type <d,<d,<e,t>>:

$\lambda y \lambda x \lambda s.s \in [SISTER] \wedge A_1(s)=x \wedge A_2(s)=y$
The relation that holds between x and y and s if s is a state of x being sister to y.

What I assume happens first in semantic incorporation is that the relational indefinite shifts with scope shift to this relation of type <d,<d,<e,t>>, and that this relation gets **thematicized** (meaning that it gets two roles A_1 and A_2 to assign):

Semantic incorporation stage 1 – Thematicization of the relational indefinite:
SISTER of type <d,<d,t>> shifts to:
$\lambda y \lambda x \lambda s.s \in [SISTER] \wedge A_1(s)=x \wedge A_2(s)=y$ of type <d,<d,<e,t>>
<A_2,A_1>

Stage two of semantic incorporation is just intersection:

Semantic incorporation stage 2 – Rethematicization:
The **thematicized** "sister" relation **intersects** with the **dethematicized** "have" relation:
$\lambda y \lambda x \lambda s.s \in [SISTER] \wedge A_1(s)=x \wedge A_2(s)=y \cap \lambda y \lambda x \lambda s.s \in S \wedge x \in D \wedge y \in D$
<A_2,A_1>   **<-,->**

which gives a **rethematicized relation**:

$\lambda y \lambda x \lambda s.s \in [SISTER] \wedge A_1(s)=x \wedge A_2(s)=y$ of type <d,<d,<e,t>>
<A_2,A_1>

The final stage completes the incorporation. The A_2 role in a thematic relation would normally be assigned to the object, but, since we have reinterpreted the relational noun phrase as a thematic relation, and hence affected the object, we don't really have an object noun phrase to assign it to. The situation is much like that of passive: in passive too, we have affected the object position, and cannot assign the first role in the theta grid to it. Instead we remove the subject role from the theta grid (and existentially close it), and make what was the object role the remaining role in the theta grid.
    I propose that exactly this happens in the third and final stage of semantic incorporation:

Semantic incorporation stage 3:
The rethematicized relation is **semantically passivized**:
PASS[$\lambda y \lambda x \lambda s.s \in [SISTER] \wedge A_1(s)=x \wedge A_2(s)=y$] =
        <A_2,A_1>
$\lambda y \lambda s.s \in [SISTER] \wedge \exists x[A_1(s)=x] \wedge A_2(s)=y$ of type <d,<e,t>>
<A_2>

Thus, with semantic incorporation, we derive a **one-place predicate**:

have a sister $\rightarrow \lambda y \lambda s.s \in$ [SISTER] $\wedge \exists x[A_1(s)=x] \wedge A_2(s)=y$ of type <d,<e,t>>
$\quad\quad\quad\quad$ <A$_2$>

This applies to the interpretation JOHN of subject *John*, bringing us to type <e,t>, maximalization takes place, which gives:

$\exists s[s \in$ [SISTER] $\wedge \exists x[A_1(s)=x] \wedge A_2(s)=$JOHN$]$ $\quad\quad$ of type t.

This is equivalent to:

$\exists x \exists s[s \in$ [SISTER] $\wedge A_1(s)=x \wedge A_2(s)=$JOHN$]$

and with the correspondence principle we get for (32):

(32) John has a sister.
$\quad\quad\exists x[$SISTER$(x,$JOHN$)]$
$\quad\quad$Somebody is a sister to John.

Thus, through semantic incorporation we derive the correct non-possessive reading of (32). We predict the definiteness effects, because the semantic incorporation process relies crucially on the possibility to shift the relational indefinite with scope shift from type <d,<d,t>> to type <d,<d,<e,t>>, the same type as the interpretation of dethematicized *have*: it is because the interpretation of the relational indefinite is born as a relation of type <d,<d,t>> that the incorporation works. Since definites and quantificational noun phrases based on a relational noun are not born at type <d,<d,t>>, they cannot be incorporated. Since non-relational noun phrases are not of the relational type either, they cannot be incorporated either. Hence semantic incorporation into *have* only applies to relational indefinites.

9.3 Incorporation in Verbs of Change of Possession

9.3.1 The lexical semantics of verbs of change of possession

We are concerned with the verbs *buy* and *sell*. I am first of all concerned with the question of which thematic roles are **semantically defined** for events of buying and selling. I will not be creative (or deeply theoretically inspired) in choosing my role labels, but will follow roughly what we see in (33):

(33)a. Fred bought a book from the auctioneer for Dafna.
$\quad$ b. The auctioneer sold a book for the collector to Fred.

Individual roles are functions from E into D.
Examples: Ag, Th, From, To, For.

Individual roles semantically defined for *buy*: Ag, Th, From, For.
Individual roles semantically defined for *sell*: Ag, Th, To, For.

We have above defined possession states and possession roles: a **possession state** is a state for which the roles Po and Th_P are defined. We can reformulate this:

Let **PO** be the set of all possession states.
Possession roles are functions from PO into D: Po, Th_P.

You may have noticed that I haven't yet included the traditional roles of Goal and Source. I will include those, but in a different way from usual. I assume that the roles of Goal and Source are responsible for the possessive interpretation of *buy* and *sell*. These verbs are verbs of change of possession of the theme.

The **Source** specifies who possesses the theme before the transaction.
The **Goal** specifies who is intended to possess the theme as a consequence of the transaction (and usually does).

I will not analyze these roles directly as individual roles, but indirectly as possession state roles:

Possession state roles are functions from E into PO: Go, So.

Possession state roles semantically defined for *buy*: Go, So
Possession state roles semantically defined for *sell*: Go, So

Thus, the possession state role of Source associates with an event of buying a possession state, specifying the initial possessor of the theme, while Goal associates with that event the later possessor. The same for selling. Thus, both Source and Goal are semantically defined for *buy* and *sell*.

The roles Source and Goal hence associate with each buying and each selling event two possession states: a source state and a goal state. Each of these states has a possessor and a possessed theme. The latter are **semantically linked** to the buying or selling event by the following semantic linking constraints:

Semantic linking constraints:
SLC 1: $\forall e \in \text{BUY} \cup \text{SELL}: Th_P(\text{Go}(e)) = Th_P(\text{So}(e)) = \text{Th}(e)$
The **possessed theme** of the **source** state and of the **goal** state of a **selling/ buying** is the **theme** of the selling/buying event.

SLC 2: $\forall e \in \text{BUY}: \text{Po}(\text{So}(e)) = \text{From}(e)$
The **possessor** of the **source** state of a **buying** event is linked to the
From role of that buying event.
$\forall e \in \text{SELL}: \text{Po}(\text{Go}(e)) = \text{To}(e)$
The **possessor** of the **goal** state of a **selling** event is linked to the **To** role of
that selling event.

SLC 3: $\forall e \in \text{BUY}: \text{Po}(\text{Go}(e)) = \text{Ag}(e) \vee \text{Po}(\text{Go}(e)) = \text{For}(e)$
The **possessor** of the **goal** state of a **buying** event is linked to the **Ag** role
or to the **For** role of that buying event.
$\forall e \in \text{SELL}: \text{Po}(\text{So}(e)) = \text{Ag}(e) \vee \text{Po}(\text{So}(e)) = \text{For}(e)$
The **possessor** of the **source** state of a **selling** event is linked to the **Ag** role
or to the **For** role of that selling event.

These linking constraints express the obvious possession facts about buying
and selling events. It's all a question of *who has the book when* in (33a) and (33b):

(33)a.   Fred bought a book from the auctioneer for Dafna.
   b.   The auctioneer sold a book for the collector to Fred.

The linking constraints tell us that, in (33a), before the buying, the auctioneer
has the book, while after the buying Fred or Dafna has the book. In (33b), before
the selling, the auctioneer or the collector has the book, while after the selling
Fred has the book.

From now on, when I talk about roles Goal, resp. Source being linked to a
role, I mean that in the relevant events the possessor of the Goal, resp. Source
state is linked to that role. So far, we have only dealt with roles that are semantically defined for the event types of buying and selling. We now come to **lexical selection** of roles. I assume that *buy* and *sell* both have a two-place meaning (of type $<d^2,<e,t>>$) and a three-place meaning (of type $<d^3,<e,t>>$), and
they lexically select the following individual roles:

Lexical selection of individual roles:
buy^2 lexically selects: $<\text{Th},\text{Ag}>$
buy^3 lexically selects: $<\text{Th, For},\text{Ag}>$
$sell^2$ lexically selects: $<\text{Th},\text{Ag}>$
$sell^3$ lexically selects: $<\text{Th},\text{To},\text{Ag}>$

So far the system has been completely general. We now introduce a lexical peculiarity of the three-place verb *buy*:

Lexical linking constraint on buy^3:
let α be the interpretation of buy^3:
$\forall x,y,z: \forall e \in \alpha(x,y,z): \text{Po}(\text{Go}(e)) = \text{For}(e)$

Thus, if the For-role is lexically selected by *buy* – which is the case in the three-place verb – then the Goal role is linked to that selected role. Look at the difference between (34a) and (34b):

(34)a.   Fred bought a book for Dafna, though when he bought it, he intended
            to give it to Netta.
    b.   #Fred bought Dafna a book, though when he bought it, he intended to
            give it to Netta.

Both in (34a) and (34b), Dafna fills the For role. In (34b) *buy* can only be *buy*^{3}. This means, by the lexical constraint, that in (34b) Dafna must be the Goal. In (34a), the For role is expressed through a prepositional phrase. I will not assume that this means that *buy* must be *buy*^{2}, but, of course, I will assume that this means that *buy* can be *buy*^{2}. That means that (34a) allows an interpretation where the For role is not lexically selected by the verb, and hence in (34a) the Goal can be either Fred or Dafna.

This explains the contrast in felicity between (34a) and (34b): while in (34a) out of the blue you might expect Dafna to be the Goal (the one who is intended to have the book as the outcome of the buying event), the linking constraints for *buy*^{2} allow Fred to be the Goal (the one who actually has the book as the outcome of the buying event), and Dafna be something else, like a beneficiary. In other words, if I buy a book, my goal can either be for me to have the book (at least temporarily), or for someone else to have the book (specified by the For role).

The situation is different in (34b). In the dative construction, *buy* must be *buy*^{3}, hence the For role is lexically specified, and hence, by the lexical constraint, only it can be the Goal: if I buy Dafna a book, the goal of the buying is Dafna having a book, not me having a book. This is what the lexical constraint imposes.

There is no analogous constraint for Source for *sell*, so there is a real asymmetry between *buy* and *sell* here.

I have defined the notion of lexical selection for the individual roles for *buy* and *sell*. I will define in terms of that a notion of lexical selection of the possession state roles Goal and Source:

Lexical selection of the roles Goal and Source by *buy* and *sell*:
A **possession state role** is **lexically selected** by a verb if it is linked to an individual role which is lexically selected by that verb.

The results are summarized in the following table. Boldface indicates lexically selected roles. I have added a characteristic example for each case.

1.	I	*sold*³	John	the book	for Bill
	Ag		To	Th	For
	↑		↑		
	So		Go		

(35) The art collector sold the museum a painting for his son, so that he could go to college.

2.	I	*sold*³	John	the book	for Bill
	Ag		To	Th	For
			↑		↑
			Go		So

(36) The auctioneer sold the museum a painting for an art collector in financial trouble.

3. ▪	I	*sold*³	the book	to John	for Bill
	Ag		Th	To	For
	↑			↑	
	So			Go	

(37) The art collector sold a painting to the museum for his son, so that he could go to college.

4.	I	*sold*³	the book	to John	for Bill
	Ag		Th	To	For
				↑	↑
				Go	So

(38) The auctioneer sold a painting to the museum for an art collector in financial trouble.

Hence: three-place *sell* lexically selects a Goal linked to the To role, and optionally lexically selects a Source linked to the Ag role.

5.	I	*sold*²	the book	to John	for Bill
	Ag		Th	To	For
	↑			↑	
	So			Go	

Also (37).

6.	I	*sold*²	the book	to John	for Bill
	Ag		Th	To	For
				↑	↑
				Go	So

Also (38).

Hence, two-place *sell* optionally lexically selects a Source linked to the Ag role.

7.	I	*bought*³	John	the book	from Bill
	Ag		For	Th	From
			↑		↑
			Go		So

(39)a.   The maecenas bought the museum a painting from an art collector.

    b. #With the side aim of decorating his house, the art collector bought the cancer fund a painting from a philanthropist, since he knew that the philanthropist would donate the money to this fund.

Example (39b) shows that, with the For-role lexically selected, the Goal cannot be linked to the Agent.

8.	I	*bought*³	the book	for John	from Bill
	Ag		Th	For	From
				↑	↑
				Go	So

(40)   The maecenas bought a painting for the museum from an art collector.

Hence, three-place *buy* lexically selects a Goal linked to the For role; it does not lexically select a Source.

9.	I	*bought*[2]	the book	for John	from Bill
	Ag ↑ **Go**		**Th**	For	From ↑ So

(41)   The art collector bought a painting from a philanthropist for the cancer fund, since he knew that the philanthropist would donate the money to them.

Here we see that if the For role is not lexically selected, the Goal can be the agent.

10.	I	*bought*[2]	the book	for John	from Bill
	Ag		**Th**	For ↑ Go	From ↑ So

(40) again.

Hence, two-place *buy* optionally lexically selects a Goal linked to the Ag role, it never lexically selects a Source.

The important generalization is the following:

Lexical selection of Goal and Source by *buy* and *sell*:
Sell allows **two** possession state roles, Goal and Source, to be lexically selected.
Buy allows only the possession state role, Goal, to be lexically selected.

From all this, we can construct ten semantic interpretations for the verbs *buy* and *sell*. I will give only one example here:

1.	I	*sold*[3]	John	the book	for Bill
	Ag ↑ **So**		**To** ↑ **Go**	**Th**	For

(The order of the arguments in the λ-prefix is based on the Dutch order Subject–Indirect object–Direct object–Verb, but this is quite immaterial for my purposes.)

$sell^3 \rightarrow$ λzλyλxλe.SELL(e) ∧ Ag(e)=x ∧ To(e)=y ∧ Th(e)=z ∧
              So(e) ∈ {s ∈ S: Po(s)=Ag(e) ∧ Th$_p$(s)=Th(e)} ∧
              Go(e) ∈ {s ∈ S: Po(s)=To(e) ∧ Th$_p$(s)=Th(e)}
          <Th,To(Go),Ag(So)>

9.3.2   Relational nouns and lexically selected possession roles

We now come to the point of the previous discussion. And that is the following observation:

Observation:
A relational indefinite is felicitous with verbs of possession *buy* and *sell* with a relational, non-possessive interpretation iff it relates to (= incorporates into) a **lexically selected possession role** (unless it is, of course, infelicitous for independent reasons.)

We start with *sell*.

Three-place sell with both roles lexically selected

(42)   The farmer, who was in need of money, sold the illegal agency *a son*.
       So   **Go**   **Th**

In (42) *a son* can be interpreted as *a son of the farmer*, i.e. it can relate to the lexically selected Source (i.e. before the transaction, the farmer has a son). The reading where it relates to the lexically selected Goal is infelicitous for independent reasons (i.e. the context makes it implausible).

(43)   The illegal agency sold the king, who was in need of an heir, *a son*.
       So   **Go**   **Th**

In (43), *a son* cannot be related to the lexically selected Source for independent reasons. It can relate to the lexically selected Goal, and be interpreted as *a son of the king* (i.e. after the transaction, the king has a son.) We find the same facts in (44) and (45):

(44)   The farmer, who was in need of money, sold *a son* to an illegal agency.
       So   **Th**   **Go**

A son can relate to the lexically selected Source.

(45)   The illegal agency sold *a son* to the king, who was in need of an heir.
       So   **Th   Go**

A son can relate to the lexically selected Goal.

Two or three place sell, *with only the Goal role lexically selected*

(46)   #The middle man sold the illegal agency *a son* for the farmer, who was
            Ag   **Go**   **Th**   **So**
       in need of money

Of course, as we have seen, the Agent could be the Source, and then *a son* could relate to it, but that interpretation is made unwelcome by the example. The crucial question is: can the sentence mean that the middle man sold the illegal agency a son of the farmer for the farmer? That does not seem to be the case. We see: the source is not lexically selected, and the relational indefinite cannot relate to it.

   Note that the argument that the relational indefinite relates to need not be explicitly there:

(47)   The king was sold *a son*.
       Go   **Th**   **(So)**

This can both mean that due to the transaction the king got a son, or that the implicit agent's son was sold to the king.

   We now come to *buy*.

Three place buy

The dative construction involves three place *buy*. The lexical semantics of *buy* tells us that, since the For role is lexically selected, the Goal role must be linked to it, and hence the Goal role is lexically selected. The source role is linked to the From role, so it is not lexically selected. This means that the relational indefinite can only relate to the For role.

(48)   The monarchy upkeep committee bought the king, who was in need of
       Ag   **Go**
       an heir, *a son* from an illegal agency.
              Th   **So**

Example (48) shows that *a son* can indeed relate to the lexically selected Goal. Relation to the other roles is already infelicitous for independent reasons.

(49)   #The middle man had earlier bought the illegal agency *a son*, for a
       Ag   **Go**   **Th**
       reasonable price, from the farmer, who was in need of money.
                           So

In (49) we have made relating *a son* to the Goal pragmatically infelicitous. Here too, relating *a son* to the agent is pragmatically infelicitous, but the Source role is pragmatically perfectly available. Nevertheless, *a son* cannot relate to the Source role, which is not lexically selected.

Next we show that, with three place *buy*, *a son* cannot relate to the agent:

(50)   #The king, who was in need of an heir, bought the country *a son*, from
       Ag   **Go**   **Th**   **So**
       an illegal agency.

A son cannot relate to the agent *the king* in (50).

Two or three place buy

If the For role is realized prepositionally, we can have either two place or three place *buy*. This means that in principle it should be possible to relate the relational indefinite to the For role, also when realized prepositionally, since it is lexically selected, if *buy* is three place:

(51)   The monarchy upkeep committee bought *a son* for the king, who was in
       Ag   **Th**   **Go**
       need of an heir, from an illegal agency
                         So

In (51), *a son* can relate to the Goal *the king*. Again, you cannot relate to the non-lexically selected Source:

(52)   #Mary was a daring 19th century discoverer. The most difficult thing she
                                                                            Ag
       did was to buy *a wife*, for a reasonable price, from a sultan.
                     Th   **So**

While this example is set up to make pragmatically relating *a wife* to Agent implausible, and to the source plausible, the example stays infelicitous. Hence, indeed relating *a wife* to the (non-lexically selected) Source in *buy* is just impossible.

On the other hand, we expect that, if the For role is not assigned to the dative, it is always possible to assume that we are dealing with two place *buy*, and hence that the Goal role is not linked to the For role, but to the Agent role. And then it is possible that the relational indefinite relates to the agent. The contrast is nicely shown in the following minimal pair in (53), where (53a) involves three place *buy* and (53b) is ambiguous:

(53)a.   The king, who needed a caretaker for his son, bought his son *a wife*.
     b.   The king, who needed a caretaker for his son, bought *a wife* for his son.

In (53a), *a wife* can only relate to *his son*, the lexically selected Goal of three place *buy*. This reading is also possible in (53b), as expected. But (53b) allows another reading, where *a wife* relates to the Agent, *the king*: the king bought himself a wife, to take care of his son. In this case, we have two place *buy*, in which the Goal role can be linked to the Agent, and is lexically selected that way. This is, of course, what we see in clearly two place *buy* as well:

(54)   The king bought *a wife*
       Go   **Th**

A wife can unproblematically relate to the agent in (54).

9.3.3   Incorporation in verbs of change of possession

Verbs of change of possession like *buy* and *sell* differ from verbs of possession like *have* in that they do not show definiteness effects with relational nouns:

(55)a.   John **has** *a son*.
     b.   #John **has** *his son*.

(56)a.   The king **bought** *a son* from an agency.
     b.   The king **bought** *his son* from an agency.

(57)a.   The farmer **sold** *a son* to the king.
     b.   The farmer **sold** *his son* to the king.

The felicity of (56b) and (57b) is not surprising. I assume that *buy* and *sell* are normal eventive verbs, with normal argument positions, and the possessive is the standard way of making a normal definite DP out of a relational noun. The puzzle lies in (56a) and (57a): for relational **indefinites**, *buy* and *sell* pattern with *have*: the relational indefinite is perfectly felicitous. This is unexpected, because we have observed that normally relational indefinites are not.

   I analyzed possessive *have* as a **possessive relation** between individuals and possession states, and the facts about the relational indefinites followed from the assumption that this relation gets dethematicized, and the relational indefinite incorporates in it.

   While *buy* and *sell* are not themselves interpreted as possessive relations, their meanings do involve possessive relations, that is, possessive relations are part of the meanings of *buy* and *sell*, in the restriction on the possession state roles Source and Goal.

The observation from the last section can now be rephrased:

Observation:
A relational indefinite is felicitous with verb of possession *buy* or *sell* with a relational, non-possessive interpretation iff **it relates to the possessive relation restricting a lexically selected possession state role of *buy* or *sell*.**

With this, it seems reasonable to assume that what goes on for *buy* and *sell* is also a form of semantic incorporation. However, in this case, the relational indefinite doesn't simply incorporate into the lexical meaning of the verb, but actually into part of the lexical meaning of the verb. I will call this **subincorporation**:

Subincorporation:
The relational indefinite incorporates into a possessive relation restricting a lexically selected possession state role of *buy* or *sell*.

Since semantic subincorporation is about as non-compositional a process as I have ever come across, I will not try to fit it into a compositional mode here. Rather, I will describe how it can be modeled on semantic incorporation, as described earlier in this chapter. We will take (58a) as our example to work on:

(58)a. The farmer sold the king a son.
    b. The farmer had a son and sold him to the king.
    c. The farmer sold someone to the king, the goal of the selling being that person being the king's son.

As we have seen, (58a) can either mean *a son of the farmer* or *a son of the king*, i.e. the readings can be paraphrased as in (58b) and (58c). The meaning of *sell* that we're interested in is three place *sell* with the Source linked to the Agent role and the Goal linked to the To role:

$$sell^3 \rightarrow \lambda z \lambda y \lambda x \lambda e.\text{SELL}(e) \wedge \text{Ag}(e)=x \wedge \text{To}(e)=y \wedge \text{Th}(e)=z \wedge$$
$$\text{So}(e) \in \{s \in S: \text{Po}(s)=\text{Ag}(e) \wedge \text{Th}_p(s)=\text{Th}(e)\} \wedge$$
$$\text{Go}(e) \in \{s \in S: \text{Po}(s)=\text{To}(e) \wedge \text{Th}_p(s)=\text{Th}(e)\}$$
$$<\text{Th},\text{To}(\text{Go}),\text{Ag}(\text{So})>$$

I will start out with bringing this into a form where the possessive relations are explicitly represented. The following representation is equivalent to the previous one:

λzλyλxλe.SELL(e) ∧ Ag(e)=x ∧ To(e)=y ∧ Th(e)=z ∧
So(e) ∈ {s:∃x∃y[**λyλxλs: s∈PO ∧ Po(s)=y ∧ Th$_P$(s)=x**] ∩ [λyλxλe.Ag(e)=y ∧
   Th(e)=x] (s,x,y)]} ∧
Go(e) ∈ {s:∃x∃y[**λyλxλs: s∈PO ∧ Po(s)=y ∧ Th$_P$(s)=x**] ∩ [λyλxλe.To(e)=y ∧
   Th(e)=x] (s,x,y)]}
<Th,To(Go),Ag(So)>

In the interpretation, the possessive relations are in boldface. Both Source and Goal are lexically selected, which means that we have a choice for sub-incorporation. Here we will choose to incorporate into the Source. Thus, for readability, we can bring the Goal back to the equivalent simpler form:

λzλyλxλe.SELL(e) ∧ Ag(e)=x ∧ To(e)=y ∧ Th(e)=z ∧
So(e) ∈ {s:∃x∃y[**λyλxλs: s∈PO ∧ Po(s)=y ∧ Th$_P$(s)=x**] ∩ [λyλxλe.Ag(e)=y ∧
   Th(e)=x] (s,x,y)]} ∧
Go(e) ∈ {s ∈ S: Po(s)=To(e) ∧ Th$_p$(s)=Th(e)}
<Th,To(Go),Ag(So)>

We start the subincorporation by **dethematicizing** the possession role restricting the Source, in the same way as we did for incorporation earlier in this chapter. We get:

λzλyλxλe.SELL(e) ∧ Ag(e)=x ∧ To(e)=y ∧ Th(e)=z ∧
So(e) ∈ {s:∃x∃y[**λyλxλe: e∈E** ∧ x∈D ∧ y∈D] ∩ [λyλxλe.Ag(e)=y ∧
   Th(e)=x] (s,x,y)]} ∧
Go(e) ∈ {s ∈ S: Po(s)=To(e) ∧ Th$_p$(s)=Th(e)}
<Th,To(–),Ag(So)>

Now, what happens with the indefinite? Well, *sell* is a normal eventive verb which takes a normal object noun phrase, hence we will need to feed the verbal interpretation of *sell* a normal argument interpretation of *a son* of type <<d,t>,t>.

a son → λP.∃z[SON(z,c) ∧ P(z)],   where c is a context variable
                                        of type <<d,t>,t>

This means that we get:

λyλxλe.SELL(e) ∧ Ag(e)=x ∧ To(e)=y ∧ ∃z[SON(z,c) ∧ Th(e)=z] ∧
So(e) ∈ {s:∃x∃y[**λyλxλe: e∈E** ∧ x∈D ∧ y∈D] ∩ [λyλxλe.Ag(e)=y ∧
   Th(e)=x] (s,x,y)]} ∧
Go(e) ∈ {s ∈ S: Po(s)=To(e) ∧ Th$_p$(s)=Th(e)} <To(Go),Ag(–)>

Thus, the contextual argument interpretation of *a son* connects to the theme role of *sell*. If nothing else happened, we would expect this, out of the blue, not to be very felicitous (as with other verbs).

But, of course, we assume that **subincorporation** takes place. The relational interpretation SON of type <d,<d,t>> gets **thematicized** in the same way as earlier in this chapter:

$\lambda y \lambda x \lambda s.s \in [SON] \wedge A_1(s)=x \wedge A_2(s)=y$ of type <d,<d,<e,t>>
$<A_2,A_1>$

And this relation **incorporates** into the dethematicized relation, which means it intersects. Thematically, I will assume that this establishes a **rethematicized Source** So$[A_2,A_1]$.

$\lambda y \lambda x \lambda e.SELL(e) \wedge Ag(e)=x \wedge To(e)=y \wedge \exists z[SON(z,c) \wedge Th(e)=z] \wedge$
So(e) $\in \{s:\exists x \exists y[\lambda y \lambda x \lambda s.s \in [SON] \wedge A_1(s)=x \wedge A_2(s)=y] \cap$
    $[\lambda y \lambda x \lambda e: e \in E \wedge y \in D \wedge x \in D] \cap [\lambda y \lambda x \lambda e.Ag(e)=y \wedge Th(e)=x] (s,x,y)]\} \wedge$
Go(e) $\in \{s \in S: Po(s)=To(e) \wedge Th_p(s)=Th(e)\}$
    $<To(Go),Ag(So[A_2,A_1])>$

This we can simplify to:

$\lambda y \lambda x \lambda e.SELL(e) \wedge Ag(e)=x \wedge To(e)=y \wedge \exists z[SON(z,c) \wedge Th(e)=z] \wedge$
        So(e) $\in \{s \in [SON]: A_1(s)=Th(e) \wedge A_2(s)=Ag(e)\} \wedge$
        Go(e) $\in \{s \in S: Po(s)=To(e) \wedge Th_p(s)=Th(e)\}$
$<To(Go),Ag(So[A_2,A_1])>$

The king goes in next, then *the farmer*, we maximalize and get:

(58)a.   The farmer sold the king a son.

$\exists e[SELL(e) \wedge Ag(e)=\sigma(FARMER) \wedge To(e)=\sigma(KING) \wedge \exists z[SON(z,c) \wedge$
    $Th(e)=z] \wedge$
        So(e) $\in \{s \in [SON]: A_1(s)=Th(e) \wedge A_2(s)=Ag(e)\} \wedge$
        Go(e) $\in \{s \in S: Po(s)=To(e) \wedge Th_p(s)=Th(e)\}]$

Now look at the statement:

So(e) $\in \{s \in [SON]: A_1(s)=Th(e) \wedge A_2(s)=Ag(e)\}$

With the correspondence principle we can simplify this to:

SON(Th(e),Ag(e))

Hence, the above interpretation of (58a) is equivalent to:

$\exists e[SELL(e) \wedge Ag(e)=\sigma(FARMER) \wedge To(e)=\sigma(KING) \wedge \exists z[SON(z,c) \wedge Th(e)=z] \wedge$
        SON(Th(e),Ag(e)) $\wedge$ Go(e) $\in \{s \in S: Po(s)=To(e) \wedge Th_p(s)=Th(e)\}]$

But this means that the semantics already provides a setting for contextual value c: hence the obvious setting, c = Ag(e), is provided by the semantics, so we can again simplify:

(58)a.   The farmer sold the king a son.

$\exists e[SELL(e) \wedge Ag(e)=\sigma(FARMER) \wedge To(e)=\sigma(KING) \wedge SON(Th(e),Ag(e)) \wedge$
$Go(e) \in \{s \in S: Po(s)=To(e) \wedge Th_p(s)=Th(e)\}$]

There is a selling event with the farmer as agent, a son of the farmer as theme, and the king filling the To-role, and the goal of the selling being the king having possession over the farmer's son.

So, with subincorporation, we derive the intended interpretation for (58a). The other interpretation is derived through subincorporating into the Goal role. That interpretation will be:

There is a selling event with the farmer as agent, a son of the king as theme, and the king filling the To-role, the source of the selling being the farmer having initial possession over the theme.

Of course, with the Goal role there is more to be said about at what point of time the SON relation should hold between the theme of the selling and the king. But it seems the interpretation derived is perfectly suited for tagging further temporal (and modal) detail on.

In sum, with subincorporation we can explain the following facts.

1. *Buy* and *sell* differ from *have* in not showing definiteness effects with relational nouns.
2. *Buy* and *sell* are similar to *have* in allowing relational indefinites unproblematically,
3. Since subincorporation is restricted to possession relations restricting **lexically selected** possession state roles, we can explain the facts about which arguments the indefinites can relate to.

Chapter 10

Definite *Time*-Adverbials and Event Measures

10.1   Rothstein's Analysis of Bare Noun Phrase Adverbials

As we know, noun phrases do not normally occur in adjunct positions. We have, of course, been extensively concerned with noun phrases that, according to our analysis, do occur in adjunct position, namely the adjoined subjects in *there*-insertion constructions. In this chapter, and the next, we look at a different construction where that seems to be the case: bare noun phrase adverbials.

Bare noun phrase adverbials were discussed in Larson (1985), Rothstein (1995, 2000). These are expressions that look like noun phrases, but occur in adverbial position (examples based on Rothstein 2000):

(1)a.   The pope said mass *every place he went.*   PLACE
   b.   Sebastian varied the theme *every way he knew.*   MANNER
   c.   A train leaves for Amsterdam *every hour.*   TIME
   d.   I opened the door *every time (that) the bell rang.* TIME/EVENT

While normally noun phrases need a preposition to be allowed in adverbial position (and hence, what we find there is not noun phrases but prepositional phrases), the cases in (1) occur without a preposition.

Crosslinguistically, the cases (1c,d) are the most stable: we find corresponding examples in many languages. The cases in (1a,b) are more language dependent: cases like (1a) seem very marginal in Dutch, while (1b) is straightforwardly impossible:

(2)a.   De paus *droeg* een mis   *op* ?(op) elke   plaats waar   hij ging.
       The pope said a   mass up at   every place where he went
       (with the verb *opdragen* with separable prefix *op*)
   b.   Sebastian varieerde het thema #(op) elke   manier dat hij wist.
       Sebastian varied   the theme at   every way   that he knew

In this chapter (and the next) I will not be concerned with temporal cases as in (1c), nor with temporal interpretations of (1d). I will be concerned with the event-interpretations of cases like (1d), discussed in Rothstein (1995). On this usage *time* is not a temporal expression, but a **counting** expression (as becomes clear when the expression is translated into, say, French or Dutch):

	English	French	Dutch
Temporal:	*time*	*temps*	*tijd*
Event:	*time*	*fois*	*keer/maal*

Rothstein has shown that examples like (1d) have interpretations where what is counted is events, and not moments of time. An example that illustrates this out is (3)):

(3) [A big panel with thousands of little lamps. In front of it Amos W. Steinhacker (from Marten Toonder: *De Bovenbazen*).]
AWS: Every time a light goes up, I am exactly $10 billion richer.
[Five lights light up simultaneously.]
AWS: Another $50 billion.

AWS's continuation is perfectly felicitous, which it wouldn't be if *time* were counting moments of time. Clearly, then, on the intended reading in (3), we are not counting moments of time at which a light goes up, but lights-going-ups, events of a light going up.

Rothstein (1995) discusses two puzzles (the first was already discussed by Larson (1985):

The grammar puzzle (Larson/Rothstein):
How can noun phrases be adverbials?

This is, of course, exactly the question that we have asked before.

The puzzle of the matching effect (Boolos/Rothstein):
Adverbial event noun phrases impose **injections (one–one functions into)**.

Look at the cases in (4a):

(4)a. Every time (that) the bell rang I opened the door.
   c. There were at least as many door openings as bell ringings.

Rothstein (1995) argues that the event reading of (4a) entails (4c). Rothstein calls this the **matching effect** and argues convincingly that the effect is semantic, and not pragmatic. The puzzle is how to account for the matching effect.

Rothstein (1995) provides the following solution:

Rothstein's Analysis:
1. *Every time the bell rang* in adverbial position is **not** a noun phrase, **but a prepositional phrase with an empty preposition**.

This, of course, does away with the first problem: if the event expressions have an empty preposition – [$_{PP}$ [$_P$ Ø] [$_{DP}$ *every time the bell rang*]] – they are not noun phrases but prepositional phrases, and they are expected in adverbial position.

Rothstein's Analysis:
2. The empty preposition is interpreted as a **role M (the matching function)** which specifies an **event value**, i.e., of type <e,e>.

This means that M only differs from other prepositions in that it is a (partial) function of type <e,e>, instead of <e,d>. With this, Rothstein interprets the relevant prepositional phrases along the following lines:

Ø *the three times the bell rang* →
$\lambda e.M(e)=\sigma(\lambda f.RANG(f) \wedge Th(f)=\sigma(BELL) \wedge |f|=3)$
The set of events that matching function M maps onto the sum of three bell ringings.

Rothstein gives a simple compositional derivation of (4a) with interpretation (4b), which entails (4c), i.e. Rothstein predicts the matching effect.

(4)a. Every time the bell rang I opened the door.
  b. For every bell ringing event **e**, there is a door opening event **f such that M(f)=e**.
  c. There were at least as many door openings as bell ringings.

Example (4b) doesn't simply say that for every bell ringing there is a door opening, but that for every bell ringing there is a door opening which M maps on that bell ringing. Since M is a function, you cannot make (4b) true by choosing the same door opening for two bell ringings. Hence, (4c) follows.

We now come to some effects that will be our concern here. As an aside in her paper, Rothstein notes an asymmetry in felicity for these event phrases when they occur in adverbial position and when they occur in argument position.

External definiteness effects (Rothstein 1995):
1. External definiteness effects in normal adverbial position.
In normal adverbial position, bare event adverbials with relative clauses must be definite or based on a definite (i.e. have a definite or universal determiner, or a partitive based on a definite). Indefinites are not felicitous:

(5)a.   I opened the door, *the three times the bell rang / every time the bell rang.*
   b.   I opened the door *three of the times the bell rang.*
   c.   #I opened the door *three/many times the bell rang.*

External definiteness effects:
2. No external definiteness effects in noun phrase positions.
In English (and Dutch), these event expressions can occur in positions
where normal noun phrases can occur, like argument position and the
adjoined subject position in *there*-insertion. In these positions, they do not
show the matching effect, and no external definiteness effects (i.e. they behave
like normal noun phrases).

(6)a.   I remember with pleasure *seven times (that) I had dinner with him.*
   b.   There were *many times that I could have strangled him.*

I will make a comment on the data here. The effects discussed here are widely
observed in a variety of languages. The definites in cases like (5) are always
fine, and the indefinites are problematic. However, in some cases, and for some
speakers, the indefinites in cases like (5) are not completely infelicitous.
Rothstein notes this, and hypothesizes that in such cases the indefinites might
be "rescued" by reinterpreting them as partitives: so when felicitous, (5c) is
rescued through (5b).
   There is some evidence that this hypothesis is correct. It comes from what I
call Dutch contexts of "spontaneous irritation." The context is exemplified in (7):

(7)   Het is me vandaag, verdomme, *elke keer dat dat kreng ging* gebeurd dat ik
       de trap opstommelde en dan was er weer geen antwoord.
       It happened today, damn it, *every time that that rotten thing rang* that I stum-
       bled up the stairs, and then once again there was no answer.

In contexts of spontaneous irritation, the partitive is not felicitous, because it
is the wrong register: it is too formal for contexts of spontaneous irritation (8a).
If so, then we expect, with Rothstein's hypothesis, that, in this kind of context,
"rescue through partitive reconstruction" is not possible. This means that in
this kind of context, indefinites should be robustly infelicitous. This is indeed
the case (8b):

(8)a.   ??Het is me vandaag *wel tien van de keren dat dat kreng ging* gebeurd, dat
         ik de trap op stommelde, en dan was er weer geen antwoord.
         It happened today, damn it, *at least ten of the times that that rotten thing
         rang* that I stumbled up the stairs, and then once again there was no
         answer.
   b.   #Het is me vandaag *wel tien keer dat dat kreng ging* gebeurd dat ik de
         trap op stommelde, en dan was er weer geen antwoord.
         It happened today, damn it, *at least ten times that that rotten thing rang*
         that I stumbled up the stairs, and then once again there was no answer.

The data in (8) support Rothstein's hypothesis, and with that, they support her observations in (5). Rothstein observes the external definiteness effects discussed here, but she does not present an analysis for them. And in fact, they raise a puzzle for her own analysis:

A puzzle for Rothstein's analysis:
On Rothstein's analysis, you don't expect external definiteness effects at all.

Rothstein analyses the event adverbials as prepositional phrases with an empty preposition. But the DP complement position of prepositions is a normal argument position. This means that on Rothstein's analysis, the event noun phrases in (5) are as much in argument position as the noun phrases in (6). But that means that, on her analysis, the cases in (5) should pattern with the cases in (6), and you shouldn't find any external definiteness effects.

10.2   Degree Relatives: Grosu and Landman's Analysis

It was pointed out in Grosu and Landman (1998) that Rothstein's data concerning external definiteness effects are the same as the data discussed in chapter 3 for relative clauses with the gap in a position effected by the variable constraint:

(9)a.   #The three books *which* there were – on the table were mine.
   b.   The three books (*that*) there were – on the table were mine.

(10)a.   *The three* books (that) there were – on the table were mine.
    b.   *Every* book (that) there was – on the table was mine.
    c.   #*Three/many* books (that) there were – on the table were mine.

I discussed in chapter 3 the Carlson/Heim analysis of the cases in (9) and (10):

The infelicity of (9a) (Carlson/Heim):
which requires an **individual variable** to abstract over.

I argued in chapter 3 that this creates a conflict with the variable constraint.

The felicity of (9b) (Carlson/Heim):
that does not require an individual variable.

Rescue strategy for (9b) (Carlson/Heim):
Reinterpret the gap in the relative clause, by semantically interpreting the head *books* internally (as found in many languages in internally headed relative clauses), **with a free degree variable**, that relativization with *that* can abstract over:

(11)   that there were (**n many books**) on the table.
       $\lambda n.\exists x[BOOKS(x) \wedge |x|=n \wedge ON\ THE\ TABLE(x)]$

Grosu and Landman argue that, for this idea to work, a change in the semantics of numerical expressions and measures is needed: degrees cannot be simply numbers, they must be more fine-grained objects (triples, in Grosu and Landman 1998, for simplicity, pairs here).

The type (d×n) of degrees.
Type **(d×n)** is the type of expressions denoting **degrees**. Its semantic domain is the Boolean algebra with domain:
$DEG_D = \{<d,n>: d \in D\ and\ n \in N\ and\ |d|=n\}$

So, a degree is a pair consisting of an object and its cardinality. We have variables of the type of degrees, and also expressions of that type such as the following:

If α is an expression of type d, $<\alpha,|\alpha|>$ is of type (d×n), denoting the degree consisting of the interpretation of α and its cardinality.

If β is an expression of type (d×n), $[\beta]_1$, $[\beta]_2$, are of type d and type n respectively, denoting the first, resp. second element of the interpretation of β.

In previous chapters, the cardinality measure C was the function $\lambda x.|x|$ of type $<d,n>$. Now it is going to be a function of type $<d,(d×n)>$:

Cardinality measure C:
$C = \lambda x.<x,|x|>$ of type $<d,(d×n)>$.

I will add an operation δ from type $<n,t>$, the type of sets of numbers, to type $<(d×n),t>$, the type of sets of degrees:

Let k be a variable of type (d×n).
$\delta: <n,t> \rightarrow <(d×n),t>$
$\delta[\alpha] = \lambda k.\alpha([k]_2)$

I will assume, as before that *three* denotes 3 of type n, and *at most* denotes $\leq$ of type $<n,<n,t>>$. In chapter 1, the number phrase *at most three* was interpreted as $\leq(3)$ of type $<n,t>$. I will now assume that the interpretation of the number phrase is $\delta(\leq(3))$ of type $<(d×n),t>$. This means that I will assume the following interpretation:

at most three $\rightarrow$ $\delta(\leq(3))$ =
                   $\lambda k.[k]_2 \leq 3$ of type $<(d×n),t>$

The measure phrase is interpreted with composition, as before:

at most three Ø → δ(≤(3)) o λx.<x,|x|> =
                    λk.[k]₂≤3 o λx.<x,|x|> =
                    λx.[<x,|x|>]₂≤3 =
                    λx.|x|≤3   of type <d,t>.

Thus, ultimately, the semantics of *at most three* Ø stays as it was.

Finally, I assume that the empty numerical relation Ø can express identity at type <n,<n,t>>, but also at type <<(d×n), <(d×n),t>>.

The rescue strategy now reconstructs inside the relative clause in (10a) the noun phrase in the following way:

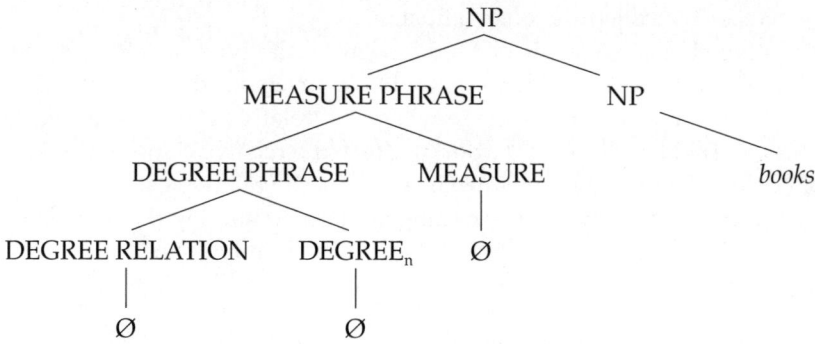

where:

$[_{degree}$ Ø$_n]$ → z$_n$ of type (d×n)

The interpretation for the whole noun phrase is:

$[(=(z_n))$ o λx.<x,|x|>$] ∩$ *BOOK =
λx.<x,|x|>=z$_n$ ∧ *BOOK(x)   of type <d,t>.

The felicity of (10a) and the infelicity of (10c) (Grosu and Landman):
Relativization **abstracts over degree variable z$_n$**, which gives a set of degrees; and it involves maximalization: it derives **the maximal degree** in that set.

The new analysis of the relative clause in (11) is:

(12)   that$_n$ there were (**z$_n$ many books**) on the table.
       {**MAX**[λz$_n$.∃x[BOOKS(x) ∧ <x,|x|>=z$_n$ ∧ ON THE TABLE(x)]]}

which reduces to:

$\{<\sqcup(\lambda x.*BOOK(x) \wedge ON\ THE\ TABLE(x)), n>\},$ of type $<(d \times n),t>$
where $n = |\sqcup(\lambda x.*BOOK(x) \wedge ON\ THE\ TABLE(x))|$
The singleton set containing the degree, which consists of the sum of all the books on the table, and its cardinality.

We have derived an interpretation for the relative clause as a singleton set. This means that, due to maximalization, the relative clause is already definite. It is this, we proposed in Grosu and Landman (1998), that creates the external definiteness effects.

We follow the rest of the analysis for the cases in (10). Semantically, the head noun *books* is already interpreted inside the relative clause. We argued in Grosu and Landman (1998) that it nevertheless also has a semantic effect outside the relative clause. We called the effect **substance**.

The relative clause, so far, is of type $<(d \times n),t>$, the type of sets of degrees. But the head noun *books* is of type $<d,t>$: books are individuals of type d, not degrees. We assume that at the stage where the relative clause is turned into an NP the external head *books* has a **sortal effect**: the relative clause must denote a set of books. The operation of substance brings the relative clause from type $<(d \times n),t>$ to type $<d,t>$, by taking the singleton set containing the first element of the pair in the relative clause. Thus, we get an **inherently definite** noun phrase interpretation:

$\sqcup(\lambda x.*BOOK(x) \wedge ON\ THE\ TABLE(x))$

Next, the numeral *three* combines appositively with this noun phrase, which means roughly that it adds the cardinality statement as a presupposition. The external definiteness effect is, finally, expressed at the level where a full DP is formed.

> **Assumption:**
> The **indefinite** determiner (singular *a*, plural $\emptyset$) cannot combine with this inherently definite noun.
> The **definite** article *the* can combine.

This gives (13):

(13)   The three (books) that$_n$ there were (z_n **many books**) on the table.
      $\sqcup(\lambda x.*BOOK(x) \wedge ON\ THE\ TABLE(x))$
      Presupposition: $|\sqcup(\lambda x.*BOOK(x) \wedge ON\ THE\ TABLE(x))| = 3$

Thus, the noun phrase denotes the sum of the books on the table, with presupposition that there are three. (From there on, this can be the input for partitives. The *every* case is analyzed by assuming that *every* can be the composition of the distributivity operator and the definiteness operator.)

10.3   Solving the Puzzle for Rothstein's Analysis

I have shown the Grosu and Landman analysis of the relative clauses cases in (10) in some detail, because of the parallel data we have seen for the event adverbials. Thus, I will assume that these event adverbials allow in essence the same analysis as the cases in (10). More precisely, the analysis of *the three times that the bell rang* will follow the analysis of the previous section exactly, up to the relative clause level. Hence, there is abstraction over a degree variable (of type $(e \times n)$), and maximalization. Thus, at the relative clause level we derive:

> *that$_n$ the bell rang (z$_n$ many times)* →
> $\{<\sqcup(\lambda e.\text{RING}(e) \wedge \text{Th}(e)=\sigma(\text{BELL})), n>\}$, of type $<(e \times n),t>$
> where $n = |\sqcup(\lambda e.\text{RING}(e) \wedge \text{Th}(e)=\sigma(\text{BELL}))|$
> The singleton degree consisting of the sum of the bell ringings and its cardinality.

The next stage is the stage where a noun phrase is formed. In the case of the books, above, we saw that the external head *books* obligatorily triggers substance, which brings the noun phrase from type $<(d \times n),t>$ to type $<d,t>$. In the event cases, the external head is the expression *time(s)*. I will argue in the next chapter that *time* is not a normal noun, but a classifier, and that its semantics is different from that of nouns. What I will be assuming is that, for the present cases, this makes a difference exactly at this stage:

Assumption one:
Unlike normal nouns, the classifier *time* need not trigger **substance**.

I am not assuming that *time* cannot trigger substance: it can, and then you derive a normal noun phrase. But it need not, and then you derive a noun phrase with an interpretation at type $<(e \times n),t>$. It is this possibility that we will exploit below.

Before that, let us briefly consider the case where you do trigger substance. In that case, you will derive a noun phrase interpretation for *the three times that the bell rang* at the normal argument type for noun phrase interpretations, hence an interpretation which can occur in argument position. Like the interpretation of (13), this interpretation has external definiteness effects: that is, this way of deriving an argument interpretation can derive a felicitous argument interpretation for the definite *the three times that the bell rang*, but not for the indefinite *three times that the bell rang*. This would be a problem, if this were the only way of deriving argument interpretations for these noun phrases, because then we would expect, contra to fact, external definiteness effects in argument position as well.

But I am not assuming that. I am assuming that the noun phrases *the three times that the bell rang/three times that the bell rang* also have derivations of interpretations at the normal argument types for noun phrases which do not go through the degree type. Since the argument interpretations are not my topic here, I will not propose details of an analysis: for my purposes, Rothstein's own analysis is good enough.

More precisely: assume Rothstein's analysis of these noun phrases, which derives interpretations at argument types without going through degree types. This generates **felicitous argument** interpretations of *the three times that the bell rang* and of *three times that the bell rang*, that is, without external definiteness effects. As we have seen, with substance, we also derive the same argument interpretation of the definite *the three times that the bell rang* in a derivation that does go through degree types. But since felicitous indefinite argument interpretations are generated anyway, this does not show up in the data as external definiteness effects in argument position.

The only further thing that we must ensure is that from derivations that do not go through the degree type, you cannot derive interpretations at the degree type. Thus, unlike Rothstein, I assume that there is no empty preposition which takes these argument interpretations as complement. More generally, I assume that there is no lifting operation that lifts interpretations at an argument type to interpretations at a degree type. With those assumptions, you can only get **adverbial** interpretations of these expressions by going through the degree strategy, with the associated external definiteness effects. I will make these assumptions explicit in the course of following the derivation of the adverbial cases. So let's come back to their derivation.

In the derivation where we do not trigger substance, we have a noun phrase with interpretation at type $<(e \times n),t>$. We assume that we can add the interpretation of numerical *three* to this as a presupposition, and we apply the definite article. We assume that at this stage the same external definiteness constraints apply as in the case in the previous section: indefinites cannot be felicitously formed from noun phrases with an interpretation as a singleton set of degrees. We derive:

$[_{DP[degree]}$ *the three times that the bell rang* $] \rightarrow$
$<\sqcup(\lambda e.RING(e) \wedge Th(e)=\sigma(BELL)), 3>,$ of type $(e \times n)$
where $|\sqcup(\lambda e.RING(e) \wedge Th(e)=\sigma(BELL))| = 3$

(For the partitives based on it, or expressions with *every*, a generalized quantifier interpretation based on type $(e \times n)$ will be derived.) Since the derivation process does not allow for the derivation of indefinite noun phrases, this derivation shows external definiteness effects.

Now we come back to the puzzle for Rothstein's analysis. Rothstein assumed that Ø *the three times the bell rang* is a prepositional phrase, and Ø is a preposition. The problem was, as we have seen, that this incorrectly predicts that indefinite event adverbials with relative clauses cases are felicitous, since the complement of a preposition is an argument position, and indefinite event noun phrases are perfectly felicitous in argument position.

We will now part ways with Rothstein with the following assumption, which we can express syntactically or semantically:

Assumption two:
DP[degree] cannot occur in argument position.
The type of degrees (e×n) is not an argument type.

We are making progress now. The derivation of the event noun phrase as a degree noun phrase shows external definiteness effects, it does not allow for the derivation of indefinite cases. As discussed above, **indefinite** event noun phrases with relative clauses can be derived with interpretations of type <e,t>. Those will be good to derive argument interpretations of type <<e,t>,t>, and as such they can occur in argument position. But:

Assumption three:
Interpretations of event noun phrases based on the normal type shifting triangle e, <e,t>, <<e,t>,t> cannot shift to the degree triangle based on (e×n).

With these assumptions it follows that degree noun phrases cannot occur in argument position, and they show external definiteness effects (because the only way we can derive them is through the procedure that involves maximalization).

Now we need to address the question of how degree noun phrases can be allowed in adverbial position. Here we follow the lead of the analysis of the DP as being of the type of degrees:

Assumption four:
Degree noun phrases can form **adverbial measure phrases**.

This means in essence that I propose the following analysis:

the three times the bell rang is analyzed as:

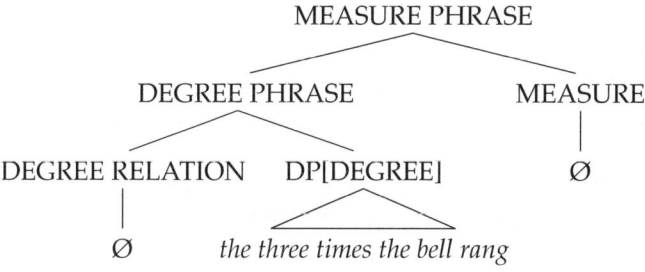

The measure [$_{\text{measure}}$ Ø] is the **default adverbial measure**. As we know, the **default adjectival measure** is C, the cardinality function. I will call the default adverbial measure CANTOR:

Assumption five:
$[_{\text{adverbial measure}}\ \varnothing\ ] \rightarrow$ CANTOR   of type $<e, (e \times n)>$

The degree relation = is of type $<(e \times n), <(e \times n), t>>$.
The interpretation of *the three times the bell rang* is of type is of type $(e \times n)$.
The interpretation of the degree phrase $=(<\sqcup(\lambda e.\text{RING}(e) \wedge \text{Th}(e)=\sigma(\text{BELL})), 3>)$
is of type $< (e \times n), t>$. CANTOR is of type $<e, (e \times n)>$. The two compose to give
the interpretation of the measure phrase at type $<e, t>$:

$(=(<\sqcup(\lambda e.\text{RING}(e) \wedge \text{Th}(e)=\sigma(\text{BELL})), 3>))$ o CANTOR $=$
$\lambda e.\text{CANTOR}(e)= <\sqcup(\lambda e.\text{RING}(e) \wedge \text{Th}(e)=\sigma(\text{BELL})), 3>$ of type $<e, t>$

Hence, we derive a perfectly legitimate adverbial interpretation of type $<e, t>$.
This can be adjoined at the event type interpretation of *Dafna opened the door*,
and we get, after maximalization:

(14)   The three times the bell rang, Dafna opened the door.
       $\exists e[*\text{OPEN}(e) \wedge *\text{Ag}(e)=\text{DAFNA} \wedge *\text{Th}(e)=\sigma(\text{DOOR}) \wedge$
       $\text{CANTOR}(e) = <\sqcup(\lambda e.\text{RING}(e) \wedge \text{Th}(e)=\sigma(\text{BELL})), 3>$
       There is a sum of door openings by Dafna, and Cantor maps that sum
       onto the degree of the three bell ringings.

CANTOR is a different formalization of Rothstein's matching intuition. The
intuition behind CANTOR is the following:

The Cantor Intuition – indirect counting:
CANTOR counting is counting by means of one–one functions.

You count a sum of events by contextually postulating a given sum of events
and providing a one–one function with it. The function CANTOR is a natural
generalization of the function C:

(c] = {b: b $\sqsubseteq$ c}
(c], the ideal generated by c is the set of c's parts.

Isomorphism:
b $\cong$ **c** iff (b] $\cong$ (c]
b and c are isomorphic iff their generated ideals are isomorphic.

The Cantor Constraint:
CANTOR is a function of type $<e, (e \times n)>$ such that:
for every e $\in$ E: e $\cong$ [CANTOR(e)]$_1$

Hence CANTOR maps every sum of events onto the degree of an isomorphic
sum of events. In this way CANTOR is a counting measure, because isomorphic
sums of events have, of course, the same cardinality.

With this constraint (14) means:

> There is a sum of door openings by Dafna, and CANTOR maps that sum onto the pair consisting of the sum of bell ringings and its cardinality 3, meaning – by the semantics of CANTOR – that this sum of door openings by Dafna and this sum of three bell ringings are isomorphic.

This entails that there are at least three door openings as well, hence, the matching effect follows from the semantics of CANTOR.

The current analysis agrees with Rothstein in the assumption that the event adverbials in question are allowed in adverbial position because they are in fact not noun phrases. The analysis also agrees with Rothstein in that it is assumed that some function needs to account for the matching effect. The analysis disagrees with Rothstein in what it assumes the expressions to be, and what accounts for the matching effect. For Rothstein, they are prepositional phrases, and the matching effect comes from the interpretation of an empty preposition as a **role** specifying event values. This, I have argued to be problematic. On my analysis, the expressions are measure phrases, and the empty element that accounts for the matching effect is an empty counting measure, CANTOR.

On this analysis, then, event adverbials are **counting adverbials**, constructed with **indirect counter** CANTOR: CANTOR counts sums of events in the main clause event type by specifying for each such sum of events e a definite, given, sum of events isomorphic to e. This is indirect counting, because we do not count the sums of events e directly in terms of their atoms, but indirectly in terms of the isomorphism with $[CANTOR(e)]_1$.

The counting through CANTOR is an attractive feature of the analysis, in comparison to Rothstein's analysis, since it directly encodes the intuition that the matching effect is a **counting** effect, and that counting is done by counters, that is, measures (and not by roles).

Carlson, Heim, and Grosu and Landman assumed for independent reasons a degree analysis of maximalizing relatives in the nominal domain. Grosu and Landman connect the external definiteness effects of these relatives to the degree of abstraction involved. Really the only additional assumption needed is a plausible one: in exceptional cases, namely with the classifier *time*, the derivation can stay at the type of sets of degrees. In such exceptional cases, the grammar will derive definite noun phrases with a degree interpretation. This gives us the external definiteness effects for these expressions as well, and, of course, brings us exactly to the right type for interpreting the expression straightforwardly as a counting adverbial. Just as number expression *three* denotes the value of the implicit adjectival counting measure C for cardinality, the definite degree noun phrase denotes the value of the implicit adverbial counting measure CANTOR. Thus, assuming that the external definiteness effects have the same source in both constructions where we find them makes a natural and plausible analysis of the event adverbials as measure adverbials possible.

Chapter 11

Indefinite *Time*-Adverbials and the Counting-Grid

11.1   Indefinite Counting Adverbials

We have analyzed definite expressions that look like noun phrases with *time*, but occur in adverbial position with a counting-events-interpretation, as adverbial measure phrases, counting events indirectly with measure CANTOR. But there are also things that look like **indefinite** noun phrases with *time* – without relative clauses this time – that occur in adverbial position, also with a counting-events-interpretation. These are the simple indefinites *three times/many times*, etc.

(1)a.   Dafna jumped *three times*.
   b.   Dafna jumped *many times*.

Now obviously, the analysis given in the previous section does not carry over to those, because that analysis only derived definite noun phrases with a degree interpretation, and precisely not indefinites. So we again need to raise the same question as before:

The grammar puzzle again:
How are noun phrases like *three times* allowed in adverbial position?

I first want to argue that the indefinite *time*-adverbials that we are dealing with here are not the same construction as the definite *time*-adverbials that we have discussed in the previous chapter. There are three strong arguments for this.

Argument 1

If the indefinite cases in (1) were the same construction as the definite cases from the previous chapter, then we have no alternative but to assume that the indefinites in (1) are to be systematically reanalyzed as implicit partitives, since that's the only way the indefinites from the previous chapter can be made vaguely felicitous. This means that the cases in (1) ought to be systematically reanalyzed as the cases in (2):

(2)a.   Dafna jumped *three of the contextually specified times (events)*.
   b.   Dafna jumped *many of the contextually specified times (events)*.

But the cases in (2) don't even entail the cases in (1)! Take (1b) and (2b). If the contextually specified events are events of me winning the lottery, (2b) would be true if, say, I win the lottery five times and Dafna jumps four times. But, if you know Dafna, that doesn't make many jumpings for Dafna, i.e. it doesn't make (1b) true.

Argument 2

Rothstein (2000) shows that the effects that we have discussed for **definite** *time* adverbials in the previous chapter, hold too for **definite** *place* adverbials (3a). But English has nothing with *place* corresponding to the simple **indefinites** with *time*: simple **indefinites** with *place* are infelicitous (3b):

(3)a.   The pope said mass *every place he stopped*.
   b.   #The pope said mass *three places*.

If the definite and the simple indefinite cases were the same construction, one would expect the simple indefinites with *time* and *place* to be licensed in the same way (since the definites are). But they are not, indicating that we are dealing with different constructions.

Argument 3

The definite and indefinite cases do not have the same meaning. Look at the contrast in (4):

(4)a.   Dafna jumped *every time/the three times*.
   b.   Dafna jumped *three times/many times*.

There is a strong intuition that, while the time adverbials count both in (4a) and (4b), they do not count in the same way. With the definite counting adverbials in (4a), jumping events are counted **indirectly** through contextually specified events, i.e. through CANTOR. But the indefinite counting adverbials count jumping events **directly**.

That is, (4a) expresses that the set of Dafna's jumping events and a specified set of contextual events are in one–one correspondence. But (4b) just says that there were three/many jumpings events of Dafna. And we observe:

Definiteness effects:
The possibility of getting a **direct count** interpretation shows definiteness effects:
All and only bare indefinite counting adverbs count directly.

In the other cases of definiteness effects discussed in this book (*there*-insertion, *have* with relational noun phrases), the definiteness effects showed up as a distinction in **felicity**: only indefinites are felicitous in these contexts. In the present case, the definiteness effects show up as a distinction in **interpretation**: only bare indefinite counting adverbials allow a direct counting interpretation. I will argue in this chapter that the definiteness effects that we are concerned with here ultimately have the same source as the definiteness effects discussed before: access to the type of sets.

In earlier talks and manuscripts I proposed what would seem to be the obvious analysis of these definiteness effects:

The Obvious Analysis:
[$_{DP}$ Ø *three times*] → λe.|e|=3   of type <e,t>.
Indefinite time adverbials are born at the type of sets of events, the same type as adverbials, and can shift into the adjunction domain.

I now want to provide two arguments that the Obvious Analysis is actually wrong.

Argument 1

The Obvious Analysis works too well to provide an adequate solution to the grammar puzzle. If it is just the fact that indefinite event noun phrases are born at type <e,t> that allows them in adverbial position, then one should in fact expect all indefinite event denoting noun phrases to be felicitous in adverbial position (just like all indefinite noun phrases are felicitous as adjoined subjects in *there*-insertion contexts). But this is not the case. We have already in the previous chapter seen the case of indefinite *time*-adverbials with relative clauses (5a). But also indefinite event denoting noun phrases like *three burnings* cannot felicitously be used adverbially (5b):

(5)a.   #Dafna answered the door *three times the bell rang*.
  b.   #They burned the documents #(in) *three burnings*.

In both cases we have perfectly fine event denoting indefinite noun phrases, yet they are infelicitous in adverbial position. The Obvious Analysis has no explanation for this.

Argument 2

The Obvious Analysis actually gets the semantics of the indefinite *time* phrases wrong. The operation ADJUNCT shift interpretations at the set type <e,t> to

intersective modifier interpretations. This is fine for expressions that it is meant for, e.g. event adverbials like *quickly*. As Parsons (1990) has argued, the intersective analysis encoded in ADJUNCT is precisely what we want to explain the intersective, **scopeless** behavior of such adverbials: such adverbials can be permuted while preserving truth value. However, as Doetjes (1997) has pointed out, such an intersective, scopeless analysis is wrong for expressions like *three times*. Look at (6):

(6)   Two girls kissed Dafna *three times*.

The **intersective** analysis proposed by the Obvious Analysis would generate (6) with the following interpretation:

$\exists e[*KISS(e) \wedge *GIRL(*Ag(e)) \wedge |*Ag(e)|=2 \wedge *Th(e)=DAFNA \wedge |e|=3]$
There are three kissing events with Dafna as theme; one of them has a girl as agent, and the other two have another girl as agent.

This is clearly not what the sentence means, so the Obvious Analysis is obviously wrong.

11.2   *Time* as a Classifier

The classifier construction in English is the construction: CLASSIFIER (of) NOUN. Here the classifier can be a measure, as in *liter (of) water* or a classifier proper, as in *bucket (of) water*. In English, in context, many nouns can be used as classifiers proper (inventing aesthetically pleasing ones is part of English recreational linguistics), and, in context, many classifiers can be used as measures. Semantically, the difference between the measure interpretation and the classifier proper interpretation is that the measure interpretation is **intersective** on the noun interpretation, while the classifier proper interpretation is not. Example (7) nicely shows the ambiguity of the classifier *bottles*:

(7)   Three bottles of wine were flushed through the toilet.

On the measure interpretation, (7) describes a simple action: wine to the quantity of three bottles was flushed through the toilet. On the classifier proper interpretation, (7) describes a problematic action: three bottles containing wine went down. In the classifier construction, the classifier takes a noun as complement to form a complex noun. Semantically, classifiers proper parcel the interpretation of their complement to fit into another semantic domain: for instance, mass entities like sums of water are parceled by the classifier *bottle* to fit into bottles, and these parcels can be counted that way.

In English, the classifier construction takes the particle *of* (which is optional in cookbooks):

(8)a. Three **buckets** (of) *water* (classifier: **buckets**, from mass to count)
  b. Three **liters** (of) *water*   (measure: **liters**, water to the amount of three liter)
  c. Three **groups** (of) *boys*   (classifier: **groups**, from sums to group atoms)

In Dutch, the classifier construction does not have an *of* particle:

(9)a. Drie **flessen** water
  b. Drie **liter** water
  c. Drie **groepen** jongens

In Dutch there is a very useful diagnostic principle to indicate for some expressions whether they are classifiers or normal nouns:

Diagnostic principle in Dutch (Doetjes 1997):
Normal nouns always show **obligatory** number agreement.
Many classifiers, in particular, measures, show **optional** number agreement, with the **non-agreeing** form preferred.

(10)a. #drie jongen/drie jongen**s**
     #three boy   /three boy**s**
  b. Drie   liter/liter**s** water
     Three liter/liter**s** water
  c. Drie   pond /pond**en** gerookte knoflook worst
     Three pound/pound**s** smoked garlic   sausage

We see in (10a) that the plural numeral *drie* requires plural morphology on the noun *jongen*. In (10b,c) *liter* and *pond* are classifiers, and, even though there is the same plural numeral *drie*, plural morphology is not required on the classifier. (Not all classifiers allow the non-agreeing form. But, when the non-agreeing form is allowed, it is clearly the preferred one. In fact, judgments differ among speakers about how good the agreeing forms are in this case. My dialect, for instance, accepts the agreeing forms more easily than Doetjes' dialect. See Doetjes (1997) for further discussion.)

Doetjes points out that in the *time*-adverbials *time* patterns with classifiers on the agreement facts:

Event classifiers (Doetjes):
In Dutch, *keer/maal* (*time*) shows **optional** number agreement in the adverbial *time* phrases.

(11)a. Dafna sprong *de drie keer/keren dat de bel ging.*
     Dafna jumped the three time/times that the bell went
  b. Dafna sprong *drie keer/keren.*
     Dafna jumped three time/times.

A nice additional fact is the following: if the indefinite *time* phrase occurs in **argument** position, *time* patterns with nouns, and not with classifiers: it shows obligatory number agreement:

(12)   Ik herinner   me zeven keren/#keer dat ik met hem dineerde.
       I remember self seven times/#time that I with him dined
       I remember seven times that I had dinner with him (on the interpreta-
       tion: seven dinner events).

That is, in (12), if we use the non-agreeing form, *zeven keer* can only be interpreted as modifying adverbially *herinnert* (i.e. seven memory events).

These facts are very promising for our purposes. What we want to explain
is how expressions that look like noun phrases can occur in adverbial position.
Well, we now see that, on the adverbial use, what looks like their noun, *time*,
is not a normal noun, but a classifier.

To come to terms with the semantics of *time* as a classifier, I turn to the nominal domain first. We are interested in the collective interpretations of (13):

(13)a.   Four *times* three boys met in the park.
    b.   Vier *keer* drie jongens kwamen samen   in het park.
         Four time three boys   came   together in the park

Note the non-agreeing form of *time* in the Dutch case. (13) has an interpretation where *time* is just interpreted as multiplication:

  A group of twelve boys met in the park.

But (13) has another interpretation, and that is the one that we are interested
in here:

  Four groups of three boys met in the park (say, each at a different corner).

This reading is what I have called in Landman (2000) a "distribution to collections" reading, and I have argued in Landman (2000) that the grammatical
availability of such readings is evidence for a **gridding** operation of **group formation**. In fact, (13) shows the need for grammatical gridding even more strongly
than the cases I discussed in Landman (2000).

   The operation of group formation originates in Link (1984): the operation
shifts the semantically plural interpretation of a noun phrase like *the boys* as
$\sigma(*BOY)$, the sum of the boys, to a corresponding semantically singular interpretation $\uparrow(\sigma(*BOY))$ as a **group atom**: *the boys* regarded as a singular entity
in its own right, i.e. with its part-of structure of singular boys, so to say, ignored.
In Landman (2000), I added group formation for the domain of type d. Here
I will add it for the type of events as well.

The domains D and E are complete atomic Boolean algebras. For each domain, the set of atoms ATOM is sorted into two non-overlapping sets:

Sorting the domains:
ATOM = IND ∪ GROUP
IND is the set of singular individuals or individual events.
GROUP is the set of singular collections of individuals or events.
SUM, the domain of sums of individuals or individual events, is *IND

The operation of **group formation** ↑ shifts pluralities (sums), which are strictly determined by their parts, to **group atoms**, so to say, more than the sum of their parts:

Group formation ↑:
If $\alpha \in$ SUM – IND, then ↑(α) $\in$ GROUP
If $\alpha \in$ IND,   then ↑(α) = α

The operation of membership specification brings you back:

Membership specification ↓:
If $\alpha \in$ GROUP, then ↓(α) $\in$ SUM
If $\alpha \in$ IND, then ↓(α)=α

Connecting ↑ and ↓:
if $\alpha \in$ SUM: ↓↑(α) = α

The diagram illustrates a partial picture of a domain with sums and groups:

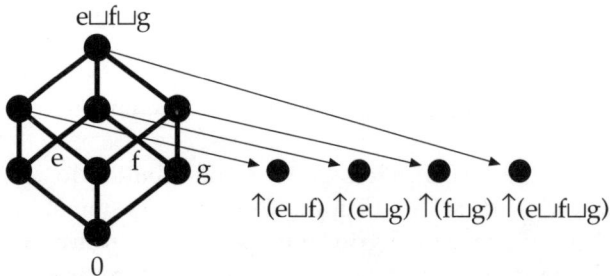

I specify here domains of sums and groups for type d and type e. In the theory of plurality developed in Landman (2000) these domains are linked by singular and plural roles, R and *R. When adding group events, it becomes useful to also add **group roles**, "groupifications" of plural roles. I use the notion ↑*R for this, and I set:

↑*R(↑(e)) = ↑(*R(e))

This means that if a sum of singing events e takes the sum of the boys, $\sigma(*BOY)$, as **plural agent** (meaning that the atomic boys together make up the agents of the atomic singing events making up e), then the corresponding group of the boys, $\uparrow(\sigma(*BOY))$, forms the **group agent** of the corresponding group event. Similarly, we can define for verbal predicates: $^\uparrow *V = \{\uparrow(e): e \in *V\}$.

I add a brief comment for the "plurality buffs" who have followed through the ins and outs of the discussion of collectivity in Landman (2000). If you're not one of them, you can safely skip the following paragraph.

Adding groups of events and group roles allows for a more finegrained analysis of collectivity than I presented in Landman (2000). The above discussion entails that a representation of the interpretation of a sentence may be formulated strictly in terms of an atomic event ($\uparrow$e), an atomic role ($^\uparrow *R$) and an atomic value for the role ($\uparrow$x), and nevertheless not be a representation of a collective reading, because the definition of the atomic role $^\uparrow *R$ allows us to reduce the representation to one which does not involve atoms. That is, an expression like:

$$\exists e \in ATOM[^\uparrow *V(e) \wedge {}^\uparrow *R(e)=\uparrow(x)]$$

is equivalent to a distributive statement:

$$\exists e \in ATOM[*V(\downarrow(e)) \wedge *R(\downarrow e)=x]$$

Thus, it is only when true collective aspects of interpretation are added that we get true collectivity. Such would be a representation:

$$\exists e \in ATOM[^\uparrow *V(e) \wedge R(e)=\uparrow(x)]$$

Here an **atomic role** R is applied to an atomic group of events, and this cannot be reduced to an interpretation which doesn't rely on groups. But cases of partial reducibility are possible too, say, an interpretation of the above atomic role R satisfying the following equivalence for group events:

$$R(e)=\uparrow(x) \text{ iff}^\uparrow *R(e)=\uparrow(x) \wedge \text{IN-COORDINATION}(e)=\uparrow(x)$$

On this interpretation, $\exists e \in ATOM[^\uparrow *V(e) \wedge R(e)=\uparrow(x)]$ would be equivalent to: $\exists e[*V(e) \wedge *R(e)=x \wedge \text{IN-COORDINATION}(\uparrow(e))=\uparrow(x)]$. Such an interpretation would be collective, because it contains an irreducible reference to groups, but it would entail the distributive $\exists e[*V(e) \wedge *R(e)=x]$.

What this brief discussion shows is that introducing group events and group roles opens up a plethora of interesting possibilities for refining existing theories of collectivity (or, if you're not a plurality buff, a can of worms).

We come back to (13a):

(13)a.   *Four times* three boys met in the park.

I assume that on the reading we are interested in, *time* is a classifier proper: *time* **parcels** the interpretation of its complement *three boys*, λx.*BOY(x) ∧ |x|=3, the set of sums of boys of cardinality three into appropriate parcels. The appropriate parcels are **countable** parcels, which will be counted by Ø *four* Ø in the usual way. The underlying intuition about the semantics of *time* is one that I already expressed in Landman (1989):

> **The counting intuition (Landman 1989):**
> Sums cannot be counted directly. Only atoms can be counted.
> Classifier *time* parcels a set of non-countable sums into a set of countable atoms.

This means that if you insist on counting a set of sums, pluralities, the grammar must make them countable by turning them into group atoms. This is, I claim, what happens in the interpretation we are after for (13a).

It will be useful for the analysis later on to express this counting intuition in the type theory. For this reason I will introduce the sets of atoms of types d and e as types in the type theory (note that the atoms of type d will include both individual atoms and group atoms, the same for type e). And for reasons explained below, I invent a fancy notation for these types: <↑,<d,t>>, and <↑,<e,t>>. (It will be helpful to think of the symbol ↑ in these types as analogous to Montague's symbol s in his intensional types.)

> **The counting types:**
> <↑,<d,t>>, <↑,<e,t>> ∈ TYPE
> The domains of these types are ATOM$_d$ and ATOM$_e$ respectively.
> Thus, <↑,<d,t>> is a subtype of <d,t> and <↑,<e,t>> a subtype of <e,t>.

The types <↑,<a,t>> and <a,t> (where a is d or e) are related by counting operators $^↑$ and $^↓$.

> **The counting operator $^↑$:**
> Let a be type d or e.
> If α ∈ EXP$_{<a,t>}$, then $^↑α$ ∈ EXP$_{<↑,<a,t>>}$
> $[^↑α]_{M,g} = \{↑(x): x ∈ [α]_{M,g}\}$

If α is an expression of type <a,t>, denoting a set of sums, then $^↑α$ is an expression of the counting type <↑,<a,t>>, denoting the set of atomic groups corresponding to the sums in α. Note that if α already denotes a set of atomic events, then $^↑α$ and α have the same denotation, but not the same type. Thus $^↑$ shifts α to the counting type <↑,<a,t>> of sets of atoms.

> **The counting operator $^↓$:**
> Let a be type d or e.
> If α ∈ EXP$_{<↑,<a,t>>}$, then $^↓α$ ∈ EXP$_{<a,t>}$
> $[^↓α]_{M,g} = [α]_{M,g}$

In this case α is an expression of the counting type $<\uparrow,<a,t>>$, denoting a set of atoms. $^{\downarrow}\alpha$ has the same interpretation as α, but not the same type: $^{\downarrow}$ shifts α from the counting type $<\uparrow,<a,t>>$ to the full type $<a,t>$. (Note that counting operator $^{\downarrow}$ has nothing to do with membership specification operator $\downarrow$.)

Introducing the types $<\uparrow,<a,t>>$ allows me to use the operations $^{\uparrow}$ and $^{\downarrow}$ as type shifting operators. We now specify the semantics of classifier *time*:

The semantics of classifier *time*:
Let z be a variable of type $<\uparrow,<a,t>>$ (a either type d or e).
$[_{classifier} \; time \;] \rightarrow \lambda z.^{\downarrow}z$ of type $<<\uparrow,<a,t>>,<a,t>>$

This means that, semantically, *time* denotes the **identity function** on the set of atoms in type $<a,t>$. The real semantic effect of *time* is encoded in the **types**: *time* requires as input an expression of the counting type $<\uparrow,<a,t>>$, hence denoting a set of atoms, and gives as output an expression with the same interpretation, but of type $<a,t>$.

Let us see how this works in example (13a). Classifier *time* combines with its complement *three boys*:

time three boys $\rightarrow$ APPLY[$\lambda z.^{\downarrow}z,$ $\lambda x.{}^{*}BOY(x) \wedge |x|=3$]
$<<\uparrow,<d,t>>,<d,t>>$ $<d,t>$

We have a type mismatch: *time* is fed a set of sums of type $<d,t>$, while it requires a set of atoms of type $<\uparrow,<d,t>>$. Creating this type mismatch was, of course, the whole point of the semantics given to *time*. Of course, the mismatch is resolved with counting operator $^{\uparrow}$:

time three boys $\rightarrow$ APPLY[$\lambda z.^{\downarrow}z,$ $^{\uparrow}\lambda x.{}^{*}BOY(x) \wedge |x|=3$] =
$<<\uparrow,<d,t>>,<d,t>>$ $<\uparrow,<d,t>>$
$\lambda z.^{\downarrow}z \; (^{\uparrow}\lambda x.{}^{*}BOY(x) \wedge |x|=3) =$
$^{\downarrow\uparrow}\lambda x.{}^{*}BOY(x) \wedge |x|=3$ of type $<d,t>$.

This expression is equivalent to:

$\lambda x.{}^{*}BOY(\downarrow(x)) \wedge |\downarrow(x)|=3$ of type $<d,t>$

Thus we get so far:

time three boys $\rightarrow \lambda x.{}^{*}BOY(\downarrow(x)) \wedge |\downarrow(x)|=3$ of type $<d,t>$
The set of all groups corresponding to sums of three boys

This is semantically pluralized, and we get:

times three boys $\rightarrow$ * $\lambda x.{}^{*}BOY(\downarrow(x)) \wedge |\downarrow(x)|=3$ of type $<d,t>$
The set of all sums whose atoms are groups corresponding to sums of three boys.

The measure phrase Ø *four* Ø combines with this plural noun in the normal way, and we get:

Ø *four* Ø *times three boys* → λu. [* λx.*BOY($\downarrow$(x)) ∧ |$\downarrow$(x)|=3](u) ∧ |u|=4
The set of all sums that have four atoms below them and that are sums whose atoms are groups corresponding to sums of three boys.

The remaining derivation is standard: we form the argument interpretation, combine with *met in the park*, which I will simplify as: λxλe.*MEET(e) ∧ *Ag(e)=x. Maximalization will derive:

(13)a.   Four *times* three boys met in the park.
         ∃e[*MEET(e) ∧ [* λx.*BOY($\downarrow$(x)) ∧ |$\downarrow$(x)|=3](*Ag(e)) ∧
                  |*Ag(e)|=4]
         There is a sum of meeting events e. The agent of each singular meeting event which is part of e is a group corresponding to a sum of three boys. The singular meeting events making up e involve in total four such group agents.

   In sum, with just the assumption that *time* is a counting classifier, we derive, without any further work, the correct interpretation for (13a): four groups of three boys met in the park.

11.3   Slashed Modifier Categories

I am now going to import a bit of categorial grammar into the grammar. A salient feature of categorial grammar is that it allows **slashed categories** in the grammar. Slashed categories are categories of the form A/B, where A and B are categories. A useful way to think about slashed category A/B is the following:

Slashed categories:
A tree with topnode A/B can be thought of as a tree with topnode A with an empty B-node in it.

On this perspective, the simplest kind of slashed category tree is the gap:

Slash introduction by slashed gaps:
Slashed gap [$_{A/A}$ Ø] can be thought of as a tree with topnode A, with A **itself** empty.

Slashes, once introduced, can percolate up the tree by principles of the following sort:

Slash percolation:
If the grammar allows $[_D C A]$ and the grammar allows A/B, then the grammar can allow $[_{D/B} C A/B]$.

Thus, the grammar can build **chains** of slashed categories from daughter to mother up from slashed gaps. Such chains of slashes end when the slash is resolved:

Slash resolution:
The grammar resolves the slash in category A/B in a structure $[_A A/B B]$

B can be thought of as introducing the head of the chain in A/B.

Categorial grammar and its slashes have, of course, a long history. The idea of using the slashes for syntactic chain constructions based on gaps goes back to Gerald Gazdar's (e.g. 1981) work. Many recent applications are discussed and/or provided in Jacobson (1999).

The semantic interpretation of the slashed category mechanisms is in essence straightforward. It is based on the following simple ideas:

Semantics of extensional gaps:
1. slashed categories: type(A/B) = <type(B),type(A)>
2. gaps: $[_{A/A} \varnothing] \rightarrow \lambda x.x$ the identity function on type(A)

Semantics of percolation and resolution:
3. slash percolation = COMPOSE
4. slash resolution = APPLY

The operation of APPLY is generalized functional application (see Landman 2000), which applies a function to an argument, while allowing the type shifting theory to resolve type mismatches along the way.

The operation of COMPOSE is similarly **generalized function composition**, which similarly composes two functions while allowing the type shifting theory to resolve type mismatches along the way. For our purposes here we can define COMPOSE in the following way:

Generalized function composition:
COMPOSE$[\alpha,\beta] = \lambda z.$LIFT$[$APPLY$[\alpha,\beta(z)]]$

As normal in function composing α with β, we apply function β to a variable. We apply α to the result, resolving type mismatch if necessary (that is what APPLY does). If the result is already at the required output type, LIFT will be identity, otherwise we LIFT the result to the required type. And finally, we abstract over the variable, as usual.

Above I have given the semantics for extensional gaps. In many cases the above mechanism will work adequately, but there are cases where it is not good enough. Take example (14):

(14)   A unicorn, Dafna believes that Netta kissed Ø.

Though *a unicorn* is topicalized in (14), (14) allows a *de dicto* interpretation, where *a unicorn* takes scope under the intensional verb *believe*. If you analyze the gap in (14) as a slashed gap which percolates and gets resolved by the topicalized expression, the interpretation of the gap cannot be the identity function at an extensional type, because that will only derive *de re* readings. For that reason we assume that the gap [$_{A/A}$ Ø] can have an interpretation as the identity function at the **intensional type** <s,type(A)>. And if you start with the gap at the intensional type, the percolation and resolution mechanisms will also be intensionalized:

Semantics of intensional gaps:
1.   slashed categories: type(A/B) = <<s,type(B)>,<s,type(A)>>
2.   gaps: [$_{A/A}$ Ø] → λx.x   the identity function on <s,type(A)>

The idea is the following:

Inheritance of the semantic nature of the slashed gap in a chain:
The semantic nature of the gap influences the types of the slashed categories in a chain based on it:
- if the slashed gap is of extensional type <b,b>, the types of the slashed categories in the chain will be extensional function types of the form <b,c>
- if the slashed gap is of intensional type <<s,b>,<s,b>>, the types of the slashed categories in the chain will be intensional function types of the form <<s,b>,<s,c>>.

Let us show the idea. Assume:

Category C has type <a,c>.
Category A has type a.
Category D has type c.
The grammar allows structure [$_D$ C A].

Next assume: The grammar allows slashed category A/B of **extensional type** <b,a>. If so, we assume that slash percolation forms:

[$_{D/B}$ C A/B] of **extensional type** <b,c>

Assume:

C → α   of type <a,c>
A/B → β   of type <b,a>
Then [$_{D/B}$ C A/B] → COMPOSE[α,β] =
                    λz.α(β(z))   of type <b,c>
                              (i.e. z is a variable of type b)

This is the extensional case.

Let us now assume that the grammar allows slashed category A/B of **intensional type** $<<s,b>,<s,a>>$. In that case, slash percolation forms:

$[_{D/B}$ C A/B] of **intensional type** $<<s,b>,<s,c>>$

We assume:

C $\rightarrow$ α   of type $<a,c>$
A/B $\rightarrow$ β   of type $<<s,b>,<s,a>>$
Then $[_{D/B}$ C A/B] $\rightarrow$ COMPOSE[α,β] =
                 $λz.^(α(^(β(z))))$ of type $<<s,b>,<s,c>>$.
                            (i.e. z is a variable of type $<s,b>$)

Thus, indeed, the nature of the gap determines the nature of the types of the slashed categories in the chain built on it; generalized composition resolves the type mismatches along the road.

The point of all this discussion is that the inheritance of the semantic nature of the gap is not tied just to extensional versus intensional types. I will make the very same assumption for the counting types:

Inheritance of the semantic nature of the slashed gap in a chain (continued):
- if the slashed gap is of **counting** type $<<↑,b>,<↑,b>>$, the types of the slashed categories in the chain will be counting function types of the form $<<↑,b>,<↑,c>>$.

Assume again:

Category C has type $<a,c>$.
Category A has type a.
Category D has type c.
The grammar allows structure $[_D$ C A].

And assume that the grammar allows slashed category A/B of **counting type** $<<↑,b>,<↑,a>>$. In that case, slash percolation forms:

$[_{D/B}$ C A/B] of **counting type** $<<↑,b>,<↑,c>>$

We assume:

C $\rightarrow$ α   of type $<a,c>$
A/B $\rightarrow$ β   of type $<<↑,b>,<↑,a>>$
Then $[_{D/B}$ C A/B] $\rightarrow$ COMPOSE[α,β] =
                 $λz.^↑(α(^↓(β(z))))$ of type $<<↑,b>,<↑,c>>$.
                            (i.e. z is a variable of type $<↑,b>$)

With this, we turn to the indefinite *time*-adverbials.

11.4   Counting Modifiers

We are back to examples like (15):

(15)   Dafna jumped *three times*.

We are assuming that in (15) *time* is a classifier proper with the following semantics:

The semantics of classifier *time*:
$[_{\text{classifier}}\ time\ ] \rightarrow \lambda z.^{\downarrow}z$ of type $<<\uparrow,<e,t>>,<e,t>>$
                        (i.e. z is a variable of type $<\uparrow,<e,t>>$)

If *time* is a classifier proper, and classifiers proper take complements, we need to raise the question: where is its complement?

Doetjes (1997) raises this question and resolves it by providing a non-standard syntax, where in essence the verb phrase is the complement of the classifier. I will make a much less non-standard assumption and assume that in this construction the classifier *time* takes a **null complement**. However, and this is where the categorial grammar comes in: I assume that the null complement of the *time* classifier is a **slashed gap of category PRED/PRED**, and interpretation of the counting type:

The semantics of the counting gap:
$[_{\text{PRED/PRED}}\ \emptyset\ ] \rightarrow \lambda z.z$ of type $<<\uparrow,<e,t>>,<\uparrow,<e,t>>$
                       (i.e. z is a variable of type $<\uparrow,<e,t>>$)

With slash percolation, the grammar will derive DP/PREDs of the following form:

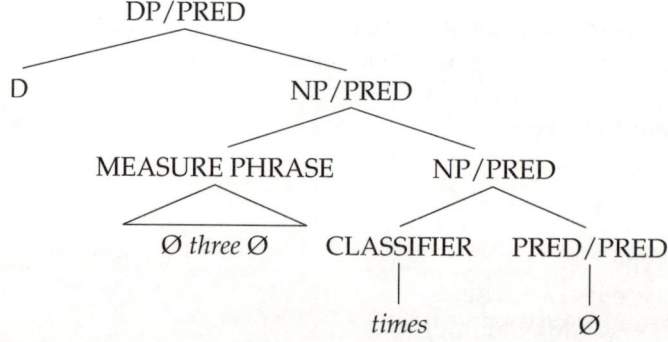

Let us look at the semantics. The interpretation of the classifier *time* composes with the slashed gap, to give the interpretation of the NP/PRED:

time Ø → COMPOSE[λu.$^{\downarrow}$u, λv.v] =
λz.LIFT[APPLY[λu.$^{\downarrow}$u, λv.v(z)]] =
λz.LIFT[APPLY[λu.$^{\downarrow}$u, z]] =
λz.LIFT[((λu.$^{\downarrow}$u)(z))] =
λz.LIFT[$^{\downarrow}$z] =
λz.$^{\uparrow\downarrow}$z = (since z denotes a set of atoms)
λz.z of type <<↑,<e,t>>,<↑,<e,t>>

The interpretation of the measure phrase is:

Ø *three* Ø → λe.|e|=3   of type <e,t>

This composes with the interpretation of *times* Ø to give the interpretation of the top NP/PRED:

Ø *three* Ø *times* Ø →
COMPOSE[λe.|e|=3, λu.u] =
λz.LIFT[APPLY[λe.|e|=3, λu.u(z)]] =
λz.LIFT[APPLY[λe.|e|=3, z]] =
λz.LIFT[APPLY[ADJUNCT[λe.|e|=3], z]]

Now, z is not of the right type to do the adjunction. The first thing we need to do is to shift it to type <e,t>:

λz.LIFT[APPLY[ADJUNCT[λe.|e|=3], $^{\downarrow}$z]]

We have another mismatch left, which is not expressed in the types. $^{\downarrow}$z denotes a set of atoms, hence is a semantically singular predicate. But the adjunct λe.|e|=3 requires a semantically plural predicate. This mismatch is resolved by pluralizing $^{\downarrow}$z:

λz.LIFT[APPLY[ADJUNCT[λe.|e|=3], *$^{\downarrow}$z]]

Now adjunction will give:

λz.LIFT[λe.|e|=3 ∧ [*$^{\downarrow}$z](e)]

We need to get to type <<↑,<e,t>>,<↑,<e,t>>>, so LIFT will finally apply $^{\uparrow}$:

λz.$^{\uparrow}$λe.|e|=3 ∧ [*$^{\downarrow}$z](e)   of type <<↑,<e,t>>,<↑,<e,t>>

We can stop here for the moment. We have derived the NP/PRED *three times* with interpretation:

$\lambda z.^{\uparrow}\lambda e.|e|=3 \wedge [*^{\downarrow}z](e)$ of type $<<\uparrow,<e,t>>,<\uparrow,<e,t>>$

The function which takes a set of atoms z and maps it onto the set of atoms corresponding to the set of sums of events that are sums of events with three atoms and that are sums of events of the atoms in z.

The computations we have gone through may be heavy going, and the resulting interpretation may not be immediately perspicuous, but note that I haven't really made any special assumptions, except for the semantics of the classifier and the assumption that its complement is a counting gap. Given these assumptions, the semantics derived for the NP/PRED just follows from completely general principles.

When we go one level up from here we come to the level of DP/PRED. In the adjectival theory, different types of determiners will give us different types of DP/PREDs:

Definite determiners:
DP/PRED is of type $<<\uparrow<e,t>>,<\uparrow,e>>$.
I will call the category derived with definite determiners: DP[IND]/PRED.

Quantificational determiners:
DP/PRED is of type $<<\uparrow<e,t>>,<\uparrow,<<e,t>,t>>>$.
I will call the category derived with quantificational determiners: DP[Q]/PRED.

Indefinite determiners: Ø
DP/PRED is of type $<<\uparrow<e,t>>,<\uparrow,<e,t>,>>$.
I will call the category derived with quantificational determiners: DP[PRED]/PRED.

Thus we derive:

$[_{DP[PRED]/PRED}$ Ø Ø *three* Ø *times* Ø $] \rightarrow \lambda z.^{\uparrow}\lambda e.|e|=3 \wedge *^{\downarrow}z(e)$
                     of type $<<\uparrow,<e,t>>,<\uparrow,<e,t>>$

In categorial grammar, slashed categories of the form A/A are **modifier categories**. What this means is that these categories are **legitimate categories** for modifier expressions, and that the chain of slashes gets resolved by combining the modifier with the expression it modifies. Hence, the grammar contains the following resolution principle for modifier categories:

Modifier resolution:
From modifier category A/A with interpretation α and head A with interpretation β, we can form $[_A$ A/A A] with interpretation APPLY$[\alpha,\beta]$.

Montague (1970) and Kamp (1975) use these modifier categories as the categories of prenominal adjectives and adverbials. Of course, for intersective adjectives and adverbials, we have here, of course, chosen a different analysis: we generate these at the type of sets, and shift them with intersective adjunction to modifier types. But that analysis obviously does not extend to non-intersective adjectives and adverbials, like intensional adjectives. And the extension of the grammar with the categorial grammar mechanism allows us to assume that they are in fact generated as modifier categories:

Proposal:
Non-intersective adjuncts are generated as expressions of modifier categories.

On this view, there are different categories for what we would call modifiers: intersective adjuncts are generated in categories that are not slashed categories. They become modifiers semantically through ADJUNCT. Non-intersective modifiers start out syntactically in modifier categories: slashed categories of the form A/A. I will now make the crucial assumption:

Assumption:
The category DP[PRED]/PRED is a legitimate modifier category:
DP[PRED]/PRED can count as PRED/PRED.

That is, even though the category DP/PRED doesn't officially have the form of a modifier category, in the case of the indefinite determiners, we get a modifier type, and I think it is reasonable to assume that in this case the label PRED can take priority.

Consequence:
All and only bare **indefinite** DP/PREDs form legitimate adverbial modifiers by this construction.

We now have an answer to the grammar puzzle. The puzzle was: how are indefinite noun phrases like *three times* allowed in adverbial position? The answer is that they are not indefinite noun phrases at all, but **adverbial modifiers** built from a **counting gap**: i.e. they are not DPs, but PRED/PREDs.

Secondly, it is clear that, if we are successful in interpreting this construction as a **direct counting** construction, we predict the definiteness effects discussed earlier. Only **indefinite** *time* phrases form PRED/PREDs, definite and quantificational *time* phrases do not receive an interpretation at a modifier type and cannot be assigned to a modifier category. Hence definite and quantification time phrases do not allow direct counting interpretations. (For the indefinites with relative clauses, I am assuming that the counting gap PRED/PRED does not allow modification with relative clauses. Hence these cases cannot occur as direct counting adverbials either.)

11.5   Direct Counting and Scope

We are now interested in the examples in (16).

(16)a.   Two girls kissed Dafna three times.
     b.   Three times, two girls kissed Dafna.

In (16a), the reading that we are interested in is the reading where there are two girls and for each of these girls there are three events of that girl kissing Dafna. Thus, *three times* takes scope under *two girls*. In (16b), the most prominent reading is where there are three clusters of events, each involving two girls kissing Dafna (so this could involve six different girls). We have given adverbial *three times* the following semantics:

$$[_{\text{DP[PRED]/PRED}} \text{ three times }] \rightarrow \lambda z.^{\uparrow}\lambda e.|e|{=}3 \wedge {}^{*\downarrow}z(e)$$
$$\text{of type } <{<}{\uparrow},{<}e,t{>>},{<}{\uparrow},{<}e,t{>>}$$

Now this analysis is tailored to complements of type $<e,t>$ (saturated predicates). Arguably, we must extend this analysis so that it can apply to complements of type $<d,<e,t>>$, so that *three times* in (16a) can be a VP adverbial. This can be done, but adds yet another level of complication. For the sake of exposition, I will provide the same syntactic analysis for (16a) and (16b), with *three times* an event type modifier, adjoined, for the sake of exposition, to IP:

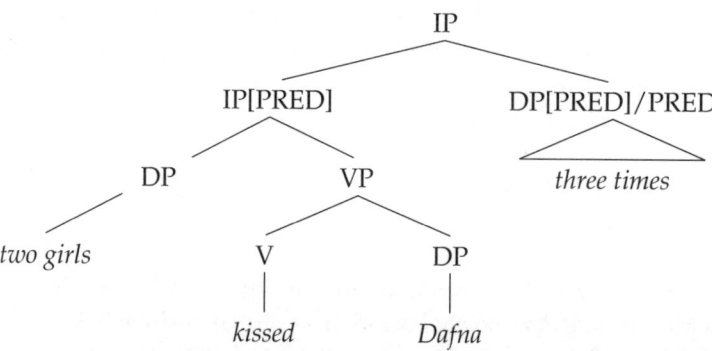

We will derive the two different readings by assuming in (16a) that the subject *two girls* is quantified in, while in (16b) it is analyzed in situ. (If we were to add a VP modifier interpretation for *three times*, we could analyze (16a) directly with *three times* a VP modifier, and the subject in situ in (16a) as well.)

  We start with the intended reading in (16a). We assume that *two girls* is stored. Given that assumption, we can, without loss of generality, assume that the IP-event type is an **atomic** event type:

$$x_n \text{ kissed Dafna} \rightarrow \lambda e.\text{KISS}(e) \wedge \text{Ag}(e){=}x_n \wedge \text{Th}(e){=}\text{DAFNA}$$
$$\text{of type } <e,t>$$

The set of atomic kissing events with x_n as agent and Dafna as theme.

three times → $\lambda z.{}^{\uparrow}\lambda e.|e|=3 \wedge [*{}^{\downarrow}z](e)$
      of type $<<{\uparrow},<e,t>>,<{\uparrow},<e,t>>$

x_n *kissed Dafna three times* →
APPLY$[\lambda z.{}^{\uparrow}\lambda e.|e|=3 \wedge [*{}^{\downarrow}z](e), \lambda e.KISS(e) \wedge Ag(e)=x_n \wedge Th(e)=DAFNA] =$

APPLY$[\lambda z.{}^{\uparrow}\lambda e.|e|=3 \wedge [*{}^{\downarrow}z](e), {}^{\uparrow}\lambda e.KISS(e) \wedge Ag(e)=x_n \wedge Th(e)=DAFNA] =$

$[\lambda z.{}^{\uparrow}\lambda e.|e|=3 \wedge [*{}^{\downarrow}z](e)]\, ({}^{\uparrow}\lambda e.KISS(e) \wedge Ag(e)=x_n \wedge Th(e)=DAFNA) =$

${}^{\uparrow}\lambda e.|e|=3 \wedge [*{}^{\downarrow}{}^{\uparrow}\lambda e.KISS(e) \wedge Ag(e)=x_n \wedge Th(e)=DAFNA](e) =$ (since the kissing event type was a set of atoms to start with)

${}^{\uparrow}\lambda e.|e|=3 \wedge [*\lambda e.KISS(e) \wedge Ag(e)=x_n \wedge Th(e)=DAFNA](e)$
The set of atomic events corresponding to sums of events that have three
atomic events and that are sums of events of x_n kissing Dafna.

We do maximalization on this event type and we get:

x_n *kissed Dafna three times* →
$\exists f[{}^{\uparrow}\lambda e.|e|=3 \wedge [*\lambda e.KISS(e) \wedge Ag(e)=x_n \wedge Th(e)=DAFNA](e)](f)$
There is an atomic group event corresponding to a sum of events that con-
sists of three atomic events and that is a sum of events of x_n kissing Dafna.

The scope mechanism from Landman (2000) will turn this into a scopal predicate of type $<d,t>$, which gets shifted to a derived one place predicate of type
$<d,<e,t>>$ (with argument role A_1), which applies to the stored interpretation
of the subject. With the Correspondence Principle, we will derive the following interpretation for (16a):

(16)a.   Two girls kissed Dafna three times.
         $\exists x[*GIRL(x) \wedge |x|=2 \wedge \forall a \in ATOM(x):$
         $\exists f[[{}^{\uparrow}\lambda e.|e|=3 \wedge [*\lambda e.KISS(e) \wedge Ag(e)=a \wedge Th(e)=DAFNA](e)](f)]]$
         There is a sum of two girls and for each of these girls there is an atomic
         group event corresponding to a sum of events that consists of three
         atomic events and that is a sum of events of that girl kissing Dafna.

The truth of (16a) postulates the following: there are two girls $a,b \in GIRL$ such
that:

1.   There is an atomic group event ${}^{\uparrow}(f_1)$, where f_1 is a sum $e_1 \sqcup e_2 \sqcup e_3$,
     and $e_1,e_2,e_3 \in KISS$ and $Ag(e_1)=Ag(e_2)=Ag(e_3)=a$ and $Th(e_1)=Th(e_2)=Th(e_3)=$
     DAFNA.
2.   There is an atomic group event ${}^{\uparrow}(f_2)$, where f_2 is a sum $e_4 \sqcup e_5 \sqcup e_6$, and
     $e_4,e_5,e_6 \in KISS$ and $Ag(e_4)=Ag(e_5)=Ag(e_6)=b$ and $Th(e_4)=Th(e_5)=Th(e_6)=$
     DAFNA.

Thus, (16a) tells us that there are two girls a and b, and six events: three of girl a kissing Dafna, and three of girl b kissing Dafna. This is, of course, the intended interpretation.

Let us now turn to (16b). As explained, we assume the same structure for (16b) here, but this time, *two girls* is not quantified in. This means that the event type that *three times* operates on is the following:

> *two girls kissed Dafna* →
> λe.*KISS(e) ∧ *GIRL(*Ag(e)) ∧ |*Ag(e)|=2 ∧ *Th(e)=DAFNA
> of type <e,t>
> The set of sums of kissing events with two girls as plural agent and Dafna as theme (meaning that each atomic part event has one of these girls as agent, and each atomic part event has Dafna as theme).

We apply modifier *three times*:

> *three times two girls kissed Dafna* →
> APPLY[λz.$^\uparrow$λe.|e|=3 ∧ [*$^\downarrow$z](e),
>   λe.*KISS(e) ∧ *GIRL(*Ag(e)) ∧ |*Ag(e)|=2 ∧ *Th(e)=DAFNA] =
>
> APPLY[λz.$^\uparrow$λe.|e|=3 ∧ [*$^\downarrow$z](e),
> $^\uparrow$λe.*KISS(e) ∧ *GIRL(*Ag(e)) ∧ |*Ag(e)|=2 ∧ *Th(e)=DAFNA] =
>
> $^\uparrow$λe.|e|=3 ∧ [*$^{\downarrow\uparrow}$λe.*KISS(e) ∧ *GIRL(*Ag(e)) ∧ |*Ag(e)|=2 ∧ *Th(e)=DAFNA](e)

Since, unlike the previous case, in this case the input event type is a plural event type, the $^{\downarrow\uparrow}$ do not cancel out. Maximalization will derive:

> ∃f[$^\uparrow$λe.|e|=3 ∧
>   [*$^{\downarrow\uparrow}$λe.*KISS(e) ∧ *GIRL(*Ag(e)) ∧ |*Ag(e)|=2 ∧ Th(e)=DAFNA](e)] (f)]

This is equivalent to:

> ∃e[|e|=3 ∧ [*$^{\downarrow\uparrow}$λe.*KISS(e) ∧ *GIRL(*Ag(e)) ∧ |*Ag(e)|=2 ∧ Th(e)=DAFNA](e)]

So we derive for (16b):

(16)b. Three times, two girls kissed Dafna.
> ∃e[|e|=3 ∧ [*$^{\downarrow\uparrow}$λe.*KISS(e) ∧ *GIRL(*Ag(e)) ∧ |*Ag(e)|=2 ∧
> Th(e)=DAFNA](e)]
> There is a sum of three atomic group events and each of these atomic group events corresponds to a sum of events of two girls kissing Dafna.

The truth of (16b) postulates a sum of events f which consists of three atomic group events: $^\uparrow$(f$_1$), $^\uparrow$(f$_2$), and $^\uparrow$(f$_3$). Here f$_1$, f$_2$, and f$_3$ are sums of kissing events each with a sum of two girls as plural agent, and Dafna as theme. The following would be a situation that makes (16b) true:

$f = \uparrow(f_1) \sqcup \uparrow(f_2) \sqcup \uparrow(f_3)$
$f_1 = e_1 \sqcup e_2$, $f_2 = e_3 \sqcup e_4$ and $f_3 = e_5 \sqcup e_6 \sqcup e_7$
$Ag(e_1) = a$, $Ag(e_2) = b$, $Ag(e_3) = c$, $Ag(e_4) = d$, $Ag(e_5) = g$, $Ag(e_6) = h$, $Ag(e_7) = h$
$a,b,c,d,g,h \in GIRL$
$Th(e_1) = Th(e_2) = Th(e_3) = Th(e_4) = Th(e_5) = Th(e_6) = Th(e_7) = DAFNA$

Thus, in this situation, there are all together seven kissing events: all of a,b,c,d,g, and h kiss Dafna, and in fact, h kisses Dafna twice. Since we are talking about groups of kissings, it is natural to assume that these groups of kissings are contextually coherent: the kissings of a and b of Dafna belong together, the kissings of c and d of Dafna do too, and the kissing of g of Dafna and the two kissings of h do too. Thus in (16b) we're counting three groups of kissings of Dafna, each group involving two girls. Again, this is the intended interpretation.

11.6   The Scope of Counting Modifiers

We have analyzed adverbial *three times* as a counting modifier of type $<<\uparrow,<e,t>>,<\uparrow,<e,t>>>$. Counting modifiers count events in event types. But events in event types are standardly pluralities, and pluralities cannot be directly counted, only atoms can. Thus there is a mismatch between the counting modifier and the head it modifies. This triggers **gridding**: the denotation of the head as a set of plural events is shifted to the set of corresponding group atoms. Counting takes place by pluralizing this set and adjoining the counting phrase *three*. As we have seen, the switch to group atoms creates a scope relation between the counting modifier, and scopal elements that the event type of the head is built from.

In this way, the mechanism of counting modifiers forms a new type of **scope mechanism**, different from the scope mechanism of argument noun phrases. The parallel is not with argument noun phrases, but with intensional operators; intensional operators create intensional contexts, which scopally interact with noun phrase interpretations. In the same way, counting operators create "counting contexts" that also interact scopally with noun phrase interpretations. What I am arguing is that, while adverbial *three times* looks like a noun phrase, it is, in fact, a modifier (comparable with intensional adverbs). Thus, we do not need to assume that the interpretation of *three times* must be scoped with the noun phrase scope mechanism, in order to get the correct scopal interpretations (which is roughly what Doetjes assumes).

If counting adverbials are scopally similar to intensional operators, and not to argument noun phrases, we may actually expect that their scopal behavior is different from the scopal behavior of argument noun phrases. As is well known, indefinite argument noun phrases take wide scope freely. But the scope mechanism of counting modifiers is an in situ mechanism: they create what we could call a "scope screen" locally. From this, we might expect that, unlike indefinite argument noun phrases, adverbial *three times* does not freely take wide scope. Look at (17):

(17)   Fred believed that Dafna jumped exactly three times.

Example (17) has, of course, a *de dicto* reading for *exactly three times*: Fred believed that there were exactly three jumping events of Dafna. A *de re* reading would be: there are exactly three events of which Fred believed that they were jumpings of Dafna. For instance, Fred, without his glasses on, is visually exposed to a scene where a big ball bounces exactly three times. In his blurred vision, he thinks he sees four movements up and down, he thinks it is Dafna jumping, so he interprets what he sees as four events of Dafna jumping. Thus, Fred would assent to "Dafna jumped exactly four times," not to "Dafna jumped exactly three times" (hence the *de dicto* reading of (17) is false). The question is: does (17) have this *de re* reading?

I think there is no such reading, and I think that this shows that indeed adverbial *three times* does not allow the wide scope possibilities that argument noun phrases do.

Adverbial indefinite *time* phrases of the form *three times* are not noun phrases, but counting modifiers: they get their semantics as counting modifiers from the assumption that *time* is a classifier which takes as its complement a slashed counting gap [$_{PRED/PRED}$ Ø]. The definiteness effects follow from this: only indefinite *time* phrases form DP[PRED]/PREDs, and can, as such, function themselves as modifiers. Also, the scopal effects follow from this: the mistake of the Obvious Analysis was to assume that sets of sums of events can be counted directly by giving *three times* an interpretation as an intersective event adjunct. But sets of sums of events cannot be counted that way: they need to be gridded, turned into sets of atoms in order to be counted.

We now come back to the definite adverbial definite *time* phrases from the previous chapter. We interpreted *the three times that the bell rang* as a measure phrase, with the semantics of an **indirect counting adverbial** of type <e,t>:

$\lambda e.CANTOR(e)=<\sigma(\lambda e.{}^*RANG(e) \wedge {}^*Th(e)=\sigma(BELL)),3>.$

The analysis so far would suggest a difference between direct counting and indirect counting: when you count directly you can only count atomic events, not sums of events, but when you count indirectly, according to the analysis so far, you can apparently count sums of events directly, because the measure phrase, in the analysis so far, is added intersectively to the event type.

However, there is no such difference: the measure phrase analysis developed in the previous chapter is problematic in exactly the same way as the Obvious

Analysis was. The reason is that it actually is the Obvious Analysis, for indirect counters. This can be seen in (18):

(18)   *The three times the bell rang*, Dafna jumped **two times**.

Example (18) expresses that, for each of the three bell ringings, there were two events of Dafna jumping. The event type of *Dafna jumped two times* is the set of sums of events that have two atomic parts, each of which is or corresponds to a jumping of Dafna. If we **intersect** that with the set of events that CANTOR maps onto the degree of three bell ringings, we get the set of sums of events that have two atomic parts, each of which is or corresponds to a jumping of Dafna, and that are isomorphic with the sum of three bell ringing events. This is, of course, no good. the problem is exactly the same problem that we noticed before for the Obvious Analysis. The conclusion should be:

Counting sums through counting atoms:
Counting is counting of atoms, whether it is direct counting, or indirect counting.

This means that it is not sufficient to derive *the three times the bell rang* as an intersective measure phrase. My proposal is:

Counting modifiers:
Adverbial counting phrases are always counting modifiers.

This means that we must turn the adverbial measure phrase *the three times the bell rang Ø* into a counting modifier. I propose the following final analysis:

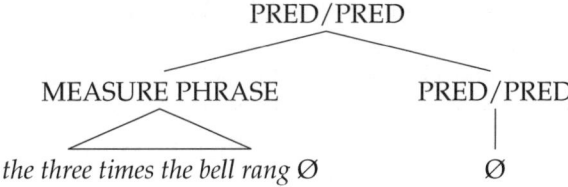

The interpretation of the measure phrase is as before:

the three times the bell rang Ø →
$\lambda e.\text{CANTOR}(e)=<\sigma(\lambda e.{}^{*}\text{RANG}(e) \wedge {}^{*}\text{Th}(e)=\sigma(\text{BELL})),3>$
of type $<e,t>$.

The interpretation of slashed gap is as a counting gap:

$[_{\text{PRED/PRED}}\ Ø\ ] \rightarrow \lambda z.z$ of type $<<\uparrow,<e,t>>,<\uparrow,<e,t>>>$

We compose, and get:

$\lambda z.$LIFT[APPLY[ADJUNCT[$\lambda e.$CANTOR(e)=<$\sigma(\lambda e.$*RANG(e) $\wedge$
*Th(e)=σ(BELL)),3>], $\lambda u.u(z)$]]

=

$\lambda z.$LIFT[APPLY[ADJUNCT[$\lambda e.$CANTOR(e)=<$\sigma(\lambda e.$*RANG(e) $\wedge$
*Th(e)=σ(BELL)),3>], z]]
= (by bringing z to the correct type <e,t> for adjunction)

$\lambda z.$LIFT[APPLY[ADJUNCT[$\lambda e.$CANTOR(e)=<$\sigma(\lambda e.$*RANG(e) $\wedge$
*Th(e)=σ(BELL))3,>], $^{\downarrow}$z]]
= (by pluralizing z for adjunction)

$\lambda z.$LIFT[APPLY[ADJUNCT[$\lambda e.$CANTOR(e)=<$\sigma(\lambda e.$*RANG(e) $\wedge$
*Th(e)=σ(BELL)),3>], *$^{\downarrow}$z]]
= (by adjunction)

$\lambda z.$LIFT[$\lambda e.$CANTOR(e)=<$\sigma(\lambda e.$*RANG(e) $\wedge$ *Th(e)=σ(BELL)),3> $\wedge$ [*$^{\downarrow}$z](e)]] =

[$_{\text{PRED/PRED}}$ *the three times the bell rang* Ø Ø] $\rightarrow$
$\lambda z.^{\uparrow}\lambda e.$CANTOR(e)=<$\sigma(\lambda e.$*RANG(e)$\wedge$*Th(e)=$\sigma$(BELL)),3> $\wedge$ [*$^{\downarrow}$z](e)]
of type <<$\uparrow$,<e,t>>,<$\uparrow$,<e,t>>>

Now let's look at (18). For simplicity, we can assume that the event type *Dafna jumped* is an atomic event type, which means that adding counting modifier *two times* gives:

Dafna jumped two times $\rightarrow \lambda e.$*JUMP(e) $\wedge$ *Ag(e)=DAFNA $\wedge$ |e|=2
of type <e,t>.

We combine this with counting modifier *the three times the bell rang* Ø Ø and get:

APPLY[$\lambda z.^{\uparrow}\lambda e.$CANTOR(e)=<$\sigma(\lambda e.$*RANG(e)$\wedge$*Th(e)=$\sigma$(BELL)),3> $\wedge$
[*$^{\downarrow}$z](e)], $\lambda e.$*JUMP(e) $\wedge$ *Ag(e)=DAFNA $\wedge$ |e|=2]

=

APPLY[$\lambda z.^{\uparrow}\lambda e.$CANTOR(e)=<$\sigma(\lambda e.$*RANG(e)$\wedge$*Th(e)=$\sigma$(BELL)),3> $\wedge$
[*$^{\downarrow}$z](e)], $^{\uparrow}\lambda e.$*JUMP(e) $\wedge$ *Ag(e)=DAFNA $\wedge$ |e|=2]

=

$^{\uparrow}\lambda e.$CANTOR(e)=<$\sigma(\lambda e.$*RANG(e)$\wedge$*Th(e)=σ(BELL)),3> $\wedge$
[*$^{\downarrow\uparrow}\lambda e.$*JUMP(e) $\wedge$ *Ag(e)=DAFNA $\wedge$ |e|=2](e)]

With maximalization, we derive:

$$\exists f\ [^\uparrow \lambda e.CANTOR(e)=<\sigma(\lambda e.*RANG(e)\wedge *Th(e)=\sigma(BELL)),3>\ \wedge$$
$$[*^{\downarrow\uparrow}\lambda e.*JUMP(e)\ \wedge\ *Ag(e)=DAFNA\ \wedge\ |e|=2](e)]\ (f)$$

which is equivalent to:

(18)   The three times the bell rang, Dafna jumped two times.
$$\exists e\ [CANTOR(e)=<\sigma(\lambda e.*RANG(e)\wedge *Th(e)=\sigma(BELL)),3>\ \wedge$$
$$[*^{\downarrow\uparrow}\lambda e.*JUMP(e)\ \wedge\ *Ag(e)=DAFNA\ \wedge\ |e|=2](e)$$
There is a sum of atomic groups events that is isomorphic to the sum of three bell ringings, and each of these atomic group events corresponds to a group of two jumpings events of Dafna.

This means that we find, corresponding to each of the three bell ringings, a group event corresponding to two jumpings of Dafna. Hence, indeed, now that we have lifted the measure phrase *the three times the bell rang* to a counting modifier, we get per bell ringing, two jumpings of Dafna. So we derive the correct interpretation.

This final reformulation does not affect the earlier account: the reason *the three times the bell rang* can occur in adverbial position is that it is not a noun phrase, but a counting modifier, based on a measure phrase, which is in turn based on a degree noun phrase. The external definiteness effects follow, as before, from the derivation of *the three times the bell rang* as a degree noun phrase.

To summarize, there are two ways of counting events with adverbial *time* phrases:

1.   **Indefinite** adverbial *time* phrases like *three times* are counting modifiers that count event types **directly** in terms of their atoms.
2.   **Definite** adverbial *time* phrases like *the three times the bell rang* are counting modifiers based on measure phrases than count event types **indirectly** through CANTOR.

Both are counting modifiers, which means that they must **grid** plural event types into atomic group event types before they can count them. This makes them **scopal** operators.

The external definiteness effects of definite adverbial *time* phrases follow from their derivation as degree denoting noun phrases. The indefiniteness effects of indefinite adverbial *time* phrases (only indefinite ones can count directly) follow from the fact that with composition up from the slashed counting gap complement of the *time* classifier, only indefinites get to the type of counting modifiers.

References

Bartsch, Renate, 1973: The semantics and syntax of numbers. In: Kimball, J. (ed.), *Syntax and Semantics 2*. New York: Academic Press.

Barwise, Jon and Cooper, Robin, 1981: Generalized quantifiers and natural language. *Linguistics and Philosophy* 4.

Bennis, Hans, 1986: *Gaps and Dummies*. Dordrecht: Foris.

Bittner, Maria, 1994: Cross-linguistic semantics. *Linguistics and Philosophy* 17: 1.

Bonomi, Andrea and Casalegno, Paolo, 1993: *Only*: association with focus in event semantics. *Natural Language Semantics* 2: 1.

Boolos, George, 1981: For every A there is a B. *Linguistic Inquiry* 12.

Bowers, John, 1991: The syntax and semantics of nominals. In: Moore, Steve and Wyner, Adam (eds.), *Proceedings of SALT 1*. Ithaca, NY: CLC Publications.

Bowers, John, 1993: The syntax of predication. *Linguistic Inquiry* 24.

Buering, Daniel, 1998: Identity, modality, and the candidate behind the wall. In: *Proceedings of SALT 8*. Ithaca, NY: CLC Publications.

Carlson, Greg, 1977a: *Reference to Kinds in English*, PhD dissertation, University of Massachusetts, Amherst. Published, 1980, New York: Garland.

Carlson, Greg, 1977b: Amount relatives. *Language* 53: 520–42.

Carlson, Greg, 1991: Cases of really direct reference: perception and ostension. Handout of talk given at *SALT 1*. Ithaca, NY.

Chierchia, Gennaro, 1989: A semantics for unaccusatives and its syntactic consequences. Manuscript, Ithaca, NY: Cornell University.

Chierchia, Gennaro, 1993: Questions with quantifiers. *Natural Language Semantics* 1.

Chierchia, Gennaro, 1995: Individual level predicates as inherent generics. In: Carlson, Greg and Pelletier, Jeffrey (eds.), *The Generic Book*. Chicago: University of Chicago Press.

Chierchia, Gennaro and McConnell-Ginet, Sally, 1990: *Meaning and Grammar*. Cambridge, MA: MIT Press.

Diesing, Molly, 1990: *Indefinites*. Cambridge, MA: MIT Press.

Dobrovie-Sorin, Carmen and Laca, Brenda, 1996: Generic bare NPs. Manuscript, University of Paris.

Doetjes, Jenny, 1997: *Quantifiers and Selection: The Distribution of Quantifying Expressions in French, Dutch and English*, PhD dissertation, Leiden University.

Doron, Edit, 1983: *Verbless Predicates in Hebrew*. PhD dissertation, University of Texas, Austin.

Dowty, David, 1982: Grammatical relations in Montague grammar. In: Jacobson, Pauline and Pullum, Geoffrey (eds.), *The Nature of Syntactic Representation*. Dordrecht: Kluwer.

Dowty, David, 1985: On recent analyses of the semantics of control. *Linguistics and Philosophy* 8.

Dowty, David, 1986: A note on collective predicates, distributive predicates, and *all*. In: Marshall, F. et al. (eds.), *Proceedings of ESCOL 86*. Columbus, OH: Ohio State University Press.

Dowty, David, 1989: On the semantic content of the notion of thematic role. In: Chierchia, Gennaro, Partee, Barbara, and Turner, Raymond (eds.), *Properties, Types and Meaning*, vol. 2. Dordrecht: Kluwer.

Dowty, David, 1991: Thematic proto-roles and argument selection. *Language* 67.

Engdahl, Elisabet, 1986: *Constituent Questions*. Dordrecht: Kluwer.

Fehringer, Carol, 1999: *A Reference Grammar of Dutch*. Cambridge: Cambridge University Press.

von Fintel, Kai, 1993: Exceptive constructions. *Natural Language Semantics* 1.

Frege, Gottlob, 1892: Ueber Begriff und Gegenstand. *Vierteljahrschrift für wissenschaftliche Philosophie* 16. Reprinted in: Patzig, Guenther (ed.), 1962: *Funktion, Begriff, Bedeutung: Fuenf Logische Studien*. Göttingen: Vandenhoek.

Gazdar, Gerald, 1981: Unbounded dependencies and coordinate structure. *Linguistic Inquiry* 12.

van Geenhoven, Veerle, 1996: *Semantic Incorporation and Indefinite Descriptions: Semantic and Syntactic Incorporation in West Greenlandic*. PhD dissertation, University of Tübingen.

van Geenhoven, Veerle, 1998: On the argument structure of some noun incorporating verbs in West Greenlandic. In: Butt, Miriam and Geuder, Wilhelm (eds.), *The Projection of Arguments: Lexical and Compositional Factors*. CSLI Lecture Notes, Stanford University, CA.

Groenendijk, Jeroen and Stokhof, Martin 1982: Semantic analysis of wh-complements. *Linguistics and Philosophy* 5.

Grosu, Alexander and Landman, Fred 1998: Strange relatives of the third kind. *Natural Language Semantics* 6.

Heim, Irene, 1987: Where does the definiteness restriction apply. Evidence from the definiteness of variables. In: Reuland, Erik and ter Meulen, Alice (eds.), *The Representation of (In)definiteness*. Cambridge, MA: MIT Press.

Higginbotham, James, 1987: Indefiniteness and predication. In: Reuland, Erik and ter Meulen, Alice (eds.), *The Representation of (In)definiteness*. Cambridge, MA: MIT Press.

Horn, Laurence, 1972: *On the Semantic Properties of Logical Operators in English*. PhD dissertation, UCLA. Distributed 1976, IULC, Bloomington, IN.

Jacobs, Joachim, 1980: Lexical decomposition in Montague Grammar. *Theoretical Linguistics* 7.

Jacobson, Pauline, 1999: Towards a variable free semantics. *Linguistics and Philosophy* 22:2.

de Jong, Franciska, 1983: Numerals as determiners. In: Bennis, Hans and van Lessen Kloeke, W. (eds.), *Linguistics in the Netherlands*. Dordrecht: Foris.

de Jong, Franciska, 1987: The compositional nature of (in)definiteness. In: Reuland, Erik and ter Meulen, Alice (eds.), *The Representation of (In)definiteness*. Cambridge, MA: MIT Press.

de Jong, Franciska and Verkuyl, Henk 1985: Generalized quantifiers: the properness of their strength. In: van Benthem, Johan and ter Meulen, Alice (eds.), *Generalized Quantifiers in Natural Language*. Dordrecht: Foris.

Kadmon, Nirit, 1987: *On Unique and Non-Unique Reference and Asymmetric Quantification*. PhD dissertation, University of Massachusetts, Amherst. Published 1993, New York: Garland.

Kadmon, Nirit, 2001: *Formal Pragmatics*. Oxford: Blackwell.

Kadmon, Nirit and Landman, Fred 1993: *Any. Linguistics and Philosophy* 16:3.

Kadmon, Nirit and Roberts, Craige 1986: 'Prosody and scope: the role of discourse structure. In: *CLS 22, Papers from the Parasession on Pragmatics and Grammatical Theory*. Chicago: University of Chicago Press.

Kamp, Hans, 1975: Two theories about adjectives. In: Keenan, Edward (ed.), *Semantics for Natural Language*. Cambridge: Cambridge University Press.

Keenan, Edward, 1987: A semantic definition of *indefinite NP*. In: Reuland, Erik and ter Meulen, Alice (eds.), *The Representation of (In)definiteness*. Cambridge, MA: MIT Press.

Keenan, Edward and Faltz, Leonard 1985: *Boolean Semantics for Natural Language*. Dordrecht: Kluwer.

Keenan, Edward and Stavi, Yonatan 1986: A semantic characterization of natural language determiners. *Linguistics and Philosophy* 9.

Kratzer, Angelika, 1995: Stage-level predicates and individual-level predicates. In: Carlson, Greg and Pelletier, Jeffrey (eds.), *The Generic Book*. Chicago: University of Chicago Press.

Krifka, Manfred, 1989a: Nominal reference, temporal constitution and quantification in event semantics. In: Bartsch, Renate, van Benthem, Johan, and van Emde Boas, Peter (eds.), *Semantics and Contextual Expression*. Dordrecht: Foris.

Krifka, Manfred, 1989b: Boolean and non-Boolean *and*. Manuscript, University of Texas, Austin.

Krifka, Manfred, 1991: A compositional semantics for multiple focus constructions. In: Moore, Steve and Wyner, Adam (eds.), *Proceedings of SALT 1*. Ithaca, NY: CLC Publications.

Krifka, Manfred, 1999: At least some determiners aren't determiners. In: Turner, K. (ed.), *The Semantics/Pragmatics Interface from Different Points of View*. Amsterdam: Elsevier.

Krifka, Manfred, Pelletier, Jeffrey, Carlson, Greg, ter Meulen, Alice, Link, Godehard, and Chierchia, Gennaro 1995: Genericity, an introduction. In: Carlson, Greg and Pelletier, Jeffrey (eds.), *The Generic Book*. Chicago: University of Chicago Press.

Landman, Fred, 1986: Pegs and alecs. In: Landman, Fred, *Towards a Theory of Information. The Status of Partial Objects in Semantics*. Dordrecht: Foris.

Landman, Fred, 1989: Groups, 1 and 2. *Linguistics and Philosophy* 12.

Landman, Fred, 1991: *Structures for Semantics*. Dordrecht: Kluwer.

Landman, Fred, 1995: Plurality. In: Lappin, Shalom (ed.), *Handbook of Contemporary Semantics*. Oxford: Blackwell.

Landman, Fred, 1998: Plurals and maximalization. In: Rothstein, Susan (ed.), *Events and Grammar*. Dordrecht: Kluwer.

Landman, Fred, 2000: *Events and Plurality*. Dordrecht: Kluwer.

Landman, Fred, 2003: Predicate–argument mismatches and the Adjectival Theory of Indefinites. In: Coene, M. and D'hulst, Y. (eds.), *From NP to DP*. Amsterdam: John Benjamins.

Larson, Richard, 1985: Bare NP-adverbs. *Linguistic Inquiry* 16.

Lasersohn, Peter, 1995: *Plurality, Conjunction and Events*. Dordrecht: Kluwer.

Link, Godehard, 1983: The logical analysis of plurals and mass terms: a lattice-theoretic approach. In: Bauerle, Rainer, Schwarze, Christoph, and von Stechow, Arnim (eds.), *Meaning, Use, and the Interpretation of Language*. Berlin: de Gruyter.

Link, Godehard, 1984: Hydras. On the logic of relative clause constructions with multiple heads. In: Landman, Fred and Veltman, Frank (eds.), *Varieties of Formal Semantics*. Dordrecht: Foris.

Link, Godehard, 1987: Generalized quantifiers and plurals. In: Gardenfors, Peter (ed.), *Generalized Quantifiers: Linguistic and Logical Approaches*. Dordrecht: Kluwer.

McNally, Louise, 1998: Existential sentences without existential quantification. *Linguistics and Philosophy*, 21:4.

Milsark, Gary, 1974: *Existential Sentences in English*. PhD dissertation, MIT, Cambridge, MA.

Mittwoch, Anita, 1998: Cognate objects as reflections of Davidsonian event arguments. In: Rothstein, Susan (ed.), *Events and Grammar*. Dordrecht: Kluwer.

Montague, Richard, 1970: English as a formal language. In: Visentini, Bruno et al. (eds.), *Linguaggi nella Societa e nella Technica*. Milan: Edizione di Communita. Reprinted in: Thomason, Richmond (ed.), 1974: *Formal Philosophy*. New Haven, CT: Yale University Press.

Montague, Richard, 1973: The proper treatment of quantification in ordinary English. In: Hintikka, Jaakko, Moravcsik, Julius, and Suppes, Patrick (eds.), *Approaches to Natural Language*. Dordrecht: Kluwer. Reprinted in: Thomason, Richmond (ed.), 1974: *Formal Philosophy*. New Haven, CT: Yale University Press.

Parsons, Terence, 1990: *Events in the Semantics of English*. Cambridge, MA: MIT Press.

Partee, Barbara, 1987: Noun phrase interpretation and type shifting principles. In: Groenendijk, Jeroen, de Jongh, Dick, and Stokhof, Martin (eds.), *Studies in Discourse Representation Theory and the Theory of Generalized Quantifiers*. Dordrecht: Foris.

Prince, Ellen, 1981: Towards a taxonomy of given/new information. In: Cole, Peter (ed.), *Radical Pragmatics*. New York: Academic Press.

Reuland, Erik, 1988: Indefinite subjects. In: *Proceedings of NELS 18*, distributed by GLSA, Amherst, MA: University of Massachusetts.

Roberts, Craige, 1987: *Modal Subordination, Anaphora and Distributivity*. PhD dissertation, University of Massachusetts, Amherst. Published 1990, New York: Garland.

Roberts, Craige, 1996: Information structure in discourse: towards an integrated formal theory of pragmatics. In: *OSU Working Papers in Linguistics 49: Papers in Semantics*. Ohio State University, Columbus.

Rothstein, Susan, 1983: *The Syntactic Forms of Predication*. PhD dissertation, Cambridge, MA: MIT. Distributed 1985, Bloomington, IN: IULC.

Rothstein, Susan, 1988: Conservativity and the syntax of determiners. *Linguistics* 26.

Rothstein, Susan, 1995: Adverbial quantification over events. *Natural Language Semantics* 3.

Rothstein, Susan, 2000: Domain selection in relative clauses. Handout of a talk presented at the Workshop on Relative Clauses, Tel Aviv University.

Rothstein, Susan, 2001: *Predicates and their Subjects*. Dordrecht: Kluwer.

Rullmann, Hotze, 1989: Indefinite NPs in Dutch. In: *Papers on Quantification*. NSF Grant Report, Amherst, MA: University of Massachusetts.

Rullmann, Hotze, 1995: Geen eenheid. *Tabu* 25.

Sag, Ivan, 1982: NP-movement dependencies. In: Jacobson, Pauline and Pullum, Geoffrey (eds.), *The Nature of Syntactic Representation*. Dordrecht: Kluwer.

Schaeffer, Jeannette, 1998: Object placement, specificity and referentiality in early Dutch and Italian grammar. Handout of a talk given at Tel Aviv University.

Sevi, Aldo, 1998: *A semantics for* almost *and* barely, MA thesis, Tel Aviv University, Tel Aviv.

Sharvit, Yael, 1999: Functional relative clauses. *Linguistics and Philosophy* 22.

Sharvy, R., 1980: A more general theory of definite descriptions. *The Philosophical Review* 89.

Stump, Gregory, 1985: *The Semantic Variability of Absolute Constructions.* Dordrecht: Kluwer.

de Swart, Henrietta, 2000: Scope ambiguities with negative quantifiers. In: von Heusinger, Klaus and Egli, Urs (eds.), *Reference and Anaphoric Relations.* Dordrecht: Kluwer.

de Swart, Henrietta, 2001: Weak readings of indefinites: type shifting and closure. In: *Linguistic Review* 12.

Verkuyl, Henk, 1981: Numerals and quantifiers in X′-syntax and their semantic interpretation. In: Groenendijk, Jeroen, Janssen, Theo, and Stokhof, Martin (eds.), *Formal Methods in the Study of Language.* Amsterdam: Mathematical Centre Tracts.

Ward, Gregory and Birner, Betty 1995: Definiteness and the English existential. In *Language* 71.

Williams, Edwin, 1983: Semantic vs. syntactic categories. *Linguistics and Philosophy* 6.

Winter, Yoad, 1998: *Flexible Boolean Semantics.* PhD dissertation, Utrecht University.

Zimmermann, Ede, 1993: On the proper treatment of opacity in certain verbs. *Natural Language Semantics* 1.

Zucchi, Alessandro, 1995: The ingredients of definiteness and the definiteness effect. *Natural Language Semantics* 3.

Index